The Impact of the Russo-Japanese War

The Russo-Japanese War was the major conflict of the first decade of the twentieth century. The struggle for mastery in northeast Asia, specifically for control of Korea and Manchuria, was watched very closely at the time by observers from many other countries keen to draw lessons about the conduct of war in the modern industrial age. The defeat of a traditional European power by a non-white, non-Western nation served as a trigger for the deterioration in the balance on the eve of World War I, and became a model for emulation and admiration among people under, or threatened with, colonial rule. This book examines the very wide impact of the war. It explores the effect on the political balance in northeast Asia, looks at reactions in Europe, the United States, East Asia, and the wider colonial world, and considers the impact on different sections of society, on political and cultural ideas and ideologies, and on various national independence movements. It concludes that the global impact of the Russo-Japanese War was far more important than the effect of any colonial war, and probably any other conflict, that took place between the Napoleonic wars and the outbreak of World War I.

Rotem Kowner is Professor of Japanese History at the University of Haifa, Israel. His recent works include *The Forgotten Campaign: The Russo-Japanese War and Its Legacy*, *Historical Dictionary of the Russo-Japanese War*, and the edited collection *Rethinking the Russo-Japanese War: Centennial Perspectives*.

D1714884

Routledge Studies in the Modern History of Asia

The Impact of the
Russo-Japanese War

Edited by
Rotem Kowner

LONDON AND NEW YORK

First published 2007
by Routledge
2 Park Square, Milton Park, Abingdon, Oxon OX14 4RN

Simultaneously published in the USA and Canada
by Routledge
270 Madison Ave, New York, NY 10016

Routledge is an imprint of the Taylor & Francis Group, an informa business

Transferred to Digital Printing 2009

© 2007 Editorial matter and selection, Rotem Kowner;
individual chapters, the contributors

Typeset in Times New Roman by
Florence Production Ltd, Stoodleigh, Devon

British Library Cataloguing in Publication Data
A catalogue record for this book is available from the British Library

Library of Congress Cataloging in Publication Data
The impact of the Russo-Japanese War/edited by Rotem Kowner.
    p. cm.—(Routledge studies in the modern history of Asia; 43.)
    Includes bibliographical references and index.
    1. Russo-Japanese War, 1904–1905. I. Kowner, Rotem. II. Series:
    Routledge studies in the modern history of Asia (2007); 43.
    DS517.I54 2007
    952.03′1–dc22   2006016645

ISBN10: 0–415–36824–3 (hbk)
ISBN10: 0–415–54582–X (pbk)
ISBN10: 0–203–02804–X (ebk)

ISBN13: 978–0–415–36824–7 (hbk)
ISBN13: 978–0–415–54582–2 (pbk)
ISBN13: 978–0–203–02804–9 (ebk)

To my parents,
Carmela and Leon Kowner

Contents

Maps

Notes on contributors

Patrick Beillevaire is Research Director at the National Centre for Scientific Research, France, and head of the Japan Research Centre at the École des Hautes Études en Sciences Sociales in Paris. He is a specialist in Okinawan history and French–Japanese relations. He has published numerous articles on these topics and is the editor of *Ryūkyū Studies: Western Encounter* (10 vols) and *Le Voyage au Japon: Anthologie de textes français, 1858–1908*.

Peter Berton is Distinguished Professor Emeritus of International Relations at the University of Southern California. He specializes in Great Power diplomacy and territorial/maritime disputes in East Asia. He is the author of over 150 publications on East Asian and Russian affairs, among them *International Negotiation*; *The Russo-Japanese Territorial Dilemma*; and *The Russo-Japanese Alliance of 1916*. He is currently completing two research projects on the Japanese Communist Party and Russo-Japanese relations during World War I.

Peter Duus is William H. Bonsall Professor of History Emeritus at Stanford University and served as the president of the American Association of Asian Studies. His special field is the history of modern Japan. His recent works include *The Abacus and the Sword: The Japanese Penetration of Korea, 1895–1910*; *Modern Japan*; and *The Japanese Discovery of America*. He is currently doing research on late Meiji Tokyo.

Cord Eberspaecher is participating in a project on Sino-German relations at the Secret Central Archive Prussian Heritage Foundation, Berlin, and is a specialist on German naval history and Sino-German relations. He is the author of *The German Yangtze-Patrol: German Gunboat Diplomacy in China in the Age of Imperialism 1900–1914* (in German) and is currently working on the relations between Prussia/Germany and China in the nineteenth century.

Jonathan Frankel is the Tamara and Saveli Grinberg Professor of Russian Studies and Professor in the Institute of Contemporary Jewry (both emeritus) at the Hebrew University of Jerusalem. Among his books are *Vladimir Akimov on the Dilemmas of Russian Marxism*; *Prophecy and*

Politics: Socialism, Nationalism and the Russian Jews, 1862–1917; and *The Damascus Affair: "Ritual Murder," Politics and the Jews in 1840.*

Sharon Halevi is a lecturer in American History at the University of Haifa, Israel, and is currently serving at the Director of the Women's Studies Program. Her main research interest is the history of identities, in particular the relationship between gender and national identities. She has published several articles on these issues; her latest work deals with the impact of the American Revolution on women's gender identity.

Joseph M. Henning is Associate Professor of History at Rochester Institute of Technology and is a specialist on the history of US foreign relations. He is the author of *Outposts of Civilization: Race, Religion, and the Formative Years of American-Japanese Relations* and is currently writing on Herbert Spencer and American thought.

Rotem Kowner is Professor of Japanese history and culture at the University of Haifa. His recent works include *The Forgotten Campaign: The Russo-Japanese War and Its Legacy* (in Hebrew); *Historical Dictionary of the Russo-Japanese War*; and the edited volume *Rethinking the Russo-Japanese War: Centennial Perspectives*. He is currently working on a book on the role of Western racial and bodily images in shaping Meiji Japan.

Michael Laffan is Assistant Professor of History at Princeton University. He is the author of *Islamic Nationhood and Colonial Indonesia* and contributor to, and co-editor of, a recent volume of *Islamic Law and Society* on the place of Islamic juridical opinion in Indonesia. Specializing in colonialism, lexicography, and informants in Southeast Asian contexts, he is currently working on a book on the evolution of notions of tradition and modernity in Indonesian Islam under Dutch colonialism.

T.G. Otte is Lecturer in Diplomatic History at the University of East Anglia. He specializes in nineteenth-century Great Power relations, and has published widely in scholarly journals and books. His latest book is the edited volume *The Makers of British Foreign Policy: From Pitt to Thatcher*. He is also the Reviews Editor of *Diplomacy and Statecraft*.

Guy Podoler teaches Korean history at the Hebrew University of Jerusalem and is a specialist in modern and contemporary Korea. He has published a number of articles on the connection between history and memory in South Korea, and is currently preparing a manuscript based on his dissertation on the construction of colonial history in Korea through museums and monuments.

Michael Robinson is Professor of Korean history in the East Asian Languages and Cultures Department of Indiana University, specializing in the intellectual and cultural history of Korea during the period of Japanese colonial rule. He is the author of *Cultural Nationalism in*

Colonial Korea and co-editor of *Colonial Modernity in Korea, 1910–1945*. His new book *History of Twentieth Century Korea* is about to be published.

T.R. Sareen retired as Director, Indian Council of Historical Research, and was formerly Assistant Director, National Archives of India. He has many published works to his credit, including *Indian Revolutionary Movement Abroad 1905–1929*; *Russian Revolution and the Indian National Movement*; *Subhas Chandra Bose and the Japanese Occupation of Andamans 1942–45*; and *British Intervention in Transcaspian 1917–19*. At present, he is working on a book project on Japanese prisoners of war in India, 1942–6.

Matthew S. Seligmann is Senior Lecturer in History at the University of Northampton. He specializes in Anglo-German relations and the origins of World War I, and has written extensively on these topics. He is the co-author of *Germany from Reich to Republic, 1871–1918* and the author of the recently published *Spies in Uniform: British Military and Naval Intelligence on the Eve of the First World War*.

Yigal Sheffy is Assistant Professor at the program for Security Studies, Tel Aviv University, and specializes in military history of the Middle East and of World War I. His books include *British Military Intelligence in the Palestine Campaign, 1914–1918*. He is currently working on British–Ottoman peace negotiations during World War I.

Harold Z. Schiffrin is Professor Emeritus of Chinese Studies, Hebrew University of Jerusalem, and specializes in the rise of Chinese nationalism during the early twentieth century. He is the author of *Sun Yat-Sen and the Origins of the Chinese Revolution* and *Sun Yat-Sen: Reluctant Revolutionary* and has co-edited volumes dealing with China's 1911 revolution.

Yitzhak Shichor is Professor of Political Science and East Asian Studies at the University of Haifa and a senior research fellow at the Harry S. Truman Research Institute for the Advancement of Peace, the Hebrew University of Jerusalem. His research and publications cover China's politics and international relations, focusing on China's military modernization and defense conversion; Middle East policy and labor export; international energy policy; Muslim–ethnic relations; and East Asian democratization processes.

Tal Tovy is Lecturer in Military History at Bar Ilan University, Israel, and also teaches at the IDF's Command and General Staff College. He specializes in American military history and his most recent book is entitled *Like Eating Soup with a Knife: The American Experience in Vietnam, 1959–1973*.

Preface

History seems at times to be a partial and even unfair judge. Not only does it focus on certain events and personalities and overlook others, it also tends to display preference for the recent over the earlier, and concentrate on what is at hand rather than what is important. Furthermore, the current importance of a specific event is often determined not necessarily because of its significance once it occurred or for its repercussions afterwards, but rather because of its place within certain historiographical trends and fads —the outcome of various needs and transient agendas. No wonder, then, that the chronicles of humanity are full of instances in which certain trivial events drew more attention than they deserved, whereas other more significant events were ignored all the way through, and sometimes even eventually faded into total oblivion.

The Russo-Japanese War may serve as an example of a historically underrepresented event. Certainly, it has never vanished completely from public memory nor has it ever been ignored, but it definitely received at certain times and places less attention than it probably deserved. Despite its resounding echoes at the time of its occurrence, it took this war, in fact, less than a decade after its conclusion to start fading from public memory, notably in the West. Within a few decades it received very few references in the records of Japan and Russia (by now the mighty Union of Soviet Socialist Republics) as well, turning into another negligible and futile conflict, off-center and seemingly unrelated to the great conflicts of the twentieth century.

This is no longer the case, however. In recent years this first armed conflict between Russia and Japan has emerged from being long forgotten to return to the limelight of historical research. Due to the changing political circumstances in Japan since the 1980s and in Russia since the 1990s, and partly perhaps also because of its centennial celebrations, the war has been given much attention recently. It has been commemorated in public ceremonies, scholarly conferences, and exhibitions, and through many popular as well as academic publications. Most of this recent commemoration has dealt with its origins, its military record, and even its artistic representation and place in collective memory, but it has overlooked the sweeping impact of the war.

This book is the first endeavor, definitely in English, devoted solely to providing a broad comprehensive assessment of the international impact of the war.[1] I undertook this enterprise not because it has not been done before, but because I firmly believe that in its repercussions, and perhaps only in this respect, the Russo-Japanese War has changed from being considered a peripheral conflict, one more in a series of "colonial wars," to being regarded as an event of global significance. When examined in this perspective, it is evident how far-reaching and pervasive have been the ramifications of the Russo-Japanese War. Some of its repercussions lasted only a decade, as in the case of the European balance of power, although they led indirectly to the outbreak of a still more pivotal event—World War I. Other repercussions of the war lasted four decades, as in the case of the continental grip of the Japanese Empire, whereas some resonate even now, as in the case of the divided Korean peninsula.

The massive clash between Russia and Japan heralded the rise of the Japanese Empire and shaped the features of East Asia until 1945. As for Europe, far removed from the battle arena, the long-standing, delicate equilibrium between the powerful nations broke down, and thenceforward a rapid deterioration began toward direct military confrontation known later as World War I. Globally, the greatest loser of the war was tsarist Russia, and the humiliating blow it suffered hastened the coming of the Bolshevik Revolution. Another significant outcome is evident among the nations under colonial rule. As a global turning point, the role of the war is recognizable in the newer definition of race relations in the world. This was the first modern conflict in which an "oriental," "non-white" nation overcame a "Western," "white" nation. For the first time the myth of the superiority of the "white man" was shattered. For this reason, the Japanese victory caused strong reverberations not only among the Powers but also among the nations then living under colonial rule, and even more so among future revolutionaries. It led to renewed fears in Europe of the "yellow peril" in Germany, France, and Britain, which shared growing concern for the fate of their Asian colonies. In the United States, notably on the west coast, it stimulated American opposition to Japanese immigration. The Russo-Japanese War was probably also the first "modern" war—a conflagration on sea and land enormous in its scope and logistic requirements—in which many warfare patterns were tested on a large scale for the first time, only to appear in full maturity a decade later.

It is not a simple task to determine the consequence of a historical event, or to identify the cause-and-effect relations between two events. Rarely, if ever, are events of major significance, let alone social or political processes, the result of a single factor. In most cases, complex human actions are determined by interactions between far-reaching and proximate causes. Among the various chapters in this book one may discern different approaches to the question of historical causality, and consequently divergent willing-ness to link the war with increasingly remote events and developments in the future. This variance notwithstanding, it is evident that all contributors believe the war had far-reaching consequences, often of immense import-ance, for their respective topics.

During this project I had the good fortune to discuss various issues related to this book with numerous colleagues. Several of them ended as contrib-utors to it. However, many others with whom I have met and corresponded in recent years, too many to name here, contributed indirectly by sharing with me their insights regarding the significance of this historical event. The financial support provided by the Research Authority at the University of Haifa was essential and is highly appreciated, and similarly the research environment facilitated by Kenneth Grossberg at the Institute of Asia Pacific at Waseda University was beneficial for the completion of this project. I thank Ido Blumenfeld for his assistance in designing the maps in this book, and I am grateful also to Peter Sowden of Routledge for initiating this project and supporting it throughout its long gestation.

The book is dedicated to my parents, Carmela and Leon Kowner, who have instilled in me the urge for learning and taught me the importance of history.

Rotem Kowner

Note

1   For partial attempts to account for the war's impact, regionally or globally, see Kang, 1981; Hirama, 2004. For book sections devoted to the repercussions of the war, see Steinberg *et al.*, 2005; Kowner, 2007.

Notes on conventions

The names of persons mentioned in the book follow several transliteration systems. The Russian names are written according to the improved transliteration system of the Library of Congress (but without diacritical marks and ligatures) and in consultation with the *Historical Dictionary of the Russo-Japanese War* (Kowner, 2006), except for the names so familiar in English that to translate them otherwise would mislead the reader (e.g. Nicholas II rather Nikolai II, Witte rather Vitte). Similarly, Russian names of German origin are written in accordance with what is common in that language or in contemporary European literature. Japanese names are written according to the Hepburn transliteration system and in consultation with the *Kodansha Encyclopedia* (1983 edition). The macron above some vowels in the Japanese names indicates a long vowel. Chinese names are written according to the Pinyin transliteration system, and Korean names according to the McCune-Reischauer transliteration system. All East Asian names are written with the family name given first, followed by the personal name.

Names of locations in Manchuria and in China are written according to the Wade-Giles system, in consultation with the *Historical Dictionary of the Russo-Japanese War*. While today the Pinyin transliteration system is widely used, most books in European languages dealing with this period, and certainly all books written during the war and in the half a century that followed, rely on the Wade-Giles system. Moreover, many of the place names in Manchuria and the names of battle sites are not in use today, partly because they stem from local dialects or non-Chinese languages. Therefore, the use of current Chinese names or of old names in Pinyin transliteration may mislead the reader and make it impossible to identify the location of these places. However, to allow the reader to identify the battle sites and link them with present-day locations, the Pinyin transliterations are added in the index. Place names in Japan are written according to the Hepburn transliteration system, in consultation with the *Kodansha Encyclopedia* (first edition) and the fourth edition of the *Kenkyusha New Japanese-English Dictionary*. Names of places of current importance are written in present-day transliteration, such as Tokyo (which a century ago was written Tokio) and Beijing (Peking).

The dates in this book are according to the Gregorian calendar (the calendar commonly used today in the West and most of the world), rather than the Julian calendar, which was used in tsarist Russia until 1918, or the modern Japanese calendar, which is still in use today. The Julian calendar, which is used in many books on Russian history, was 12 days "behind" the Gregorian calendar during the nineteenth century and 13 days "behind" during the twentieth century. Therefore, the date of the outbreak of the war, which was January 26, 1904 according to the Julian calendar in Russia, and the eighth day of the second month of the thirty-seventh year of the Meiji Era in Japan, appears in this book as February 8, 1904.

Military ranks are given according to the British system at the beginning of the twentieth century. The units of measurement are given in the metric system, but, to facilitate the reading for those unfamiliar with it, figures still in use in the United States or under certain military conventions appear in parentheses.

1 Between a colonial clash and World War Zero

The impact of the Russo-Japanese War in a global perspective

Rotem Kowner

On the morning of February 6, 1904, Japan severed its diplomatic relations with Russia. The same day, the Japanese Combined Fleet under the command of Admiral Tōgō Heihachirō set sail for the shores of Korea. Off the port city of Chemulpo, in the vicinity of the capital Seoul, the force split into two. Most of the warships made for Port Arthur while a small naval force under Rear Admiral Uryū Sotokichi remained to protect the landing of the army on Korean soil. On the night of February 8, ten Japanese destroyers attacked Russian warships anchored in the harbor of Port Arthur but did not inflict much damage. The following morning the Japanese forces of the First Army took control of the Korean capital while Uryū's naval force demanded of the Russian naval detachment in Chemulpo that it leave the port. The Russians obeyed, but, following a short offshore engagement, they returned to the port and scuttled the cruiser *Variag* and the gunship *Koreets* rather than hand them over to the enemy. These seemingly trivial episodes were but the prologue to a colossal struggle. The next day Japan declared war, whereupon a 19-month war began officially.[1]

From a broad historical perspective, the Russo-Japanese War was the long-anticipated flashpoint of the enmity between two expanding powers. On the western boundaries of Asia the Russian Empire had been advancing relentlessly southeastward for centuries, while on the eastern fringe of this continent the Japanese Empire had been spreading westward for three short decades. The difference in the extent of their imperialist expansion, however, did not diminish the magnitude of the conflict, and additional dissimilarities only made its resolution by diplomatic means ever less feasible. In fact, apart from their imperialist aspirations, their recent modernization, and their technologically advanced armies, there was little similarity between the two states. They differed in the size of their territory, population, and economy, as well as in their racial composition, language, and religion. Eventually, the encounter between them took place in the killing fields of Manchuria and Korea, areas both sides were eager to control. It was not their first or their last confrontation, but certainly it has exerted the greatest impact on both.[2]

Historiographically, views on the significance of the Russo-Japanese War have undergone tremendous fluctuations since its outbreak and throughout the subsequent century, shifting from sensation to amnesia and recently revived recollection. Present readers might be surprised to discover that the Russo-Japanese War was not an unknown event at the time of its occurrence. On the contrary, for such a peripheral conflict, it generated enormous reverberations. It was an astounding war, and millions around the globe kept abreast of the news of the surprising victories of "little" Japan over the "mighty" Russian Empire.

In the following years many prominent figures who shaped the history of the twentieth century referred to the Russo-Japanese War and remembered acutely the sensation it created. Adolf Hitler, for example, was one of those who took the war seriously, so much so that it might have contributed to his early evolving *Weltanschauung*. Serving his sentence in Landsberg prison two decades after the Russo-Japanese War and writing his fateful manifesto *Mein Kampf*, Hitler's memory of it was still vivid. In 1904 the future Führer was 15 years old, and the war found him "much more mature and also more attentive" than during the Boer War, in which he also took, he confessed, great interest. He at once sided with the Japanese, and considered the Russian fiasco "a defeat of the Austrian Slavic nationalities."[3] Hitler, of course, was not alone in understanding the importance of that event. Many others, particularly in Asia, regarded the war as a formative event in their political upbringing. During the hostilities India's future leader of independence, Mohandas Gandhi, for example, grasped from remote South Africa that "the people of the East seem to be waking up from their lethargy."[4] Similarly, Sukarno, Indonesia's first president after its independence, appraised Japan's victory in retrospect and viewed it as one of the major events affecting "the development of Indonesian nationalism."[5]

Less than a decade after its conclusion, however, the war was hardly mentioned again, and after another three decades its claim to fame had vanished completely. Overshadowed by two global conflicts, and suffering from the demise of both regimes that took part in it, the Russo-Japanese War was virtually forgotten in the second half of the twentieth century. It was more or less destined for such a fate, as from an early stage this titanic struggle was customarily labeled merely one more clash in a series of colonial wars that afflicted the world throughout the nineteenth century.[6] No wonder, therefore, that most history books dealing with the modern age make no more than a brief mention of it, and even today some fundamental issues of the war, such as the decision-making on both sides during the war, and the military campaign, still await a comprehensive examination that takes into account all sources available.[7]

A typical example of the prevalent disregard for the war can be found in Barbara Tuchman's book *The Proud Tower* (1966), in which she sought to provide a portrait of "the world" in the three decades before World War I. In her preface this influential historian admitted that she adopted a very selective view in attempting to describe the image of the world during that critical period. Tuchman had no hesitation in stating that it might have been possible to include a chapter on the Russo-Japanese War, as well as a plausible chapter on the Boer War, Chekhov, or the everyday shopkeeper. But no, she chose to deal with what she believed were the main issues. Her writing is decidedly Eurocentric, and almost inevitably Tuchman ends by focusing on the Anglo-Saxon world, and then in descending order on Western Europe and tsarist Russia, while devoting only a few lines to the Russo-Japanese War—a critical juncture along the road to World War I.[8]

Among Western historians Tuchman is obviously not an exception. In fact, her tendency to look at the world through European spectacles and to ignore events outside the sphere of Europe and North America is rather the rule. Still, the blame for this historiographic amnesia about the Russo-Japanese War should not be attributed to Western myopia alone. Much of it was due to the proximity of the war to an even more important event, at least from a European point of view. There is no doubt that World War I (1914–18) was an event on a different scale. It changed the face of Europe and of the entire world, and created not only a new international system but also a different way of perceiving the modern era. Apart from the shadow cast by this subsequent colossal event, the Russo-Japanese War was forgotten simply because it happened "out there" at the distant edge of Asia, in remote and sparsely populated areas. The Japanese and Russians who fought it were considered the "Other," obscure and anonymous troops, and their losses did not affect the hearts and minds of the public in the West. The military campaign was conducted amidst a local population that barely recorded its history, and the relatively few journalists who went to cover the fighting were kept under tight control and strict censorship. Their reports were also not immortalized by many visual mementos, since photographing equipment was heavy and the battle arena too distant, motion pictures had only just emerged, and live television broadcasts were still many decades in the future.

No less important, the two opponents themselves played an active role in diminishing the importance of their conflict. In Russia, soon to be transformed into the Soviet Union, the defeat emerged as just one more event in a long despicable series of fiascos associated with the "old" regime. With the Bolsheviks' rise to power 12 years after the conclusion of the Portsmouth Peace Treaty, the defeat against Japan was turned into a war of the tsar and not of the people who fought to overthrow him.[9] In Japan, by contrast, the victories of the war became an invaluable asset in the brief military legacy of the imperial forces. Nevertheless, at the time of its surrender to the Allies in 1945 Japan too began a process of suppression and denial of its imperial past, in a manner somewhat recalling what had happened to its Russian arch-rival several decades earlier. With such tortuous legacies, it would have been most unlikely for the memory of the war not to fade from national consciousness on both sides.

In the last few years the war has been widely commemorated and has received much more attention than in previous decades. Benefiting from the emergence of national consciousness in Japan since the 1980s and the collapse of the Soviet Union in the early 1990s, it became again a valid topic for research and reflection. With the hindsight of a century it is possible to examine the war from an appropriate historiographic distance. By now all available documents related to the conflict have been declassified and analyzed, its heroes have all died, and the sensationalism that enveloped the battles is long gone. Today more than ever, it becomes clear that the war was not only of great importance at the time it occurred, but that it had an important impact on the entire history of the twentieth century.

A recent edited volume, *The Russo-Japanese War in Global Perspective: World War Zero*, seems to reflect the greater role that the war is given in current historiography. The editors of this volume contend that the modern era of global conflict began with the Russo-Japanese War rather than in 1914. In their brief introduction, they suggest that the war deserves this designation since it was fought between two powers, a European and an Asian, and was sponsored by a third party money market.[10] While the title *World War Zero* admittedly sounds appealing, the Russo-Japanese War was not a global conflict. Not only did it involve directly only two adversaries, but for both of them it was far from a total war in the form they would experience in the following world wars. From Russia's perspective, in fact, the clash with Japan was not a total war even in the sense of the Napoleonic Wars. During most of the campaign only a small segment of the Russian military machine was involved, and Russian casualties in Manchuria were far lower than those even in the Crimean War.[11] No less important, no other power assisted either of the belligerents, and even their closest allies— Britain on Japan's side and France on Russia's side—did their utmost to avoid taking any active part in the conflict. Finally, the war did not witness the introduction of any revolutionary weapon, certainly not on the scale of the airplane, tank, or submarine, as was the case in World War I. All in all, it seems to resemble much more the Crimean War or even the American Civil War than any global conflict of the scale the world would experience twice within a 35-year period later on.

If the Russo-Japanese War carried any global significance it lay not in its origins in the actual warfare, in the diplomatic alliances, or in financial support obtained during the war, but in its repercussions. Although these were associated directly with the decline of Russia and the rise of Japan, they had a wide-ranging effect on numerous nations, regions, and spheres. Furthermore, these repercussions did not involve only immeasurable sentiments, such as fear, joy, or envy, but touched upon the economies and military organizations of every power in the early twentieth century, and its

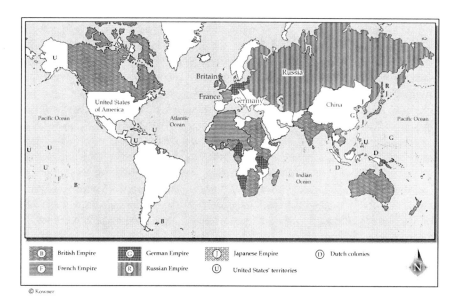

Map 1 World empires, 1904–14.

balance of power with others. Through this, the war affected the stability of Europe, Russia in particular, the equilibrium between the United States and Japan, and the territorial status quo in northeast Asia.

Implications for Europe: deterioration of the power balance

The Russo-Japanese War did not cause any instant or visible upheaval in Europe but its ultimate impact on this continent was devastating. It did not lead immediately to a substantial rise in military expenditure; nor did it start an arms race. It did not prompt any new radical attitude either, and even some of the political processes associated with it had begun to crystallize before the war broke out.[12] More than anything, its impact in Europe was linked with Russia's debacle in the battlefields of Manchuria and the consequent instability at home in the wake of the 1905 revolution. The status of Russia had in turn tangible, arguably even radical, repercussions on the power balance in Europe. Its impact was initially of a psychological nature and took shape in part during the war and in part after it, leading to a new balance, or rather imbalance, of power. The new political arrangement that emerged in Europe during 1904–5 was one of the precipitants, if not the main one, of the deterioration that led to the outbreak of the Great War less than a decade later.

Russia was not reduced to a marginal power following its final defeats in Mukden and Tsushima during the first half of 1905, but it unquestionably became second-rate in its image, its military capabilities, and its actual ability to influence others. The collapse of this mighty power undermined the political and military equilibrium that had endured in Europe since the Napoleonic era. While Russia lost its former military status, Germany had just completed a ten-year period of military build-up and during the war emerged as Europe's supreme military and industrial power. The German rise was not a new phenomenon, but the Russian defeat suddenly high-lighted the continental hegemony of Germany. The ascent of Germany had begun more than four decades earlier, and even before the war other European powers perceived it as jeopardizing the stability of the continent. However, the exposure of Russia's military weakness, its naval losses, finan-cial burden, and internal instability swung the already uneven military balance in Europe still more to Germany's favor. In the subsequent decade the fluctuating balance between these two powers determined the fate of the continent. During 1904–14 this fragile equilibrium was in large measure, as David Herrmann convincingly argues, "the story of Russia's prostration, its subsequent recovery, and the effects of this development upon the strategic situation."[13]

Much of the road to the Great War was therefore associated with chang-ing perceptions of this military balance by the German leadership.[14] But, despite its economic and military hegemony, pre-war Germany was isolated and lacked a large empire overseas. The war in Manchuria provided Germany with a unique opportunity to reverse its prolonged failing diplo-macy, which had begun to deteriorate since its last successful diplomatic collaboration in 1895 (the "Three Power Intervention" with France and Russia), aimed not by chance against Japan. Due to the sudden change of military power in 1905, Germany was able to pose a threat of war against its western neighbor France. The reluctance to give up the geopolitical advantages gained during the war, together with the desire to disrupt the recent Anglo-French Entente of 1904, was the underlying motive for the kaiser's landing in Tangiers in March 1905 and contesting French attempts to turn the area into its protectorate. Five months later the flamboyant kaiser turned to Germany's eastern neighbor Russia, in another attempt to disrupt the position of France, this time by driving a wedge between Franco-Russian ties. He ventured into an abortive exercise in personal diplomacy too by signing a treaty with Tsar Nicholas II at Björkö, Finland, believing the latter could be wooed at a time of debacle abroad and crisis at home (see Map 2, p. 10). The kaiser was momentarily right, perhaps, but German leaders underestimated the forces in Russia that prevented it from abandoning France and entering into alliance with Germany. Hence, in a short time the treaty seemed "little more than a curious episode in Russian diplomacy."[15]

German prospects for a successful offensive on its western border were probably better in 1905 than nine years later on the eve of World War I.[16] Concluding that Russia could not help France, German strategists were plan-ning during the Russo-Japanese War an offensive ("preventive war") against

France. Their scheme did not materialize since the ambitious kaiser was still unready for the undertaking. He probably did not realize the full array of consequences of the war and revolution for Russia, but nonetheless he orchestrated the plans, albeit without sufficient coordination.[17] Although the remote conflict in Manchuria exposed the weaknesses characterizing German governmental structure, German planners did update their drafts and completed the notorious Schlieffen Plan in December 1905. Their French counterparts did not remain idle, revising simultaneously their own Plan XV and completing it in 1906.[18] Hesitating to go to war, the kaiser nonetheless appointed Helmut von Moltke on January 1, 1906 as his new Chief of Staff, replacing the 72-year-old Alfred von Schlieffen, believing the latter was too old to lead the troops effectively should an armed conflict break out.[19]

The desire of Germany, and to a lesser extent of Austro-Hungary, to maintain its continental hegemony acquired during 1904–5 was one of the cardinal causes of the outbreak of World War I. These two nations perceived the Russo-Japanese War as a window of opportunity in which they could exploit their momentary hegemony. Germany in particular, argues Matthew Seligmann (Chapter 7, this volume), was painfully aware that its relative power was diminishing during the decade that followed the war and that this window was rapidly closing. The sense that the period of grace was about to end became acute in 1914 and turned into one of the most decisive undercurrents, at least on the German and Austrian side, of the war against Russia and France in 1914. This sentiment can be plainly discerned, for example, in Moltke's view, expressed at a meeting with his Austrian counterpart Franz Conrad von Hötzendorf on May 12, 1914: "To wait any longer means a diminishing of our chances; as far as manpower is concerned we cannot enter into a competition with Russia." Eight days later, recalled the German Foreign Minister Gottlieb von Jagow, Moltke lectured him that "there was no alternative to waging a preventive war in order to defeat the enemy as long as we could still more or less pass the test."[20]

As for Russia, the impact of the war with Japan was both concrete and psychological. It was not the only cause of the Russian Revolution in 1905, but it served as its main catalyst. The link between the war outside Russia and the events occurring within its territory is unquestionable. The constraints of a large and unexpected colonial war, far from home and costly in both human lives and material, aggravated social divisions, damaged agrarian economy, led to financial crisis, and enhanced political opposition to the autocratic regime.[21] While the upheavals in Russia prevented the political system from acting with full force against Japan, the war outside Russia made it difficult to respond harshly to the revolution within. Witnessing the weakness of the autocratic regime for the first time, the public were powerfully affected by the Russian defeat and their trust in the tsar never fully recovered.

As Jonathan Frankel notes (Chapter 4, this volume), the most apparent outcome of the war was Nicholas's readiness to set up a legislative council called the Duma, and to grant the people a constitution. The first Duma was received in the palace of the tsar in 1906, but from the very start it struggled to obtain political and civil rights, and to implement plans that were not included among the concessions the tsar granted at the end of 1905. The battle for a less autocratic rule during the war did not prevent the formal dissolution of the first Duma within ten weeks, but this institution continued to function up to 1917. The inability of Nicholas to cope simultaneously with a foreign enemy and an internal rebellion, as evident in the Russo-Japanese War, was to recur with even greater intensity after 1914, and to lead to his downfall three years later.[22]

Except for Russia and Germany, Britain seemed to be affected the most by the war. During the military campaign in Manchuria and in the following years, Britain improved its geopolitical position, consolidating alliances with France and Russia, its two arch-rivals during the previous decades. Of the two, the rapprochement with France had the greatest significance. Only a few years earlier Britain had been uncertain about the identity of its allies in Europe.[23] In April 1904, however, Britain rendered its final verdict when, together with France, it renewed their Entente Cordiale, according to which France agreed to British control over Egypt in return for recognition of French hegemony in Morocco. To many the Entente was a surprising turn-around, since only four years earlier Britain had still manifested a desire for an alliance with Germany against France and Russia. Very few could have foreseen then that within seven years Britain would make an alliance with both, and regard Germany as its most menacing rival.[24]

The sudden outbreak of the Russo-Japanese War accelerated the Anglo-French rapprochement as both were bound by specific clauses of their respective alliances with the two combatants: the Anglo-Japanese and the Franco-Russian alliances. Threatened by a direct conflict against each other, the two settled their differences within two months and concluded their Entente, which lingered in some way throughout the twentieth century.[25] Historians tend to disagree as to the extent to which this Anglo-French alliance was originally intended to isolate Germany, since there was nothing in the agreement that could be construed as an anti-German measure. Nonetheless, many in Britain and France expressed relief at the fact that German foreign policy could no longer count on the tension between the two states. Thereafter, Britain abandoned its long "splendid isolation" and became fully involved in the worsening continental quagmire, leading to its fateful participation in the European conflict of 1914, side by side with its new allies.[26]

The British alliance with Japan since 1902 and the successful exploits of the Imperial Japanese Navy during the war enabled the Royal Navy to concentrate its warships in the Atlantic and the Mediterranean. Enhanced by its new alliance with France, Britain regained its naval hegemony, and forced

Italy, with its long and vulnerable coastline, to join its side. Through its improved ties with France, Britain was destined to enhance its contacts with Russia as well. Completing its containment in 1905, as Thomas Otte (Chapter 6, this volume) illustrates, it was ready now to signal its willingness to appease its arch-rival hitherto.[27] Russia could not respond appropriately during the conflict with Japan, but once defeated and no longer the menace to Britain it was earlier, it shifted its policy toward its arch-rival after the conclusion of the war. Retiring from an almost century-long wide-ranging border conflict with Britain across Asia (whimsically entitled "the Great Game"), Russia now turned its focus back to Europe, the Balkans in particular. As the Russo-Japanese War ended, Britain, or at least a few of its leading figures, was convinced that in the event of a continental war in Europe, it must send troops to support its new ally France. This decision to intervene in European conflict was not modified until August 2, 1914.[28]

Eventually, the sudden rise of Germany, at least in relative terms, the rapprochement between Britain and France, and its own defeat in Manchuria drove Russia after the war into the arms of Britain, its arch-rival during most of the nineteenth century. In 1907, two years after the war ended, a new de facto balance between the European powers came into existence, and remained in force until the outbreak of World War I. Thenceforward, they were divided into two blocs: a diplomatic alliance of Great Britain, France, and Russia on the one hand, and a central defensive alliance of Germany, Austria-Hungary, Italy, and Romania on the other. The road to an all-European war was not irreversible, but on the diplomatic front no change occurred in the power relationships over the next several years, and no new alignment was formed to divert Europe from a major conflict.[29]

The impact of the war on Europe was also felt strongly in the Balkans, where the diminished status of St Petersburg contributed further to the destabilization of the region. Russia's weakness exposed in northeast Asia caused Austria-Hungary to seek rapprochement initially, and on October 15, 1904 the two nations signed a secret protocol to maintain the status quo in southeast Europe. Austria-Hungary's growing sense of confidence during the war was one of the causes of the deterioration of its diplomatic relations with Italy, leading soon to a virtual war scare and to unresolved suspicions and mutual armament during the following decade.[30] Although weakened, Russia resumed its active meddling in the Balkans after the war even more intensively than before. Although Russia had earlier expressed its consent, an Austrian move to annex Bosnia and Herzegovina in 1908 without notifying St Petersburg resulted in a six-month crisis with Russia. An armed clash was averted through boycotts, threats, and reparations, but the successful annexation left Austria-Hungary and its ally Germany in a greater mutual commitment and with a sense of vindication. Thereafter, the conflict with Russia exacerbated, culminating in the outbreak of World War I. Russia's diminished power was manifested again in 1912, when it was unable to prevent the Balkan League from declaring war on the Ottoman Empire.

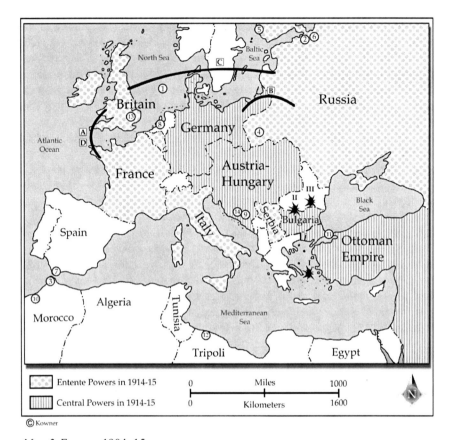

© Kowner

Map 2 Europe, 1904–15.

Key

Conflicts: I Italo–Turkish War (1911–12); II First Balkan War (1912–13);
III Second Balkan War (1913).

Treaties: A Anglo-French Entente (Entente Cordiale) (1904); B Treaty of Björkö (1905);
C Anglo-Russian Entente (1907); D Anglo-French Naval Agreement (1912).

Events:
 1 The Dogger Bank incident (1904)
 2 St Petersburg—Revolution of 1905
 3 Tangier—Landing of the German emperor and the First Moroccan Crisis (1905)
 4 Lodz Uprising (1905)
 5 Treaty of Björkö (1905)
 6 St Petersburg—The First Duma (1906)
 7 Algeciras Conference (1906)
 8 Hague Peace Conference (1907)
 9 Annexation of Bosnia and Herzegovina (1908)
 10 Agadir—The Second Moroccan Crisis (1908)
 11 Istanbul—Constitutional Revolution (1908)
 12 Tripoli—Annexation of Tripolitania (1911)
 13 London Peace Conference (1913)
 14 Sarajevo—Assassination of Archduke Franz Ferdinand (1914)

Note: The borders in the Balkans are pertinent to the period between the peace treaties signed
in August–September 1913 and August 1914.

Similarly, its secondary role in the Triple Entente did not prompt its allies, Britain and France, to lend support to its position in this turbulent region during the entire period until the Great War.[31]

The echoes of the Russo-Japanese War were felt even on the western periphery of the Russian Empire—Scandinavia and Poland in particular— and they gave rise to uprisings and demands for greater freedom. For Sweden, Russia's defeat merely heralded a relief from the neighborly menace,[32] but for the semi-independent duchy of Finland the revolution of 1905 stirred a national awakening together with attempts at radical activities against Russia, to the extent of collaboration with Japanese agents.[33] After several years of tightened Russian control over Finland, the demonstrations and general strikes that swept the country during 1905 led in November that year to the restoration of the *status quo ante* until 1899, and to the reinstatement of the rights of the local parliament. Divided between Russia, Germany, and Austria-Hungary, Poland too displayed a burst of hope for independence during the revolution. Finnish and Polish hopes during the revolution of 1905 should not be a surprise. It was, Hugh Seton-Watson argued:

> as much a revolution of non-Russians against Russification as it was a revolution of workers, peasants, and radical intellectuals against autocracy. The two revolts were of course connected: the social revolution was in fact most bitter in non-Russian regions, with Polish workers, Latvian peasants, and Gregorian peasants as protagonists.[34]

While Poles swept the streets with anti-Russian riots, Josef Pilsudski and Roman Dmowski, leaders of two movements for the unification of Poland, ventured to Japan and examined ways of cooperation with the Japanese.[35] Their eventual moderation paid off. Less than a year after the war, 36 Polish delegates were elected to the first Duma. Signs of greater freedom were apparent also in the field of education, and in the coming years the idea of Polish unity under the protection of the Russian Empire grew stronger. However, as a result of Russian counteraction all these achievements were gradually lost, and Poland's movement for independence, like Finland's, was forced to wait until 1918 before its vision became a reality, at the cost of much bloodshed.

A dress rehearsal for the Great War: military aspects

The disturbance of the balance of power in Europe during the Russo-Japanese War was not only in the diplomatic realm but also in the military sphere. In many ways this confrontation between two large and modern armies served as virtually the last general dress rehearsal for the colossal military spectacle that was to take place in Europe a decade later. In a speech in the British House of Commons in 1901, a young Member of

Parliament named Winston Churchill foresaw with a fine degree of accuracy that "Democracy is more vengeful than governments" and that the wars of nations "will be more terrible than the wars of kings."[36] Churchill was right about the outcome but not about the sources of this phenomenon. Relative to the number of participants, the Russo-Japanese War proved a terrible slaughter. Yet compared with subsequent wars of the twentieth century, such as the two world wars, and even the Korean and Vietnam Wars, the death toll was rather low. The number of dead was only 1 percent of the loss of life suffered in World War I, and about 7 percent of the loss in the Korean War. The lower figures of casualties in the Russo-Japanese War were not so much due to the character of the regimes involved but to the weapons available and the reluctance of both belligerents to utilize all national resources to win the war. In addition, both kept their engagements far away from civilians, and were ready to reach a compromise in the early stages of attrition.[37]

This unwillingness to keep on fighting was due mainly to the fact that neither side fought on its own territory, and that each had much to lose at home. Furthermore, the conflict did not approach the totality of the wars or the ideological struggles, nor was it motivated by abysmal hatred and dehumanization, all of which would characterize many subsequent conflicts of the twentieth century. Paradoxically, this conflict might have been one of the last "gallant" wars, as well as one of the first "humane" ones— a conflict in which both sides maintained rather strictly the traditional rules of decency but also provided reasonable treatment to the wounded and prisoners of war according to the humane and unprecedented standards that began to be instituted at the end of the nineteenth century.[38] The Russo-Japanese War, therefore, may provide some hints not only as to the means to prevent escalation, but also, as Peter Berton shows (Chapter 5, this volume), as to ways for a rapid rapprochement between belligerent nations.

Despite its remote location, the war attracted the attention of the world's principal armies and navies, and military observers dispatched to Manchuria recorded their conclusions in thick tomes.[39] They witnessed a number of large-scale battles, notably the battle of Mukden in which about half a million soldiers participated—the largest number in military history until then. As Yigal Sheffy points out (Chapter 16, this volume), the Russo-Japanese War was overwhelming proof for those still in doubt as to the importance of firepower as the dominant factor in military combat. Skilled observers, and an unprecedented number of them were in this campaign, did not have to wait for the fighting in 1916 around the trenches of Verdun. In the battlefields of Manchuria they could see the deadly and decisive effect of the use of intensive artillery in general, and the machine-gun in particular, as a result of which the tactical range in front of the defense lines became impenetrable. These observers' reports notwithstanding, the strategic planners of all the major European armies did not absorb this insight. They overlooked the growing superiority of defense in a war that lacked a revolutionary offensive weapon, miscalculating (on the German side) that the coming war in Europe would be "over by Christmas." Oddly enough, the successes the Imperial Japanese Army gained at terrible cost served to preserve existing beliefs and prevailing doctrines regarding the supremacy of offense over defense. The reluctance or inability of the European armies to emulate the tactical or strategic lessons of the war, in face of the dramatic increase in firepower in warfare, led to the horrendous slaughter a decade later.

The naval arena witnessed some dramatic improvements in weaponry and tactics after the war, but paradoxically the lessons of the war itself hardly contributed to the radical transformation of naval warfare that took place in the next two global conflicts, nor did it undermine substantially the contemporary balance of power among the major fleets. The war presented a long-awaited opportunity to test new weapons systems, and naval observers of all major navies, as Cord Eberspaecher shows (Chapter 18, this volume), followed closely the engagements between the Imperial Russian Navy (the world's third largest fleet) and the Imperial Japanese Navy (the world's sixth largest). The battle of Tsushima, which concluded the naval campaign, was the most important naval engagement since Trafalgar, and has remained ever since the last decisive battle between two major surface fleets. The sinking of a considerable part of the Imperial Russian Navy placed the British Royal Navy, the biggest fleet in the world, in an even stronger position than it had been throughout the previous two decades, and allowed it, and Britain as a whole, to concentrate on the German naval threat. Burdened by budgetary constraints, the Royal Navy accelerated the construction of a new and revolutionary class of battleship—the *Dreadnought*. The idea to launch such an all big-gun capital ship, which ultimately was armed with ten big guns of the same caliber, instead of the four big guns in the standard battleship until then, arose before the war, but the lessons of its naval battles, notably the battle of the Yellow Sea and the battle of Tsushima, provided the final affirmation for this novel concept. After the completion of the *Dreadnought* in 1906 more than 100 battleships of earlier classes were rendered obsolete and a new global naval arms race commenced, reflecting this time more exactly, as Phillips O'Brien noted, a nation's economic and technological capabilities.[40]

The war also demonstrated some significant improvement in military logistics as both sides conducted the campaign for a long period and far from their home bases. While Japan efficiently sustained its troops on the continent, its logistic achievements did not match those of Russia, which supplied the needs of a large army at a distance of nearly 10,000 kilometers (about 6,200 miles) from its capital, using only a single railway track. Another complex and unprecedented operation from a logistic perspective was the voyage of the Russian Baltic Fleet to East Asia, which involved enormous difficulties of refueling along the 33,000 kilometers (about 17,800 nautical miles) covered by this armada from its departure point to the place of its defeat. The logistic capabilities demonstrated by both sides served as a catalyst for further improvements and new fuels that fully materialized in both world wars.

The rise of new rivalry across the Pacific

Geographically remote from the two belligerents, the United States exploited the war as another step in its steady rise to global supremacy. While acting as a mediator in the peace process concluding the war, it changed from a sympathetic supporter of Tokyo at the outbreak of the war to a worried onlooker at Japan's emergence as a regional power at the end of the conflict. The following decades were marked by mutual suspicion and American attempts to check Japan's continental ambition and naval hegemony in the Pacific. As such, the war signaled the beginning of a struggle for control of the Pacific Ocean, culminating 37 years later in the Pacific War.

The 19-month period of the Russo-Japanese War was characterized by international awareness of the increasing political importance of the United States. In the 15 years since 1890 its population had grown tremendously, making it the second most populated power after Russia. By the turn of the century it was a leading economic power, but it still lacked the foresight and experience to use its economic achievements for geopolitical means and exert decisive international influence. Throughout the war the United States, under the dynamic presidency of Theodore Roosevelt, maintained its neutrality although it subtly changed its attitude to the Japanese. As the latter did not lose a single battle throughout 1904, Roosevelt's hopes of seeing both belligerents exhausted soon faded.[41] By the end of that year he was concerned by the prospects of a Japanese victory and its consequences for East Asia, wondering whether the Japanese did not lump all Westerners, together with the Russians, as "white devils inferior to themselves ... and seek to benefit from our various national jealousies, and beat us in turn."[42] This concern notwithstanding, Roosevelt played the role of host and mediator at the Peace Conference that brought the war to its conclusion. During the negotiations at Portsmouth, New Hampshire, he demanded that Japan conduct an "Open Door" policy in Manchuria, and return the area to Chinese sovereignty. Unwilling to enter into conflict with Japan, the United States signed an agreement with that country in July 1905, in which it recognized Japanese control over Korea in return for a similar recognition by Japan of American control over the Philippines.

At the outbreak of the war, many influential Americans, as Joseph Henning demonstrates (Chapter 10, this volume), held positive attitudes to Japan and regarded it as the underdog, and certainly more civilized than Russia. Some of them even tended to perceive the Japanese as semi-whites despite being non-Christian. As Japan gained the upper hand, however, a growing number of Americans, including Roosevelt, became aware of the dangers it constituted for the American presence in East Asia, the Philippines in particular; in the following years, even at home anti-Japanese sentiments outpaced the work of Japan's friends in the United States. Many more Americans, notably those residing along the west coast, likewise considered the war another sign of the "Yellow Peril" and became opposed to further Asian immigration to the United States.

The initial goodwill on both sides of the Pacific before and during the clash in Manchuria turned into slow diplomatic deterioration, and the first signs of a new conflict surfaced as early as in 1905. Both were rising powers that saw clearly for the first time the threat each posed to the other's interests and aspirations to control the ocean expanse and access to the markets of East Asia. This new outlook had some military implications, and consequently in 1907 the Americans updated their "Orange Plan" to protect the waters of the Pacific Ocean against the Japanese menace, fearing Tokyo might take over American outposts in the Philippines and Hawaii, and might even blockade the Panama Canal (completed in 1914). American apprehension of Japan, slightly premature but not too unrealistic, tightened the restrictions on Japanese immigration to the United States, and was the first step toward a suspicious and much more hostile policy on Japan in the 1920s. Hence, the Russo-Japanese War marks the beginning of relationships which Tal Tovy and Sharon Halevi justly term (Chapter 9, this volume) "a cold war" between the United States and Japan, ending in full military confrontation in December 1941.

The impact on East Asia

Japan's victory and Russia's defeat in the war had vital and lasting repercussions for Asia in general and its northeastern region in particular. The war marked the onset of Japan's firm grip on the continent and the takeoff point in its imperialist expansion. Only after the war was Japan regarded by others, and more especially by its own leaders, as being on an equal footing with all other imperialist forces involved in East Asian affairs, and only then did it become, at least from a military perspective, the strongest nation in the region (see Chapter 2, this volume). Russia, on the other hand, lost its colonial momentum in East Asia and returned to intervene in the local affairs of the region only in the 1930s. Additionally, the war had a bearing on the stability of the imperial regime in China as well as a decisive and long-term impact on Korean sovereignty.

The victory over Russia did not diminish Japanese military requirements, since the takeover of territories on the mainland created massive defense needs. Still, Japan and Russia, as Peter Berton illustrates (Chapter 5, this volume), were quick to overcome their previous animosity, and, following a series of four agreements (1907–16), were able to maintain a peace until the demise of the tsarist regime (see Map 3, p. 17). Nonetheless, two years after the war Japan drafted a national security plan that defined Russia, France, and, for the first time, the United States, as possible foes.

All maintained diplomatic relations with Japan, but they also had interests in East Asia and in the Pacific Ocean not necessarily congruent with Japan's national security. At home, Japanese society for the next 40 years viewed the war as firm evidence of its invincibility. With the removal of the sup- posedly existential threat against the nation, and with overwhelming proof of its successful modernization, Japanese intellectuals turned to deal with questions of national identity. The war thus intensified the ongoing debate with regard to two dialectical views on culture, "Japanese" and "Western," and laid the foundations for the bitter struggle Japan waged against the West from the early 1930s until its surrender in 1945.

In China, the war accelerated widespread political activities resulting six years later in the revolution of 1911 and the elimination of the Qing dynasty after 267 years. Already in 1905, as Harold Z. Schiffrin notes (Chapter 11, this volume), an infrastructure for a constitutional monarchy had been laid, and at the same time the first modern political movement was founded. Sensing its power undermined, after the war the Chinese government began to introduce several reforms, among them the establishment of elected assemblies and a campaign to eradicate the smoking of opium. During the war the Chinese public had expressed some solidarity with the Japanese, regarding them as brothers in a racial struggle, and, soon after, thousands of young Chinese flocked to Japan to study at its universities. They found it to be an appropriate role model for a successful modernization process that China could emulate. Within three years, however, this sentiment changed into deep suspicion toward the Japanese, who not only showed disrespect for the Chinese, but were also determined to snatch Manchuria from their hands. In this sense, the Russo-Japanese War, rather than its predecessor—the Sino-Japanese War of 1894–5—marks the onset of the great divide between these two East Asian giants.

The development of Manchuria, today a major industrial region with a population exceeding 100 million, is closely related to the consequences of the Russo-Japanese War. Its control of southern Manchuria made Japan regard this region as an entity separate from China, thereby placing the two nations on a collision course culminating in a Japanese takeover of the entire region in 1931. Japanese encroachment on Chinese soil began during the first Sino-Japanese War, a decade before the war against Russia, but at the end of that conflict the Three-power Intervention had forced Japan to give up its hold in Manchuria. In 1905, however, no power could take away Japan's coveted prize. The Japanese presence in southern Manchuria led to increased frictions with the Chinese authorities there, but also to a desire to become involved in the internal affairs of China itself. Japanese aspirations came to light a decade later with the notorious "Twenty-one Demands," which Japan submitted to the president of the new Chinese republic, and which eventually materialized beyond anything imaginable during the conquest of China starting in 1937. Such a move against China

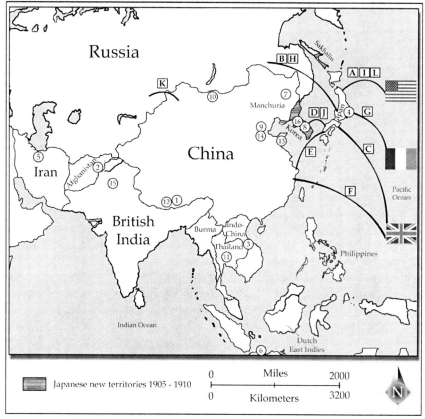

© Kowner

Map 3 Asia, 1904–19.

Key

Treaties: A Katsura-Taft Agreement (1905); B Portsmouth Peace Treaty (1905);
C Anglo-Japanese Alliance (1905, 1911); D Protectorate Agreement (1905);
E Treaty of Peking (1906) (Japan–China); F Anglo-Chinese Alliance (1906);
G Franco-Japanese Agreement (1907); H Russo-Japanese Agreements (1907, 1910, 1912,
1916); I Takahira-Root Agreement (1908); J Treaty of Annexation (1910);
K Treaty of Kyakhta (1915) (Russia, China, and Mongolia); L Lansing-Ishii Pact (1917).

Events:
 1 Lhasa—British opening of Tibetan trade (1904)
 2 Kabul—British request for concessions (1904)
 3. Laotian revolt (1904–6)
 4 Tokyo—Hibiya riots (1905)
 5 Tehran—Constitutional Revolution (1906)
 6 Jakarta (Batavia)—Establishment of the first nationalist movement (1908)
 7 Harbin—Assassination of Itō Hirobumi (1909)
 8 Seoul—Korean annexation (1910)
 9 Beijing—Chinese Revolution (1911)
10 Ulan Bator—Mongolian independence (1911)
11 Thailand—Military coup (1912)
12 Lhasa—Tibetan independence (1912)
13 Tsingtao—Japanese takeover (1914)
14 Beijing—Twenty-one Demands (1915)
15 Amritsar massacre (1919)
16 Seoul—March 1st Movement (1919)

was impossible at the end of the nineteenth century, but in the wake of the war with Russia, and even more after the Chinese Revolution of 1911, it no longer seemed far-fetched.

The greatest impact of the war on a single nation was undoubtedly on Korea. This backward and politically weak kingdom at the time was rapidly losing its sovereignty, until it was finally annexed by Japan in 1910. After the war the Japanese felt confident enough to seize control of almost all aspects of life in Korea, and began to dispatch settlers without international protest. They correctly concluded that no power could prevent them from annexing Korea, and in the course of less than five years they did not hesitate to realize their ambition ruthlessly. From a Korean viewpoint, the end of the Russo-Japanese War marked the beginning of prolonged suppression and an orchestrated attempt to destroy their national identity—a period that ended only with the fall of Japan in 1945. As Guy Podoler and Michael Robinson point out (Chapter 12, this volume), the annexation of Korea has left its deep scars on the nation's psyche until today. The fracture of the Korean society and national identity during 35 years of Japanese rule made possible the territorial division of Korea, no less than the political division between American and Soviet forces, which respectively installed a capitalist regime in the south and a communist regime in the north. This political division characterizes the two states of the Korean peninsula to the present day. Not only does the great hostility between them endanger peace in the area, but both states still bear a grudge against Japan for its occupation. Furthermore, North Korea has never established diplomatic relations with Japan and continues to seek compensation for the suffering endured by its people during the colonial era.

The war also served as a catalyst for the foundation and activities of many radical movements and organizations all over East Asia. Spanning a political and ideological spectrum from socialists to nationalists, anarchists, and even communists, these movements were a source of fermentation for many dramatic developments that characterized Asia from a political perspective in the following decades. The war, Yitzhak Shichor suggests (Chapter 13, this volume), contributed to the radicalization of moderate socialist movements in the area, to the de-legitimization of parliamentary democracy, and to an emphasis on the national aspect. Extremist movements sprang up during the war in China and Japan, but also in countries that were under colonial rule, such as Vietnam and the Philippines. In the ensuing years they worked for the independence of their countries, albeit with no marked success at that time.

Echoes of the war in western Asia and the colonial world

In colonial terms, the Russo-Japanese War signaled the final stage of the "Age of Imperialism," heralding Japan's 40-year colonial rule in Asia. The most significant and concrete spoil of the war was Korea, but it served as a spur for the takeover of all Manchuria 26 years later. Japan and the United States mutually enhanced their colonial hold by signing two agreements in 1905 and 1908, which consolidated their control over Korea and the Philippines, respectively. Further to the west, Russia and Britain reached an agreement in August 1907 on Tibet and Persia, making the former a buffer state and dividing the latter into two spheres of influence.[43]

In spite of these developments, the main impact of the war on the colonial world was psychological rather than territorial. Colonial subjects across the world—from Southeast Asia and the Indian subcontinent to the Middle East—were all thrilled by the war. When Sun Yat-sen, a revolutionary who several years later became the first provisional president of the Republic of China, was voyaging down the Suez Canal during the war, a local man approached him and asked if he was Japanese. "The joy of this Arab, as the son of a great Asian race," Sun noted, "was unbounded."[44] Sun's keen observation was made at the zenith of a symbolic turning point in the history of the colonial world: a non-European power employing modern technology could defeat a European power. From that time on, the victory was associated with a drive for more active and conscious nationalist movements in colonial Asia. This first significant rupture of the long-standing conceptions of superior "West" and inferior "East" created a new mindset, in which Japan served as a role model. With such a mindset nationalist and revolutionary ideas could thrive in the hope of future realization. During the war new sectors of the colonial population, Asian in particular, began to share their distress over the foreign rule and manifest a desire for a national self-definition. More radical segments of this population viewed the victory of Japan, a developing Asian country, over a major European power as a symbol, and as a portent for their own prospects of breaking free of colonial rule and taking the course of modernization on the Japanese model.

Apart from joy at the Russian defeat, national movements across the Arab world, much of it still under the rule of the Ottoman Empire, saw the war as a sign that they too could win soon their independence.[45] Further to the east, a revolution erupted in Iran that put into power, for the first time, a constitutional government. This political upheaval one year after the war was much affected by the weakening of Russia, but was also inspired by the knowledge that the victor was an Asian power with a constitution, whereas the vanquished was the only European power without a constitution.[46] Two years later another revolution broke out, this time at the heart of the Ottoman Empire itself. There too Japan served as a model of a country that had succeeded in adopting modern technology without losing its national identity. All in all, the war instilled belief in the Young Turks that they had the strength to cope with Western imperialism and encouraged them to rebel in 1908. Ultimately, however, the clash in Manchuria and the resulting political constellation in Europe were indirectly associated with Istanbul's decision in the aftermath of the Balkan wars to accept the overtures of Germany. The two nations signed, on August 2, 1914, a formal treaty of alliance, leading to immediate general mobilization, a declaration of war in October, and the entire collapse of the empire four years later.

The same year, young upper-class Javanese students in the Dutch East Indies established the first nationalist movement, the Budi Utomo, devoted to the promotion of Javanese culture. Throughout Muslim Southeast Asia, Michael Laffan finds (Chapter 14, this volume), Japan emerged after the war as "the light of Asia." Suddenly it materialized as a savior from Dutch colonialism, but it also featured as one of several lodestars, including the Ottoman Empire, for accomplishing a "hybrid modernity."[47] In India too "the reverberations of that victory," as the British Viceroy Lord Curzon became aware, "have gone like a thunderclap through the whispering galleries of the East."[48] Long subjugated under British colonialism, India experienced an unmistakable psychological impact from the Japanese triumph, argues T.R. Sareen (Chapter 15, this volume), which stirred up a wave of excitement and gave rise to the emergence of a new group of more radical leaders.[49]

Only six years after the American takeover and the consequent suppression of the Filipino uprising against the new rulers, the war reignited hopes for independence in the Philippines. American authorities were aware of the potential Japanese threat to the stability of their rule on the archipelago but in reality their fears were ungrounded, at least at this stage. The new political status of Japan after the war in northeast Asia led its leaders to prefer a settlement with the United States rather than further encouraging the nationalist aspirations of their southern neighbors. In the aftermath of colonial understanding with the United States, Japanese officials limited their contacts with Filipino nationalist leaders. Although impressed by the Japanese victory, disappointment with Tokyo's new policy led Filipino nationalists to cooperate pragmatically with the Americans in an effort to win greater rights.[50]

In retrospect, however, the psychological effect and the political repercussions of the Japanese victory on movements for independence in the colonial world were rather limited, notably in comparison with the repercussions of the war in other regions discussed here.[51] The colonial powers were determined to maintain their control, whereas most of the local movements were still at the incubation stage of formulating their policy vis-à-vis colonial rule. The ultimate proof that this impact of the war was minor is the fact that no colonial rule collapsed in the following three decades. Hence, although some nationalist movements grew stronger and more determined, it was only Japan's move against the West in December 1941 that brought about the final demise of Western colonialism, even if it resurged momentarily with Japan's surrender four years later.

Conclusion: the question of causality and the impact of the war

While the lack of public interest in the Russo-Japanese War, as discussed earlier, seems somewhat understandable, one may still wonder why historians have overlooked such a wide array of seemingly important repercussions. After all, they virutally affected every major nation involved in the chronicles of the early twentieth century. Could it be that the cause-and-effect relations between the fighting in remote Manchuria and subsequent events elsewhere were simply weak and indirect? Or could it be that historians encounter difficulty identifying such relations?

The question of causality is one of the fundamental issues in the study of history. In his classic study *What is History?* Edward H. Carr asserts that historical inquiry is the inquiry of reasons.[52] Historians indeed attribute extreme importance to causes and effects, and implicitly deal with the relations between one event or action and another in almost every one of their works. Causality is also the underlying motif of this book: the effect of the Russo-Japanese War on subsequent events throughout the world. Still, historical causality is often a precarious issue. It is a simple task to link an event to another immediate occurrence and argue for causal relations, but it is increasingly harder and less evident as the occurrence becomes more remote.

When dealing with causality, historians show preference for the study of the origins of a single event over its outcomes and impact. The preference is associated perhaps with the propensity historians have to view their discipline as a science, that is, a field governed by rules that might be applied for future use. The study of the origins of wars, as such, can be used for preventing them, whereas the study of the impact of wars seems more like an intellectual exercise. Moreover, the study of causes culminates in a single event, whereas the study of the outcomes of a single event expands and multiplies into countless events as the retrospective becomes broader and more distant. For this reason, we find a large number of studies, and even full discourses ("historical debates"), regarding the origins of wars but much less concerning the impact those wars have had.[53]

It is reasonable to assume that the effect of the Russo-Japanese War on the outbreak of World War I in 1914 did not resemble its effect on the much later outbreak of the Pacific War in 1941. Similarly, its effect on the annexation of Korea in 1910 was obviously much more crucial than the impact it had on the ongoing and wide-ranging events in China that culminated in the revolution of 1911. Nonetheless, causal relations involve more than that. While all contributors to this volume assume that the Russo-Japanese War had a substantial impact on their respective field of inqury, to them the term *impact* does not necessarily mean the same. This implicit meaning is important. Do they all take it that the war was a preliminary condition, a precipitant, an accelerator, or only a trigger for the occurrence

of a given subsequent event? Do they imply that the war was a sufficient condition or an imperative condition for this event to occur?[54] Do they
believe the war was the only cause, the crucial cause, or merely one out of
many causes of this event?

Most of the contributors have overlooked these semantic differences.
They have done so not only because the study of history barely provides
the methodological means to identify the sort of causal relations that exist
between two consequent events (thus we often prefer the term "influence"
to "impact"), but also because they have all dealt with a vast array of events
and could not examine in detail the type of impact each of them had. Despite
this methodological constraint and space limitation, their studies, separately
and together, invariably suggest that the Russo-Japanese War, although not
a global conflict in itself, had extremely broad and consequential repercussions. With a century's hindsight, one may even argue that the global impact
of the Russo-Japanese War was far more important than the effect of any
colonial war, and probably any other conflict, that took place between the
Napoleonic wars and the outbreak of World War I.

Notes

1 Many publications on the war and the military campaign were written in the
   first decade after the war by various reporters, military observers, and general
   staffs. Notable among them are multi-volume official histories published by
   Austria-Hungary, 1910–14; France, 1910–14; Germany, 1910–11, 1911–12;
   Great Britain, 1906–10, 1910–20; Japan, 1906, 1912; and Russia, 1910–13,
   1912–18. Although we still anticipate an authoritative overview of the military
   campaign, which will take into account archival materials and documents of
   both belligerents as well as their observers, in recent decades there have been
   a number of publications that survey all or certain aspects of the land and naval
   warfare, such as Connaughton, 1988; Jukes, 2003; Levitsky, 2003; Menning,
   1992; Ōe, 1988; Shinobu and Nakayama, 1972; Tani, 1966; Warner and Warner,
   1974; and Zolotarev and Kozlov, 1990.
2 Relatively speaking, there has been much written on the origins of the war and
   Russo-Japanese conflict in general, notably Duus, 1995; Lensen, 1959, 1982;
   Malozemoff, 1958; Nish, 1985; Romanov, 1952; and Stephan, 1994.
3 Hitler, 1939: 205.
4 In an article published on October 28, 1905, in Gandhi, 1961, V: 115; see also
   Gandhi, 1960, IV: 466–7. Similarly, Jawaharlal Nehru, the first prime minister
   of India after its independence, who was 15 years old at the outbreak of the
   war, recalled how the war assisted Indians to free themselves from their feeling
   of inferiority. In Nehru, 1934–5: 455, 514.
5 Cited in Gotō, 1997: 301–2.
6 David Thomson, for example, labeled the Russo-Japanese War the "fifth major
   colonial dispute." In Thomson, 1966: 518.
7 For additional examples, see Shillony and Kowner, 2007.
8 "In choice of subjects the criterion I used was that they must be truly representative of the period in question and have exerted their major influence on
   civilization before 1914, not after." In Tuchman, 1966: xv.
9 On the war in Russian historical memory, see Oleinikov, 2005: 505, 517.

10 Steinberg *et al.*, 2005: xix–xxi.
11 Toward the end of the war, Russia mobilized to Manchuria most of its regulars from Europe, the Caucasus, and Central Asia, but refrained from mobilizing most of its reserves, ending with about 500,000 of them in Manchuria out of more than three million. See, for example, Bushnell, 2005, 342–3, 346. The Russian death toll in the Crimean War was at least five times greater than in the Russo-Japanese War, amounting to about 256,000 dead. In Arnold, 2002: 39.
12 Two European nations witnessed a substantial shift in their military expenditures during the war or immediately after it: Russian expenditure declined sharply whereas German expenditure rose. In Stevenson, 1996: 2–8.
13 Herrmann, 1996: 7.
14 On the post-war negative image of the Russian national character in general and the capabilities of the Russian army in particular among the British, German, and Austro-Hungarian military authorities, see Herrmann, 1996: 93–5.
15 McDonald, 1992: 77. On the kaiser's schemes at Björkö, see McLean, 2003.
16 See Kennedy, 1988: 325.
17 On the German plans for a preventive war in 1905, see Moritz, 1974.
18 On the German overlapping and outdated government structure, see Steinberg, 1970.
19 The German operational war plan against France (known as the Schlieffen Plan) was designed soon after of the Russo-Japanese War and affected by its outcome. This daring but purely military plan was finalized by General Alfred von Schlieffen, the German Chief of Staff, and formed the basis for the German attack in 1914 with regular annual revision. Following the Russian defeat, Schlieffen argued that, in the coming war, the decisive theater would be in western Europe, and that the relatively weak armies of Russia could be held by defensive operations during the first weeks. On the Schlieffen Plan, see Bucholz, 1993; and Zuber, 2002; and on its repercussions in 1905, see Mombauer, 2001: 72–80. On the decision to replace Schlieffen, see Ritter, 1958: 111. On the French Plan XV, see Herrmann, 1996; Luntinen, 1984; and Tannenbaum, 1984.
20 Fischer, 1975, 164–7; Geiss, 1967, docs 3, 4, cited in Ferguson, 1999: 100. In another memorandum regarding Russia's future potential written in 1914, Moltke estimated that the Russian army would be fully fitted from 1917 onwards, concluding: "There cannot be any more serious doubt about the fact that a future war will be about the existence of the German people." Cited in Mombauer, 2001: 176. For a similar conclusion regarding Moltke's view of "war now or never," see Mombauer, 2001: 288.
21 See Ascher, 1988; Bushnell, 2005; Galai, 1973; and Kusber, 1997, 2007.
22 See Erickson Healy, 1976; Galai, 1973; and Walkin, 1962.
23 Even in late 1901, slightly before Britain concluded its alliance with Japan, Arthur Balfour, a supporter of an alliance with Germany and soon Britain's prime minister, argued that "the Japanese Treaty, if it ends in war, bring us into collision with the same opponents as a German alliance, but with a much weaker partner." In Balfour Papers, Add. Mss 49727, Balfour to Lansdowne, December 12, 1901. Cited in Charmley, 1999: 301.
24 For example, Kennedy, 1981: 118–39.
25 See Kennedy, 1988: 324–7.
26 For example, Andrew, 1968; Charmley, 1999; Monger, 1963; and Rolo, 1969.
27 Gooch, 1974: 171, 175; Monger, 1963: *passim.*
28 Ferguson, 1999: 56–81.

29 Ignoring the complex motives and strong fears of Germany in Britain in 1908–14, several historians have argued simplistically that Britain's decision to join the war in August 1914 was spurred by fears of Russia becoming too strong an empire in case of victory over Germany and the repercussions of such a scenario for the British Empire. In a similar manner, an attitude of "appeasing the strong" can be observed in 1903–4. If we accept this line of argument, the Russo-Japanese War did little to alleviate these fears, but it did help Britain to appease Russia. Furthermore, Germany accordingly did not pose the greatest threat to Britain either in 1904 or in 1914, although this does not necessarily mean that during the Russo-Japanese War German threats did not grow substantially. See, for example, Ferguson, 1999: 54–5; and Wilson, 1985.

30 See Behnen, 1985: 100.

31 On Russian diplomatic weakness after the war and on Russian policy in the Balkans, see Anderson and Hershey, 1918; McDonald, 1992, 2005.

32 See Edström, 1998: 13.

33 On Finnish political status during and after the war, see Hodgson, 1960. On Finnish revolutionary activities during the war and collaboration with Japan, see Copeland, 1973; Fält, 1976, 1979, 1988; Kujala, 1980; and Zilliacus, 1912.

34 Seton-Watson, 1977: 87.

35 On Polish attempts to collaborate with Japan during the war, see Bandō, 1995; Fountain, 1980; Inaba, 1992; and Lerski, 1959.

36 James, 1974, I: 82.

37 For the figures on the casualties, see Kowner, 2006: 80–1.

38 On the humane aspects of the military campaign, see, for example, Kowner, 2000a; and Towle, 1975.

39 For studies on the military observers in the Russo-Japanese War, see Greenwood, 1971; and Towle 1998, 1999.

40 O'Brien, 1998: 32.

41 See, for example, Trani, 1969: 36.

42 Roosevelt to Cecil Spring Rice on December 27, 1904. In Morison, 1951–4, IV: 1085–6.

43 On the British takeover of Lhasa during the war, see Stewart, 2007.

44 Cited in Jansen, 2000: 441.

45 On the public interest in the war in Egypt, see Bieganiec, 2007; and Marks, 2005.

46 Whereas the general public and military personnel throughout the Ottoman Empire were enthusiastic about the Japanese triumph, the official reaction was ambivalent, partly because of the Sultan's fears that Japan's victory might be interpreted as a victory of a constitutional state over an autocracy. On the reactions to the Japanese victory in the Ottoman Empire, see Akmese, 2005: 30–1, 72–8.

47 On the reactions to the war in the Dutch East Indies, see also Rodell, 2005.

48 Quoted in Passin, 1982: 14.

49 On the impact of the war in India, see also Dua, 1966; Dutta, 1969; and Marks, 2005.

50 On the relations of the Philippines with Japan and the United States before and after the war, see Yu-Jose, 1992. Rodell (2005) argues that nationalist movements in the Philippines and Vietnam were the only ones in Southeast Asia at a sufficiently advanced stage to be significantly affected by the war. See Rodell, 2005: 635–52.

51 On the difficulty associating the war with the revolt in Laos in 1904–6, the abortive military coup in Thailand in 1912, or the nationalist undertaking in Burma, see Rodell, 2005: 644, 631–3.

52 Carr, 1961.
53 See, for example, the historical debate in Germany on the origins of World War I (e.g. Mombauer, 2002), as well as the origins of German behavior in modern times ("der deutsche Sonderweg") and the writings in the early 1960s in Japan on the origins of the Pacific War (e.g. *Taiheiyō sensō e no michi: kaisen gaikō shi* [The Road to the Pacific War: A Diplomatic History of the Origins of the War]).
54 In his *Enquiries Concerning Human Understanding*, David Hume defines causes in imperative terms. That is, if one object does not exist, the subsequent object cannot exist either. In Hume, 1777 [1975]: 76.

Part I
The belligerents

2   The war as a turning point in modern Japanese history

Rotem Kowner

In the aftermath of the riots that hit Tokyo at the conclusion of the Russo-Japanese War, the Japanese government embarked on a widespread campaign of re-indoctrination. The target was the seemingly frustrated public, and the means was mainly displays of military prowess. The campaign began with a ceremonial review of the returning navy on October 23, 1905, followed by a series of marches and victory parades in the capital, and reached its climax in a huge victory review in the presence of Emperor Meiji on April 30, 1906. On the morning of that spring day, the 54-year-old monarch surveyed the vast spoils of enemy armaments arranged in precise order. Dressed in a new khaki uniform, he then passed through a triple triumphal arch 18.5 meters high that had been erected in honor of the event, and strode toward another grand spectacle. Waiting for him in the outer square were more than 30,000 soldiers, representing the 17 Japanese divisions that had taken part in the combat, as well as about 40,000 dignitaries and invited spectators.[1]

The review was followed by a military parade through the city streets under the rapt gaze of hundreds of thousands of citizens, and lasting until the evening hours. Behind the emperor's open carriage some of his close relatives galloped on fine horses, accompanied by a Korean prince and the British military attaché. The choice of riders was not fortuitous. The emperor's family members symbolized the growing importance of the imperial establishment and its place in the hearts of the Japanese nation, while the presence of the two foreign representatives reflected the elevated international status of Japan in the aftermath of the long war. The representative from Great Britain, the world's foremost power still, signified Japan's strong and steadfast foreign relations, and the Korean representative in a secondary position served as an indication for the ascent of Japan to the level of a regional power.

This international message notwithstanding, the demonstration was primarily for internal needs, to settle the recent turbulence that had erupted in the Hibiya riots. This popular disorder in the wake of the Portsmouth Peace Conference seemed initially to reflect a patriotic protest, but soon developed into sheer violence by an infuriated mob.[2] The retrospective design of the display emphasized the positive aspects of the war, but only a few of the spectators could have foreseen the great changes that were to take place in the following years. The next decade was not characterized by public prosperity or national grandeur, nor did it betray any indication of the significance of the war for Japan. This began to manifest itself only after World War I, when Japan turned "suddenly" into a world power.

The discussion of the place of the war in the modern history of Japan began only after World War II, when it was possible to analyze the local strain of imperialism in retrospect. After 1945 it became obvious that the Russo-Japanese War was the greatest conflict in which Japan was involved in the first 70 years of its modernization, overshadowed only by the eight years of continuous warfare (1937–45) on the Asian continent and the Pacific Ocean. Historians of modern Japan customarily view the Meiji Restoration of 1868 and the surrender in 1945 as two "turning points," or decisive events, in the modern chronicles of this nation. At the first turning point Japan abandoned the feudal system and the traditional, isolationist worldview, and began a rapid modernization; at the second Japan ceased to employ military force and to expand into territories beyond its archipelago. The elimination of militarism at the end of the Pacific War curbed Japan's estrangement from the West and directed it onto the path of economic development, combined with a certain degree of political detachment from Asia. In light of these events, how may we view the place of the Russo-Japanese War?

During the 1960s a number of Japanese historians debated the importance of the Russo-Japanese War, and two decades later the issue re-emerged in *Japan Examined*, a volume devoted to major themes in modern Japanese history. One of its chapters examined the legacy of the war, focusing on the role of the war in accelerating Japanese imperialism.[3] In spite of its narrow perspective on the implications of the war, the issue presented there still seems as relevant as ever before. With this background in mind, the following chapter seeks to examine the repercussions of the war on Japan and to determine to what extent it too might be considered a "turning point" in the modern history of this nation.

The rise of Japanese imperialism

At the end of World War I, Japan was regarded one of the world's Great Powers. As one of the Big Five powers at the Versailles Peace Conference, Japan won a permanent seat on the Council in the newly established League of Nations in 1919. This rise to the status of a world power was meteoric but not instantaneous. Fourteen years earlier, at the end of the Russo-Japanese War, Japan had been already considered as a regional power. Back then, it satisfied most of the criteria that may be applied to define such a designation: it had a sizeable military force, definitely the strongest in East Asia; it was recognized as a power in a series of agreements with other powers; it played a role in keeping order among the powers in the region under its control; and it had general interests outside its national borders, even though most of them were only in northeast Asia.

World War I did not alter Japan's position substantially, and, except for a brief military engagement against German forces stationed in Tsingtao, Japan did not take an active part in the war; nor did it make any considerable territorial gains.[4] By and large, its regional position grew only relatively, since at that time the involvement of other powers in East Asian affairs diminished dramatically. After the war against Russia, Japan was able to establish an array of mutual agreements with other powers and thus to fortify its "special position" in northeast Asia. Proponents of "Greater Japanism" were winning out, as Hata Ikuhiko points out, with every further agreement.[5] Strong Japan also meant retention of the Powers' control of East Asia and the perpetuation of Chinese disintegration.

Renewing their alliance in 1905 and again in 1911, Great Britain remained Japan's most valuable ally. Despite growing tension and suspicion, the United States recognized Japanese hegemony in Korea in return for Japan's recognition of its control over the Philippines in two agreements, signed in 1905 and 1908. In late 1906 Japan began negotiations also with France regarding a mutual agreement, and three months later it began to negotiate even with Russia. The negotiations in St Petersburg were a swift and unexpected realization of the vision of Sergei Witte, who only a year and half earlier, in Portsmouth, had spoken of a future alliance with Japan. Eventually, in June 1907 Japan signed an agreement with France (the Franco-Japanese Entente) and in July completed the first series of agreements with its former arch-enemy. The Russo-Japanese Agreement of 1907 ratified the Treaty of Portsmouth, supported the territorial integrity of China and an open-door economic policy within its boundaries, and also contained a secret protocol marking the sphere of control of each nation in Manchuria. Now, for the first time, Russia recognized fully Japan's interests in Korea and even committed itself to non-intervention, while Japan reciprocated by recognizing Russian interests in Outer Mongolia.

In territorial terms, at the end of war against Russia Japan acquired the southern half of Sakhalin and control over the southern tip of the Liaotung peninsula in Manchuria (renamed the Kwantung Leased Territory). Following the Treaty of Portsmouth and the subsequent agreement with China in late 1905, Japan was allowed to deploy troops in southern Manchuria to guard the tracks and concessions along the South Manchuria Railway. The agreement brought about the establishment of the Kwantung army (*Kantōgun*), Japan's military garrison in Manchuria, which played a decisive role in Japanese meddling in Manchuria and the eventual takeover of the whole region in 1931. Korea, Japan's most coveted prize, still remained independent, but not for long. In the following years Japan grew confident of its power to annex Korea without fearing any Western interference. In November 1905 it took its boldest step toward full control of the Korean peninsula by forcing a Korean official to sign the Protectorate Agreement, even though at this stage there was still no consensus in Tokyo about the desired policy vis-à-vis Korea. The first resident-general in Korea, Itō Hirobumi, for example, opposed annexation and saw his role as a mission for reform. Eventually, however, Katsura Tarō's return to power, the resignation of Itō and his assassination, as well as the stubborn Korean opposition to the Japanese presence, led in 1910 to the full annexation of Korea. This was Japan's most substantial gain in territorial and demographic terms until the early 1930s, and it reinforced Japanese confidence even more.[6]

Despite the initial modest territorial gains and incomplete military victory, some historians consider the Russo-Japanese War a turning point in the modern history of Japan due, as Peter Duus suggested in an oft-cited paper, to its being the "takeoff point" for Japanese imperialism.[7] Duus thereby challenged two other theses. The first postulates that Japanese imperialism developed in a direct, continuous, and deliberate line of expansionist exploits from the first attempts to open up Korea in the 1870s until Japan's surrender in 1945. Accordingly, the war against Russia was merely another stage, not necessarily a central one, in a chain of events that gave rise to the Japanese Empire. Supplementary to this, a second thesis assumes that, if one insists on a key point in the development of Japanese imperialism, it should be the first Sino-Japanese War (1894–5). This is because, with this conflict, for the first time in three centuries Japan embarked on a full-scale military adventure oversees, aiming to seize a continental foothold.

Duus objected the first thesis, treating it almost as an intellectual casuistry. It was never taken seriously, he averred, because most of the historical evidence unequivocally indicated that the decisions to build an empire were made only in the later stages of the Meiji period (1868–1912), and that even the decision to go to war against China was taken with great caution. Japanese imperialism was mostly opportunistic and derived from transient needs, and consequently the continental expansion cannot be regarded as an inevitable process. At every stage it could have been sped up or slowed down, and at certain times the wheel even turned back. As for the second thesis, Duus reasoned that the first Sino-Japanese War had to be measured according to its results so it could not be regarded as a turning point.[8] True, it was this conflict that created the belligerent imperialist line of action that Japan followed until 1945, and its success in the war with China gave decision makers in Tokyo the confidence to dare to challenge Russia a decade later.[9] Nonetheless, this war did not ensure Japan's position in East Asia, as is evident from its capitulation to the Three-power Intervention. In the same vein, that war did not foster Japan's taking control of Korea, and in the end it remained in 1895 without a foothold on the continent.

Duus's argument regarding the limited importance of the first Sino-Japanese War makes much sense, certainly compared with the Russo-Japanese War. A quantitative comparison leaves no doubt about the greater weight of the latter. Hostilities against Russia lasted 19 months, compared with "only" nine months against China, and they cost the Japanese treasury some 1,730 million yen as compared with the 200 million yen required a decade earlier.[10] More than a million soldiers and sailors fought in the conflagration with Russia, five times more than the figure in the previous decade, and the death toll exceeded 85,000 lives, about six times the losses in the previous war.[11] Moreover, it was only after the end of the war against Russia that foreign observers began to regard Japan as a power on an equal footing with other powers involved in East Asian affairs. Only then did Japan become, at least militarily, the strongest power in the region. After the first Sino-Japanese War some military experts were impressed by Japan's combat capacity, but most of them still professed that, as long as it did not cross swords with a Western opponent, it could not be considered a genuine military power.[12] In the wake of the war against Russia, no expert cast doubt any longer on Japan's military capabilities.[13] By now Japan was a national menace to China, and thereafter relations between the two nations changed considerably, culminating in a prolonged armed conflict that ended only in 1945.[14] Whereas until 1904 the struggle between the two states focused on Korea, a territory under the sovereignty of neither, by the end of the war with Russia Japan occupied sizeable portions of China's Manchuria. This control was to endure for the next four decades, stimulating Japan's appetite for further interference in China's internal affairs.

Another substantial impact of the war on Japanese imperialism was its commercial outcome. Following the victory the numbers of private businessmen and entrepreneurs who left for the Asian continent in search of new commercial opportunities rose substantially. Many of these enterprising individuals reached Manchuria, whose abundant resources and wide plains they regarded as a business opportunity, and they based their initiatives on Japanese involvement in the area.[15] Within a few years Japan's economic center of gravity on the continent had shifted to the north, Manchuria becoming the "promised land." The war contributed toward making imperialism a vision and goal for the entire Japanese people, who began, through mass demonstrations and protests, to exert continuous pressure for additional exploits. Paradoxically, the territories Japan took over created a sense of exaggerated military and strategic needs rather than security: victory was followed by increased military expenditure and additional military build-up.

The upsurge of Japanese militarism

The war's impact on Japanese militarism was decisive and lingered until the dissolution of the Japanese army and navy in 1945. In military terms, the clash with Russia had no precedents on that scale, and in later years as well it remained Japan's most fateful military challenge until the Pacific War (1941–5). The war enhanced the status of the military, elevated its commanders to heady fame, and helped to militarize the imperial family symbolically.[16] Both the army and the navy were aware of the significance of this, and regarded the war as a starting point and reference for training, budgetary allocations, and the creation of military ethos.[17] Critically, the war provided the two services with enormous and varied combat and logistic experience, put to use in the next conflict that they were to join four decades later.[18]

As a lesson in history, the war provided the most solid evidence that the Japanese nation was invincible. This conviction could not have emerged after the victory over China because of the seeming inferiority of the opponent and because the victory had been an isolated case. The triumph over Russia provided the required continuity: Japanese forces won two victories against foes of superior size, one Asian and the other European. The war also reinforced the belief that the national spirit in general, and its fighting spirit in particular, could make up for, if not replace, shortage of manpower and some deficiencies in advanced armament. *Yamato Damashii* (Japanese Spirit) became a major factor in comprehending Japan's victory over the supposed superiority of the numerically greater Russia. This concept had a long-standing historical background in Japan, but now it was used for military objectives. In the following decades it was to play a crucial role in promoting Japanese militarism, by spurring field commanders to take unnecessary risks in battlefield and by motivating the rank and file to fight to the point of exhaustion and to sacrifice their lives.[19]

The concept of Japanese Spirit was partly a myth, and like all myths it was detached from reality and thorough analysis. During the war many incidents occurred where Japanese soldiers did not evince much combat spirit, contrary to what Japanese propaganda after the war boasted. During the siege on Port Arthur, for example, a gradual decline in military discipline was evident, and occasionally soldiers were forced to charge. The belief in this spirit was partly responsible for the huge and needless losses incurred by General Nogi Maresuke's Third Army around Port Arthur, and also for the post-war campaign to conceal these losses and to magnify Nogi, of all commanders, as a war hero.[20] In reality, the victory over Russia was not just a "victory of spirit over matter." Russia was certainly a mighty nation with a much larger army, but throughout much of the war the bulk of its forces remained in Europe and many of the battles were conducted in a state of numerical parity, occasionally even with the advantage on the Japanese side. Ultimately, the emphasis on *Yamato Damashii* bore a catastrophic message that found expression in the military adventures Japan was to hazard later on.

A similar legacy with horrendous repercussions was the conviction that Japan could defeat a superior force by means of a surprise opening gambit and subsequently conclude the military campaign around the negotiating table. The buds of this notion surfaced in 1894, but the surprise attack on Russia on the eve of the war and the Portsmouth Peace Conference in its conclusion became the epitome of a model war. The same model would be applied optimistically 37 years later, on the eve of the Pacific

War, underlying the audacity to enter an all-out struggle against superior foes such as the United States and Great Britain. The ostensible similarity between the two events, both in scale and in their inherent risk, led Japanese decision makers in 1941 to believe they could replicate the military success against Russia, despite some significant differences in international circumstances. The resort to the successful pattern of a previous war is apparent in the memoirs of Admiral Tomioka Sadatoshi:

> Before and at the beginning of the [Pacific] war, we all believed in the concept of Limited War . . . and anticipated the course of the war as follows: firstly, to attain an overwhelming supremacy over the enemy forces in its early stages and create a strategic equilibrium against the allies; then to seek a favorable opportunity to enter into negotiations with our enemies for a compromise peace, keeping enough potential to continue the war.[21]

Nevertheless, the wars Japan waged after 1905 were not exact copies of the campaign against Russia. Not only had global circumstances been transformed substantially, and the enemies been different, but the Japanese themselves had changed. Some of patterns of their combat behavior had altered unrecognizably. The readiness for compromise had gradually narrowed, and there was a noticeable shift toward extremism in the fighting ethos. One such transformation occurred in the attitude to Japanese prisoners of war. The approximately 2,000 Japanese soldiers that returned from Russian captivity in 1906 underwent interrogation, and in accordance with the new regulations published in July 1905 they had to explain the reasons for their becoming captive. By and large, they were not imprisoned, but most of them were forced to retire from service. This attitude was still lenient compared with the combat code three decades later, which regarded falling into captivity as utter shame for the soldier and his family. While the Russo-Japanese War signaled a slight change in attitude to Japanese personnel who were taken prisoner, only in the 1930s did the authorities begin to stress combat until the "bitter end" and the dishonor of falling captive, and only then did Japan endeavor earnestly to distinguish the desired code of conduct among its soldiers from the prevalent code in the West.[22]

The quest for identity

Toward the end of the war with Russia public opinion in Japan began to expect Western recognition of its newly elevated status as a first-class power (*ittōkoku*) and a great nation (*taikoku*). True, only a few years earlier Japan finally altered the unequal treaties its had signed in the mid-nineteenth century with the Western powers, but now any indication of lack of respect or discrimination caused an uproar and triggered a sensitive sense of injury and insult. At the same time, fresh memories of the Three-power

Intervention nine years earlier resulted in intense fears of fresh Western reaction. While neither European intervention nor a second wave of "Yellow Peril" in the West materialized, the Japanese victory did intensify American animosity vis-à-vis Japanese immigration, and led to legislation restricting immigration from Asia.[23] These new restrictions were followed closely in Japan, and the psychological repercussions of this and other tokens of "national insult," argued Naoko Shimazu, had "a lasting impact on Japanese thinking." Once relatively acquiescent to Western differential treatment, the victory changed Japanese international expectations in an instant. But it was a rude awakening. Only after the war against Russia, Shimazu correctly observes, did the Japanese became fully aware of "the seemingly unbridgeable racial gap between themselves and the other great powers." [24]

In the following years Japanese society witnessed the emergence of an extensive discourse known as *jinshuron* (lit. "theories of race"). Its origins are rooted earlier, starting probably with the encounter with Western ideas of a racial taxonomy during the early Meiji era and intensified by European notions of the "Yellow Peril" in the late 1890s. Nonetheless, only after the war did Japanese intellectuals begin to question earnestly their national belonging, expressing skepticism as to whether their nation would ever be deemed as being on an equal footing with the leading powers. Twenty years before the victory over Russia, the influential reformer and thinker Fukuzawa Yukichi had advocated abandoning Asia and joining Europe, but, after the war with China, and still more in 1905, doubts were rife regarding the ability and even the need to do so.

The war reinforced earlier misgivings regarding the course Japan had chosen since the Meiji Restoration. In 1898 the aristocrat politician Konoe Atsumaro proposed the concept of "solidarity of similar races," promoting collaboration with China vis-à-vis the West via his pan-Asian movement Tōa Dōbunkai and its successor Tōa Dōshikai.[25] In the aftermath of the war such pan-Asian ideas became more popular than ever, gaining new converts. Pan-Asianists were no longer dreamers or extreme figures but included some of Japan's leading personalities. One of them was Yamagata Aritomo, a former prime minister and one of the five *Genrō* during the war, who in 1905 still subscribed to Fukazawa's idea. A few years later, however, and especially after the 1911 revolution in China, Yamagata became an ardent pan-Asianist.[26] In the post-Russo-Japanese War era, the incongruity between the two perceptions, one supporting solidarity with the West and one supporting a pan-Asian struggle against the West, grew stronger, and a bitter debate erupted over Japanese identity. In the eyes of many Japanese, however, the world for which they strove left them little choice.[27] While public opinion in the United States and Europe increasingly regarded Japan as a threat to their economic interests and colonial rule in Asia, sympathy for Japan in China and Korea rapidly dwindled. A total ban in China on Japanese merchandise in 1908, and the assassination of Japan's leading statesman, Itō Hirobumi, by a Korean patriot a year later, sent a stark message to the Japanese public that even their racial kin regarded them as an alien and hostile entity. At a time of growing need for foreign reassurance, the new circumstances left a strong feeling of isolation. Even the typically sober Itō wrote in 1907 that never before had Japan been so isolated politically.[28]

In such a state of affairs the initial public euphoria over the victory did not last long. The most perceptible feeling was soon one of disillusionment and gloom. The inadequate diplomatic achievements at Portsmouth—the supposed cause of the "Hibiya riots"—were not the sole cause for the disappointment, and at any rate they did not upset most of the intellectuals. They were simply filled with frustration and dread resulting from what they sensed even before the war as a loss of Japanese identity and its incongruity with Western culture. Early signs of this sentiment had emerged earlier, but the conclusion of the extreme national efforts aimed against Russia gave way to a rather individual quest for meaning, which now collided with still strong elements of the feudal and Confucian legacy. Sensing the *Zeitgeist*, the novelist Tokutomi Roka stated in 1905 that the conversion of Japan into a world power had done very little to strengthen its security and economy.[29] A similar mirror of the contemporary melancholy is found in the journal *Shin kōron*, which in several issues in mid-1906 dealt with the inability to stem "the tide of deterioration." In the introduction to the series, the editors reason:

> The so-called pessimism, the so-called anxiety, and suicide, all this is the product of an age of decline and has no place in the rising empire of Japan. Nonetheless, these damaging trends are swiftly becoming the sign of the times. Is this not a problem worthy of serious consideration by our intellectual leaders?[30]

Side by side with growing chauvinism and jingoism, Japan in 1906–12 underwent a significant transformation in the ideological and intellectual sphere.[31] It was now a time for reflection—a necessary stage that had been postponed before due to the existential threat of Russia. More than any other Japanese, perhaps, it was the writer Natsume Sōseki who depicted succinctly the shattered dreams the Japanese experienced after the war and their growing ambivalence vis-à-vis the West. A year before the outbreak of the war Sōseki had returned from a frustrating three-year stay in London, and thereafter he devoted the remainder of his short life to portraying the Japanese conflict with modernity. "It will be a pity," he wrote in 1905, "to lose one's own and one's country's special characteristics through too much adoration of the West."[32] By means of mainly Western military technology, Japan's elimination of the Russian threat served as proof of the success of modernization, but this was not necessarily identical with Westernization. In the following decade intellectuals felt free to return to questions of identity, and they made a concerted effort to redefine the essence of being

Japanese. Many of them believed that Japan's post-war mission was to serve as a bridge between East and West, by reconciliation or by integration.[33] The national discourse that emerged soon after the war is known as *nihonjinron* (lit."theories about the Japanese"), and with certain ebbs and flows it has engaged the Japanese society to this very day.[34]

Early *nihonjinron* writers focused on the meaning of being Japanese in a modern but non-Western society and the spirit that characterized such a society. The expression *wakon yōsai* ("Japanese spirit—Western technique") had been coined before the war, but after it a wide range of thinkers sought to redefine that spirit. In 1909 the leading psychiatrist Morita Shōma (Masatake) developed the concept of *shinkeishitsu*—a mental condition supposedly unique to Japanese that manifests itself whenever the mind is occupied with superfluous thoughts.[35] A year later Nishida Kitarō, the most eminent modern Japanese philosopher, published his *Zen no kenkyū: jitsuzai to jiko* (An Inquiry into the Good). Using Western terms, he sought to define the key concept of "pure experience"—a conscious state unique to Orientals.[36] Also in 1910 the renowned ethnologist Yanagita Kunio examined in *Tōno monogatari* oral traditions among the peasants.[37] Focusing on Japanese modernization, he argued that it was not identical with Westernization. Among the peasants Yanagita discovered the ideal of the "common Japanese man," contending that the repression and exploitation in Japan had originated from a foreign culture, imported in the past from China and in the present from the West.[38]

A year after the war the radical ideologist Kita Ikki challenged the parental relationships between the emperor and the people dictated by the Meiji oligarchy.[39] He asserted that both the emperor and the people should belong to the state, and their ties ought to transform accordingly. Kita, the future author of the manifesto of the political right in the 1930s,[40] was not the only figure to re-examine national ideology. From a single publication on this topic in 1908 the number rose two years later to ten.[41] In an article published in 1911 the economist Kawakami Hajime began to deal with cultural problems and compared Western individualism, based on a "personal framework" (*jinkaku*), with the Japanese family state, based on a "national framework" (*kokkaku*). Kawakami postulated that Japanese uniqueness lay in the identity of the particular interest of the individual with the public interest. Like many of his contemporaries, Kawakami enhanced the sense of a dialectical opposition between two completely different cultural structures—that of Japan and that of the West.[42] These two structures constituted the tension, argued Peter Dale, between the individual and society during the period of modernization. The "West" functioned in this equation as an external metaphor for all the outward aspects of the Japanese social structure during the course of modernization.[43]

The war served as a cause and trigger for the emergence of a new national self-image. Until the war, the Japanese had undergone a process that the American anthropologist Harumi Befu labeled "self-Orientalism," that is, the acceptance of the Western perception of the East as inferior by those who are the very object of that perception. After the war, however, new forces began to stress the qualities of the Japanese spirit, suggesting that Japan was equal to the West and in certain spheres even superior. In this evolving intellectual milieu, the West began to represent elements different from, and sometimes inferior to, the cultural framework Japan could offer. This view created a new sense of pride but also was the harbinger of confrontation between two dialectic images: that of Japan on the one hand and that of the West on the other.[44]

The post-war ideology also imparted greater importance to the emperor. The collision with Russia provided Emperor Meiji with many glorious moments he had never experienced before, and from then until 1945 his heirs were considered both the constitutional monarchs and the father figures of the nation. Although he remained in his Tokyo palace throughout the war against Russia, the emperor was depicted as a senior statesman involved in all strategic decisions. As the war ended he left for the temple of the Sun Goddess in Ise to report the victory, in an unprecedented act that demonstrated, some historians argue, that his divinity had been finally established.[45] Victory was the emperor's, but the "shameful peace" obtained at Portsmouth was not.[46] In the seven-year period spanning the conclusion of the war and the death of the first modern Japanese monarch in 1912, the embedding of the modern concept of "emperor," as the Meiji oligarchy had envisioned it many years before, was finally completed. At the heart of the emerging concept of a family state stood a figure whose status had received a substantial boost during the war. In post-war school textbooks the image of the emperor was further enhanced, presenting him as the symbol of Japan's national fortitude. The confused young man of 1868 was now the symbol of "Japan's advance to the level of the world powers."[47]

Political and social transformation

In the decade after the war, Japan witnessed a number of social and political developments whose repercussions echoed long afterwards. The three most significant trends associated with the war, as Banno Junji has aptly pointed out, were the emergence of the Rikken Seiyūkai party, which gained a stable majority in the Lower House before the war, the increasing interference of the army and navy in politics, and the rise of popular urban movements. In addition, the war brought about numerous subtle changes that shaped the face of Japanese society and politics as more constitutional, and somewhat more liberal, but also planted resistant seeds for future totalitarianism and ultra-nationalism.[48]

Politically, the most immediate outcome of the war was a government reshuffle. At the beginning of 1906 the 56-year-old nobleman Saionji Kimmochi was appointed prime minister, in place of the resigning Katsura Tarō. Saionji represented the Seiyūkai, although the actual leader of the party was Hara Kei (Takashi), a man considered the first genuine party politician. Still, the rise of Saionji did not proclaim any dramatic changes in Japanese politics because the gentlemanly way of appointing prime ministers remained intact. It was Katsura who recommended Saionji for this position; in 1908 the latter recommended the former as his successor, and each of them was able to lead another cabinet before 1913. Nonetheless, Katsura and Saionji did not enjoy the same power pre-war oligarchs had exerted, and after 1906 there was a significant increase in the power of the parliament, which served to balance somewhat the belligerent tendencies toward further continental expansion.[49]

In a similar fashion, the years that followed the war were characterized by further weakening of the *Genrō* position, the unofficial and manifestly non-democratic council of senior statesmen that possessed the greatest power among the oligarchy on the eve of the war. Eighteen years later all five wartime *Genrō* were dead. In 1912, three years after the assassination of Itō, Saionji was appointed as the fifth *Genrō*, and when Yamagata died a decade later he remained alone in this position until his death in 1940. Although the decline of this role constituted theoretically another step toward democracy, in the second half of the 1920s the system of checks and balances in Japanese politics was undermined by the lack of stabilizing bodies promoting general national interests as the *Genrō* had. Thus, the cessation in appointing additional figures to the position, and the lack of suitable leaders endowed with political realism and assuming national responsibility like the early oligarchs, were damaging to Japan's foreign policy and probably contributed to some of its rash and adventurous decisions in the following decades.

Another political transformation associated with the war was the growing involvement of the army and navy in internal affairs. This phenomenon had pre-war roots and would recede temporarily in the early 1920s, but the struggle with Russia definitely served as its catalysts. Of the two services, the navy was the greater beneficiary of the war, because of its intact combat record but also because it became evident that, without large annual budgets, Japan would not be able to maintain its naval hegemony in the region. With the establishment of the Ministry of the Navy in 1872, separate from the Ministry of the Army, the navy was considered a secondary service. After the war, however, the navy began to perceive itself as equal to the army, and vied for a greater share in limited resources of the state.[50] In the new political circumstances its leaders were capable now of forging a political alliance with members of the Seiyūkai party, resulting in a counter-alliance between the army and parties opposed to the Seiyūkai. In 1910 the inter-service tension reached a climax when the army demanded two additional divisions to the existing nineteen due to the annexation of Korea. Public support for the navy's expansion program, and the political commitment to this service, enabled the government headed by Prince Saionji to refuse the army's demand. The army counteracted by bringing down the government in 1912, and three years later its demands were finally met.

In the following decades the ties between the military and civilian systems continued to weaken, while both services displayed increasing involvement in politics. Starting in 1912, the army, and to a lesser extent also the navy, made manipulative and frequent use of the practice established in 1890, namely that the minister in charge of each service should be appointed from among the generals and admirals on active service. By then, each had different goals and sets of priorities, which mirrored a new post-war condition that Oka Yoshitake defined as "dissolution of consensuses."[51] The discord over national goals and the corrosion of the central process of decision-making characterized the following years. In the 1930s the growing interservice competition had a far-reaching and subversive impact on internal politics, accompanied by greater pressures for imperialist expansion.[52]

The post-Russo-Japanese War period is often considered to have heralded the "Taisho democracy" and the broadening of political participation.[53] Certainly, the "golden age of government authority," which characterized, according to Tokutomi Sohō, the early Meiji era, had ended.[54] The new period was characterized, instead, by the emergence of many popular movements, such as the movement against taxes, arguably a symptom of the political crisis that broke out at the beginning of the Taisho period (1912–13). Within this context the "Hibiya riots" are often regarded as an early sign of the popular movement that led to the political movement of the Taisho period. In fact, certain signs of the political awakening of the masses emerged even before the end of the war, stimulating Prime Minister Katsura to express his concern to Yamagata that the lower classes "are mixing politics with social questions, and now, from grooms and rickshawmen to small tradesmen, the people are raising a hue and cry about an indemnity, though they know nothing about the issue."[55] Much of the popular protest in Hibiya, and many other protests and strikes peaking in 1907, were associated merely with new a sense of deprivation, both political and economic, and of frustration in that these spheres were monopolized by the few (*tokken kaikyū*; "the privileged classes"). Nonetheless, it is difficult to discern any direct link between the riots and later political developments. All the popular movements of that period, this one included, were passing phenomena, and their influence remained limited. Even the post-war radicalism was nothing new, and its implications were marginal compared with the reactionary forces at the beginning of the Meiji and Showa eras.[56]

Was the war a turning point?

The term "turning point" carries two different usages, hence implications. On the one hand, it indicates an unusual or a sharp change from a previous trend—a sort of inverted historical course.[57] On the other hand, a turning point can be considered a mere change in intensity, consisting of significant strengthening or weakening of a persistent trend. In historiographic terms, the first usage can be seen as a breakthrough and even as the beginning of a new age, while the second serves to mark a subdivision within a period. When discussing the significance of the Russo-Japanese War as a turning point, we seem to be dealing with the second meaning. As this chapter has sought to demonstrate, the war caused no sharp turnabout in earlier trends in most spheres, but only led to their strengthening and acceleration. In this sense, the Russo-Japanese War differs from the two indisputably "genuine" turning points in the modern history of Japan—the Meiji Restoration in 1868 and the surrender of Japan in 1945, which stand as remarkable deviations from an earlier course.

In many respects, indeed, the war did not alter any earlier trends for Japan. Its aspiration for imperial expansion had made a modest start back in the 1870s, and the significant incursion into the continent took place during the first Sino-Japanese War. Even the roots of Japanese militarism went back much earlier, and the army and navy were granted large budgets and significantly augmented before the war. The transformation of Japan's military image at home and abroad had begun before the war, and were it not for such an evaluation Britain would probably have refrained from entering into an alliance with Japan in 1902. Even the indications of disappointment with the West and the desire for a distinct identity that marked the years following the war can be found in many publications at the end of the nineteenth century. Finally, the democratic tendencies that accompanied the strengthening of political parties in Japan were rooted in the establishment of a parliament in 1889 and the slow decline in power of the Meiji oligarchy. It is fairly difficult, therefore, to point to a single sphere in which the war constituted a breakthrough.

The search for spheres in which a genuine shift occurred during and after the war forces the historian to overlook many domains in which minimal changes, if any, occurred. Despite the intellectual quest for identity, the war did not lessen significantly the popular attraction of the West and its culture, and certainly did not slow down the rate of modernization. On the whole, the regime did not change and the oligarchy continued to maintain its strength in various forms for more than a decade. Most economic indices neither improved nor declined steeply, although industry continued to expand.[58] There was no drastic change in the Japanese social structure and its preconceptions since, except for marginal reforms, economic and social inequality persisted, women remained without the right to vote, the urban population continued to grow steadily, and poverty and harsh living conditions continued to characterize the rural areas.

Although disappointing for some, this broad review of the spheres in which transformation was marginal stresses the fact that the war was far from a historical turning point in the first sense of the word. Not only did it reinforce earlier trends rather than shift their direction, but in many spheres there was actually no significant change, even in the intensity of the trends. This sober perspective notwithstanding, it is difficult to imagine the development of modern Japan without the imperialist drive that characterized it from 1904 to 1945. As Peter Duus (Chapter 3, this volume) suggests, a considerable share of the foreign affairs, industrial growth, and political developments that Japan witnessed during the subsequent four decades were associated with its triumph over Russia.

There is only one alternative and positive model to that of imperial Japan that we seem able to envision. This is post-1945 Japan—a nation with a prosperous economy confined within a limited territory and practically free of territorial disputes. It is difficult to assume that Japan could have clung to such a model in 1904, when its industry was still in its infancy and the state was in the midst of its Age of Imperialism. Historians with a deterministic outlook incline to argue that the war and the imperialist development that followed were a necessary stage in the modernization of Japan. Having only one course open, history does not allow us to examine it properly. All in all, however, a broad view of the actual repercussions of the war on Japan, as well as those that did not materialize, indicates that the Russo-Japanese War was a crossroads, after which many essential processes for the making of what we know today as Japan accelerated. Therefore, we ought to regard this war as a landmark, marginal perhaps in comparison with the two other dramatic turning points, but still one of the key points in the modern history of Japan.

Notes

1 The War Ministry also organized an exhibition of unprecedented proportions in the open courtyard in front of the imperial palace. It presented Russian armaments taken as spoils from the battlefields of Manchuria: more than 70,000 rifles, swords, and spears; nearly 500 guns; and more than 2,000 wagons and carts. On the imperial review and the exhibition in spring 1906, see Fujitani, 1996: 134–6.
2 On the riots and their significance, see Okamoto, 1970, 1982.
3 "The Russo-Japanese War: Turning Point in Japanese History?," In Wray and Conroy, 1983: 149–69.
4 Japan gained the Mariana, Carolina, and Marshall Islands in the Pacific, and temporarily also the German holdings in the Shantung peninsula in northern China.
5 Hata, 1988: 271.
6 The annexation of Korea provided Japan with an additional territory of about 220,000 square kilometers and a population estimated at about 13.8–14.7 million subjects, depending on the source. For the population data of Korea in 1910, see Nahm, 1988; and Shin, 2002: 353.
7 Duus, 1983: 154. For a similar view, see also Kitaoka, 1978.
8 Compare with an earlier argument by Inoue Kiyoshi that Japanese imperialism emerged in 1899. In Inoue, 1953.

9   For an expanded discussion on the importance of the first Sino-Japanese War, see Oh, 1983.
10 On the Japanese expenditures, see Okamoto, 1970: 127.
11 There are minor inconsistencies about the number of casualties in the Imperial Japanese Army. According to one source the army suffered 60,083 killed in battle (among them 1,926 officers) as well as 21,197 who succumbed to disease (among them 278 officers); see Ono, 1935: 752. The figures for the veneration of warrior spirits at the Yasukuni National Shrine do not qualify as an accurate count of losses but give a clear idea about them. At the two ceremonies held after the first Sino-Japanese War, 12,877 warrior spirits were venerated, while at the ceremonies held after the Russo-Japanese War a total of 88,131 spirits (85,206 of the army and 2,925 of the navy) were venerated. See Yasukuni jinja, 1983, I: 319–27; and Harada, 1986: 212. Following the war the Imperial Japanese Army reported over 60,000 killed and 130,000 wounded; see Ōe, 1988: 131. For a summary of the Japanese casualties, see Kowner, 2006: 80–1.
12 For Western views on Japanese military capabilities after the first Sino-Japanese War, see Kowner, 1998: 229–36.
13 For a sample of positive descriptions of Japanese military and combat capabilities, see Ashmead-Bartlett, 1906: 485; Matignon, 1907: 93, 104, 149; Villiers, 1905: 68, 164. A few years later, however, some of the negative pre-war views of Japan's military resurfaced, notably within British intelligence. See Best, 2002.
14 For Japan's continental expansion after the war and attitude vis-à-vis China, see Kitaoka, 1978; Matsusaka, 2001.
15 On the growing importance of the Chinese market and the expanding share of Manchuria in Japanese investments and imports after the war, see Duus *et al.*, 1989.
16 On the emperor's calm and restrained conduct and attitude during the war, see Keene, 2002: 605–29. In an opinion poll on "the greatest figure in history," conducted among Tokyo factory workers in 1924, the war hero General Nogi Maresuke came second, preceded only by the then reigning emperor. Nogi rated higher than civil leaders in the war, such as Emperor Meiji (4) and Itō Hirobumi (10). In Nakamura, 1992: 51–3; cited also in Shillony, 2005: 183. After the war the rank of the emperor's aides-de-camp became higher and their authority greater. Similarly, the emperor's first male grandchild, the young Hirohito, began to undergo military education under the tutelage of the war hero General Nogi Maresuke. In Bix, 2000: 34–6.
17 In 1925 the military began to commemorate the war, and in 1930 it celebrated its twenty-fifth anniversary with even bigger festivities. In those five years many books and articles were published about the war. In 1930 the tragic heroism of General Nogi was portrayed in a kabuki play, entitled *The Fall of Port Arthur*. In Bix, 2000: 210.
18 The basic unit the Imperial Japanese Army deployed was the army, and in some battles it was able to coordinate a number of armies simultaneously. The navy too made use for the first time of a large number of modern capital ships, and executed large-scale engagements against a modern fleet as well as complex logistic operations.
19 New infantry manuals were revised to stress the importance of the human spirit in warfare, as well as the importance of the deeds of individual soldiers, thus emphasizing hand-to-hand combat and small-arms fire. In Bix, 2000: 34. On the myth of mind over matter in the Sino-Japanese War, see Lone, 1994: 51; a good example of the use of the term *Yamato Damashii* can be found in the classic wartime book *Nikudan*, published in Japanese immediately after the war

and translated into English two years later as *Human Bullets* (Sakurai, 1907). This argument about the Japanese sense of invincibility and the role of the war as a prelude to future war is presented in greater detail in Cook, 1993: 285; Dickinson, 2005: 539–42; and Wilson, 1999; 182–3.

20 On the glorification of Nogi after the war, see Matsusaka, 2005; and Shimana, 2001. On the making of Admiral Tōgō Heihachirō into a national hero of legendary proportions and its use for political ends, see Dickinson, 2005: 537–9.

21 Cited in Ikeda, 1982: 144.

22 On the change in attitude to being captured in battle, see Hata, 1996; and Straus, 2003: 17–47.

23 On the Japanese efforts during the war to mobilize public opinion in the United States and in Europe, see Kowner, 2001; and Valliant, 1974.

24 Shimazu, 1998: 101–2.

25 On Konoe, see Jansen, 1980.

26 Banno, 1977: 126–7. In February 1908 one of Japan's leading magazines, *Taiyō*, dedicated a special issue to Japan's national identity, leaving no doubt regarding its position. The issue was entitled "The Clash of the Yellow and White Peoples."

27 Similar sentiments of disappointment with the West marked the emergence of the Zionist movement, particularly the organization of the First Zionist Congress in Basel in 1897.

28 On the subjective sense of isolation, see Iriye, 1966: 49. Itō is quoted in Iriye, 1989: 778.

29 Tokutomi is quoted in Iriye, 1989: 778.

30 Quoted in Oka, 1982: 207.

31 For a classic study of the rise of chauvinistic discourse after the war, see Miyaji, 1973.

32 Sōseki is quoted in Jansen, 2000: 480.

33 Oka, 1982: 213–14.

34 On the post-Russo-Japanese War origins of *nihonjinron* and the sense of superiority vis-à-vis the West, see Minami, 1994: 29–63. For contemporary manifestations of this discourse, see Befu, 2001; and Yoshino, 1992.

35 Morita, 1926.

36 Nishida, 1910 [1921].

37 Yanagita, 1910 [1935].

38 On the intellectual transformation in 1906–12, see Dale, 1986: 201–27; and Gluck, 1985: 157–212.

39 Kita, 1906 [1959], I: 213.

40 *Nihon kaizō hōan taikō* (An Outline Plan for the Reorganization of Japan), published in 1924.

41 The figures are cited in Jansen, 1965: 82.

42 Kawakami, 1911 [1964].

43 Dale, 1986: 212.

44 On self-Orientalism in Japan, see Befu, 1995.

45 See, for example, Yasuda, 1990: 57; Shillony, however, suggests that the emperor was not treated by the Meiji oligarchy as a god, certainly not with the deference accorded to his grandchild, Emperor Shōwa. See Shillony, 2005: 165.

46 On the emperor's role during the war, see Gluck, 1985: 89–90; and Keene, 2002: 605–29. On the distinction between the emperor and the "criminals" responsible for the Treaty of Portsmouth, see Okamoto, 1982: 272.

47 On the emperor's place in late Meiji era ideology, see Gluck, 1985; 73–101.

48 Banno, 1983; on the political repercussions of general mobilization during the war, see Matsuo, 1966: 79–80.

49 See Najita, 1967: 12–30; and Ovsyannikov, 2007.
50 For the navy post-war expenditures and expansion programs, see Ono, 2007.
51 Oka, 1982: 214–15.
52 On the expanding political role of the Imperial Japanese Navy and the inter-service rivalry from 1906 to 1914, see Masuda, 1982; Schencking, 2002, 2005.
53 See, for example, Matsuo, 2001.
54 Tokutomi is quoted in Oka, 1982: 198.
55 A letter to Yamagata on September 2, 1905, in Tokutomi, 1917, II: 296; quoted in Gluck, 1985: 175.
56 On the anti-taxation movement, see Banno, 1983: 166–7. On the debate regarding the implications of the protest movement toward the end of the war, see Okamoto, 1970: 306 (n. 104), 1982.
57 For a less strict definition of turning points in general, and regarding Japan's modern history in particular, see Edström, 2002: 6–11.
58 The war resulted in a temporary large trade balance due to a rise in imports. See Bank of Japan, 1966.

3   If Japan had lost the war . . .

Peter Duus

Would modern Japanese history have changed if the Japanese had lost the Russo-Japanese War? Even before the fighting began the country's leaders recognized that the outcome was by no means certain. Kaneko Kentarō later recalled that the army projected only a 50/50 chance of defeating Russia and that the navy expected to lose half its fleet. Neither were the country's leaders confident that they could hold out very long against such a formidable power.[1] The wartime situation was so fraught with disastrous possibilities that Japan's ultimate success seems all the more astonishing. Only in retrospect does the inevitability of its victory appear obvious.

But what if General Nogi Maresuke's forces had failed to break Russian resistance at Port Arthur? What if General Ōyama Iwao's forces had met with resounding defeat on the plains of Manchuria? What if Admiral Tōgō Heihachirō's fleet had been pummeled by the Russian Baltic Fleet? What if disgruntled Koreans had launched an insurgency against the Japanese protectorate? What if President Theodore Roosevelt had refused to broker a peace settlement? And so on, and so on.

"What if" questions, of course, are ultimately unanswerable. That does not mean that they are frivolous or useless. Considering what might have been, with or without regrets, is a common human occupation. My old army commander, who spent the Pacific War as a POW captured at Corregidor, hung a quotation from Tennyson on his office wall: "The race is neither to the swift nor strong but time and chance happent to us all." It was a reminder that if he had not been in the wrong place at the wrong time he might have ended his post-war military career as a general rather a colonel. Thinking about the range of possibilities embedded in any particular historical moment can help the historian, like the individual, assess the role of contingency, accident, and error in human experience.

In one sense, counterfactual history is easier to pursue than its conventional counterpart. Shedding the troublesome burden of considering evidence is not only liberating but less time-consuming. There is no secondary literature to plod through, no voluminous archives to search for documents, no eye witness accounts to assess, and no need for footnotes.[2] On the other hand, given the multiplicity of potential turning points in any particular historical situation, speculating about alternative outcomes in history is not an easy task either. There are no quantifiable variables to juggle on one's computer, nor is there any way to interview departed historical figures about what else they might have done. About all a counterfactual historian can do is to consider the consequences of what did happen, then ruminate on what might have happened had there been no such consequences.[3]

The first and most important consequence of the victory over Russia was Japan's emergence as a major regional power—and as a potential world power. After its defeat of China in 1895 Japan had remained a marginal player in world affairs. Indeed, the so-called Triple-power Intervention by Russia, Germany, and France had forced the Japanese to back down from the peace settlement it reached with China at Shimonoseki. To be sure, the British and Americans, who were impressed by the Japanese victory and pleased by Japanese efforts to open the Chinese market wider, refused to join this diplomatic intervention, but the Japanese had to give up their territorial foothold in the Liaotung Peninsula and soon found themselves competing with Russia for a dominant position in Korea. This unexpected turn of events was a blow to national self-esteem that aroused demands for a war of revenge against the Russians. Even after the country's international status rose after its dispatch of troops to quell the Boxer Rebellion in 1900, and its signing of an alliance with Great Britain in 1902, these feelings remained intense.

In the world of high imperialism, the strong made friends easily. In 1905 the Japanese proved their military and naval strength by driving Russian forces out of southern Manchuria, demolishing the Russian fleet, and forcing the Russian government to the negotiating table. Instead of giving up their wartime gains under pressure from a coalition of Western powers as they had ten years before, Japanese leaders launched a post-war diplomatic offensive to win full acceptance by the Western powers. They struck bilateral agreements with the Russians, the British, the Americans, and the French promising not to infringe on their colonial territories and enclaves in Asia in return for their promises to recognize Japan's paramount position in Korea and southern Manchuria. The Western powers, seeing little to their own disadvantage in the post-war status quo in East Asia, accepted the Japanese as equal partners in maintaining it. The Japanese were now full-fledged members of the imperialist club.

The rise in Japan's international status would have been checked by a defeat that left Russia rather than Japan as the dominant power in Korea and Manchuria. The Japanese would have remained on the sidelines while Russia emerged as a major player in East Asian international politics—and the chief rival to Great Britain in the region. An Anglo-Russian confrontation similar to the "Great Game" played out in Central Asia two decades earlier might have prompted the Japanese to side with British rather than their old enemy Russia, but on the other hand Japan's defeat by Russia might have reduced British confidence in Japanese military power and convinced them not to renew the Anglo-Japanese Alliance. Without the alliance, the Japanese would have no real reason to participate in World War I (assuming that it took place) or the peace conference that followed, leaving Japan on the sidelines of world politics much longer.

A second consequence of Japan's victory over Russia was consolidation of its commitment to territorial expansion on the Asian mainland. By the standards of the day, the military victories and domestic reforms of the Japanese demonstrated that they were capable of ruling less "civilized" peoples, such as the Koreans. No outside power objected to the establishment of a Japanese protectorate over Korea or its eventual annexation as Japanese territory. Despite its ruthless suppression of anti-Japanese opposition movements, the Japanese colonial administration introduced administrative, technological, and economic changes with an efficiency that matched or surpassed most Western colonial regimes. Even the Americans conceded that the Koreans would be better off under Japanese control than under self-rule.[4]

The Japanese would not have remained the dominant power in Korea had they lost the war in 1905. In any peace settlement, a victorious Russia would surely have insisted on a de facto division of Korea between the two countries or complete Japanese withdrawal from the peninsula. These terms would have meant continuing friction with Russia, but the memory of a defeat in 1905 would have made Japan's leaders think twice about another "war of revenge" against their huge northern neighbor. The cost of the war had been staggering—more than six times the size of the Japanese government annual revenues—and the loss of life unprecedented. The ranks of its company grade officers had been seriously depleted on the battlefield. Even after victory, the Japanese leaders worried about the possibility of renewed hostilities with Russia. Defeat would have magnified those worries.

Defeat would also have prevented Japan from establishing a sphere of influence in northeastern China. Under the Portsmouth Treaty, the Russians ceded their railroad and leasehold concessions in southern Manchuria to Japan. A small army of petty traders, land speculators, and businessmen soon made their way there to exploit the new economic opportunities, and the Japanese government established new quasi-governmental enterprises like the South Manchuria Railway Company and the Oriental Development Bank to bolster their presence, and the Kwantung Army, a garrison force stationed in the Liaotung leasehold, was deployed to defend them. Eventually, the Japanese civilian and military community in Manchuria became a major element in supporting Japan's "rights and privileges" in Manchuria.

But, if Japan had lost the war, the Russians would not only have maintained their position in Manchuria but perhaps even established a protectorate there. The Japanese would have found their path on the Asian continent blocked not only on the Korean peninsula, but also in China north of the Great Wall. The only remaining Japanese stake on the continent would have been the rights to trade and invest in the treaty ports guaranteed by the treaty with China in 1895. Many Japanese leaders realized that rapid industrialization and proximity to the Chinese market meant that Japan had a bright future there, even in competition with the British. Optimism about Japan's economic chances in China might have strengthened support for a cautious continental policy that emphasized cooperation with the other treaty powers, especially the Anglo-Americans.

Ironically, the failure to acquire a territorial stake in Korea and Manchuria might also have reduced the sense of insecurity that plagued Japanese leaders. The country's only colony would have been Taiwan, a territory that the Ch'ing regime had let slip with little struggle, where the Japanese faced little internal resistance except from the "aborigines." The empire would have had maritime boundaries more easily defended and less cause for concern than one that included a Korea seething with anger at the Japanese presence or a Manchurian sphere of influence not only resented by the Chinese but coveted by the Russians as well. (Of course, if the Japanese had lost half their fleet in the course of being defeated by Russia, maritime boundaries would have felt more fragile—but defeat would also have provided an incentive to rely on the navy rather the army for basic national security.)

One might even speculate that, if Japan had lost the war to Russia, and if its expansionist impulses had been checked, it might have pursued what many late Meiji intellectuals, officials, and politicians envisaged as its proper role in East Asia—as a cultural and political intermediary between East and West, and as a haven for anti-colonialist nationalists from the rest of Asia. To be sure, many saw the Japanese victory in 1905 as an opportunity for Japan to champion the cause of other Asian peoples struggling against oppression and exploitation by European colonial powers.[5] But the post-war diplomatic offensive undercut this possibility. The government's desire to cultivate close ties with these colonial powers (and with the slowly crumbling Ch'ing regime as well) prompted the expulsion of nationalist leaders like Sun Yat-sen and Phan Boi Chau, who had not only sought refuge in Japan, but also wanted to learn the secrets of its successful modernization.

Even had these Asian nationalists not been rebuffed, it would have been difficult for the Japanese to identify their interests with struggling anti-colonial movements as long as they held on to their colonies and sphere of influence in China. On the other hand, a defeated Japan with reduced territorial ambitions might have been more willing to give anti-colonial activists aid and comfort, if only for pragmatic reasons. Colonial powers might be less likely to threaten Japan if confronted with native anti-colonial insurgencies. For similar reasons, army leaders appear to have supported Sun Yat-sen's early insurrections against the Ch'ing regime.[6] Certainly, a policy of supporting anti-colonial activists would have found support not only from the "liberal" forces in Japanese politics, but also from right-wing patriotic organizations, and, in the long run, it would have aligned visions of "Japan's mission in Asia" with the tides of history.

A third consequence of the victory over Russia was the heightened influence of the military in domestic politics. Far from satisfying a craving for military security, expansion on the continent did not reduce strategic anxieties; it increased them. The war had barely ended when both the army and the navy began to press for increased armament expenditure. The national defense plan formulated in 1907 assumed that the country's chief hypothetical enemies would be Russia, its ally France, and the United States. All had formally correct diplomatic terms with Japan, but all had substantial interests in East Asia that might conflict with Japan's colonial empire and sphere of influence in China. The military urged an arms build-up in anticipation of a clash with one or all of them.

Many civilian politicians, particularly party leaders in the Imperial Diet, objected to increases in the military budget. The Imperial Diet had voted enthusiastically for war appropriations in 1904–5, but when the war ended fiscal priorities shifted to domestic economic development and reduction of the enormous national debt created by wartime borrowing. Politicians were reluctant to finance future wars when the most recent one was yet to be paid for. The army leadership used its privileged constitutional power to achieve its goal and, when the Saionji cabinet attempted to postpone the expansion of the army by two divisions in 1911, the army brought it down by refusing to provide a war minister. Even though the resulting political crisis changed the formal procedure for selecting military and naval ministers, in practice the army leadership retained considerable informal influence.

The army's prestige had risen enormously after the victory over Russia. Wartime commanders like General Nogi, the victor at Port Arthur, and Admiral Tōgō, the victor in the battle of Tsushima, were enshrined as national heroes in school textbooks. The army encouraged its identification with the nation and the national interest by organizing the National Reservists Association—a network of local organizations devoted to spreading patriotism and "military spirit" among the general population. As a result, the army became an indispensable participant in any discussion of foreign policy, and a powerful player in the politics of budget-making. Inevitably civilian–military conflict, largely absent before the Russo-Japanese War, became an endemic feature of domestic politics.

A loss to Russia in 1905 would surely have diminished the military's prestige. During the Siberian expedition of 1918–22, which was an attempt to roll back the Bolshevik Revolution by giving military support to White Russian forces, public opinion turned against the army. The expedition was criticized as a pointless waste of money and manpower, and its failure to achieve its goal undermined confidence in the military. It is not difficult to imagine that a similar reaction, but one magnified by the jingoism and high hopes of victory that accompanied the outbreak of war, would have followed a defeat at the hands of Russia in 1905. It is unlikely that the army's influence over foreign policy would have been greatly diminished, but its leverage over domestic resources and domestic budget might have been.

Furthermore, it would not have been as easy for supporters of the military to rouse public opinion in favor of further military adventures overseas. In the post-war period, a popular commitment to empire became deeply embedded in public consciousness. Rhetorical appeals to a victory "bought by the blood of one hundred thousand valiant souls and billions from the national purse" quashed all debate about the legitimacy of expansion abroad. To question the sacrifices made in building the empire was cast as unpatriotic, even treasonous. Indeed, it would be no exaggeration to suggest that the victory over Russia made imperialists out of all Japanese, even the unborn who were to learn the glory of the Japanese military from primary school textbooks.

A defeat at Russia's hands would surely have strengthened anti-military and anti-imperialist sentiments, which were conspicuously rare after 1905. Pacificists were few and far between, and so were those who opposed imperial expansion. Defeat might have persuaded many that Japan had more to gain by adopting a lower position in world politics. Foreign trade was expanding, and Japanese manufactured goods, particularly textiles, were beginning to compete with those of the West. The argument advanced by Ishibashi Tanzan in the 1920s—that the costs of empire outweighed its benefits and that the country profited more from open markets and free trade abroad—might have attracted support as the public discovered that peaceful economic expansion was a plausible route to international influence.

In short, one might argue that had it not been for the victory over Russia in 1905 eventually Japan might have emerged as a less bellicose, less aggressive, and less militaristic power during the first four decades of the twentieth century than it did. Indeed, its policies in Asia might have come to resemble more and more that of the United States during the same period: a commitment to an "Open Door" policy in China, support for free trade within the treaty port system, opposition to the territorial division of China, cultural and educational support for aspiring Asian nationalists, and maintenance of a strong navy.[7] To be sure, these policies probably would have been touched with the same inconsistencies, hypocrisies, and arrogance that new nations show toward older ones and that more developed countries show toward the less developed.

The Japanese would also have been as uncomfortable with other people's revolutions, particularly in their immediate region, as the Americans were. It is difficult to imagine that any Japanese leader would have watched the collapse of the Ch'ing Empire or the ensuing internal political chaos in China passively. The temptations to intervene one way or another would be great. But, if an undefeated Russia retained a strong military or diplomatic presence in Manchuria and Korea, Japan's interventions in the Chinese Revolution would probably have focused on the treaty ports and coastal provinces south of the Great Wall, where it would have found ready collaborators in the British, the Americans, and perhaps the French. If such a coalition of collaborators had supported a strong man like Yuan Shih-kai or his warlord successors instead of the nationalist elements, the history of modern China, and perhaps East Asia, might have turned out radically different from the way it did. On the other hand, if they had supported Sun Yat-sen's Kuomintang . . . ?

As this question suggests, counterfactual history has its limits. It can never offer a definitive picture of an alternative past. The chain of contingencies stretches on ad infinitum. If my old army commander had not been captured by the Japanese at Corregidor but had fought in the Pacific, he might not have gotten his general's star anyway. So many other things might have happened to him—he might have been disastrously injured or killed in combat; he might have disgraced himself on the battlefield; he might have had a desk assignment rather than a combat role; or he might have decided after the war to retire and raise horses on his Pennsylvania estate.

Similar uncertainties hover over speculation about a Japan defeated by Russia in 1905. Would a victorious Russia have gone on to exploit its new position in Asia as assiduously as the Japanese did? Would an embittered Japanese public have demanded another "war of revenge"? Would the Japanese have been tempted to help anti-foreign elements in Korea expel the Russians? Would the collapse of the Ch'ing have created new opportunities for Japan to expand in the south? Would a more peaceful Japan oriented toward trade have been able to take full advantage of its economic opportunities in China when strong nationalist forces arose there? And so on, and so on. In sum, even if Japan had lost the war, would its leaders still have found cause—and political support—for continuing an expansionist policy?

We will never know. Japan did not lose.

Notes

1 Kaneko, 1929: 26–9.
2 The editor, however, has encouraged me to include footnotes in the chapter.
3 For recent attempts at the writing of counterfactual history, see Ferguson, 1995.
4 Duus, 1995: 189.
5 For example, see Jansen, 1954.
6 See Mukōyama, 1974.
7 This set of policies would probably have been embraced by leaders like Itō Hirobumi, who opposed the aggressive post-war stance of the army. See Inoue, 1968: 300–1.

4   The war and the fate of the tsarist autocracy

Jonathan Frankel

The Russo-Japanese War demonstrated as never before to what an extent the fate of the tsarist regime at home was tied to its policies of war and peace abroad. With political stability insecure, the danger of defeat on the battlefield (as will be examined in this chapter) could take on existential proportions. It was, of course, the French Revolution of 1789 (and thereafter) that had first exposed the political vulnerability of the *ancien régime* in Europe, thereby undermining forever the supreme self-confidence that had characterized the reformist policies of such "enlightened despots" as Frederick II of Prussia and Joseph II of Austria. In Russia, Catherine II ("the Great"), who for so long had been proud to count such radical critics of the traditional order as Voltaire and Diderot among her friends, turned savagely in the years 1790–2 against prominent local representatives of the European Enlightenment, Aleksandr Radishchev and Nikolai Novikov, even having the former sentenced (initially) to death. The final elimination of Poland, with its constitutional system of government, in 1795—a country now carved up among its three great autocratic neighbors, Russia, Prussia, and Austria—was another sign of the fear then stalking the courts of St Petersburg, Berlin, and Vienna.

Threatened by the message and mission of the revolution (the rights of man; constitutionalism; the abolition of the feudal order; the subversion of inherited hierarchies), the tsarist regime staked its future on its ability to prove itself an invincible military power even in the face of the new and overwhelming dangers. The legitimacy of the autocracy—and of the entire established order—thus depended on the ability to meet the challenge of armed conflict.

The search for stability and the drift to war

During the nineteenth century, the response of the tsarist regime to war followed a clear logic and a recurring pattern. Victory on the battlefield served to reinforce the inherent political conservatism of the Russian autocracy in the post-1789 era. Why erode or undermine the existing system as long as it could triumphantly pass the test of arms? On the other hand, military defeat inevitably raised the question of whether far-reaching political change could be avoided if Russia were not to fall behind those rival powers that, in varying degrees, were abandoning the principles of the *ancien régime*.[1] Thus, the appointment by Alexander I of Mikhail Speransky, the would-be architect of constitutional reform, as his leading minister in the years 1807–12 followed immediately on the heels of catastrophic defeat by the Napoleonic armies at Austerlitz, Eylau, and Friedland. The era of the "Great Reforms" (the emancipation of the serfs; far-reaching judicial innovation; elected government at the local levels) was prompted by the humiliating defeat of Russia by the Western powers, Britain and France, in the Crimean War (1854–6).

Conversely, the central and the heroic role played by the Russian armies, with the personal participation of Alexander I, in the war against Napoleon during the period 1812–14 introduced a 40-year period of ultra-conservatism at home and counter-revolutionary intervention abroad (Russia as "the gendarme of Europe"). Victorious wars waged against the Ottoman Empire (1828–9 and 1878–9), the Caucasian mountain nations (1830–60), and the Central Asian emirates of Bukhara, Khiva, and Kokand (1865–76) all served to reinforce the self-image of the nineteenth-century tsars as worthy heirs to Peter the Great and their other venerated Romanov ancestors. Did not the empire keep expanding its frontiers, if no longer toward the West after 1815, then at least toward (British) India in Southeast Asia and toward China and Japan in East Asia? (By the Treaty of Beijing, 1860, China yielded a vast area between the River Ussuri and the Pacific Ocean to Russia, making possible the foundation of Vladivostok as a naval port; and, by the treaty of 1875, Japan yielded recognition of the island of Sakhalin as Russian territory.)

However, in the 1890s, with the appointment of Sergei Witte as the Minister of Finance, a radical attempt was launched to break out of this cycle, which for one hundred years had witnessed alternate periods of "freeze" (seeking to safeguard the status quo in all spheres) and "thaw" (an openness to the idea of change). The reign of Alexander III (1881–94) did see a sharp swing toward the conservative, even reactionary, pole at the political level, but matching that was the extraordinary effort led by the Minister of Finance to modernize the empire at the economic level.

Witte's goal was to develop the fiscal policies—high tariffs and taxes; a stable currency tied to the gold standard; and the large-scale import of foreign capital—required to accelerate the growth of domestic industry at rates far faster than anything known hitherto. In the decade from 1892 to 1902, the length of the railway lines in the country rose by almost 50 percent; the output of coal was doubled, and that of pig-iron tripled, while government revenues per annum rose from under one billion to some two billion rubles. There was an awareness in government circles, of course, that this policy of rapid industrialization was bound to be socially disruptive and thus a potential source of danger to the regime. A peasantry loaded down by taxes, direct and indirect; an industrial proletariat growing fast and forced to live in appalling urban squalor; a rapidly expanding student body and intelligentsia, notoriously alienated from the autocratic system; and even a nobility resentful of the preference assigned industrial, as opposed to agrarian, interests—here was an explosive amalgam indeed.[2]

By the late nineteenth century, however, it was obvious even to such ultra-conservatives as Alexander III that the Russian Empire would not be able to retain its status as a great power unless it had the industrial and technological base necessary in order to supply, and resupply, the armed forces with modern weapons; in order to transport those forces rapidly from place to place; and in order to provide all the logistical support associated with modern warfare. Witte's strategy of industrialization was rooted in the same logic that encouraged St Petersburg to enter into the Franco-Russian Alliance of 1894. The Romanov Empire was not prepared to become a mere satellite of the Hohenzollern Reich, which was then enjoying astonishing levels of industrial growth, technological innovation, and military advance.

The centerpiece of Witte's strategy was the construction of the Trans-Siberian Railway, which was to link European Russia to Vladivostok, a distance of about 9,200 kilometers (some 5,700 miles), and which was almost, but not quite, completed by 1904. As Witte saw it, the railway would make possible the settlement of Siberia (so drawing off surplus population from the land-hungry regions of the empire); would open up China and Japan to Russian exports; and would provide an alternative to the Suez Canal as a key trade route between Europe and East Asia. Even though this enterprise clearly involved Russia in the race between the Great Powers to gain new markets and a preponderant influence in large regions of East Asia, neither the tsar nor the Minister of Finance were thinking in terms of war and territorial expansion. In their view, what Russia required in order to build up its industrial base, and to give at least a minimal education to its still largely illiterate population, was a prolonged period of peace. In this context, it should be recalled that Alexander III was the only tsar in modern history to have kept his country out of war.

Historians, following many contemporary observers, have demonstrated an unusual degree of unanimity in concluding that Nicholas II, who acceded to the throne in 1894, was ultimately responsible for the political decisions that made war with Japan inevitable toward the end of 1903. Witte could state without hesitation that "had Alexander III lived on there would never have been war with Japan."[3] Furthermore, in his *The History of the Russian Revolution*, Leon Trotsky conceded, for all his Marxist credo, that such a hypothesis was certainly plausible: "if Alexander III had drunk less he might have lived a good deal longer . . . and [Russia] have not become mixed up in a war with Japan." He also explained that "we do not at all pretend to deny the significance of the personal in all the mechanics of the historic process, nor the significance in the personal of the accidental."[4]

Where Witte and Trotsky differed fundamentally—and where the historians have always been divided—was over the nature of the causal relationship between the Russo-Japanese War and the revolution of 1905 (or, more strictly speaking, of 1905–7). In Witte's view, Alexander III had been absolutely correct in his belief that "[t]he unrest that had existed at the end of his father's reign had resulted from his father's wavering and not from Russia's desire for revolution. He realized that Russia wanted a quiet existence."[5] Hence, as Witte saw it, the war was to blame for the revolution.

In contrast, Trotsky argued that, even had war with Japan been avoided, the revolution would have erupted before any great length of time had elapsed. In his incompetence, Nicholas II (like Charles I of England and Louis XVI of France before him) represented not only personal weakness but, far more, the decay of the entire system—a system that had lost the inner vitality to protect itself against a method of imperial inheritance (primogeniture) that left so much to pure chance. In its final phase, wrote Trotsky:

> The monarchy loses its capacity for any kind of creative initiative; it defends itself, it strikes back, it retreats, its activities acquire the automatism of mere reflexes . . . His nearest ancestors . . . passed on to Nicholas a chaotic empire already carrying the matured revolution in its womb. If he had any choice left, it was only between different roads to ruin.[6]

Both Witte and Trotsky were, of course, writing with the benefit of hindsight: the former after the defeat of the 1905 revolution (a victory for the regime in which he personally had played a crucial role); and the latter after the triumphant Bolshevik Revolution of November 1917, which he, together with Lenin, had led. For those historians such as myself, though, who cannot rely on the certainties of the Marxist faith, and who understand not only the attraction, but also the limitations of counterfactual history, there can be no simple answers when it comes to assessing what would have happened to the tsarist regime if it had only kept itself out of war in 1904 and again in 1914.

For war with Japan to have been avoided in 1904, Nicholas II would have had to opt for a determined and energetic pursuit of diplomatic compromise. Lacking such a clear-cut commitment, there was nothing to put a stop to what was, in fact, a natural drift toward war. After all, for over an entire decade, Russia had chosen to trample roughshod over Japanese interests in order to extend its power in East Asia. Working together with other European powers, most notably Germany and France, Russia had imposed two exceptionally painful diplomatic defeats on Japan: first, the radical revision in 1895 of the Sino-Japanese Peace Treaty of Shimonoseki, thus depriving Japan of the Liaotung Peninsula; and, second, adding insult to injury, the virtual annexation in 1898 by Russia of that same strategically and commercially valuable peninsula. From the standpoint of Witte (largely shared by the Minister of Foreign Affairs, Count Vladimir Lamsdorf), it was clearly in the Russian interest to avoid any further action liable to drive Japan to desperation. Apart from anything else, he pointed out that the annexation of Manchuria to the Russian Empire would simply add a

"Chinese problem" to the pre-existing Finnish, Jewish, Polish, Armenian, and other acute nationality problems confronting the regime.[7]

That Witte's position was rejected is in no way surprising. The suppression of the Boxer Rebellion in 1900 had entailed the occupation of Manchuria by the Russian armed forces. First undertaken as a temporary measure, to be coordinated with other powers, in order to restore order in China, the occupation soon took on its own momentum. The concept of voluntarily yielding territory once occupied by the Russian army ran counter to the political culture of a country that had constantly expanded from a size of less than 40,000 square kilometers (15,000 square miles) in the fifteenth century to 22,419,700 square kilometers (8,665,000 square miles) in 1900.[8]

Russia did eventually sign an agreement with China in April 1902 to complete the withdrawal (in three stages) from the occupied Manchurian territories by October 1903, but this fact by no means signified that the tsarist government necessarily intended to honor that undertaking. Even the Minister of War, Aleksei Kuropatkin, who was generally considered a moderate, argued that there could be no justification for evacuating northern Manchuria (stage three of the agreed withdrawal) and thus yielding territory of great strategic importance for the defense of the Trans-Siberian Railway and of its branch line, which headed southward via Harbin to Port Arthur.[9] As for the members of the more militantly minded group, headed by Aleksandr Bezobrazov, State Secretary to Nicholas II, they not only refused to contemplate further withdrawals (beyond the first, completed in October 1902), but they also pressed for the expansion of Russian control beyond Manchuria into the Korean peninsula, across the Yalu river. The vehement opposition of Japan, backed by Britain and the United States, to these policies was a factor assigned no weight by these advisers. The treaty of alliance concluded between England and Japan in January 1902 was likewise counted by them as insignificant.[10]

That Nicholas II had unequivocally opted for the policies represented by Bezobrazov and his coterie became unmistakably clear when Witte was forced to resign as Minister of Finance on August 28, 1903. This fateful decision is partially to be explained in psychological terms. The tsar considered Witte, whom he had inherited as a leading minister from his father, Alexander III, to be unforgivably overbearing. He found it intolerable that he, the autocrat, the sole ruler of all Russia, should feel lorded over by one of his own subordinates. That he was of unusually short height, while his father had been very tall, every inch the emperor, undoubtedly accentuated such resentments. On the day that Witte was dismissed, Nicholas II wrote in his diary, "Now I rule!"[11]

However, a still more important factor in the decisions taken by the tsar was the fact that he simply could not imagine Japan deciding to initiate war. Given his assumption that Russia enjoyed overwhelming military superiority, his attitude was not illogical. He assured all and sundry in the latter half of 1903 that peace would certainly be maintained because he, the

Russian tsar, had decided against war. Apart from the fact that the Russian population at approximately 150 million was some three times greater than that of Japan, Nicholas II was also undoubtedly influenced in his thinking by the conviction, typical of the era, that "yellow" soldiers could never be a match for a "white" army.

The war and the revolution

The surprise attack launched by Japan against the Russian naval base at Port Arthur on February 8, 1904 did little or nothing to shake the self-confidence of the Russian regime. Even though the Russian navy, caught totally off guard, suffered very heavy losses and thus in effect yielded command of the seas in the western part of the Pacific Ocean to Japan, the assumption in St Petersburg was that this defeat meant no more than a temporary set-back. After all, the commander of Port Arthur, Lieutenant General Anatolii Stoessel, had 40,000 soldiers under his command in order to withstand a long siege if necessary, and in the meantime reinforcements in the hundreds of thousands could be brought in from European Russia.

What is more, the initial reactions of the Russian public to the war could only have encouraged the optimism of the regime. Indeed, those observers, such as Witte, who argued that the people were basically loyal to the status quo, could draw encouragement, at least until the late autumn of 1904, from the response of the population. The outbreak of hostilities brought with it many meetings and demonstrations organized to express support for the war effort; or, as Nicholas II noted in his diary: "From all quarters [there are] touching manifestations of unanimous excitement; and displeasure at the impudence of the Japanese . . .; touching expressions of popular feelings and in complete order."[12]

More significant was the remarkable drop in the level of industrial unrest. While the year 1903 had witnessed an unprecedented number of work-stoppages—140,000 workers joined 550 (illegal) strikes[13]—the first year of the war was quieter on the industrial front than at any time for a decade. Even the professional revolutionaries, many living as political exiles in Western Europe, did not attach much significance to what they tended to regard as hardly more than still another colonial adventure, many thousands of miles away and of little relevance to developments west of the Urals. As for the riots that now often accompanied the large-scale mobilization of the reserves—mainly peasants drawn from the villages—they could easily be dismissed as simply typical of behavior in a country so vast that it could never be effectively policed. (In any case, whenever circumstances permitted, the primary target of the angry recruits tended to be neither officialdom nor the nobility, but rather the hapless local Jewish population.)

However, as the war dragged on throughout the year without any end in sight, the public mood gradually began to shift. Even though the situation in the battle zone remained hazy, what news there was tended to be bad. In February, Japanese forces, exploiting their superiority at sea, landed at

Chemulpo (Inchon) in order to launch a drive northwards through Korea. A few months later, a Russian column under General M.I. Zasulich was forced back beyond the Yalu river, and in early September the important town of Liaoyang, which lay on the railway linking Port Arthur to Harbin, fell to the Japanese.[14]

It is most unlikely that this series of setbacks contributed in any way to the decision of the Party of Social Revolutionaries (SRs) to kill the Minister of the Interior, Viacheslav von Plehve. He was assassinated on July 28, at a period of the year when the significance of events in Manchuria was still little understood in European Russia. Moreover, such sensational acts of terror had become commonplace long before the outbreak of hostilities in East Asia—the Minister of Education, for example, had been assassinated in 1901 and the previous Minister of the Interior, Dmitrii Sipiagin, in 1902. Von Plehve had become a natural target for the armed wing of the SR party not because of his known support for the policies that had led to war (he was alleged to have said that "in order to prevent revolution, we need a small victorious war"),[15] but rather because of his association with relentless political repression and, rightly or wrongly, with the authorization of the Kishinev pogrom in April 1903. (The chief architect of the SR campaign of terror, Evno Azev, although a double agent who received payments from the Ministry of the Interior, was also a Jew and might well have been eager to avenge the dozens of Jews butchered in Kishinev.)[16]

Whatever exactly had motivated the assassination, there can be no doubt that the violent death of von Plehve, who, more than anybody else, had come to symbolize the impregnability of the regime, dealt a significant blow to the autocratic system. Also at that point, Nicholas II made a complicated situation still more entangled by his failure to adopt a consistent policy.

On the one hand, he now appointed as Minister of the Interior a man known for his relatively moderate (or even liberal) views, Prince Petr Danilovich Sviatopolk-Mirskii, who had previously served as the governor general of the northwestern region (the provinces of Vilna, Grodno, and Kovno). But, on the other hand, the tsar could not bring himself to accompany this move, which was clearly intended to appease the disaffected sections of the public, with any major steps toward political change. What might have been accepted in liberal circles as a genuine gesture of goodwill, thus could only be interpreted as a mark of disarray and weakness.

The first signs of significant political unrest now emerged not from the *narod* (the great mass of the population: the peasants and wage-workers), but from the *obshchestvennost* (the educated strata: the professionals, the intelligentsia, and the liberal members of the middle class and even of the nobility). It was this latter camp that could draw encouragement from the conference of oppositional forces that met in Paris in late September and early October. At this gathering, which brought together moderates and socialists (only the Russian Social Democrats refused to participate), the prominent liberal and historian Pavel Miliukov played a key role. The statement issued at the conclusion of the conference declared, *inter alia*, that "[t]he present moment is especially favorable for . . . action . . . against the autocratic government which is discredited and has been made impotent by the terrible consequences of its adventurist war policy."[17]

More significant still was another oppositional conference, likewise held in the autumn, but this time in St Petersburg, on the Fontanka, only a short distance from the Winter Palace. On December 15, over 100 representatives of the *zemstva*—the institutions of local self-government elected by the rural population—met in the capital to discuss the current political situation. In a country where there was no parliament, elected officials of any kind could claim to speak for the Russian people in a way that the bureaucracy and the tsar could not. The mere fact that a conference of this kind, which had been called together without governmental permission, was allowed to meet free of police interference clearly suggested an erosion of self-confidence within the government. The resolution, carried by the majority of the delegates, appealed to the tsar "in view of the . . . difficulty of external and internal conditions . . . [to call together] freely elected representatives of the people in order to lead our fatherland on a new path."[18]

Resolutions of this type were now adopted by a wide variety of city councils and of professional, scholarly, and cultural societies. More dramatic still, in the context of the autocratic state, was the rash of political banquets that were now organized to raise the demand for greater freedom and for elections to a parliament. All in all, no fewer than 38 banquets were held in 26 cities.[19] Gatherings of this kind, as the organizers fully realized, had been a widespread phenomenon in France in 1847, serving there as a direct prelude to revolution and the overthrow in February 1848 of Louis Philippe's Orleanist regime.

So long as such demonstrations of political discontent remained within non-violent limits, the regime manifested few signs of anxiety, and the tsar felt free to continue issuing contradictory signals. Thus, an *ukaz* (decree) of December 25 promised to prepare legislation that would, *inter alia*, extend the authority of the *zemstva* and city councils as well as easing the restrictions on the press; but at the very same time a second governmental statement reasserted the principle of autocracy and accused the liberals of undermining the war effort—"unconsciously acting not for the good of the fatherland, but for that of its enemies."[20]

However, even though it might not have been fully apparent at the time, Russia was now fast entering what Marxists were once wont to term "a revolutionary situation." Or, to turn to Crane Brinton's classic work, *Anatomy of a Revolution*, Russia now faced that same fateful combination of factors that had heralded revolution in England in the 1630s, in the American colonies in the 1770s, and in France in the 1780s: a major failure of governmental management, on the one hand, and a profound loss of governmental legitimacy within the country's elites, on the other hand. The sense of mounting crisis was greatly accentuated when the news arrived that on December 29 Port Arthur had finally fallen to the Japanese, after almost a year of courageous defense. Anybody in Russia with even a minimal knowledge of history was bound to recall the surrender of Sebastopol in 1855, another searing defeat, and one that had soon forced Russia on to the path of far-reaching reform. It took only three weeks from the surrender of Port Arthur for the political situation inside the country to take what, from the regime's perspective, was a radical turn for the worse. As with many developments that took place during the reign of Nicholas II, so too with the events of January 22, 1905 ("Bloody Sunday," as it became known), the historian finds himself astonished by the inability of the government to pursue any given policy consistently.

Thus, having launched the idea in 1901 of "police trade-unionism" (meaning the encouragement of the workers to organize themselves in pursuit of improved economic—but not political—conditions), the regime then backed away from its strategy as soon as it developed a momentum of its own. In 1903, this policy had ended in a large-scale strike in Odessa, causing acute embarrassment to the architects of this stratagem (von Plehve and Sergei Zubatov, the Moscow police chief, who was then dismissed). In 1905, a variation on this same concept produced nothing less than a major catastrophe for the regime. Eager to neutralize the influence exerted by the revolutionary socialists on the industrial proletariat, the authorities had given the green light in 1903 to an Orthodox priest, Father Georgii Gapon, to set up a workers' organization that would provide its members with a range of such social and cultural activities as lectures and dances. However, of course, given the upsurge of political excitement and unrest in late 1904, it was inevitable that an organization of this type would be drawn into the confrontation with the regime. Extraordinary flexibility and foresight on the part of the authorities would have been required in order to ensure that the protest of the workers remained, like that of the liberals, non-violent.

For his part, Father Gapon, swept along on the general tide of protest, included a number of radical clauses in the petition that he had drawn up in the name of the St Petersburg workers, with the expectation that he could present it to the tsar. *Inter alia*, it contained demands that the suffrage for the "elections to the constituent assembly be—universal, secret and equal," and that "the ministers should be responsible before the people." Likewise, it called for the "termination of the war in accordance with the will of the people" and also, paradoxically, for war manufacture to be concentrated "in Russia and not abroad." "The bureaucratic administration," it declared, "has brought the country to the brink of ruin, involved her in a humiliating war, and is leading Russia closer and closer to disaster."[21]

Perhaps 100,000 workers set out on January 22 toward the Winter Palace where, it was hoped, Father Gapon would be allowed personally to deliver the "most humble and loyal address" to the tsar. Nicholas II, though, had already left the city and orders were given not to permit the march to approach anywhere near the palace. What was not done, and what logic should have demanded, was also to issue clear orders that all possible measures be taken to avoid bloodshed. The march, it has to be remembered, was the work of an organization sanctioned and even subsidized by the government.

In the absence of such specific instructions and with the huge festive march pressing forward, the troops fired volley after volley into the crowds. The dead numbered approximately 150; the wounded, many hundreds, if not more. That Russia was by now one year into an ever more exhausting war was probably one of the factors that made possible the disaster of January 22. The demand for strict obedience to orders almost invariably becomes more insistent in wartime, and the punishment for disobedience all the harsher. Be that as it may, there could be no doubt that the massacre did more than years of revolutionary agitation had done to destroy the myth of the Russian tsar as a strict but just father figure (*batiushka*), who could be depended upon, if well enough informed, to oppose the predatory conduct of the bureaucracy. The bullets fired into the crowd in St Petersburg transformed the nature of the oppositional movement. The transition from a "pre-revolutionary situation" to revolution had begun.[22]

The tides of protest, unrest, disorder, and sheer violence ebbed and flowed, but the overall tendency soon became unmistakable. Across the vast empire, ever broader sectors of the population were turning against the government; and by the autumn of 1905 the question had astonishingly become whether the tsarist regime could survive. With growing frequency, observers now had to resort to the term *smuta* to describe the situation in the country—a reference to the disintegration of the Muscovite state, and to the anarchy that had swept across Russia, in the decade 1603–13. The *smuta* had come to an end with the establishment of the Romanov dynasty. Was that dynasty now about to fall, just short of its three-hundredth anniversary?

In immediate response to Bloody Sunday, the empire was swept by a wave of strikes unprecedented in scope and intensity. All in all, nearly half a million workers were involved in such strikes during the month of January alone, more than during the entire previous decade.[23] February witnessed the eruption of widespread violence directed against the landowning nobility by the peasantry in the provinces of Orel and Chernigov, and in much of the black-earth belt. No less ominous from the perspective of the regime was the fact that the non-Russian provinces of the empire (regions annexed in the eighteenth and nineteenth centuries)—Poland, the Baltic areas, Georgia—were from the start strongly represented in this assault on the existing order.

Adding to the perception of mounting crisis was the constant resort by anarchists and SRs to "personal terror," with the victims of assassination ranging from the Grand Duke Sergei Aleksandrovich (the tsar's uncle, murdered in February) down to policemen, soldiers, and officials on the lowest rungs of the governmental hierarchy. Violent clashes between the armed forces and vast crowds in such major cities as Warsaw, Lodz, and Odessa (clashes often associated with the funerals of revolutionary "martyrs") constituted a particularly harsh chapter in the story of 1905. Estimates of those killed in Odessa in mid-June, directly by the troops, or by the massive fires ignited during the chaos, range from one to two thousand.[24]

Not as dramatic, but no less significant, was the trend during the spring toward the formal organization and institutionalization of the anti-tsarist forces. Thus, for instance, the month of May witnessed both the formation of the Union of Unions—an umbrella organization of some 14 associations committed to the constitutionalist cause—and also the decision by a conference of peasant representatives to work toward the establishment of an All-Russian Peasant Union (its constituent conference met clandestinely in Moscow in late July).

By this stage the oppositional flood waters were rising so rapidly that the ability of the authorities to manage the crisis was clearly threatened. The decision of Nicholas II in February to yield in principle to the demand for an elected parliament had been generally received with scorn as too little and too late. The new institution was to be granted consultative but not legislative powers. A similarly hostile reception met the publication on August 6 of the electoral law that granted the vote to only a small minority of the population. That the Russo-Japanese War was meanwhile continuing not only unchecked, but drawing in an ever larger number of combatants, greatly exacerbated the situation facing the regime. News of the defeat in the battle of Mukden, in which the Russian army had deployed some 300,000 troops, could hardly have come at a worse time. Yet still more disastrous was the catastrophe that overtook the Baltic Fleet, which, having sailed some halfway around the world in order to reach East Asia, was decimated in a single day, May 27, by the Japanese navy deployed in the Straits of Tsushima.

The fact that by this time close to one million Russian soldiers were concentrated in Manchuria meant that the ability of the regime to police the empire was stretched dangerously thin. With a large number of the best-trained officers removed from their own units in the west, the reliability of those units was seriously reduced. The dependability of the reservists, recruited in very large numbers during the war, was anyway highly questionable. This problem had become so acute by the spring of 1905 that it was decided in the Ministry of War to abandon any thought of further recruitments in no fewer than 32 of the 50 provinces in European Russia.[25] Even the mobilization of Cossack units, rightly considered the backbone of the effort to maintain order in the country, could no longer be taken for granted.

To add still further to the anxieties of the regime with respect to the loyalty of the armed forces came the seizure on June 27 of the battleship *Potemkin-Tavricheskii* by its mutinous crew. The 800 rebel sailors failed in their attempt to draw the entire Black Sea Fleet over to the revolutionary side, and they eventually had to accept asylum in Romania where they abandoned their ship.[26] Nonetheless, their uprising cast such doubt on the future loyalty of the sailors that for a time it was decided to deactivate the entire Black Sea Fleet.

Adding to the multiple problems of the government was also the fast mounting fiscal crisis. The huge costs of the war effort, combined with a domestic economy in chaos, imposed an intolerable burden on the country's finances. Early in the war Russia had been able to raise loans worth half a billion rubles on foreign capital markets. But a country suffering defeat after defeat and in revolutionary upheaval could hardly expect to repeat that success. By the summer of 1905, the Minister of Finance, Vladimir Kokovtsov, had concluded that within another month or two the country would be facing bankruptcy.[27]

Under these circumstances, it is hardly surprising that, when the President of the United States, Theodore Roosevelt, offered in June to mediate between the two warring states in an effort to conclude a peace agreement, the Russian government eagerly took up the offer—as, indeed, did Japan, which, although victorious on land and sea, was finding the burden of so intensive, lengthy, and blood-soaked a war increasingly difficult to sustain. Reluctantly acknowledging the severity of the crisis facing his regime, Nicholas II now turned to Witte, whom he had shunted aside so summarily two years earlier, in order to lead the peace delegation that set sail for the United States in July. By the treaty signed on September 5 in Portsmouth, New Hampshire, Russia abandoned its control of the Liaotung Peninsula and gave up its claims to a privileged status in northern Korea and in nearly all of Manchuria. Additionally, the Russian side had to cede southern Sakhalin to Japan. As against that, however, it was agreed that Russia be spared the burden and humiliation of indemnity payments.[28]

Seen in retrospect, the conclusion of the peace treaty with Japan can be ranked as a major turning point in the course of the 1905 revolution. The appointment of Witte as head of the Russian delegation, the firm backing that he received from St Petersburg during the negotiations, and the speedy conclusion of the treaty on relatively satisfactory terms, all demonstrated that for the first time in years a certain sense of realism was gaining a hold on the mind of the tsar. There were, after all, few voices in the upper ranks of the army and the government who were advocating that the war should still be fought to a victorious conclusion. For Nicholas II to have opted firmly against that advice showed that he had finally begun to grasp just how threatening the domestic situation was becoming.

In the short run, though, the achievement of peace did nothing to halt the decline of governmental authority. On the contrary, if it had any immediate impact, it must have given still greater encouragement to the forces of opposition: a regime so thoroughly defeated on the battlefield would hardly be able to withstand revolution at home. In fact, the wave of rebellion—or, more accurately, of the rebellions, for there was little coord-ination between one region and another, or between one social class and another—reached its height in the last three months of the year.

The moment when the Romanov regime appeared to be on the actual verge of collapse came some two months after the Portsmouth Peace Treaty, in late October. A railway strike that had begun in Moscow early in the month was taken up in St Petersburg on October 25, and almost immedi-ately spread far and wide across the empire. With the telegraph and post also struck, it became impossible to maintain communications between the central government and the provinces. Indeed, within a matter of days, it was no longer clear which institution had greater control of the country: the tsarist regime or the Council—the Soviet—of Workers' Deputies, a forum hastily established to represent the industrial proletariat of St Petersburg, mobilized in entirety by the general strike. Using the Soviet as their stage, the revolutionaries, SRs and Marxists (with Leon Trotsky in a most conspicuous role), now for the first time were able to seize a leading role in a revolution that hitherto had borne a markedly inchoate character.

It was at this juncture that Nicholas II in desperation turned once again to Witte, who in a report addressed to the tsar at the height of the crisis on October 26 had called for a radical change in the nature of the regime. "The unrest," he wrote,

> which has seized the various classes of the Russian people [is not] . . .
> the consequence of the partial imperfections of the political and social
> order or . . . of the activities of organized extreme parties. The roots of
> that unrest lie deeper . . . Russia has outgrown the existing regime and
> is striving for an order based on civic liberty.[29]

Writing to his mother, the Dowager Empress Mariia Federovna, on Novem-ber 1, Nicholas II stated that he had been faced with a stark choice between appointing a dictator to crush the rebellion as ruthlessly as possible or else "to give the people their civil rights, freedom of speech, of assembly and association, press; also to have all laws confirmed by a State Duma . . . [which] would be essentially a constitution."[30] He had opted, however reluctantly, for the latter course and, on October 30, he had appointed Witte as prime minister and had agreed to issue the manifesto, which promised the Russian people "the unshakable foundations of civil liberty," a greatly expanded franchise for the elections to a Duma, and a guarantee that "no law can be put into effect without the consent of the State Duma."[31]

In the short run, for a matter of months, the October Manifesto, with its promises of freedom, constitutionalism, and (in some vaguely defined form) parliamentary government, did little or nothing to restore order in the country. In the rural areas, peasant attacks on the manor houses of the nobility now reached proportions without precedent since the Pugachev uprising in the 1770s. American historian Roberta Manning, who has written on the politics of the nobility in this period, described these jacqueries as "the terrifying 'October–November Days', a time when the old social-political order . . . appeared to be well on its way to extinction."[32]

Many regions of the country were now virtually cut off from the center and, in varying degrees, under revolutionary control. This was true of large stretches in the Baltic area; of Transcaucasia and of Siberia. Incredibly, almost all contact between St Petersburg and the million-man army in Manchuria was lost and speculation was rife that the rank-and-file soldiers had thrown off the control of their officers and were now on the side of the revolution. The unrest in Poland, Finland, and Central Asia did not abate. As for the universities, to which academic autonomy had been restored in August 1905, they had become centers of almost ceaseless revolutionary meetings and organization. Even the predominant section of the liberal movement, under Miliukov's leadership and now organized into the Constitutional Democratic Party (or the Kadets), insisted that the revolution had to continue until the principle of popular and parliamentary sovereignty was formally and finally conceded.

No less symptomatic of the continued uncertainty with regard to the future of the regime and the revolution was the willingness of the socialist leadership in Moscow (particularly the Bolsheviks) to enter in December into a direct and armed battle with the authorities.[33] The hope was that such a gamble would inspire mutiny among the soldiers and a massive wave of anti-governmental action in St Petersburg and across the country.

Despite all the appearances to the contrary, however, the conclusion of peace with Japan in August and the issue of the October Manifesto did eventually make possible a turn in the tide. Within the middle and upper classes, despite the stance of the Kadets, there was a deepening fear of the lawlessness and anarchy that were taking over the city streets and the countryside. The necessity for compromise with the regime was raised as its banner by the second major liberal party that was now established, calling itself—unambiguously—the Octoberist Party. As for the working class, the continual strikes, with their consequent loss of pay, had proved totally exhausting; and the call of the insurrectionists in Moscow for bold acts of solidarity went unheeded elsewhere.

Of decisive importance in the unfolding of events, though, was the fact that, with the Russo-Japanese War now ended, the chances of mutiny within the armed forces could be radically reduced. The soldiers no longer faced the danger of dispatch to the battle front. Moreover, the Ministry of War, under the leadership of Aleksandr Rediger, decided that the rapid release of the reservists, recruited for the war, would be one important way to deprive the revolution of potential, and armed, reinforcements.[34] As for those parts of the army that were not due for release, the funds were now found to make significant improvements in the conditions of service. In his memoirs, Rediger explained that the aim was a total transformation of the way in which the non-commissioned officers (and, to some extent, even

the privates) were to be treated. Where, previously, they had been expected
to find the leisure time to earn enough money to furnish most of their basic
needs, now they were to be provided with:

> A quarter of a pound of meat a day; lard and tea; blankets; bed linen;
> towels; handkerchiefs; soap; an increase in the money for boots from
> 35 kopecks to two and a half rubles; a complete set of underwear; and
> a shirt with shoulder bands attached.[35]

Relying at first on the Cossacks and the Guards to overwhelm the revolutionary forces and rebel populations, it gradually became possible to employ
regular army units. With the opposition now divided against itself and
with the war concluded, it became easier to restore traditional forms of
discipline in the army. Once the armed forces could be dispatched to crush
resistance, often with utter ruthlessness, the regime slowly emerged from
the crisis. During the year 1906, thousands of government employees were
assassinated by the revolutionaries; and over one thousand revolutionaries
were executed after sentencing by field courts. Violence was still endemic,
but the regime could feel more secure month by month.[36]

In ways very much reminiscent of the 1848 revolutions in central and
southern Europe, the autocratic system was able to exploit its control of the
army to roll back the initial gains made by the revolution. The government
of Nicholas II chose to follow the Prussian rather than the Austrian example,
severely curtailing—but not abolishing—the powers earlier granted to the
parliament and the constitutional framework. With the law of June 16,
1907—often, and persuasively, described as a coup d'état—the balance
established in 1906 between the tsar and the people tipped sharply, albeit
not all the way, toward the autocratic principle.

Beyond 1905

Given the obvious link between the defeat in war and the upsurge of revolution, the tsarist regime clearly needed to undertake a far-reaching review
of its intertwined foreign and military strategies. To avoid another chain
reaction along the lines of 1904–6 was a matter of nothing less than survival.
The measure of calm that gradually ensued as the revolutionary tide ebbed
provided, on the face of it, a favorable context for such a reassessment.

After all, the electoral law of June 1907 made it possible for the Duma
to become an integral part of a mixed system of government, which, combining elements of autocracy, aristocracy, and democracy, came to be widely
seen as relatively stable. In contrast to the first and second Dumas, which
had both been dispersed within a few months, the third and fourth were
allowed to live out their five-year terms—until, that is, they were inter-
rupted in the midst of World War I by the revolution of February 1917. In
constitutional terms, the Romanov Empire had thus moved much nearer to

its Hohenzollern and Habsburg neighbors (with its electoral laws particularly close to those long established in the Prussian and Hungarian subdivisions within those two states). The fact that Russia had shed its pariah status as the only strictly autocratic regime in Europe clearly reduced its vulnerability in the face of revolutionary pressure.

Developments within the economic sphere likewise offered the regime a welcome breathing space. With agriculture providing close to 70 percent of Russian exports, the buoyant grain prices on the world markets underpinned rapid rates of growth across the entire economy. Governmental revenues, which as noted above had stood at 2,000 million rubles in 1902, had risen to 3,400 million by 1914 (despite the intervening years of war and revolution).[37] Moreover, economic expansion was now financed far more by domestic rather than foreign funding, with investments from abroad down from some half of the annual total to an eighth over the ten-year period 1904–13, while this industrial expansion was increasingly underwritten not by the Russian state, but by private banks.[38]

No less significant a factor in energizing the economy was the fact that, in the wake of the major agrarian reform initiated in 1906 by Prime Minister Petr Stolypin, the peasants were far freer, if they so chose, to sell their landholdings and to join the urban labor force, thus removing a major bottleneck hampering the process of industrialization. Commenting on this developmental spiral, the noted economic historian Alexander Gerschenkron could write that, putting to one side counterfactually the questions of war and revolution, Russia by 1914 was "well on the way toward a Westernization, or perhaps more precisely a Germanization, of its industrial growth."[39]

This analysis is by no means universally accepted by the historians, who are even more divided when it comes to estimating what chance of long-term survival the tsarist regime, and indeed the empire as a single state, would have had even under the hypothetical conditions of lasting peace.[40] Only rarely, though, does anyone dispute the proposition that the risk of fighting, and hence possibly of losing, a war constituted the most immediate threat to both the dynasty and the state. This fact was broadly recognized in the governing circles, which had emerged severely chastened from the years of the recent *smuta*. However, there was no consensus regarding the strategic conclusions to be drawn from that sobering experience.

Broadly speaking, it can be argued that Russia was faced by a choice between three basic options in coordinating its military and diplomatic priorities; and these competing concepts each had its advocates in ongoing debates both within the upper reaches of government and in the public arena, particularly in the press, which had come to enjoy far greater freedom of expression than prior to 1905. One line of thought insisted that the most promising path to avoiding war was to maintain a low profile both in international relations and in the rebuilding of the armed forces. Translated into concrete terms, this meant the avoidance of radical change in the pre-existing fundamentals.

The Franco-Russian Alliance, sealed by the treaties of 1891 and 1894, had to be maintained, while stressing its defensive character. *Inter alia*, the long-standing plans for a retreat from most of Russia's Polish territories in the early stages of a war with Germany and Austria, in order to enable an orderly build-up of military strength behind shortened lines, were to be preserved and developed. A crucial benefit to be derived from such a military strategy was that it would discourage provocative policies on the part of any French government seeking to reverse the defeat of 1870 and the loss of Alsace-Lorraine, while simultaneously reassuring the regime in Berlin that Russia was seeking no more than a non-aggressive balance of power. Similarly, the decision taken by Russia in the 1890s (and confirmed at the meeting between Nicholas II and Franz Josef in 1897) to avoid entanglements in the Balkans was of no less importance within this overall conception with its preference for retrenchment rather than innovation.

Again resorting to a high level of abstraction, it can be said that it was precisely skepticism with regard to the effectiveness of such an apparently timorous strategy that prompted the alternative thinking characteristic of the second option. Overly cautious planning in both the military and the diplomatic spheres were bound, in this view, to be taken as symptomatic of a built-in structural vulnerability. The inevitable result would be, on the one hand, to expose Russia constantly to humiliation by the Central Powers, while, on the other, undermining confidence in the Franco-Russian Alliance, with France possibly leaving its eastern partner to fight a war more or less unaided. Or, no less serious, in case of armed conflict Russia might not be able to act effectively to prevent the rapid defeat of France, an outcome that would again position it in an uneven struggle against the combined forces of Austria-Hungary and Germany. The logical conclusion was that the tsarist empire had no choice but to act out the role of a great power to the full as the only effective way to uphold the balance of power and preserve the peace. To regain the respect that it had lost at home and abroad during the crisis of 1904–6, the regime would have to exploit the surge in economic growth in order to build up its armed forces both on land and sea as rapidly as possible; coordinate military planning closely with France; develop a forward military strategy, exploiting the Polish, salient as a launching pad for major offensives against the Central Powers, both in Galicia and in East Prussia; and boldly uphold its legitimate interests in the Balkans.[41]

Finally, in polar opposition to this entire standpoint was the third strategic conception. The key idea here was that the natural allies of the tsarist state with its semi-autocratic and mixed system of government were the two neighboring empires, the Hohenzollern and the Habsburg. United, these three conservative regimes could effectively defend themselves against the forces threatening their survival from without (France in possible alliance with Britain) and from within: socialism, minority nationalism, and even outright revolution. To divide off and risk war against each other was thus nothing short of suicidal.[42]

A clear-cut decision in favor of any one of the three options, and the pursuit of policies consistent with its inner logic, might have had a chance of success, albeit success of a different order in each case. A policy of cautious retrenchment could have increased the chance of preserving peace, while threatening to undermine the prestige of a regime already badly battered by the defeat abroad and revolution at home. The forward strategy, if pursued too vigorously, ran the risk of provoking the Central Powers to launch a preventive war, but it offered a real chance of victory given that Germany would have to fight on two fronts at the opening stage of the hostilities. A full-scale realignment of alliances could have left Russia highly vulnerable to heavy-handed and brutal diktats, or even outright ultimata from its would-be allies in Berlin and Vienna.[43]

Be that as it may, in the world not of hypotheses but of cold realities there was no chance whatsoever of the tsarist regime being able to select and execute a consistent set of strategic policies over any extended period of time. The lack of coherence and steady focus that had permitted the tsarist empire to entangle itself in armed conflict with Japan was, if anything, greatly accentuated by the way in which the newly established constitutional system functioned in the years from 1907 until 1914. Built-in antagonisms at the apex of the governmental pyramid were reproduced at the lower levels within the armed forces and the diplomatic service. Any decision affecting military or foreign policy was liable to be reversed, neutralized, or circumvented by its opponents who could count on being able to play off one faction in the country's leadership against another.

In rational terms, Nicholas II accepted the fact that he had no choice but to reconcile himself to the limitations placed on his autocratic power by the fundamental laws introduced in 1906, but he still profoundly resented the changes forced upon him. He regarded the Duma, despite its built-in conservative bias, with outright hostility, and bitterly rebuffed its attempts to play even a secondary role in the area of military oversight. This situation left even so able a prime minister as Stolypin, a politician with genuine leadership qualities, struggling in limbo and unable to count on reliable support from any source: not from the tsar and his court, not from either chamber of parliament (the Duma and the State Council), nor even from his fellow ministers who saw themselves as directly answerable to the tsar as well as to the premier.[44] A similar situation prevailed in the military sphere where War Minister Vladimir Sukhomlinov had to face persistent and often insurmountable opposition from influential coteries within the higher echelons of the army, particularly from the cavalry and artillery branches, associated above all with the Grand Duke Nikolai Nikolaevich, the tsar's uncle.[45]

With no single guiding hand, decisions in the crucial areas of foreign and military policy tended to be taken on an ad hoc basis without due consideration to long-term planning or a strategic vision. Suffice it here to mention a few of the initiatives that, however potentially viable, were either abandoned or not supplied with sufficient backing to ensure probability of success. Thus, for example, throughout the period between the Russo-Japanese War and World War I, a number of serious overtures were made to Berlin in search of a significant improvement in relations. At a meeting between the tsar and the kaiser off the Finnish port of Björkö in July 1905, a treaty of mutual defense was signed between the two countries; but having failed to consult with his top ministers in advance, Nicholas II was induced in essence to repudiate it as incompatible with the Franco-Russian treaties. Subsequent meetings in 1910 (at Potsdam) and in 1912 (on the Baltic) likewise indicated an awareness on both sides of the danger inherent in their opposing systems of alliance, without any coherent alternative being developed.

Russian policy in the Balkans similarly developed without adequate attention to potential consequences. The hands-off policy officially instituted in 1897 was not reversed in the wake of far-reaching analysis, but rather on a case-by-case basis. So, for instance, the disastrous debacle of the Izvolskii-Aehrenthal agreement (Russian consent to the Austrian annexation of Bosnia-Herzegovina in exchange for Austrian support for Russian claims vis-à-vis the Black Sea Straits) resulted from a hasty and personal decision by the Russian Foreign Minister.[46] More egregious still, Russian policy toward Serbia in the months leading up to the First Balkan War was determined less by the foreign ministry in St Petersburg than by the ambassador to Belgrade, Nikolai Hartwig, who had strong Pan-Slavic convictions and enjoyed excellent connections at the tsarist court.[47]

A steady hand at the helm was equally lacking when it came to overall military direction. The elaborately developed plans to concentrate the core of the peace-time army in heartland Russia and to yield large swathes of Polish territory initially in case of war against Germany were finally confirmed in 1910, only to be reversed shortly thereafter. By 1912 the line of thought adopted was to invade East Prussia in the first stage of war, thus drawing off large German forces that otherwise would be available for the invasion of France. This radical change of direction was matched by huge investments in a build-up of military strength, both on land and sea. By 1914, it has been estimated that the Russian army was receiving more funding than the German. Simultaneous changes in the organization of conscript recruitment meant that the peace-time army was expected within the space of a few years to become three times larger than the German. Given the fact that the Russian population at over 150 million was more than twice as large as that of Germany, it was inevitable that in Berlin the —"Pan-Slavic"—threat from the east now took on ever more menacing proportions and that a preventive war increasingly came to be seen as the only rational response.[48]

With such high stakes involved, it was clearly essential to concentrate every effort on assuring the success of the East Prussian campaign if, as seemed ever more likely by 1913, war were to break out. In reality, though, the competition between rival forces in the military establishment culminated in the opposite result, far more divisions being assigned to the southwestern (Galician) than to the northwestern (Prussian) front. The subsequent defeat of the Russian armies led by the generals Samsonov and Rennenkampf at the battle of Tannenberg came as early as September 1914, a few weeks after the start of hostilities.

The prolonged crisis that now overtook Europe was not primarily set in motion by the Russian Empire. Convinced that time was against them, powerful forces within the ruling elites of Austria and Germany chose to unleash the conflict. However, a considerable share of responsibility has to be assigned to the tsarist government, which, in 1912–14, as in 1902–4, proved chronically unable to foresee the way in which other states would respond to its own actions.

This failure was caused by deep structural problems, not by any lack of highly intelligent, competent, and dedicated officials; but their ideas and formulae tended to cancel each other out. In this context, the last word here should go to the extreme right-wing politician Petr Durnovo, who had served briefly as Minister of the Interior during the 1905 revolution, and whose secret memorandum of February 1914 demonstrated a truly remarkable degree of political foresight. A powerful advocate of full-scale reconciliation with Germany at the expense, if necessary, of the French connection, he spelled out his case at great length. Suffice it here to quote a few key passages:

> The central factor of the period of world history … now is the rivalry between England and Germany [which] … must inevitably lead to an armed struggle between them … The Russo-Japanese War radically changed the relations among the great powers and brought England out of her isolation … All through the Russo-Japanese War England and America observed benevolent neutrality toward Japan, while we enjoyed similar benevolent neutrality from France and Germany. Here, it would seem, should have been the inception of the most natural political combination for us. But after the war our diplomacy faced abruptly about … toward rapprochement with England …; the Triple Entente was formed with England playing the dominant part; and a clash became inevitable … with the powers grouping themselves around Germany.
>
> … Improved relations with Japan [are] hardly a result of Russo-English rapprochement … Japan does not covet our Far Eastern possessions … Possessing Korea and Formosa, Japan would hardly go further north and its desires would sooner lie in the direction of the Philippine Islands, Indochina …
>
> The fundamental groupings in a future war are self-evident: Russia, France and England, on one side; Germany, Austria and Turkey, on the

other . . . The main burden of war will undoubtedly fall on us . . . Are we prepared for so stubborn a struggle . . . We must answer. . ., without evasion, in the negative . . . We must note, first of all the insufficiency of our military supplies . . . on account of the embryonic condition of our industries . . ., while the blockade of the Baltic as well as the Black Sea will make impossible the importation of the . . . materials we lack.[49]

A struggle between Germany and Russia, regardless of its outcome, is profoundly undesirable for both sides, as . . . weakening the conservative principle of which . . . [these] two great powers are the only reliable bulwarks . . . There must inevitably break out in the defeated country a social revolution which . . . will spread to the country of the victor.

A general European war is mortally dangerous both for Russia and Germany, no matter who wins . . . An especially favorable soil for social upheavals is found, of course, in Russia. The peasant dreams of obtaining free a share of somebody else's land; the workman of getting hold of the entire capital and profits of the manufacturer . . . If these slogans are scattered far and wide, Russia undoubtedly will be flung into anarchy such as she suffered in the ever memorable period of troubles in 1905–06 . . . In the event of defeat, the possibility of which in a struggle with . . . Germany cannot be overlooked, social revolution in its most extreme form is inevitable . . . The defeated army, having lost its most dependable men during the war, and carried away . . . by the tide of the general elemental desire of the peasant for land, will prove to be too demoralized to serve as a bulwark of law and order. The legislative institutions and the opposition intelligentsia parties . . . will be powerless to stem the popular tide . . . and Russia will be flung into hopeless anarchy, the outcome of which cannot even be foreseen.[50]

This memorandum was addressed by Durnovo to the tsar. One may wonder whether he read it. If so, he must have felt some sympathy for its conservative sentiments, and recalled the Treaty of Björkö, but by February 1914 the die had surely been cast.

Notes

1 For general works on nineteenth-century Russian history, see, for example, Florinsky, 1947; Seton-Watson, 1967; and Westwood, 1981.
2 On Witte's economic strategy and its social costs, see von Laue, 1963: 71–119; see also Kahan, 1989: 1–107.
3 Harcave, 1990: 175.
4 Trotsky, 1931: 119 (English version, 1957: 95).
5 Witte, 1921: 175.
6 Trotsky, 1931, I: 122 (English version, 1957: 97–8).
7 White, 1964: 30.
8 Rogger, 1983: 164.

9   For Kuropatkin's memorandum of October 1903, arguing for the annexation of northern Manchuria, see *Krasnyi Archiv*, 1922: 87–9. On the diplomatic maneuvering that preceded the outbreak of the Russo-Japanese War, see Malozemoff, 1958; and Nish, 1985.

10 On the influence of Bezobrazov and his coterie, see White, 1964: 31–75. In his diary, Kuropatkin recorded his having told Witte in February 1903:

> Our tsar has grandiose plans in his head: to take Manchuria for Russia, and then go on to annex Korea. He dreams of having Tibet too under his rule. He wants to take Persia and seize not only the Bosphorus, but also the Dardanelles. We, the ministers, manage to hold the tsar back from acting on these dreams by referring to the specific conditions prevailing on those areas, but this results in our utterly disappointing him; he still thinks that he is right and that he understands better than us questions concerning the prestige and interests of Russia.

In *Krasnyi Archiv*, 1922: 31. For a recent study of Russian imperialist thinking vis-à-vis the Far East, see Schimmelpenninck van der Oye, 2001.

11 Quoted in White, 1964: 74.

12 Diary entries for January 27 and 30, 1904; Nicholas II, 1923: 130–1.

13 Ascher, 1988: 23.

14 Fuller, 1992: 400–1. There is a vast literature on the Russo-Japanese War; for some of the more recent studies, see, for example, Connaughton, 1988; Rostunova, 1977; and Westwood, 1986.

15 Qu, in Witte, 1921: 369. Kuropatkin quotes Lamsdorf's impression that Plehve believed "a war would distract the masses from political questions." In *Krasnyi Archiv*, 1922: II: 94.

16 See, for example, Geifman, 2000: 68–70; and Nikolaevskii, 1991: 76–7 (English version, 1934: 72–3). On Plehve's possible involvement (considered improbable by the author) in instigating the Kishinev pogrom, see Judge, 1992: 86–91, 125–33.

17 Qu, in Ascher, 1988: 61. For Miliukov's account of the Paris conference, see Miliukov, 1955, I: 242–6. See also Galai, 1973: 214–31; Riha, 1969: 59–62; and Stockdale, 1996: 120–3.

18 Vernadsky *et al.*, 1972, III: 743.

19 Ascher, 1988: 67.

20 Ascher, 1988: 72.

21 For the text of the Gapon petition, see Sablinsky, 1976: Appendix II, 344–9; for the passages quoted here: 345–7.

22 The most important and impressive study of the revolutionary period is Ascher's two-volume history *The Revolution of 1905*. See also Harcave, 1964; and Verner, 1990.

23 Harcave, 1964: 104.

24 See, for example, Weinberg, 1993: 136.

25 Fuller, 1992: 404.

26 On the *Potemkin* mutiny, see Bushnell, 1985: 55–65.

27 Fuller, 1992: 405. See also Kokovtsov, 1935: 16–17, 42–4.

28 For a detailed account of the Portsmouth Peace Conference and Treaty, see White, 1964: 229–309, 359–68.

29 Vernadsky *et al.*, 1972, III: 704.

30 *Krasnyi arkhiv*, 1927: 168. In this very uncharacteristic letter, replete as it was with politically oriented detail, the tsar also wrote that "we are in the midst of a full-scale revolution with the entire government of the country disrupted; therein lies the primary danger."

31 Vernadsky *et al.*, 1972, III: 705.
32 Manning, 1982: 177.
33 For a Soviet account of the Moscow uprising, see Iakovlev, 1957: 82–214.
34 For an analysis of the unrest in the armed forces and of the steps taken to reduce it, see Rediger, 1999, I: 474–80. Rediger writes, *inter alia*, that, in the last months of 1905, "the unrest in the forces was . . . on the increase and every day reports were received—by the dozen—of disturbances in various units" (p. 475). See, too, the convincing description of the role of the army in the revolution from late 1905 and into 1906 in Bushnell, 1985: 109–44.
35 Rediger, 1999, I: 478.
36 One estimate gives the number of political assassinations in 1906 as 1,126 and in 1907 as some 3,000, while 1,102 people were executed on the orders of the field courts during the period when they functioned (August 1906–April 1907). In Conroy, 1976: 91, 94. See also Ascher, 2001: 137–49.
37 Pushkarev, 1985: 282
38 Gatrell, 1986: 222–8.
39 Gerschenkron, 1962: 142.
40 See, for example, the well-known debate: Haimson, 1965; the comments of Mendel and von Laue; and Haimson's response, 1965. Cf. the differing assessments advanced in Walkin, 1963: 183–236; and Waldron, 1998: 178, 186.
41 On Russia's changing doctrines of military strategy, see Fuller, 1992: 412–45; cf. Stone, 1975: 17–43.
42 For an illuminating analysis of a pro-German realignment of alliances, see Lieven, 1983: 73–83.
43 Noting the complexity of these dilemmas, Fuller writes: "Thus paradoxically the Russian Empire could be destroyed through fighting a war or through not fighting one." In Fuller, 1992: 456.
44 For an excellent description of Stolypin's years as head of government (1906–11), see Ascher, 2001: 115–362, 391–9.
45 It has to be added, of course, that no governmental system is free of internal conflict and confusion; and that the hybrid constitutional arrangements instituted in Berlin, Vienna, and St Petersburg were all particularly prone to crossed lines of command. But the problem was arguably rendered particularly acute in Russia due to the personality of the tsar. Much insight into the built-in conflicts within the military establishment is provided by the memoirs of Rediger (Minister of War until 1909), 1999, II: 267–96; Polivanov (Assistant Minister of War (1906–12), 1924: 15–114; and Sukhomlinov (Minister of War from 1909), 1926: 133–215. Cf. Menning, 1992: 238–71; Wildman, 1980, I: 41–74; and Fuller, 1985: 192–263. For a valuable collection of articles comparing the varieties of confusion in the sphere of foreign policy and intelligence, see May, 1984.
46 Commenting on this diplomatic defeat, Nicholas wrote to his mother on March 18, 1909 that "the way in which the German government addressed us was harsh and we won't forget that!!" In *Krasnyi arkhiv*, 1932: 189. By the following year, however, he could write apropos of his forthcoming visit to Potsdam that "in these days it is necessary to live with our neighbors in complete friendship—something which is not difficult avec un peu de bonne volonté de part et de l'autre" (p. 191).
47 On Hartwig's "incurable Austrophobia," see Lieven, 1983: 41–3. Hartwig's role, though, should not be exaggerated. See, for example, the comments in his memoirs of the tsarist Foreign Minister on the creation of the Balkan League in 1912: "Russia's historical mission—the emancipation of the Christian peoples

of the Balkan peninsula from the Turkish yoke—was almost fulfilled by the beginning of the twentieth century; its completion could be left to . . . the liberated peoples themselves." But, he added, they were too weak "to dispense with her [Russia's] help in the event of any attempt upon their national existence by warlike Teutonism." In Sazonov, 1928: 49.
48 Stone, 1975: 37–43.
49 Vernadsky, *et al.*, 1972, III: 793–5.
50 Vernadsky, *et al.*, 1972, III: 797.

5   From enemies to allies

The war and Russo-Japanese relations

Peter Berton

In 1905, Japan and Russia ended their war and signed a peace treaty, and in 1916 the Japanese government proposed to Russia a draft of an alliance that was essentially an unlimited offensive–defensive pact.[1] How did this happen? How did the Japanese and the Russians transform their relationship from enemies to allies in a short decade? This chapter explores this transformation from the standpoint of Japanese and Russian domestic politics as well as the evolving international environment in the world, and in East Asia in particular. It touches upon Japan and Russia's evolving relationship with their respective allies, Great Britain and France, and the significance of China and Germany as contributing factors. The chapter discusses the three agreements (public and secret) negotiated by Japan and Russia in 1907, 1910, and 1912, which effectively demarcated their respective spheres of influence in Manchuria and Mongolia; the attempts of France and Russia to join the Anglo-Japanese Alliance at the beginning of World War I; and the successful negotiations in Tokyo and Petrograd that led to the conclusion of a Russo-Japanese treaty of alliance in 1916. This was the path from enmity to alliance taken by the protagonists of the war of 1904–5.

Normally, wars produce a desire for revenge on the part of the losing side, ending as preludes to the next war. One such example is the relationship between Germany and France after the Franco-Prussian War of 1870, which led to World Wars I and II. And who does not remember the picture of Hitler dictating terms of surrender in the same railway car in which the French dictated their terms of surrender to the German delegation in 1918? Some wars, however, do not end as preludes to further wars of revenge, but result in a modus vivendi between the former adversaries. Still other wars transform the protagonists into allies who face a new common enemy. Such was the historical scenario of the relationship between the United States, Britain, and France on the one hand, and their former World War II enemies Japan and Germany on the other. A long and bloody war did not necessarily lead to feelings of revenge on the part of the losers—the Germans and the Japanese—but transformed them into a close alliance with the victorious powers. I will argue in this chapter that this is what happened to the relationship between Russia and Japan after the bloody war of 1904–5.

But it takes two to tango, and I intend to look into the motives of both the Japanese and Russian military and civilian leadership: to avoid another war against Russia on the part of the Japanese, and to forgo the desire for revenge on the part of the Russians.

The Treaty of Portsmouth of 1905, which brought the Russo-Japanese War to a conclusion, was the first step toward working out a new balance of power in East Asia. After its unsuccessful war, Russia's concern was to minimize the danger of internal revolution. As its foreign policy turned westward to Europe, some guarantee of the stability of its Far Eastern possessions was desirable. In Japan, on the other hand, the military leaders, some of whom had reservations about the Anglo-Japanese Alliance and fearing a war of revenge, felt the need to come to an understanding with Russia. The rapprochement between Russia and Japan was promoted and further facilitated by their respective allies, France and Great Britain, who were anxious to align the two countries against Germany and to make it possible for Russia to concentrate its forces in Europe. In fact, the conclusion of the Anglo-Russian Convention in 1907, which settled their disputes in Persia, Afghanistan, and Tibet, ended the Great Game—the historical competition between the two powers in the heartland of Asia.

The three agreements of 1907–12

In July 1907, Russia and Japan signed a treaty of commerce and navigation, and a fisheries convention, followed by two political agreements, only one of which was to be made public.[2] In the public agreement each of the two countries "engaged to respect the actual territorial integrity of the other" and all rights accruing from treaties. They recognized the independence and territorial integrity of China and the principle of equal opportunity, and undertook to support and defend the maintenance of the status quo by all pacific means at their disposal.

The secret convention signed on the same day divided Manchuria into two spheres of influence, leaving the larger, or northern, part to Russia, and the southern part to Japan. In view of the "natural gravitation of interests and of political and economic activity in Manchuria," both governments agreed not to obstruct the initiative of the other in their respective spheres. The line of demarcation agreed upon ran roughly from the northwestern point of the Russo-Korean frontier, along the Sungari, Nonni, and Tola rivers, to the 122-degree meridian. Furthermore, Russia, recognizing "the relations of political solidarity between Japan and Korea," undertook not to interfere with further development of those relations; while Japan, recognizing "the special interests of Russia in Outer Mongolia," undertook "to refrain from any interference which might prejudice those interests." The text of the secret agreement was communicated by Russia to France and by Japan to Britain. Thus, in the secret agreement, Korea, Manchuria, and Mongolia were definitely set aside for Russian or Japanese activity, while the public convention spoke of such respectable ideas as the principle of equal opportunity and the territorial integrity of China. The conclusion of the first agreements proved that cooperation was feasible between the recent enemies, while developments in East Asia, as events proved, were to facilitate this rapprochement.

In November 1909, Philander Knox, the American Secretary of State, advanced a plan for the neutralization of the Manchurian railway. He proposed that an international syndicate be formed to make a loan to China so that it might buy out Russian and Japanese interests in the Manchurian railroads and that the railroads be internationally administered during the period of the loan. The Russian and Japanese reaction to this interference was to work more closely together. Both countries rejected the American plan in notes handed on the same day and similarly worded. The American intervention provided an impetus for new Russo-Japanese negotiations that led, once again, to the conclusion, in July 1910, of two conventions, only one of which was made public, the other to remain secret except for informing the British and French governments.[3]

In the public convention the two powers pledged friendly cooperation to improve their respective railway lines in Manchuria and to refrain from competition. This was in effect transferring into the public treaty, for the purpose of giving public notice to the other powers, an obligation already assumed in the secret agreement of 1907. Mention of the recognition of "the independence and territorial integrity of China" and of "the principle of equal opportunity," which had been included in the agreements of 1907, was dropped from the new agreement. The two countries pledged themselves to maintain and defend the status quo in Manchuria with measures "which they may deem it necessary to take,"—measures not necessarily restricted to "pacific means" alone, as was stated in the public convention of 1907. This was definitely a warning to other powers to keep hands off the Russo-Japanese preserves in Manchuria.

The secret treaty signed at the same time was also a development of the 1907 formula. By the terms of the new agreement, Russia and Japan each recognized the right of the other to take freely all measures necessary for the defense of its interests; each undertook not to hinder in any way the consolidation and further development of the special interests of the other country, and to refrain from all political and some types of economic activity within the sphere of the other. Finally, in the event of a threat to their interests, Russia and Japan pledged themselves to agree upon the measures to be taken with a view to common action or to the support to be accorded one another for the defense of their interests.

This was clearly a stronger version of the corresponding article in the public convention of 1907, with the important difference that, instead of defense of the status quo, there was a defense of special interests. This meant that Russia and Japan were not interested primarily in maintaining the status quo, because development of special interests automatically upsets the status quo. The conclusion of the Russo-Japanese treaties of 1910 was promptly followed by the Japanese annexation of Korea. During 1911 the two powers defeated an American-sponsored Four Power Loan to China and cooperated in other Chinese problems. There were consultations between the two countries when the Manchu dynasty was overthrown in China. The United States, in February 1912, proposed joint action by the powers in China, but Russia and Japan replied, after consultations, that Manchuria and Mongolia belonged to their respective spheres of influence, and must be treated as being outside of the sphere of any joint action of the powers.

Russian assistance to Mongolia became continuous after Mongolia declared its independence from China. The new developments in Mongolia made necessary a demarcation of spheres of influence there, and in 1912 secret negotiations were begun between Japan and Russia, leading to the conclusion of the third secret agreement in July of that year.[4] The new agreement extended the demarcation line of 1907, dividing Inner Mongolia into two spheres: western-Russian, and eastern-Japanese, the dividing line being the Peking Meridian. The conclusion of this treaty was followed by Russian recognition of the new regime in Mongolia in November 1912.

Thus, during the course of five years a substantial part of East Asia had been divided between Russia and Japan. Korea had been annexed, Mongolia to all intents and purposes detached from China, and Manchuria and Inner Mongolia divided into Russian and Japanese spheres of influence. After 1912 the relations between Russia and Japan were very different from those that had prevailed immediately after the defeat of 1905. A certain solidarity of action was manifested by the two governments, not only in Manchuria and Mongolia, but over the wider area. Much of the original animosity and some of the suspicion had been eliminated, and the benefits to be derived from Russo-Japanese cooperation in East Asia had been made clear even to less enthusiastic supporters of this policy.

The outbreak of World War I and triple and quadruple alliance proposals

The outbreak of the European war in 1914 found Japan in the enviable position of being allied to Great Britain and courted by Russia and France. Japan soon captured German possessions in East Asia and the Pacific and set about gaining a freer hand in the affairs of China—its defenseless neighbor—as the European powers were expending their men and wealth in a protracted war. Before Japan's declaration of war on Germany, in August 1914, France had offered Japan an alliance modeled after the Anglo-Japanese pact.[5] The motives of the French in proposing such an alliance were to facilitate Japan's entry into the war on the side of the Allies and to obtain additional security for French possessions in East Asia. The proposed pact would have given increased protection to Russia as well, thereby enabling it to concentrate the bulk of its forces in Europe; in turn, Russia's greater war effort on the eastern front would have lessened German pressure on France.

Russia was likewise interested in an alliance with Japan. However, Foreign Minister Sazonov favored Russia's adherence to the Anglo-Japanese Alliance rather than a bilateral treaty between Russia and Japan. While the French were primarily interested in strengthening relations with Japan in wartime, the Russians desired a pact, not so much to safeguard their Far Eastern possessions during the war and to allow a larger concentration of their forces in Europe, but to cement their relations with Great Britain for the distant future. Although Sazonov was in favor of closer ties with Japan, he deemed it safer to include the Allies in the agreement, otherwise Russia might have to support Japanese policy even when it ran counter to French and British interests.

The British showed little enthusiasm for new agreements. At first, Britain had requested that Japan enter the war, and when, a few days later, the Japanese had agreed to do so, the British in a sudden about-face had asked them to reconsider their decision to declare war on Germany. Apparently, Britain was torn between the desire to obtain maximum Japanese help in the war against Germany, and the fear of long-range consequences that would result in the weakening of the British position in East Asia. Moreover, the Dominions looked with suspicion upon the replacement of Germany by Japan in the Pacific, and the British trade interests in China were alarmed at the prospect of unrestricted Japanese activity. The Foreign Office thus preferred postponing any discussion of French or Russian participation in the Anglo-Japanese Alliance until the end of the war; but, having just reversed their position toward Japan's break with Germany, the British decided to cooperate should Japan be inclined to accept these French and Russian proposals.

In summary, then, Russia's motives in proposing an alliance were to induce Japan to enter the war on the side of the Allies, thereby strengthening the allied camp on the one hand, and, on the other, relieving Russia's anxiety over the security of its territories in northeast Asia ("Russian Far East"), and allowing greater concentration of its forces in Europe. This main consideration, perhaps coupled with a desire to cement relations with Great Britain, which would have been strengthened had Russia joined the Anglo-Japanese Alliance, remained even after Japan's entry into the war.

In Japan, two centers of authority maintained opposite positions on foreign relations. The Elder Statesmen, still wielding considerable power, enthusiastically recommended acceptance of the Russian and French offers. Fear of Japan's isolation in the post-war period and the necessity to contend with an "all-white" coalition was their main reason for advocating alliances with these powers. Foreign Minister Katō Takaaki, however, an exponent of British orientation in Japanese diplomacy, believed that the Anglo-Japanese Alliance would be weakened by the participation of France, and especially Russia—the original target of the pact. Katō was able successfully to resist the pressure of the Elder Statesmen and to obtain an understanding with the British Foreign Secretary Sir Edward Grey concerning the postponement of the decision respecting the Russian and French proposals until after the war.

The spring of 1915 brought Russian military disasters on the eastern front and substantial development of Japanese influence in China. Through the presentation, in January 1915, of its infamous "Twenty-one Demands," Japan attempted to establish a protectorate over China while other powers, their attention centered in Europe, were unlikely to offer resistance. The Japanese demands, after the elimination of the most humiliating fifth group, were accepted, and Japan's position in China was greatly strengthened.[6] However, this was achieved at the cost of incurring the enmity of the Chinese people, and resulted in a distinct strain in Japanese relations with the United States, Britain, and other countries. While Russian interests were not directly affected by Japan's gaining most of the "Twenty-one Demands," which included taking over Germany's position in the Shantung peninsula, Sazonov feared future Japanese ambitions. In its desperate situation, however, Russia was unable to resist Japanese attempts to achieve a predominant position in China; and, in spite of such fears, Russia, in fact, was advocating closer cooperation with Japan in order to obtain urgently needed war supplies. The deteriorating military position of Russia prompted Sazonov in the summer of 1915 to raise, again unsuccessfully, the question of an alliance with Japan, hoping that it might result in larger deliveries of war supplies from Japan and eliminate the danger of a German–Japanese rapprochement.

The Russo-Japanese Alliance of 1916

It was at this juncture, in December 1915, that Tsar Nicholas II decided to send his uncle to Japan as his personal envoy, hoping that this would speed up the delivery of Japanese munitions—an important factor in Russian military planning. Japan was even to be offered the sector of the Russian-controlled Chinese Eastern Railway in Manchuria that was situated in the Japanese sphere of influence in exchange for badly needed war supplies. Sazonov utilized this trip to send along the head of the Far Eastern Department of the Foreign Ministry, to sound out the Japanese about signing another agreement with Russia.[7] Besides placing an obligation on Japan to supply more munitions to Russia, such an agreement aimed to prevent Germany from again rising to influence in China after the war, and to restrain Japan from coming to an understanding with Germany. While Russia was tied down in Europe, a new Russo-Japanese agreement would serve as another guarantee of Russia's Far Eastern possessions.

The Japanese Foreign Ministry rejected the Russian proposals, arguing that there was no need for another agreement, and, being in doubt whether the military authorities could substantially increase the delivery of war supplies, failed to show sufficient enthusiasm over the offer of the railroad. At this point the rejection of the Russian proposals became known to Field Marshal Yamagata, the most influential of the Elder Statesmen, to whom the Russians complained about the unreceptive attitude of the Japanese Foreign Ministry. As the war progressed, German successes made victory apparent, and, recalling the "Yellow Peril" statements of William II, the Elder Statesmen were now even more afraid of German revenge. They especially feared a Russo-German separate peace, which could well lead to an alliance between those two nations. A Russo-Japanese alliance, on the other hand, they reasoned, would prevent the latter possibility, and would serve as an anti-German weapon, especially since relations with Britain had cooled off and there was disappointment in some quarters over the Anglo-Japanese Alliance.[8] The Elder Statesmen, who ever since the outbreak of war had been advocating an alliance with Russia, now took steps to ensure acceptance of the Russian offer. As in the case when they forced Katō from the cabinet, and when, several months later, they prevented him from becoming prime minister, the Elder Statesmen exerted sufficient pressure to have the cabinet adopt a new Russian policy.

The Foreign Ministry complied, and they produced a draft of a treaty that was essentially an unlimited offensive–defensive pact and that did not take into consideration the system of already existing agreements.[9] Quite conceivably such an agreement could have clashed with obligations under the Anglo-Japanese or the Russo-French pacts. Russia, on the other hand, genuinely interested in collaboration with the West in the acquisition of Constantinople and the Straits, and in pursuit of an active policy in Europe, wanted a Russo-Japanese alliance within the framework of Entente relationships. Russia wanted the agreement with Japan to run parallel to the Anglo-Japanese Alliance, allowing an eventual combination of the two into a triple alliance, and did not desire, for example, to be bound to Japan in a war against the United States. And, finally, unable at the time to think of developing its interests in China, Russia strove to check Japan's increasing influence and attempted to insert restrictive clauses in the agreement.

Sazonov and Ambassador Motono, negotiating in Petrograd, took four months to complete the agreement, most of the time being consumed by the Russian efforts to restrict Japanese activity in China.[10] Neither country emerged victorious from the negotiations. Russia succeeded in weakening the alliance by making the military commitment conditional upon receipt of assistance from France and Britain. On the other hand, Russia lost its battle to place limitations on the freedom of Japan's action in China. The public convention of 1916 is composed of two parts.[11] One part contains pledges by each country not to be a party to any combination directed against the other, and reflects the mutual suspicions held by both Russia and Japan of the possibility that either might conclude a separate peace with Germany. The second part is an article from the secret agreement of 1910, extended to cover the entire region of East Asia ("Extreme-Orient" in the original text), which dealt with the defense of special interests of the two countries. This served as a notice to China, Germany, and the United States. The fact that a clause originally incorporated in a secret agreement between Russia and Japan now appeared in a public convention was perhaps indicative of the changing power relationship in East Asia.

The secret agreement was limited to China, and was designed to prevent China from falling under the domination of a third power. Both Russia and Japan had Germany in mind, and not the United States, when they negotiated the agreement. Furthermore, the provision to lend armed assistance was linked with receiving help from their respective allies, France and Great Britain. Considering the nature of British and French relations with the United States during this period, it is therefore unlikely that the alliance would have been applied against the United States within the foreseeable post-war era and certainly not during the short duration of the alliance. At the same time, it must be noted that the fact of another Russo-Japanese agreement, as a sign of growing rapprochement between these two countries, indirectly strengthened the Japanese position vis-à-vis the United States. In regard to the immediate objectives of Japan and Russia, then, the alliance was essentially an anti-German measure, and reflected the mutual fear of Germany and the possibility that one of the partners might team up with a victorious Germany against the other.

Effects of the Russo-Japanese Alliance and future scenarios

What was the effect of the Russo-Japanese Alliance? Russia doubtlessly achieved additional assurance for the security of its Asian possessions and may have shifted some Siberian troops to the European front. Since the negotiations regarding the cession of the railroad sector progressed slowly and were not completed until the November revolution, it is doubtful whether the alliance resulted in a substantial increase in the delivery of war supplies. Whether the alliance with Japan strengthened Russia's war position is also difficult to answer in view of the effect of the February Revolution, which took place only a few months after the signing of the alliance. It is likewise doubtful that the alliance hastened China's break with Germany, which came about only after the intervention of the United States in the war. It must be conceded, however, that the conclusion of an alliance with Russia in 1916, accompanied by government-sponsored public demonstrations, helped to keep Japanese sympathies in the war on the side of the Allies, and made a separate peace with Germany a more remote possibility.

Had Russia stayed in the war until victory over Germany had been achieved, it is possible that Japan would have been more successful at the Versailles Peace Conference. It is not improbable, for example, that Russia would have supported Japan in the fight for racial equality. Moreover, had friction developed between Russia and Britain over the division of spoils in the Near East, it is possible, especially in view of the decreasing popularity and effectiveness of the Anglo-Japanese Alliance, that a Russo-Japanese bloc could have crystallized in East Asia to counter the developing Anglo-American coalition. Quite conceivably, the isolation of Japan at the Washington Conference and the return of Shantung rights to China could then have been avoided. In the decade following the Russo-Japanese War, a potential conflict between the two adversaries had been successfully resolved. It was due to the desire of the Japanese military to avoid a war of revenge by Russia and, on the part of the Russians, to the development of Westward orientation and the need to protect its interests in East Asia. The fact that both Russia and Japan were on the allied side in World War II obviously contributed to the growing rapprochement between the two former adversaries.

What was the broader impact of the Russo-Japanese War? The most immediate impact was on Korea, which promptly lost its independence and was annexed and incorporated into the Japanese Empire. The next impact was on China, which was further fragmented and practically lost control over the areas in the Japanese and Russian spheres of influence in Manchuria and Mongolia. China was further weakened in the course of World War I, when all the major powers, except the United States, were entangled in hostilities in Europe, while Japan further strengthened its position in China by issuing the infamous "Twenty-one Demands" in 1915. The victory of Japan, a country considered to belong to the yellow race, over a European power, Russia, sent a psychologically potent signal to all of Asia, which suffered under the yoke of white imperialism. Nationalist movements developed in India, China, the Dutch East Indies, French Indo-China, and other colonies and semi-colonies, but they were sadly disappointed when Japan proclaimed, under the slogan of the "Greater East Asia Co-Prosperity Sphere," the liberation of Asia from white imperialism only to supplant it with its own colonialism and imperialism imposed with great brutality.

Looking forward in the evolution of relations between Japan and the Soviet Union that emerged amid the ruins of tsarist Russia, we enter into a period of discontinuity when relations between the two neighbors took a 180-degree turn: the path from enemies to allies and from allies back to enemies. Japanese troops joined the United States and Canada in the intervention in Siberia in 1918, occupied the northern half of the island of Sakhalin in 1920, and lagged behind the European powers in recognizing the new Bolshevik regime. With the occupation of Manchuria in 1931, Japanese–Soviet relations took a turn for the worse, degenerating into armed clashes along the Manchurian–Maritime province and Manchurian–Outer Mongolian borders in the late 1930s. These clashes culminated in large-scale warfare in the battle of Nomonhan on the eve of World War II. It should be noted that Stalin referred to the defeat of Russia in the war of 1904–5 as a motive for Soviet participation in the war against Japan in the waning days of World War II. The spoils of Japan in the Russo-Japanese War, namely the southern half of the island of Sakhalin, were regained by the Soviet Union with a bonus of the entire Kurile archipelago, including four islands that historically were never part of Russia. The dispute over these four islands is still unresolved a century after the Russo-Japanese War.

Notes

1 The author wishes to thank Midori Kobayashi for research assistance and Tatiana White for editorial help. A grant from the Center for International Studies, School of International Relations, University of Southern California is hereby gratefully acknowledged. For further reading, see also Berton, 1988, 1993.
2 Price, 1933: 107ff.; Japan, Ministry of Foreign Affairs, 1914: 154–6.
3 Price, 1933: 113ff.
4 Price, 1933: 117.
5 Gooch and Temperley, 1926–38, X, XI; Itō, 1929; Japan, Ministry of Foreign Affairs, 1944 [1971]; Union of Soviet Socialist Republics, 1931–9, Series III: 1914–17.
6 MacMurray, 1921.
7 Japan, Ministry of Foreign Affairs, 1915–16; Union of Soviet Socialist Republics, 1931–9.
8 Tokutomi, 1933, III; Takahashi, 1924.
9 Japan, Ministry of Foreign Affairs Archives, 1915–16; Japan, Ministry of Foreign Affairs, 1944 [1971], II: 327ff.
10 Japan, Ministry of Foreign Affairs, 1944 [1971].
11 Price, 1933: 121ff.

Part II

Europe and the United States

6 The fragmenting of the old world order

Britain, the Great Powers, and the war

T.G. Otte

If the actual fighting during the Russo-Japanese War was confined mostly to southern Manchuria and the seas of northern China, the conflict had global ramifications. It affected all the major powers of the day, but especially Great Britain. This, in turn, was rooted in the dual nature of British power. Much emphasis has been given to its traditional concerns with the balance of power in Europe,[1] yet Britain was not an exclusively European power. Its far-flung empire consisted of two strategic blocs, or networks of possessions and interests: the British–European and the Anglo-Indian ones. If Britain's interests were defined globally, then this also necessitated a global reach of British power. Nevertheless, at the opening of the twentieth century wider changes within the constellation among the Great Powers before, during, and after the Russo-Japanese War placed constraints upon Britain's power. These constraints arose from the dual nature of British power and from the 1902 alliance with Japan. Throughout the nineteenth century Russian expansion in Asia posed the most serious threat to Britain's strategic interests. Russia was firmly part of the European Great Power system. Its Asian expansion, however, affected the Anglo-Indian strategic bloc. The 1902 alliance tied Britain to a non-European, and therefore non-systemic, power. Although the Japanese alliance protected British interests in China, it did not address Britain's core interests. The Russian threat may have been geographically confined to Central and East Asia, but it derived its significance from systemic factors. A conflict between Britain's non-systemic ally and Russia, therefore, had potentially broader ramifications.

Lastly, the global repercussions of the Russo-Japanese War were also a reflection of the gradual transformation of the international system since the 1890s. Europe remained the powerhouse of international politics, and the European Great Powers the ultimate arbiters of all international matters. Yet, in the period of "high imperialism," as the Great Powers expanded their influence overseas, European diplomacy was projected onto a broader canvas. Conversely, it also meant that tensions overseas had the potential to cause reverberations in Europe. More than any other region, East Asia

emerged as the main arena of international interest. Indeed, following the
Sino-Japanese War of 1894–5, international politics revolved around the
two poles of Europe and East Asia. The two "were fused into one political
system . . . The scope of diplomats' activity was increased. They were
compelled to follow carefully every change in the political barometer in
China and Europe—for the political situation in one sphere affected the
situation in the other."[2] Crucially, Russia's geo-strategic position, physically linking Europe and Asia, connected these two poles of international
diplomacy. Any shift in the regional balance of power in East Asia was,
thus, bound to affect relations between the Great Powers in the European
core area.

A strategic umbrella: the Anglo-Japanese Alliance

The prospect of a military conflict between Russia and Japan had been a
concern for British policy makers since the end of the Sino-Japanese War of
1894–5.[3] The eventuality of such a conflict was brought considerably closer
as a result of the 1902 Anglo-Japanese Alliance. The alliance itself was the
result of earlier failures of British diplomacy to halt Russia's advance on the
Asian mainland either by means of a direct deal with Russia, or through an
agreement with Germany and Japan. While the approaches to Russia and
Germany envisaged exclusively diplomatic means to ameliorate the effects
of isolation, financial and naval factors affected the notion of a Japanese
understanding. Treasury demands for expenditure curbs and the perceived
naval advantages of an arrangement with Japan created a new dynamic in
British strategic and foreign policy thinking. Combined, the two brought the
Japanese option into sharper focus. Technological advances in battleship
design and the rise of foreign navies had led to a substantial increase in naval
and imperial defense costs. The estimates for the 1901–2 building program
alone had risen by 20 percent, as compared with the preceding year. Overall,
during the period between the adoption of the "Two-power Standard" under
the 1889 Naval Defence Act and 1904 the production cost per battleship
doubled, while that of cruisers rose fivefold.[4]

As British war-planning was still principally concerned with the eventuality of a conflict with the Franco-Russian combination, the expansion and
acceleration of the French and Russian naval armament programs forced
the Admiralty to increase Britain's narrow margin of superiority.[5] Lord
Selborne, the First Lord of the Admiralty, argued that Britain's naval
strength was "inadequate if applied to a possible war against France in
alliance with Russia." In light of its global dispersal, and more especially
its Chinese commitments, Selborne noted, the Royal Navy had little more
than a bare equality of strength in the Mediterranean and the home waters.
Highlighting the systemic nature of the Franco-Russian threat, he warned
that "bare equality at the heart of Empire is a dangerous risk." Britain's

strategic position, however, could be improved by means of a Japanese alliance. Selborne envisaged a naval defense pact, which would allow Britain to reduce the number of vessels on the China Station, and to concentrate forces in European waters, where the decisive battles in a contest with the *Franco-Russe* would be fought.[6] The Admiralty's concern about the Far Eastern regional balance of power and the Treasury's anxiety for fiscal restraint reinforced each other, so accelerating a dynamic that ultimately led to the conclusion of the Japanese alliance.[7] Ultimately, the Treasury–Admiralty–Foreign Office axis in Whitehall prevailed over those who feared Asian complications as a result of a Russo-Japanese War. Such concerns were most strongly articulated by the Prime Minister, the Marquis of Salisbury, and his deputy and chosen successor Arthur Balfour. In the Foreign Secretary's, the Marquis of Lansdowne's, rationale the alliance was to safeguard British interests in China, without involving European commitments, thereby also avoiding additional expenditure. Thus, the Anglo-Japanese Alliance emphasized Britain's continued aloofness from Europe, rather than marking the end of "splendid isolation."[8] The combination of British and Japanese naval forces established a new balance of power in northern China and in Korea. Though delicately poised, it provided something of a strategic umbrella protecting Britain's own interests in the Middle Kingdom. As a defensive policy it was not entirely without risks. Above all, the alliance did not reduce the likelihood of a Russo-Japanese conflagration.

"Keeping the ring": Britain and the war in Asia

The Anglo-Japanese Alliance did not improve Britain's strategic position to the extent its advocates had anticipated. By April 1902, the Admiralty had reluctantly come to the conclusion that "Germany is building *against* us"; and "the German factor" had now to be taken into consideration more than hitherto.[9] Therein lay the problem. It meant that a reduction in naval expenditure, the anticipated result of the Japanese alliance, would not materialize. A strictly regional pact with a non-European power proved to be useless as a means of checking the naval advances of European competitors. Even in Far Eastern waters, Russia's Pacific squadron now outnumbered the Royal Navy vessels on the China Station.[10] Instead of allowing for financial retrenchment, without sacrifice of defense requirements, the combination with Japan yielded no "alliance dividend." Selborne's estimates for the 1903–4 building program projected a further, substantial increase in naval expenditure; and the Treasury, though concerned about the constraints on the nation's finances, had to submit to Admiralty demands.[11]

Still, the ramifications of the alliance were not all negative. Britain's diplomatic position had improved to some degree. While officially making "*bonne mien à mauvais jeu,*" Russian diplomacy was alarmed at the conclusion of the Anglo-Japanese Alliance.[12] The Russian Foreign Minister, Count Vladimir Nikolaevich Lamsdorf, sought to neutralize the combination of the two naval powers through *"un acte analogue"*—an extension of the Franco-Russian Alliance—which should be open to other powers, more especially Germany.[13] Lamsdorf's hasty attempt to revive the 1895 Far Eastern three-power alliance came to nothing. The much narrower Franco-Russian agreement of March 20, 1902 pledged the two powers to maintain the status quo in China.[14] Even so, it heightened concern in London that, in the event of a Russo-Japanese conflict, the *casus foederis* under the Japanese alliance might be triggered after all. Still, Britain's arrangement with Japan exercised a considerable degree of restraint on Russian diplomacy in the region. Russian pressure on China over Manchuria, a potential international flashpoint since the winter of 1900–1, eased perceptibly and the revised Sino-Russian agreement of April 1903 provided for the phased evacuation of Russian troops from the province.[15] The lull in Far Eastern affairs in 1902–3 was deceptive. The vagueness of some of its terms had facilitated the speedy conclusion of the alliance. Its real test, however, came with a Russo-Japanese clash over Korea. Indeed, some months after the outbreak of the conflict, Lansdowne reflected that, while the alliance had

> not [been] intended to encourage the Japanese Government to resort to extremities, [it] had, and was sure to have, the effect of making Japan feel that she might try conclusions with her great rival in the Far East, free from all risk of a European coalition such as that which had [in 1895] . . . deprived her of her fruits of victory.[16]

By the summer of 1903 conflict between the two Asiatic powers was increasingly imminent. By the end of the year both antagonists were set on a war course. Over the Christmas period, of all times, senior cabinet ministers discussed the probable strategic ramifications of a war in East Asia. Selborne was *"very anxious* about the Far East." The imminent prospect of conflict made it incumbent upon the cabinet to decide upon a policy to meet that eventuality. Implicit in Selborne's earlier advocacy of an alliance with Japan had been the assumption "that we could not allow to see Japan smashed by Russia." This imperative had gained in strength with the conclusion of the alliance. However, the First Lord of the Admiralty warned that "our intervention might also entail that of France, and we and France might be driven into war, an appalling calamity!!" Selborne made a vague suggestion of some Anglo-French diplomatic initiative to deter Russian aggression.[17] Arthur Balfour, by now prime minister, acknowledged the need for the government to formulate a line of policy prior to any conflict in East Asia. All policy considerations, however, depended on Japan's preferred course of action, and on its chances of success in a contest with Russia.[18] Austen Chamberlain, the Chancellor of the Exchequer, was more optimistic than either Selborne or Balfour, and advocated ruthlessly Bismarckian precepts. A Russo-Japanese War would be "the proper time for us to secure and to secure promptly, whatever we want in places where Russia is our rival." Russia, preoccupied with the Japanese threat to its East Asian ambitions, would be vulnerable to British pressure.[19]

The Foreign Secretary was not enamored of the Chancellor's recommendation to "take a leaf out of the notebook of German diplomacy," and poured cold water on the Chancellor's neo-Bismarckianism. The Whitehall axis between Foreign Office and Admiralty was still in place at this stage, for Lansdowne, too, envisaged a joint initiative with France, and possibly the United States, to extract from St Petersburg the outline of a Manchurian agreement that would be acceptable to Japan. Britain would then "tell the Japanese distinctly that they must be content with the bargain they can get as to Corea."[20] Balfour was not persuaded of the merits of mediation, and now inclined toward Chamberlain's position. Once Russia had augmented its naval forces in the Pacific, it would enjoy a numerical superiority over Japan. With its sea lines of communication threatened, it would no longer be able to pursue a land campaign in Korea. In spite of its superior strength, however, Russia could neither invade Japan nor force it to its knees by means of a naval blockade. The first entailed "an impossible military operation"; the latter was rendered impossible by Japan's self-sufficiency, and by Britain's naval presence in Far Eastern waters. A Russo-Japanese War, Balfour predicted, was likely to develop into a prolonged stalemate; and Japan should be left to "work out her own salvation in her own way."[21]

This was not an attempt to justify a policy of equivocation. Rather, it was a closely reasoned, if cynical, exposition of Balfour's principles of statecraft. He had opposed the alliance with Japan at the end of 1901, and he did not accept it now as unconditionally committing the British government to Japan. He was adamant that Britain ought not to interfere in the Russo-Japanese stand-off, unless asked to do so by Japan. He insisted that under the terms of the alliance "[w]e are only required to 'keep the ring'." For the present Britain should remain aloof.[22] This view ran counter to the Admiralty–Foreign Office axis in Whitehall. Even King Edward VII entered the fray, urging Balfour to offer Britain's good offices to prevent war.[23] The prime minister was immovable. On December 29 he brought the discussions to a conclusion, and laid down the principles of Britain's policy in the event of a war in East Asia. While admitting the formal obligations of the 1902 alliance, he stipulated that British policy be guided "solely in the light of British interests, present and future." These interests dictated that Japan was not allowed to be "crushed"; but that eventuality was not likely to occur. Balfour's analysis went to the core of Britain's "Russian problem." The Russian Empire was a factor in British strategic calculations "chiefly as (a) the ally of France; (b) the invader of India; (c) the dominating influence in Persia; and (d) the possible disturber of European peace." On all four counts, even a Russian victory over Japan would reduce the Russian threat to key British strategic interests. Balfour concluded with a flourish, reiterating his earlier observation to Selborne: Russia's "diplomacy, from the Black Sea to the Oxus [a river in Central Asia], might be weakened into distantly resembling sweet reasonableness."[24]

British non-intervention in the Far Eastern conflict also extended to the field of international finance. Balfour vetoed a Japanese request for financial assistance as this would amount to an "act of war" against Russia. Lansdowne, meanwhile, was asked to draw up the outline of a possible agreement with Russia.[25] The prime minister prevailed along the whole line; and he moved quickly to implement his ideas. A meeting of the Committee of Imperial Defence (CID) was convened to discuss British policy in the event of a Russo-Japanese conflict. The military planners concluded that the theater of operations would be extended to India if Britain entered the war.[26] Throughout January and early February, the CID and the armed services departments considered the various logistical and strategic problems that might arise if hostilities broke out in East Asia.[27] Senior British diplomats, meanwhile, regarded the mounting tensions as a "dangerous game of American poker—the stakes in this game being the peace of the Far East, and indirectly of the world." If they anticipated the poker game to end in war, Japan's lightning strike against the Russian fleet at Port Arthur on February 8 still came as a surprise to them.[28]

Once hostilities had commenced, Balfour decided that it would be best to await further developments, although foreign diplomats in London noted that senior officials at the Foreign Office "strongly sympathized with Japan."[29] Assurances by Japanese officials and financiers well connected in government circles in Tokyo that Japan did not seek "continental responsibilities," which would result from territorial annexations in Korea or Manchuria, but merely sought economic opportunities, helped to allay latent suspicions of Japanese ambitions.[30] British diplomacy now concentrated on ensuring the localization of the conflict. Lansdowne pursued this aim simultaneously in Europe and in China. Assurances were easily obtained from the French Foreign Minister Théophile Delcassé, who was as anxious as Lansdowne himself to remain aloof from the war.[31]

In fact, relations with France had improved markedly in the course of the past year. In the summer of 1903 Lansdowne and Paul Cambon, the French ambassador in London, had resumed talks about a settlement of outstanding colonial disputes. Following the outbreak of war, Lansdowne and Cambon resolved speedily to settle the few remaining points. Even so, the Foreign Secretary in particular was determined to make the arrangement stand on its own merits.[32] The result was the Anglo-French Entente of April 8, 1904, in reality a series of colonial agreements, with the Morocco–Egypt barter at their core. Ironically, an understanding with France had always been seen principally in terms of its utility as "a stepping stone with Russia," for only an Anglo-Russian understanding could produce "some reduction in our enormous military and naval expenditure."[33] Now, Russia's involvement in a war in Asia hastened the conclusion of the French Entente. Thus, the 1902 alliance with Japan, far from keeping Britain aloof from Europe, had set in motion the process of Britain's gradual involvement in continental affairs.

France was only one factor in the European equation. Fortunately for Lansdowne, the German government was also determined to avoid being dragged into the war, though no proclamation of neutrality was issued.[34] British diplomats argued that a weakened Russia would be to Germany's advantage in Europe: "the real German tradition is to wait until she sees to which side victory inclines, and then joins in falling upon the underdog."[35] This reading of German diplomacy was at least partially correct. Berlin's prognoses that the war would last some time were carefully noted. More attention, however, was paid to reports that Germany was surreptitiously allowing Russian vessels to replenish supplies at Germany's Chinese naval base at Kiaochow.[36] Such reports seemed to vindicate earlier rumors, transmitted from Vienna, that the German emperor had offered his Russian cousin support against the other powers.[37] Although this particular rumor proved ultimately to be without foundation, it demonstrated the extent to which Britain was implicated by the outbreak of war between its Asian ally and a continental European power.

At Beijing, meanwhile, the British minister, Sir Ernest Satow, was instructed to concentrate his efforts on keeping China neutral. Given the checkered history of recent Russo-Chinese negotiations this was entirely sensible. Chinese participation in the war would have torpedoed all efforts to localize the conflict. If China joined Russia against Japan, the *casus foederis* would be triggered; and if it jumped in the other direction, Russia was likely to call upon the assistance of France, in which case Britain would also be drawn into the war. At the very least, Sino-Japanese cooperation would give Russia the necessary pretext to reinforce its troops in Manchuria, possibly even to occupy Beijing and Tientsin. Chinese neutrality, therefore, was as vital to the localization of the war as were French or German non-interference. It was also essential to the safeguarding of Britain's regional interests.[38]

As regards Russia, events repeatedly brought the two countries to the edge of the abyss. The unprovoked seizure of a British steamer in the Red Sea by the Russian warship *Petersburg* led the cabinet to decide to adopt naval measures to prevent or, if they occurred, to meet any further Russian attacks on British shipping.[39] From the summer of 1904 British warships shadowed the movements of the Russian squadrons.[40] However, when on October 21, 1904 the Russian Baltic Fleet en route to the East Asian theater of war sank Hull fishing trawlers off the Dogger Bank in the North Sea, both countries seemed destined to slither over the brink of war.

Public opinion in Britain was inflamed. Lansdowne immediately demanded an official Russian apology, compensation payments for the relatives of the trawlermen, and "security against the recurrence of such intolerable acts."[41] Balfour was prepared to use the Royal Navy to intercept by force Vice-Admiral Zinovii Petrovich Rozhestvenskii's Baltic Fleet to "exact explanation and reparation."[42] In conversation with the Russian ambassador, Count Aleksandr Konstantinovich von Benckendorff, the Foreign Secretary used "language which could not be regarded as otherwise than menacing." Britain would use force, if necessary, to stop Rozhestvenskii at Vigo, where the officers responsible for the incident were to be left behind.[43] His warning that British warships were being concentrated at Gibraltar made some impression on Russian diplomacy. Nevertheless, the risks were high, as Lansdowne admitted a little later: "it looked to me as if the betting was about even as between peace and war."[44] For 48 hours war seemed imminent. It was averted only by an ignominious Russian climb-down, though it still took another three weeks to draft the final text of the agreement that brought the matter to a close.[45]

It was now that German diplomacy struck. The Wilhelmstrasse had ruthlessly exploited Russia's weakness in the summer of 1904. The friendly signals, sent in supplying the Baltic Fleet with coal, were counteracted by forcing on Russia a new, less favorable commercial treaty in July. It was a classic Bismarckian move to demonstrate to St Petersburg the benefits that would accrue from improved relations with Germany, as well as the latter's ability to cause problems for Russia if relations did not improve. At the end of October, shortly after the Dogger Bank incident, the kaiser proposed to the tsar a Russo-German defensive alliance as a first step toward a continental league with France, and with a stance against Britain and Japan. Nicholas II agreed to his imperial cousin's project.[46] The major stumbling block, however, was France. Whereas Berlin envisaged a bilateral agreement with Russia that would force France to join, the *Pevcheskii Most* (literally "Choristers' Bridge," the location of the Tsarist Foreign Ministry) would not move without prior consultation with the Quai d'Orsay, not least because of Russia's de facto dependence on French financial assistance. Lamsdorf and Delcassé were anxious, moreover, lest the kaiser's project escalated the Asian conflict into a wider war between the Great Powers. From Germany's perspective, trilateral negotiations—as opposed to a Russo-German alliance to which France acceded—ran the risk of significantly reducing Berlin's position in the new continental bloc, and, in consequence, the matter was dropped.[47]

Rumors of improved Russo-German relations also reached London, where it was widely accepted "that Germany is anxious to see us at loggerheads with Russia."[48] A further twist came in July 1905, when Wilhelm II foisted upon his hapless imperial cousin the ultimately abortive alliance—his exercise in personal diplomacy known as the Treaty of Björkö. Coming a little over a week before the opening of the peace negotiations, news of the treaty triggered speculations in London that German assurances to Russia might prolong the war after all.[49] The kaiser's Baltic surprise ensured that the focus of British diplomacy was now firmly on Germany. Lansdowne was filled with disquiet: "What may not a man in such a frame of mind do next."[50] Despite the many complications caused by the war, Britain's global strategic position improved significantly in 1904–5. This was due to shrewd diplomacy and to that rarest of political commodities, good luck.

Lansdowne's efforts to keep the war localized and the conclusion of the French Entente mended diplomatic fences with France, but also made it more difficult for Germany to play a more forceful role while the war continued. Moreover, until Tsushima there had been the risk "of important fragments of China being dominated by more warlike and aggressive powers."[51] This risk no longer existed. Japan's victories over Russia at sea and in Manchuria had profound implications for Britain and the other powers. The complete annihilation of the Russian Baltic Fleet at Tsushima on May 27–28, 1905 dealt a fatal blow not only to Russia's war efforts. Maurice Paléologue, special assistant to Delcassé at the Quai d'Orsay, drew a parallel with Philip II of Spain's Armada. Just as the defeat of the Spanish fleet had ushered in the decline of Spanish predominance in Europe, so Tsushima "*a marqué la fin de la domination russe en Asie.*"[52] In terms of Britain's global strategy, following the "catastrophe in the Korean Straits" Russia's traditional threat in Asia ceased to be a pressing concern for British policy makers. It eliminated Russia as a naval factor for the foreseeable future.[53]

While Japan's forces were advancing on the Asian mainland, the question of renewing the 1902 alliance came to occupy the governments in London and Tokyo. The latter had taken the initiative in this matter in December 1904, even though the alliance was not due to expire for another two years.[54] Without a renewal of the 1902 compact, Britain ran the risk of losing influence in East Asia to a more assertive Japan. While this was an incentive to pursue the talks with Japan, it could not remove lingering doubts about the wider strategic utility of the alliance. A mere renewal of the existing treaty had few attractions for policy planners in Whitehall. The military planners in Whitehall were agreed that Russia's double crisis—external military defeat and domestic political turmoil—had merely weakened the Russian threat to India, but had not permanently removed it. For about a decade or so, Russia would not be in a position to mount another major military campaign; Russia's current weakness, therefore, opened a strategic window of opportunity.[55] To exploit it, and in anticipation of Russia's future revival, the CID insisted that a renewed Japanese alliance should be extended in its geographical scope to include India, and that it should come into operation in the event of an attack upon one of the two parties by a third power, with Japan committing troops to the defense of India.[56]

The CID also suggested that a statement be inserted in the treaty committing both parties to maintaining the status quo in the East. This "might tend to reassure France, who is nervous as to her Indo-China frontier."[57] It was also indicative of the extent to which the Japanese alliance had come to affect Britain's relations with other powers. The geographical extension and the substantive tightening of the alliance committed Japan to the defense of the Indian frontier, and held out the prospect of an Anglo-Japanese naval bloc. Thus, both Russian forward policy in Central Asia and naval expansion in the Pacific were blocked. The Japanese accepted these terms and, in return, obtained Britain's recognition of Japan's new position in Korea. The revised and extended alliance was signed on August 12, 1905, just after the commencement of the American-sponsored Portsmouth peace talks. Lansdowne stressed the defensive nature of the new compact. By extending the scope of the alliance, Britain had merely "raise[d] the wall of [its] back garden to prevent an over-adventurous neighbor or that neighbor's unruly or overzealous agents from attempting to climb it."[58]

The system deranged: the aftermath of the war

Lansdowne's reference to Russia is indicative of the true purpose of the revised alliance. The common need to contain Russian expansion in Asia had brought London and Tokyo together in 1902; and the treaty revision of 1905 completed Russia's containment. But international politics, and alliances more especially so, are constantly evolving. In many ways, the years between 1902 and 1905 marked the highest point of Anglo-Japanese cooperation. Thereafter, the alliance began to wane. This was, perhaps, not immediately noticeable. In October 1905, following a British initiative, the two governments decided upon the reciprocal upgrading of their respective diplomatic missions in each other's capital from the rank of legations to that of embassies. It was a symbolic recognition of Japan's newly acquired status of a first-rate power, the result of Mukden and Tsushima as much as of the renewed alliance. Of similar symbolic significance was the Duke of Connaught's mission to Tokyo in February 1906 to bestow the Order of the Garter upon the Emperor of Japan.[59] Lansdowne's Liberal successor as Foreign Secretary, Sir Edward Grey, was ready to honor Britain's alliance commitment to Japan. This gave Japan increased leverage over Britain; and the Tokyo government was willing to exert pressure to ensure that Britain remained fully committed in northern China, for instance in 1906–7 over the issue of Britain's retention of its Weihaiwei naval base on the Shantung promontory. Still, although the Foreign Office in London bowed to the wishes of the Japanese ally for Britain to remain at that place, the British naval squadron in Chinese waters was gradually reduced after 1907.[60]

The outcome of the Russo-Japanese War and the conclusion of the 1905 alliance had wider ramifications for Britain's strategic foreign policy and for the constellation between the Great Powers in general. Commenting on the outcome of the war, Satow at Beijing observed:

this part of the world is going to be the scene of important events for some decades to come, and ... the centre of political interest will be removed here ... The rise of Japan has so completely upset our equilibrium as a new planet the size of Mars would derange the solar system.[61]

The scholar-diplomat's prognostication was only partially correct, for the impact of Russia's defeat went far beyond the Far Eastern subsystem of international politics. If anything, Far Eastern diplomacy now ran in quieter channels. By 1910 there was a perceptible rapprochement between Tokyo and St Petersburg. In March 1907, the Paris bourse had raised a loan of 300 million French francs for the Japanese; and the Quai d'Orsay was eager to complement financial ties with a political agreement. The resulting Franco-Japanese agreement of June 1907 gave Japanese commerce access to French Indo-China. It pledged both parties to maintain China's political and territorial integrity, though, in a secret exchange of notes, both recognized their respective spheres of influence in the Middle Kingdom. This agreement was speedily followed up by one with France's ally and Japan's recent enemy. The Russo-Japanese agreement of July 1907 provided for the reciprocal recognition of effective domination over Mongolia and Korea as well as the delimitation of spheres of influence in Manchuria.[62] The division of Manchuria into a Russian and a Japanese sphere was confirmed again in a second Russo-Japanese agreement of March 1910, which cemented closer ties between the two former belligerents. Combined, the Russo-Japanese rapprochement and Japan's outright annexation of Korea in August 1910 stabilized the Far Eastern pole of international politics. It was followed, in 1911, by an Anglo-Japanese commercial treaty and a renewed alliance. The cumulative effect of these developments was that East Asia remained relatively quiet.

In terms of Anglo-Japanese relations, the two countries continued slowly to drift apart. Already in 1911 there had been some opposition among senior British diplomats to the renewal of the alliance.[63] The strains in Anglo-Japanese relations were to become more pronounced as a result of the Chinese Revolution of 1911–12 and of Japan's expansionist ambitions during World War I. Growing suspicions of Japan and Britain's inability to reconcile the desirable object of continuing the Japanese alliance, albeit in a much diluted form, with the new post-war strategic imperative of forging closer ties with the United States of America, the other new Great Power, meant that the alliance was allowed to run out in 1921–2.[64]

In the more immediate aftermath of the Russo-Japanese War, Satow's prediction of future international tensions was correct, only these were to occur in Europe rather than in Asia. The tectonic plates of the Great Power system had shifted as a result of Russia's defeat. In the short term, in so far as the Russians were concerned, British diplomats were confident that they "w[oul]d find them easier to deal with than before", and that some form of an arrangement with Russia was once again within the realm of practical politics.[65] However, whether such hopes would be realized, and whether Russian policy would "lose its predominating character of military aggression" depended on the outcome of the protracted power struggle between competing factions at St Petersburg.[66] That an influential section at the imperial court favored realignment with Germany, and that the Wilhelmstrasse was working hard at a Russo-German rapprochement, was well understood by senior British diplomats.[67] In the summer of 1905 this was by no means an unrealistic prospect, as the Treaty of Björkö of July demonstrated. This treaty was not a mere coincidence with, but was the direct result of, the war in East Asia.

The failure of Russian arms in Asia and Russia's current domestic and financial difficulties meant that one of the two continental alliance groups was disabled. Since 1894 the relative stability of Europe had rested on the equilibrium between the Franco-Russian dual alliance and the German-led triple alliance. Russia's defeat in Asia, then, not only brought to a close the final phase of the Chinese question, which had preoccupied the chancelleries of Europe since the mid-1890s; it also destroyed the military balance of power in Europe. Until the Russo-Japanese War the Franco-Russian combination had acted as a restraint on Germany. It was a kind of military-diplomatic vice. With the diminution of Russia's military strength that vice had cracked open. As a result German diplomacy was less restricted than at any stage since the mid-1890s. Herein lay the true significance of the Russo-Japanese War for British foreign policy and for European Great Power relations in general. Without the might of Russia's arms in Germany's rear, France was now exposed to German pressure.[68]

This was a considerable reversal in Germany's international position. In the spring of 1904, news of the conclusion of the Anglo-French Entente had plunged senior diplomats in the Wilhelmstrasse into "a profound depression"; the settlement of the Egyptian question, a bone of contention between London and Paris for nearly a quarter of a century, had removed from the tool-kit of German diplomacy an important instrument for the manipulation of Anglo-French relations.[69] It was widely accepted at the German foreign ministry that "[w]e need a success in our foreign policy."[70] If, at the beginning of the Russo-Japanese War, Germany's diplomatic room of maneuver seemed restricted, Russia's eventual defeat in East Asia shifted Europe's equilibrium in Germany's favor. Already in 1905, Russian diplomacy in Europe was noticeably more cautious.[71] German pressure on France over Morocco was the direct result of this. The kaiser's Baltic surprise at Björkö was the premature, and ultimately failed, attempt to formalize this new constellation by breaking the Franco-Russian Alliance. Berlin's decision to provoke the Moroccan crisis, the CID secretary observed, "is based on the belief that [France] cannot count upon our support or that of Russia."[72] It was widely accepted within the British diplomatic service that in the new, post-war international environment "Germany is the principal danger," and this contributed to the determination of British diplomacy, now under Sir Edward Grey, to support France.[73]

In the longer term, Russia's spectacular humiliation at the hands of Japan, combined with the tightened 1905 Anglo-Japanese Alliance, halted the Russian advance in Asia, and so placed British imperial security in the region on a much firmer footing. St Petersburg's evident desire for a *recueillement*, moreover, furnished an opportunity to negotiate a settlement of Anglo-Russian differences. Common concerns about German economic penetration of Persia provided an opening. The Anglo-Russian Convention of August 1907 brought to a conclusion the efforts of successive British foreign secretaries to obtain some form of *modus vivendi* with Russia. Ranging from Persia and Afghanistan to Tibet, the convention was, on paper at any rate, "a milestone that ended nearly a century of Anglo-Russian hostility."[74] It was the culmination of repeated British efforts since the mid-1890s to arrive at an understanding with Russia. The convention settled, or at least eased, a number of points at issue between the two countries.

The partition of Persia into a British, a Russian, and a neutral sphere extended a security glacis around India's western flank. Following the partition, the strategically vital Seistan province no longer bordered on a Russian-dominated part of Persia. All of this helped to stabilize India's volatile northwestern frontier region. Russia also formally recognized Afghanistan as an exclusively British sphere of influence. Finally, with respect to Tibet, Britain obtained Russian acceptance that, while Tibet was to remain under Chinese control, Britain would enjoy special and exclusive rights and interests there.[75] Over the next few years, Anglo-Russian relations focused on the Near and Middle East, the Balkans, and Persia. In this they reflected the dual—European and imperial—nature of British power. The 1907 convention was an imperial arrangement, with the aim of safeguarding Britain's Indian and Russia's Central Asian interests. Yet, subcontinental security could not easily be divorced from European affairs, as Sir Charles Hardinge, the Permanent Under-Secretary at the Foreign Office, observed to Britain's ambassador at St Petersburg: "our whole future in Asia is bound up with the possibility of maintaining the best and most friendly relations with Russia."[76] This consideration, and the dislocation of the balance of power in Europe, meant that British diplomacy required a strong Russia. It was, as Hardinge impressed upon Lamsdorf's successor, Aleksandr Petrovich Izvolsky, in the summer of 1908, "in the interest of peace and the maintenance of the balance of power that Russia is as strong at sea water and on land."[77] Russia had to be strong enough to contain an increasingly restless Germany in Europe, yet also willing not to renew its past challenge to Britain's imperial interests.[78]

There was a profound irony about this. Russia's current weakness, above all the annihilation of the Russian fleet, had facilitated the Anglo-Russian rapprochement of 1907. Yet, Russia's continued weakness gave way to new threats to British interests. This was particularly noticeable in the naval sphere. The elimination of Russia as a naval factor and the closer ties with France rendered Britain's "two-power standard" meaningless. Germany, Britain's most likely naval adversary, did not yet pose a serious threat. However, the Russo-Japanese War coincided, but did not cause, the adoption by the British Admiralty of a new design of an all big-guns battleship. While the genesis and the underlying strategic rationale of the so-called "*Dreadnought* revolution" remain subject to some debate, its consequences are more clearly discernible.[79] Britain's strengthening diplomatic ties with France and Russia rendered obsolete the navy's previous strategic premises based on the global reach of battle cruisers to defend Britain's far-flung imperial interests against a Franco-Russian naval combination.

But with Germany now emerging as a likely enemy, the *Dreadnought* also emerged as the weapon of choice for any future confrontation in the North Sea. The unprecedented success of Japan's long-range gunnery in the Russo-Japanese War, moreover, was widely held to be one of the lessons of that conflict, and served to underline the attraction of the *Dreadnought* with its ten 12-inch guns paired in five turrets. The revolutionary design and technological superiority of this new capital ship rendered obsolete all Pre-Dreadnought battleships. This, in turn, stimulated the rush by other naval powers to build their own dreadnoughts. The unforeseen consequence of the "*Dreadnought* revolution" and the changes in the diplomatic landscape was the Anglo-German naval race between 1907 and 1912, a central factor in the rise of Anglo-German antagonism before 1914.[80]

After 1907 Russia's expansionist ambitions were diverted to northern Persia and increasingly to the Balkans. Here, these ambitions clashed with the interests of Germany and Austria-Hungary, and the Russian government could ill afford to compromise or, worse still, to be thwarted, in light of the latent domestic pan-Slav sentiments. And here the tension, inherent in Germany's restless *Weltpolitik* ambitions, between security in Europe and Germany's ill-defined desire for world power status, became insoluble. It is not without irony that Germany's refusal in March 1901 to support Britain over Manchuria for fear of incurring the wrath of Russia ultimately led to that very same constellation—only this time under much more adverse conditions, with Germany in relative isolation, the *locus* of conflict in Europe rather than in Asia, and policy makers in Britain no longer inclined to side with it.

The Russo-Japanese War had political repercussions well beyond its actual theater of war. It disturbed the European equilibrium, and so began the fragmentation of the old world order, as established at the end of the last major European war in 1815. This was not merely a question of the "objective realities" of the balance of power. It also affected the accepted norms of international behavior. In November 1904, during their abortive alliance talks, Kaiser Wilhelm II suggested to his cousin the Tsar Nicholas II "to carry revolution to India."[81] In essence, this meant accepting the annihilation of one of the Great Powers, upon whom the existing international order rested. Under the blows of Mukden and Tsushima, the accepted norms of the old world order had begun to disintegrate as well. Europe had begun its descent on the road to Sarajevo. For Britain, French and Russian weakness after 1905 meant that the affairs of Europe could not be ignored. Good relations with Russia especially were no doubt desirable in view of British interests in Central Asia. But when German diplomacy settled for the "calculated risk" of a continental war, European calculations superseded narrowly imperial considerations.[82]

Notes

1 For a survey, see Otte, 2003: 77–9.
2 Joseph, 1928: 416–17.
3 Rosebery to Kimberley, April 10, 1895, Rosebery Mss, National Library of Scotland, Mss 10070; Satow to Salisbury (private), April 6, 1898, Salisbury Mss, Hatfield House, 3M/A/126/38.
4 Neilson, 2002; for details, see Sumida, 1993: 18–20.
5 "Memorandum on Present Arrangements for War in the Mediterranean with France and Russia," March 1902, Admiralty Papers (hereafter ADM), The National Archives (formerly Public Record Office) (hereafter TNA (PRO)) ADM 121/75; memo. Altham, "Military Needs of the Empire in a War with France and Russia," August 10, 1901, War Office Papers (hereafter WO), TNA (PRO), WO 106/48/E3/2.
6 Memo. Selborne, "Balance of Power in the Far East," September 4, 1901, Cabinet Papers (hereafter CAB), TNA (PRO), CAB 37/58/81; also Steiner, 1959: 29–31.
7 Hicks Beach to Salisbury (private), September 16, 1901, Salisbury Mss, 3M/E/Hicks Beach (1899–1902); memo. Hicks Beach, "Financial Difficulties: Appeal for Economy in Estimates," October 1901, CAB 37/58/109; memo. Selborne, "The Navy Estimates and the Chancellor of the Exchequer's Memorandum on the Growth of Expenditure," November 16, 1901, CAB 37/59/118.
8 The argument developed by *inter alia* Howard, 1974: 92–3; also Goudswaard, 1952: 92–3.
9 Kerr to Selborne, April 28, 1902, Boyce, 1990: 144.
10 Satow to Lansdowne (private), August 27, 1903, Lansdowne Mss, TNA (PRO), FO 800/120.
11 Memo. Selborne, "Naval Estimates, 1903–4," October 10, 1902, CAB 37/63/142; memo. Ritchie, "Public Finances," December 23, 1902, CAB 37/63/170; see Sumida, 1993: 24–6.
12 The Russian reaction as reported by the Netherlands minister in London, Loudon to Lynden de Melvil (no. 82/19), February 26, 1902, Smit, 1957–62, (3) I: no. 545.
13 Telegrams Montebello to Delcassé (nos. 9 and 15), February 12 and 15, 1902, in Ministère des Affaires Étrangères, 1930–46, (2) II: nos. 79 and 91; telegram Alvensleben to Auswärtiges Amt (no. 43), February 19, 1902. In Lepsius *et al.*, 1922–7, XVII: no. 5049.
14 For the text, see Ministère des Affaires Étrangères, 1930–46, (2) II: no. 145.
15 Townley to Lansdowne (no. 161, very confidential), April 23, 1903, Foreign Office Papers (hereafter FO), TNA (PRO), FO 17/1598. For the text of the agreement, see MacMurray, 1921, I: 326–9.

16 Lansdowne to Edward VII, April 18, 1904, Lansdowne Mss, FO 800/134; Nish, 1985: 256.

17 Selborne to Lansdowne (private), December 21, 1903, Balfour Mss, British Library, Add. Mss 49728.

18 Balfour to Selborne (private), December 21, 1903, Selborne Mss, Bodleian Library, Ms Selborne 34.

19 Chamberlain to Balfour (private), December 21, 1903, Balfour Mss, Add. Mss 49728.

20 Lansdowne to Balfour, December 22, 1903, Balfour Mss, Add. Mss 49728.

21 Memo. Balfour, "Japan and Russia," December 22, 1903, CAB 17/54. Balfour had substantially completed the paper before receiving Lansdowne's letter of December 22; see draft memo. Balfour, December 21, 1903, Balfour Mss, Add. Mss 49728.

22 Balfour to Selborne (private), December 23, 1903, Selborne Mss, Ms Selborne 34.

23 Edward VII to Balfour (private), December 25, 1903, Balfour Mss, Add. Mss 49683; Lee, 1927, II: 282–3.

24 Memo. Balfour, "Situation in the Far East," December 29, 1903, CAB 37/67/97; Neilson, 1995: 242–3.

25 Balfour to Lansdowne (private), December 31, 1903 (two letters), Balfour Mss, Add. Mss 49728; memo. Lansdowne "Proposed Agreement with Russia," January 1, 1904, CAB 37/68/1.

26 CID, minutes of twenty-ninth meeting, January 4, 1904, CAB 2/1.

27 CID, minutes of thirtieth and thirty-first meetings, January 27 and February 8, 1904, CAB 2/1. For a detailed survey, see Neilson, 1989: 63–87.

28 Scott to Sanderson (private), January 6, 1904, Lansdowne Mss, FO 800/115; Hardinge to Bertie (private), February 8, 1904, Bertie Mss, British Library, Add. Mss 63016.

29 Gericke van Herwijnen to Lynden de Melvil (no. 74), February 9, 1904, Smit, 1957–62, (3) II: no. 144; Balfour to Lansdowne (private), February 11, 1904, Balfour Mss, Add. Mss 49728; Nish, 1985: 298–332.

30 MacDonald to Lansdowne (no. 158, confidential), May 27, 1904, FO 46/578; also Kajima, 1976–80, II: 124.

31 Monson to Lansdowne (private), February 23, 1904, Lansdowne Mss, FO 800/126; Delcassé to Cambon, January 14, 1904, Cambon, 1940–6, II: 107–9.

32 Lansdowne to Monson (private), December 28, 1902, Monson Mss, Bodleian Library, Ms. Eng. hist. c.595; Lansdowne to Bertie (private), March 30, 1904, Bertie Mss, Add. Mss 63016; Andrew, 1968: 201–16; Rolo, 1969: 228 and 243–4.

33 Cromer to Balfour (private), October 15, 1903, Cromer Mss, TNA (PRO), FO 633/6; Hardinge to Bertie (private), April 22, 1904, Bertie Mss, Add. Mss 63016; Otte, 2000: 15–16.

34 Lansdowne to Lascelles (no. 27), February 11, 1904, FO 244/636; and vice versa (no. 46), February 12, 1904, FO 64/1593; see Steinberg, 1970: 1970–1.

35 Satow to Lansdowne, February 25, 1904, Lansdowne Mss, FO 800/120; also Lascelles to Lansdowne (no. 236), November 21, 1903, FO 244/626.

36 Lascelles to Lansdowne (nos. 58 and 131), February 26 and May 18, 1904, FO 64/1593; and (no. 202), August 26, 1904, FO 64/1594.

37 Lascelles to Barrington, March 4, 1904, Lascelles Mss, FO 800/12; Neilson, 1995: 247.

38 Satow to Lansdowne (private), December 29, 1903, Lansdowne Mss, FO 800/120.

39 Balfour to Edward VII, July 21, 1904, CAB 41/; see Neilson, 1995: 251.

40 Selborne to Balfour, August 28, 1904, Balfour Mss, Add. Mss 49708.
41 Telegram Lansdowne to Hardinge (no. 174), October 24, 1904, FO 65/1729.
42 Telegram Balfour to Selborne, October 24, 1904, Selborne Mss, vol. 39.
43 Lansdowne to Hardinge (no. 377), October 26, 1904. In Gooch and Temperley, 1926–38, IV: no. 13.
44 Lansdowne to Hardinge (private), October 29, 1904, Hardinge Mss, Cambridge University Library, vol. 7.
45 Walder, 1973: 190–202.
46 Telegram Wilhelm II to Nicholas II, October 27, 1904, Bernstein, 1918, 72–3; Shebeko to Lamsdorff, November 15, 1904, Serge'ev, 1932: 56–65.
47 Paléologue diary, November 3, 4, and 9, 1904, Paléologue, 1934: 158–61 and 171; Bülow to Holstein and vice versa, both December 15, 1904, Rich and Fisher, 1956, IV: nos. 869–70; see Vogel, 1973: 201–16; Long, 1974: 220–4.
48 Mallet to Sandars, November 1, 1904, Balfour Mss, Add. 49747; also Spring-Rice to Ferguson, November 10, 1904, Gwynn, 1929, I: 432–3.
49 The text is in *Krasnyi arkhiv*, 1924: 24–6; Hardinge to Lansdowne (private), August 1, 1905, Lansdowne Mss, FO 800/141; see McLean, 2003: 119–42.
50 Lansdowne to Tower (private), August 20, 1905, Lansdowne Mss, FO 800/130.
51 Balfour to Spring-Rice (private), January 17, 1905, Balfour Mss, Add. Mss 49729.
52 Paléologue diary, May 29, 1905, Paléologue, 1934: 336.
53 Hardinge to Lansdowne, June 7, 1905, Hardinge Mss, vol. 6.
54 MacDonald to Hardinge, December 23, 1904, Hardinge Mss, vol. 7; Nish, 1985: 299–300.
55 Memo. Clarke, "The Afghanistan Problem," March 20, 1905, CAB 38/8/26; see Towle, 1980: 114–15.
56 Memo. Clarke, April 10, 1905, CAB 17/54; CID, minutes of seventieth meeting, April 12, 1905, CAB 2/1; see Gooch, 1974: 218–20; Wilson, 1993: 324–56.
57 Clarke to Balfour, June 11, 1905, Whittinghame Muniment Mss, National Archive of Scotland, GD 433/2/39; see min. Clarke, May 4, 1905, Sydenham Mss, British Library, Add. Mss 50836.
58 Lansdowne to Hardinge, September 4, 1905, Hardinge Mss, vol. 7; Esthus, 1986: 144–5; Lowe, 1969: 18–19.
59 Nish, 1976: 345–8.
60 Otte, 2005: 21–5.
61 Satow to Dickins, January 27, 1905, Satow Mss, TNA (PRO), PRO 30/33/11/6.
62 For details, see Edwards, 1954: 340–55; Hayne, 1993: 178–83; and Nish, 1985: 359–60.
63 Lowe, 1969: 38–43.
64 Goldstein, 1994: 7–12; Nish, 1967: 369–84.
65 Hardinge to Lansdowne, August 16, 1905, Hardinge Mss, vol. 6; Lansdowne to Bertie (private), January 19, 1905, Bertie Mss, Add. Mss 63017.
66 Sanderson to Hardinge, September 19, 1905, Hardinge Mss, vol. 7.
67 Hardinge to Lansdowne (private), May 25, 1904, Hardinge Mss, vol. 6; see Lieven, 1980: 34–54.
68 Mallet to Bertie, January 17, 1905, Bertie Mss, Add. Mss 63017; Williams, 1974: 105–7.
69 Spitzemberg diary, April 15, 1904, Vierhaus, 1960: 439.
70 Memo. Lichnowsky, April 23, 1904, Lepsius *et al.*, 1922–7, XX: 1, no. 6516.
71 For example, in the matter of the break-up of the Union between Sweden and Norway—a matter that had security implications for northern Europe and the Baltic region; Jungar, 1969: 107–14.

72 Clarke to Balfour, June 13, 1905, Whittinghame Muniment Mss, GD 433/2/39; Raulff, 1976: 80–94.
73 Spring-Rice to Lansdowne (private), August 6, 1905, Lansdowne Mss, FO 800/116; Otte, 2003: 83–8.
74 I am following the assessment by Steiner and Neilson, 2003: 90; also Williams, 1963: 360–73.
75 For the text, see Gooch and Temperley, 1926–38, IV: app. I; Neilson, 1995, 279–88.
76 Hardinge to Nicolson (private), March 26, 1909, Nicolson Mss, TNA (PRO), FO 800/342; also Neilson, 1995: 304–10.
77 Izvolsky to Benckendorff, June 5/18, 1908, Siebert, 1928, I: no. 3; also Grey to Spring-Rice (private), December 22, 1905, Spring-Rice Mss, FO 800/241.
78 By 1912, Anglo-Russian relations became more strained again owing to Russia's renewed advance in Persia. For a comprehensive treatment, see Neilson, 1995: 333–40; Siegel, 2002: 175–96.
79 Fairbanks, 1991: 246–72; Sumida, 1993: 50–61.
80 Kennedy, 1980: 415–31; 1989: 129–60.
81 Wilhelm II to Nicholas II, November 17, 1904, Levine, 1920: no. 39.
82 Otte, 2000: 26–8.

7 Germany, the Russo-Japanese War, and the road to the Great War

Matthew S. Seligmann[1]

For Germany's international relations the Russo-Japanese War was a significant watershed. As this chapter will argue, the outcome of this conflict
shaped German attitudes toward both Japan and Russia in the succeeding
decade. The consequences could be felt on two continents. In Asia, Germans
were fearful that the rise of this new regional power would weaken their
political position and undermine their colonial pretensions in China. They
were also anxious about the racial challenge an "Asiatic" nation posed to
their cozy assumptions of white supremacy. Nevertheless, they hoped to
exploit Japan's growing prominence to their advantage. In particular, it was
believed that Japanese expansionism could be used to put a spoke in the
burgeoning Anglo-American friendship and German diplomacy was mobilized to this end. In Europe, the result of the Russo-Japanese War was the
forging of a new set of perspectives about peace and security. In the short
term, Russia's definitive military defeat ensured that Germany would experience a new sense of certainty that its place in the Great Power system was
a secure one. However, the comforting assumptions created by the Russo-
Japanese War would ultimately prove more destabilizing. As Russia
recovered from its calamitous debacle in the Far East, the Reich would
experience a growing sense of insecurity that would act as a powerful
impetus toward World War I, a conflict in which, ironically, Germany would
find itself ranged against both Japan and Russia.

Germany, Japan, and power politics in Asia and the Pacific

Even before Japan had decisively announced its arrival as a major player
on the international stage by comprehensively defeating Russia in the war
of 1904–5, both the German government (the *Reichsleitung*) and the German
people had already formed a highly ambivalent attitude toward this new,
distant, and rising nation. The basis for their mixed feelings was the sense
that both major opportunities as well as significant dangers existed in the
emergence of this new Asian (regional) and "Asiatic" (non-white) power.
Encapsulating simultaneously both threat and opportunity, Japan was for

Germans a perplexing and worrying dichotomy. The reasons for this are clear to see.

On the positive side, as many commentators and officials were quick to recognize, the expansion of Japanese influence represented a potential boon of the greatest magnitude for German diplomacy. As a regional Asian power eager to increase its political authority in the territories that surrounded it, a vibrant and assertive Japan was bound, sooner or later, to come into conflict with other nations in the vicinity. In particular, it seemed unavoidable that the government in Tokyo would enter into competition with Russia, the other state seeking to expand its political role in the area. The development of such a rivalry was eminently to Germany's advantage. As there were distinct limits to Russian strength, the tsarist regime could only pursue its ambitions in East Asia by turning away from other potential areas of interest. Hence, the positioning of St Petersburg's gaze to the east inevitably necessitated a reduced concentration on the nations of the Balkans. Given that these southeast European territories were an area where Russian interests clashed with those of Germany's ally Austria-Hungary, the Balkans represented a dangerous fault line in Russo-German relations that had often in the past threatened to poison the diplomatic interaction between them. Consequently, the shift of Russian attention to Asia had a calming influence on Russo-German relations. Japan, being a diversion from the major source of discord between them, acted, in effect, as a balm to the European rivalry between Berlin, Vienna, and St Petersburg. Yet, it did more than just provide a welcome distraction. The greater the tension between Japan and Russia, the more the tsarist government sought the cooperation and friendship of those of its neighbors in a position to provide assistance. German support being particularly prized, the rise of Japan actually placed a premium on Berlin's amity for the policy makers in Russia. Inevitably, therefore, the rise of Japanese power left many members of the *Reichsleitung* smiling.

However, despite such substantial diplomatic gains, many Germans felt decidedly uncomfortable about the entry of an "Asiatic" power into the international arena. None was more vocal on this point than the German emperor, Kaiser Wilhelm II, who famously expressed his feelings on this matter through the medium of the visual arts. In 1895, this most unsubtle of monarchs commissioned his favorite painter, Hermann Knackfuss, to produce an iconographic work that gave full vent to all his fears and prejudices. Completed from Wilhelm's original sketch, the finished canvas depicted the nations of Europe, portrayed in allegorical form as beautiful warrior goddesses, being led by the Archangel Michael, patron saint of Germans, "against the Yellow Peril," symbolically represented by the figure of a distant Buddha hovering malignantly over a desolate scene of conflagration and carnage. To complete the image (and the metaphor), a large shining crucifix was fixed in the western heavens, casting its radiance over Europe's maiden and presumably Christian soldiers. The picture's blunt message, with its obvious overtones of both racial and religious struggle, was compounded by the equally unambiguous inscription "*Völker Europas, wahrt eure heiligsten Güter!*" (Nations of Europe protect your holiest goods!). Thus, in both word and image, Wilhelm's drawing was a clarion call for a prophesized ethnocultural and religious crusade against the orient.[2]

To ensure that the message was heard, Wilhelm had an engraving made of the drawing so that it could be reproduced in lithographic form. These prints were disseminated in large numbers, even to the extent of being incorporated in popular books, periodicals, and newspapers and being sold as postcards.[3] Wilhelm also ordered German steamship lines—including those that sailed to the east—to hang copies of the picture in their ships.[4] Additionally, at the end of September 1895, Wilhelm sent a full-size copy to Tsar Nicholas II. Lest the tsar should somehow miss the point of the picture—although it is hard to see how he could have done so!—an accompanying letter, delivered by Wilhelm's personal adjutant, spoke directly about "the danger to Europe and our Christian faith" from "the development of the Far East" and of the resultant need "to unite in resisting the inroad of Buddhism, heathenism, and barbarism for the defense of the Cross." In this way, art and diplomacy combined in Wilhelm's actions to send a powerful message of his distaste and discomfort at the rise of an "Asiatic" military power.[5] Many Germans, including most obviously the purchasers of Wilhelm's picture, shared their emperor's view.

If, as we can see, even before the advent of the Russo-Japanese War, there were evidently mixed feelings in Germany about the rise of Japan, the outbreak of the conflict and its subsequent resolution in Japan's favor did little to resolve matters. Indeed, the war and its outcome exacerbated the coterminous sense of threat and opportunity among Germans about the arrival on the international scene of Japan, an Asian and "Asiatic" nation.

In terms of the perception of a Japanese threat, the defeat of Russia, one of the great European powers, by an Asian nation, one moreover that had only opened itself up to contact with the rest of the world a mere 50 years previously, heightened this feeling considerably. As ever, Kaiser Wilhelm II was in the vanguard of expressing such views, pontificating to anyone who would listen about the threat to Christian nations and to European civilization and culture posed by the Mikado's hordes from the East. As he explained to the tsar in a typical outburst at the end of December 1907, the Japanese were "going in for the whole of Asia, carefully preparing their blows against the white race in general! Remember my picture, it's coming true!"[6] He was certainly not alone in these extreme views. Another vocal exponent of the theory that Japanese expansion was a threat to the white race and, hence, to Christian civilization was the radical colonial publicist Baron von Falkenegg. In a 52-page pamphlet, entitled *Japan, die neue Weltmacht: Politische Betrachtungen* (Japan the New World Power: Political Considerations), published in the immediate aftermath of the war, Falkenegg prophesized that Japan's rise would mean Europe's downfall.

As he explained in vaguely Mackinderesque terms, in light of their victory, the Japanese would now adopt the slogan "Asian for the Asians" and, with that phrase as their watchword, they would first attempt to kick the Europeans out of the Orient and then, having taken control of this region, attempt to use it as a springboard to dominate the world. His explanation for this theory was an unhealthy *mélange* of right-wing politics, historical misappropriation, and racism. As he put it:

> Even today there are thousands of Europeans, supposedly educated in historical matters, who are rejoicing wildly over the victory of Japan over Russia. But they are not well educated historically, and do not see that in Manchuria, not Russia, but Europe was beaten . . .
>
> The idea of world power is not confined to the Caucasian race alone; the Mongoloids can also refer in their history to the fact that they several times succeeded in shaking the Western world to its foundations, and that three times they came near to establishing a powerful world empire—under Attila, Genghis Khan and Tamerlane [Timur] . . .
>
> The Clever Japanese . . . have enough understanding of historical matters to interpret Mongoloid history, and from this understanding to draw the conclusion that as soon as the mighty will of an energetic ruler set in motion the elementary nationalist fervor of the Mongoloid people, they are irresistible.
>
> With the increasing success of the Japanese, might not the idea have taken root in the mind of Emperor Mutsuhito that he was destined by Providence to lead Japan to a high position of world power, far superior to that of the West?
>
> . . . Japanese policy, supported by the power of success, can only have one aim in sight; Asia for the Asians, or, more so, Asia for the East-Asians, at whose head stand the Japanese, who only need to re-organize vast densely-populated China, to become ruler of the world. The 55 million Japanese at the head of 400 million Chinese, whom the former will arm and fill with enthusiasm for war—now feel called to the forefront of the world powers, and to dictate the law to Asia, and perhaps Europe.[7]

This belief that a militarily strong Japan now represented a danger—to the European powers in general and the Germans in particular—manifested itself in a number of ways. Above all, there was a growing concern that Germany's position in East Asia was now under the shadow of Japanese power. Even before Japan's military victories over Russia there had been some concern in Berlin that the German colonial outposts in the region —in particular, the German concession in China, the port of Tsingtao (Kiaochow)—would be difficult to defend against a Japanese onslaught. Nevertheless, despite the doubts that existed on this score, plans had been laid to do so and Tsingtao had even been fortified. Emplacements for two 240-millimeter, four 210–millimeter, and seven 150-millimeter guns had been put in place and German warships in the region were instructed to aid in the defense.[8] Now, in the aftermath of the war, it was clear that any prospect of a prolonged resistance was near impossible. At best, local German contingents might attempt to hold out until a relief force arrived from Europe. However, given the historical precedent provided by the annihilation of the Russian Baltic Fleet in its attempt to relieve Port Arthur, this did not seem a promising prospect.

The vulnerability of German colonial possessions in Asia to Japanese attack had wider ramifications. Among those to comment upon this was Commander Philip Dumas, the British naval attaché in Berlin, who reported on May 24, 1906 that the near impossibility of defending Tsingtao made Germany very susceptible to Japanese political pressure, a fact that was clearly understood in Tokyo. According to Dumas, the Japanese saw the German concession in China as a hostage guaranteeing German good behavior. As his Japanese counterpart, Captain Yashirō Rokurō, explained to him: "Japan had considered the question of demanding that the Germans should evacuate Kiautschou [*sic*] but had decided not to do so as the presence of the Germans there would always prove a useful lever should questions arise between the two nations." The British naval attaché further recorded Yashirō as saying that, for this reason, the Japanese were determined to keep the Germans there. Thus, although it was known in Tokyo that the Chinese wanted the German occupation of the port to end, "he was sure that Japan would do her best to preserve the present state of affairs from the above-named considerations."[9] The Germans were not oblivious to the pressure that could be applied on them by the Japanese. On July 19, 1907, Dumas noted that "the German Emperor has said that he recognized that, should the Japanese say the word, they—the Germans—must clear out of Kiautschou [*sic*] forthwith."[10]

The German sense of weakness in East Asia vis-à-vis Japan led to various efforts to persuade the Japanese that Germany was still a force to be reckoned with. An example of this was the decision in 1907 to invite a Japanese squadron to participate in the *Kieler Woche* (Kiel Week)—Germany's premier annual maritime festival. The object of the exercise was to impress Japan's visiting naval officers with the spectacle of the assembled German fleet. According to the July 5 edition of the *Wilhelmshavener Tageblatt*— a minor local newspaper, but one well-informed on naval matters—this plan did not unfold as had been hoped, as it was the sight of the Japanese vessels rather than the German ones that proved the more impressive. Their correspondent noted with alarm:

> The great difference between the Japanese armored cruiser the *Tsukuba* and our own battleships is apparent even to laymen, as was shown

during the Kiel Week. The uninitiated may find our battleships very stately, but even they can see the Japanese ships are the stronger. Does it not give one a feeling of shame that Germany is not in a position to defend her colonies and that the yellow fellows can take away Kiautchau [*sic*] from us any day that they may wish to do so. The necessity for increasing our fleet was never so apparent as at Kiel.[11]

Yet, if there were Germans who took fright at the rise of Japan as an Asian great power, there were others who realized that this self-same situation opened numerous strategic possibilities for the Reich. One appealing prospect was that the enhanced international status of Japan might provide numerous diplomatic complications for Great Britain, one of Germany's principal European rivals, and that these complications might be exploitable for the benefit of Germany's geopolitical position. The logic behind this thinking related to the nature of British diplomacy. In 1902, in an effort to deal with the growing threat from Russia in the Far East, the British government had signed an alliance with Japan. In the short term, this decision proved a sound one. Yet, it was not without some cost, for, while the Anglo-Japanese Alliance gave London extra security in its dealings with Russia, it also created difficulties for Britain in its diplomatic relations with the United States. Owing to its ever greater predominance in the western hemisphere and its growing international reach, the United States was a country that Britain was eager to court. As there were few areas where the two nations' interests clashed, this was a goal that seemed readily achievable and great strides were made in the enhancement of amicable Anglo-American relations, particularly as London was willing to compromise on most issues of disagreement between them.

Consequently, settlements were reached regarding points of contention as diverse as Alaska and Venezuela. Unfortunately, there remained one point of possible contention. As a power with growing interests in the Pacific Ocean and in Asia, interests that at times clashed with those of Japan, the United States regarded the growing regional prominence of this Asian nation with some unease. The dramatic outcome of the Russo-Japanese War greatly enhanced this sentiment. So long as Japanese influence had been balanced by the counter-pressure of strong rivals, American anxiety had been muted by the knowledge that Japan's freedom of action was circumscribed by its dealings with other powers. However, the annihilation of Russian influence in the Far East had destroyed this equilibrium, leaving Japan as the only possible rival for the United States in the Pacific. Accordingly, tensions between the two nations slowly began to build and these tensions could not but help complicate matters for Japan's only ally, Great Britain. Consequently, owing to the outcome of the Russo-Japanese War, circumstances arose in which Britain's alliance with Japan threatened to tarnish its growing friendship with the United States. This was a situation that many Germans attempted to exploit to their advantage.

One group that endeavored to do so were Germany's diplomatic representatives in the United States. They went to considerable trouble to propagate the notion in their discussions with American policy makers that a collision between Japan and the United States was inevitable—something that many Americans already feared themselves—and to use this supposed "fact" to spread discord between Britain and the United States by reminding leading American statesmen of the ties that bound the United Kingdom to Japan. The purpose of linking these two ideas was, of course, to imply that Britain was an untrustworthy friend for the United States because in a crisis it would and did support Japan. Thus, for example, on September 9, 1907, Hermann Speck von Sternburg, the German ambassador in Washington, informed President Theodore Roosevelt that "Japan was doubtless aiming at control of the Pacific Ocean, extension of her territory southwards and domination in China." Having, thus, pandered to American fears of a Japanese threat, Speck then reminded Roosevelt that Kaiser Wilhelm "had for years recognized this danger which threatened the Christian nations of the world" and followed this up by criticizing any European power—implicitly, Britain—that might remain neutral in such a conflict. Such a country would, Speck emphasized to his interlocutor, "be responsible if the Christian powers were destroyed."[12]

Efforts to cultivate an undercurrent of distrust between Britain and the United States were not confined solely to diplomatic discourse in Washington. German officials in Berlin also spoke freely on the matter, repeatedly informing the American representatives in the Reich of their belief in the inevitability of an American war with Japan. So much gossip was exchanged on this point that the German capital soon became the global center for alarmist rumors about Japanese intentions in the Pacific. In this case, piquancy was added to this prediction by the discomforting news that professional military opinion in Germany regarded Japan as the likely winner.[13]

Needless to say, this discourse both about a future war between the United States and Japan and about Britain's complicity in this future catastrophe also made it into the German media. A typical example of this was a 14-page pamphlet that appeared in 1907, entitled *Der japanisch-amerikanische Krieg des Jahres 1907* (The Japanese-American War of the Year 1907). This self-serving and tendentious polemic articulated a simple thesis. Japan, it asserted, wished to fight the United States in order to conquer the Philippines and to impose upon the United States a victor's indemnity of such magnitude that would "on the one hand put an end to Japan's financial difficulties and on the other hand provide the means to make the Japanese navy the finest in the world." To this end, the Asian state was making secret preparations to ready its navy for battle and to arrange for the landing of an army corps on the long and difficult to defend American Pacific coastline. All of this, the pamphlet maliciously asserted, was made possible by the Anglo-Japanese Alliance:

> The great success of Japanese diplomacy is to be seen in the fact that
> Japan is the only power which may go to war with America unpunished.
> What England would oppose in any other power on the earth, namely
> an attack on the United States, a country bound to England by years
> of friendship and closely related to her by a common heritage, she
> cannot oppose in her ally Japan.[14]

The impact such ideas were intended to have upon American opinion is
clear: it was an argument for an end to the ever deepening Anglo-American
rapprochement. Frustratingly for many Germans, although the point was
often made, it was not one that seemed to exercise a decisive influence on
either British or American thinking. Nevertheless, it remained an axiom
of German diplomacy that this message should be ventilated with great
regularity.

The war, Germany, and the balance of power in Europe

It is evident from the above that friction in the post-war relations between
the United States and Japan was welcome in Berlin both as a potential
embarrassment for British diplomacy and as a specific means of undermining the efforts of London to get closer to Washington. However, valuable
though such opportunities for disrupting Britain's foreign policy were, this
useful by-product of the Russo-Japanese War was not the major strategic
benefit that the fighting conferred. In reality, the greatest advantage bestowed
upon Germany by this conflict lay in the impact it had on the European
balance of power.

Throughout the nineteenth and early twentieth centuries, at the heart of
all German security considerations was the geo-strategic imperative created
by the Reich's position as a country in the center of Europe. Located directly
between two major powers—France and Russia—both of which maintained
substantial armies, the German Empire's military posture was determined
by the necessity of being able to fight a war on two fronts against dangerous,
capable, and well-equipped opponents. As a result, the nightmare scenario
for Germans of all descriptions was that their nation, though strong, might
nevertheless be crushed by a simultaneous and irresistible onslaught from
both east and west. However, for this fear to have either potency or
immediacy, it was necessary for Germans to hold a real belief in the military capabilities of France and Russia to undertake such an operation. Prior
to the Russo-Japanese War, doubts on this score had existed, but had been
muted. However, the onset and outcome of the war destroyed the belief in
such an eventuality, at least as far as Russia was concerned.

While the Russo-Japanese War had numerous and significant consequences for the development of strategic thinking and operational doctrine
around the globe, above all else, it had a dramatic effect upon the international reputation of the Russian armed forces and upon assessments of

the military potential of the Romanov state. In the view of most Germans, the calamitous series of debacles suffered by Russia—namely, the elimination of the Russian Pacific and Baltic Fleets and the constant retreat of the Russian armies in Asia—proved beyond doubt that neither the Russian army nor navy were competent practitioners of the arts of modern warfare. In the realms of strategy and tactics as well as in the areas of morale, equipment, leadership, and stamina, the tsar's armed forces proved not only to be less capable than their Japanese opponents, but also to have fallen below the standard expected of a modern military power of the first rank. This poor performance on the battlefields of Korea and Manchuria naturally lessened German fears of the dangers of a Russian attack in Europe. If the tsar's armies could be defeated by Japan, sending the country into revolution and turmoil in the process, it seemed doubtful that the Russian government would risk fighting Germany, the premier military power in the world. However, should the regime prove so foolish as to attempt such a thing, there seemed no prospect but that it would suffer another defeat, one probably even more crushing than that suffered at the hands of the Japanese.

Russia's newly proved military incompetence was not the only reason for Germans to be less fearful of a Russian attack. It was also the case that the battering it had received appeared to have rendered the tsarist military machine *hors de combat*. In fighting Japan, the Russian armies had expended a great deal of ammunition, had seen a lot of equipment lost or captured, and had suffered high casualties, including close to 100,000 men at the battle of Mukden alone.[15] Furthermore, those units that were defeated in the field and were forced as a result into constant retreat saw their effectiveness degraded in other ways, including a growing loss of confidence in their commanders (and, ultimately, also in the tsarist regime itself) as well as an increasing unwillingness to stand and fight. Worse was to befall the Russian navy, which witnessed nearly all its finest ships sunk, crippled, or captured, while the remainder were bottled up ineffectually in port, with devastating effects on the *esprit de corps* of the sailors. Thus, in terms of all the major indices of military potential—manpower, *matériel*, leadership, and morale—the tsarist armed forces emerged from the war a seemingly broken tool. Consequently, it was obvious to most observers that, until their reserves had been restocked and their formations had been re-equipped, retrained and restored in their discipline and fighting spirit—a work of many years—there appeared to be no possibility of their embarking upon another major campaign. An offensive against Germany, the most difficult of all the tsar's possible opponents, was, therefore, totally out of the question.

Inevitably, the knowledge that Russia's capacity to embark upon a new armed conflict had been rendered negligible by the consequences of their defeat at the hands of the Japanese revolutionized Germany's geo-strategic position. Freed from the fear of an imminent two-front war, Germany's politicians, soldiers, and diplomats were at liberty to reshape German foreign and security policy. Naturally, they seized this opportunity. As a first step, they attempted to alter the European alliance system to their benefit. Recognizing that Russia's weakness would make the regime in St Petersburg feel vulnerable, the Germans took this opportunity to offer the tsar the possible security of a defensive pact with Germany. On July 24, 1905, at Björkö, off the southern coast of Finland, the kaiser attempted to lure Nicholas II into entering into an alliance. On the face of it, he succeeded. Under considerable pressure from Wilhelm and at a moment of near psychological collapse, Nicholas did indeed put his signature to the document that Wilhelm placed before him. However, the German triumph was short lived. When the Russian Foreign Ministry learnt of the tsar's actions they raised strong objections and the treaty never came into effect. Germany's postwar *Rußlandpolitik* was, thus, a failure. The consequences of this would be evident a decade later.[16]

Much more significant than the ultimately unsuccessful efforts to woo Russian friendship were the moves made to recast the Reich's military position. The Russo-Japanese War had a major impact on the thinking of Germany's military leadership. First of all, it reaffirmed their long-held neo-Clausewitzian belief in the value of war as an instrument of policy. As Karl von Einem, the Prussian Minister of War, succinctly put it, the conflict in Asia made it clear that "only weapons can arbitrate serious disputes between nations." His colleague, the world-renowned military author General Colmar von der Goltz, expressed a comparable view, adding that the Russo-Japanese War had the additional advantage that it would end the "constant bawling about peace."[17] Second, the conflict reinforced their existing presumptions about the best means of undertaking military operations, namely going on the offensive. As is abundantly clear from the German general staff's own "Official History" of the Russo-Japanese War, in the opinion of the chief planners of the German army, Russia's defeat could be ascribed to the passivity and irresolution of its commanders, who sat "paralyzed" on the defensive and who "had not the strength of mind to fight the battle to the bitter end." By contrast, the Japanese victory could be put down to their much greater energy, superior initiative, and bolder, more offensive spirit. As the text pithily judged matters, in the Japanese case, "the will to conquer, conquered."[18] In short, the war seemed to validate the social Darwinist view that dash and targeted aggression would always persevere in modern conflict.[19]

Significantly, if the Russo-Japanese War acted as a fillip to the army's belief in the utility of war as an instrument of policy and provided further grounds for a belief in the power of the offensive, it also engendered circumstances in which the Reich's military planners could integrate the above two presumptions into their work. The reason for this was that the fiasco suffered by the Russian army gave the *Reichsleitung* the opportunity to break away from their traditional concern of preparing for the rigors of a war on two fronts. As Friedrich von Holstein, the head of the Political Department of the German Foreign Office, put it: "Our situation has eased

... the danger of France and Russia together falling upon Germany can be set aside for the foreseeable future."[20] Alfred von Schlieffen, the Chief of the Great General Staff, thought likewise. On June 10, 1905 he informed the Chancellor, Bernhard von Bülow, that there was not the slightest prospect of Russia posing a military challenge to Germany for many years to come. Indeed, he went much further. His analysis of Russian martial capabilities in the light of their recent performance denigrated almost every facet of the Russian military apparatus, including the likelihood that Russian commanders could oversee a program of improvements. He stated emphatically:

> For a long time, it was known that the Russian army possessed no significant leaders, that the majority of its officers were of limited value, and that the training of the troops could only be seen as insufficient. On the other hand, the individual Russian soldier was seen as one of the best in the world. His unquestioning obedience, his infinite patience, his quiet contempt for death were all recognized as inestimable characteristics.
>
> Now however, the experience of the war in the Far East has shaken greatly our belief in these characteristics. The Russian soldier's obedience proved not to be so blind. Many cases have come to light in which the officers did not command their troops, but rather begged, debated and entreated with them. In other cases, the troops resisted and turned against their superiors in the most insolent way. The authority of the Russian officers and the obedience of their troops are very questionable. Moreover, the Russian troops did not display their famous stoicism. In the Manchurian campaign, panic often broke out. The troops did not hold out until the very end. The war has shown that the famous Russian obedience was based less on attention to duty and a feeling of honor than on dullness and a fatalistic resignation. Further, it has shown also that the inherited characteristics of the Slavic race last only so long, but then they degenerate into brutality.
>
> Above all, the Russian soldier is not properly trained. He does not understand how to fire and maneuver in battle. In earlier times, one could still do something with brave but poorly schooled troops. Today, however, improvements in weapons require a soldier to possess careful and thorough training. Since the Russian soldiers did not receive this, they are not up to the standards of other armies and are altogether unfit for the offensive.
>
> In short, the East Asian war has shown that the Russian army is less competent than had been assumed previously by informed opinion and that the war has worsened the Russian army rather than made it more efficient. ...
>
> It is very questionable whether or not an improvement will take place. The Russians lack enough self-awareness to carry this out. They see

the origins of their defeat not in their own imperfections, but rather in the enemy's superiority in numbers and in the ineffectiveness of particular commanders. The Russian army lacks the men capable of carrying out the required reforms and who possess the necessary moral fortitude.

Therefore, recent history would suggest that the Russian army will not improve, but instead will grow more ineffective.[21]

Schlieffen's contempt for the Russian army could not have been clearer. Thus, despite the widely aired views of Terrence Zuber, who recently claimed that German military intelligence analyses for 1905–6 provide no indication that the Germans believed that Russian martial capabilities had been degraded by the conflict in the Far East,[22] it is clear that, in the wake of the Russo-Japanese War, the most senior planner in the German army felt able to downplay the military significance of Russia for years to come. This was a new development in the geo-strategic environment that opened up enormous possibilities. For, if a Russian offensive on Germany's eastern border was no longer to be expected, then there would no longer be any necessity to deploy large military assets in the east to defend against this eventuality. The vast majority of Germany's military manpower and resources could instead be redirected to the west. As a result of this, in December 1905, Schlieffen advocated a new war strategy in which Germany would focus all its initial energies on a rapid offensive campaign against the French. Outlined in a memorandum entitled simply "War against France," this document would later become infamous as the Schlieffen Plan. Most historians agree that, despite a few minor alterations, the concept advanced in this *Denkschrift* served as the basis for German war planning from 1906 to 1914.[23]

It seems clear, then, that one significant consequence of the Russo-Japanese War was a major reorientation of Germany's military posture. While the Great General Staff continued out of habit to consider the possibility of an *Ostaufmarsch* (eastern deployment)—finally abandoning this only in April 1913—from 1906 onwards an attack on France through the flat and less heavily fortified terrain of Belgium became the primary German war plan. As we have seen, this strategic transformation was one born out of confidence. After observing the lamentable performance of the tsar's forces in the Russo-Japanese War, the Germans, who were already full of self-belief in their own military capabilities, became highly dismissive of those of their eastern neighbor. This sense of superiority inspired them to be bold and to adopt, without any major concerns or reservations, a plan that involved leaving the Reich's eastern border largely undefended for the first two months of a future European war. So confident were German planners that Russia was militarily abject that no thought was given to what would happen if circumstances changed. Yet, change they did. Within the space of only a few years, Germans would find themselves assailed by a new feeling of self-doubt, a sentiment that, no less than the confidence described above, was also a consequence of the Russo-Japanese War. The source of this sense of national anxiety—which would have significant and unfortunate consequences—was the Russian response to their 1905 defeat and the German assessment that, contrary to expectations, these Russian reactions had major implications for their own diplomatic and security position.

In regard to matters of foreign policy, it was largely inevitable that, following the humiliation of their attempt at dominance in the Far East, the tsarist government should lose its enthusiasm for Asian expansion and, instead, seek to refocus its attention back upon the other geographical region of greatest concern to it, namely Europe. Thus, after 1905, Russian interest in the Balkans began to increase. This was extremely unwelcome in Berlin, as the natural consequence of any renewed Russian activity in southeastern Europe was to place Russia on a collision course with Germany's ally, Austria-Hungary. This was inevitably destabilizing for the region and corrosive for Russo-German relations. As crisis followed crisis in the Balkans, the deterioration in Austro-Russian relations that ensued not only undermined the possibility of Russo-German friendship, but actually engendered frictions between Berlin and St Petersburg that made a wider conflict involving Germany and Russia seem increasingly likely.

Had Russia remained militarily supine, then this growing friction in diplomatic relations would have caused only limited anxiety in Berlin. Unfortunately, despite Schlieffen's optimistic predictions of 1905, Russian weakness in the wake of the Russo-Japanese War showed every appearance of being a temporary phenomenon. Much to the surprise of most informed observers, the tsarist state responded to its defeat in the Far East with uncharacteristic vigor. In particular, major efforts were made to remedy those deficiencies in the army that had been so vividly demonstrated by the Japanese and to learn the lessons of modern warfare. To this end, the Russian military authorities embarked upon a thorough program of reform. They pensioned off incompetent and underperforming officers, promoting in their place younger and supposedly more capable leaders. They rewrote the procedures for military training, re-equipped the army with more modern and efficient artillery, increased the number of specialist units, and experimented with new technology, such as aircraft and airships. In addition, a comprehensive reorganization was undertaken of the Russian order of battle that led to new units being created, many of which were based in the interior of Russia. The rationale was to create formations that could be deployed as needed to any of Russia's borders and that were, also, invulnerable to a pre-emptive strike by any of Russia's neighbors (i.e. Germany). Finally, measures were taken to speed up Russian mobilization by a systematic remodeling and simplification of the call-up procedures and to accelerate deployment times by the building of new railroads designed to make it possible for newly mobilized units to be fed more rapidly to the front.[24] The impact of all these reforms was dramatic. The Russian army, which had so thoroughly disgraced itself in combat with the Japanese, appeared to most observers—including those in Berlin—to be rapidly honing itself into a most formidable military machine.

Thus, as we can see, the reorientation of tsarist foreign policy toward the Balkans took place at the same time as a major reform of the Russian army and, as a result, the increasing Russo-German diplomatic friction of this period occurred against a backdrop of the resurgence of Russian military power. Because of this, the tsarist regime, which in the past had had little option but to back down to German demands—as, for example, over Bosnia in 1908—was becoming ever more willing to contemplate taking matters with Germany to a head. In January 1914, for instance, Nicholas II outlined his perspective on Russo-German relations to the senior French statesman Théophile Delcassé. Speaking of "the perhaps inevitable and imminent collision between German ambitions and Russian interests," he noted with remarkable and misplaced nonchalance: "We will not let them tread on our toes and, this time, it will not be like the war in the Far East: the national mood will support us."[25]

In contrast to this increasing Russian confidence, the assurance of German leaders was ebbing. German military planners, in particular, were conscious that Russian military reforms were progressively undermining all the strategic assumptions upon which Germany's post-1905 plans were based. Russian weakness, which was the condition that had permitted the concentration of most military assets in the West, was no longer a given and, consequently, it was by no means clear that the Schlieffen Plan would continue to be viable in the face of the Russian "steamroller." Particular anxiety was caused by the ongoing enhancement of Russia's strategic railroad network, which threatened upon completion to place an enormous army on the Russo-German border within record time. As Schlieffen's successor, Helmuth von Moltke the younger, explained to Chancellor Theobald von Bethmann Hollweg in July 1914, the Russians would soon be able to deploy two-thirds of its substantial military manpower against Germany in 13 days.[26] In the face of this "Slavic horde," the small East Prussian defense forces risked being swamped and, with them thrust aside, Germany itself risked being overrun. How should German military leaders respond to this predicament? One option, never seemingly considered, would have been to abandon Schlieffen's offensive concept and change the war plan to meet the new conditions. Another possibility was to call for "preventive war." It would be preferable, Moltke noted on several occasions, to resort to arms and deal with Russia before the situation became unmanageable. In the summer of 1914, another crisis in the Balkans—the assassination of Franz Ferdinand at Sarajevo—would allow Moltke to push this argument to a successful conclusion. Thus, in August 1914, the plan devised by Schlieffen, in a moment of confidence inspired by Russian weakness, was implemented by Schlieffen's successor in response to his fears of Russian strength. The irony of this is self-evident.

Epilogue

World War I, which broke out less than a decade after the conclusion of the Russo-Japanese War, was not the inevitable consequence of this earlier conflict, but it was partly inspired by it. Germans responded to the events in the Far East by reassessing their strategic outlook. This led to a recognition that Germany's military position in Asia was probably untenable, but also a comforting belief that the Reich's security in Europe had been enhanced. This latter phenomenon, however, proved all too temporary. As the Russians recovered their military strength, new anxieties emerged that made war seem desirable. The reality would, of course, prove rather different, but, by the time this was known for sure, it was already too late.

Notes

1 The author thanks Dr Jim Beach for his careful editing suggestions.
2 Röhl, 2004: 754–6, 909–10.
3 Lehmann, 1978: 149–50.
4 Cecil, 1996: 38.
5 Rich, 1965, II: 445.
6 Röhl, 1994: 204.
7 Lehmann, 1978: 173–6.
8 Lambi, 1984: 234–5.
9 The National Archives (formerly Public Record Office) (hereafter TNA): FO 244/665.
10 TNA: FO 371/261, f. 418.
11 TNA: FO 371/261, f. 418.
12 Dugdale, 1930: 262–3.
13 Braisted, 1958: 198, 209.
14 TNA: FO 371/270, ff. 323–9.
15 Various estimates suggest that the Russian forces in Mukden had over 20,000 dead or missing in action, about 50,000 wounded, and more than 20,000 prisoners of war.
16 McLean, 2003: 119–42.
17 Brose, 2001: 127.
18 Cox, 1992: 397.
19 Mackenzie, 1999: 33.
20 McLean, 2003: 121.
21 Foley, 2003: 159–61.
22 Zuber, 1999: 296.
23 Mombauer, 2001: 72–105.
24 Stevenson, 1996: 150ff.
25 McLean 2004: 67–8.
26 Foley, 2005: 76.

8   The impact of the war on the French political scene

Patrick Beillevaire

Of all the Western powers, France, its political leaders and its ordinary citizens alike, appears to have been the most intimately affected by the outbreak of the Russo-Japanese War. Not that the French harbored an exaggerated fear of the "Yellow Peril," or that their colonial interests in Asia were more directly threatened by Japan's continental expansion, although this latter point cannot be altogether dismissed. In fact, France was then bound to Russia by a treaty of alliance regarded as the cornerstone of its foreign policy. Concluded in 1891 on France's own initiative and insistence, the treaty had been completed the following year by a military agreement, or "defense pact," requiring from both countries "an immediate and simultaneous mobilization" in case either one would be attacked. Since the humiliating defeat of 1870, French foreign policy was aimed at containing Germany with the underlying hope of eventually recovering the lost provinces of Alsace and Lorraine, and the alliance with Russia was naturally meant to match the Triple Alliance between Germany, Austria, and Italy.

France, the ally of Russia

Though somewhat against nature, the rapprochement between the secular French Republic and tsarist Russia, often referred to as the "sister nations" for the purpose, had been steadily celebrated for more than a decade by a succession of much publicized official visits accompanied, at least on the French side, by important popular festivities. With the backing of French politicians and of a bribed press, Russia had taken advantage of that friendly climate to float a series of loans on the French market, a large share of which had been subscribed by small investors. By 1904 France had thus become Russia's main creditor, the total of loans and direct investments benefiting the latter being estimated at one-quarter of all the French foreign assets.[1] As reflected in the popular press, that situation explains why a majority of the French, indifferent to the already receding *japoniste* vogue, were definitely Russophile when the protracted negotiations between the two parties finally resulted in open hostilities.[2]

The outbreak of war first sparked a wave of panic among French financiers. More seriously, it soon raised the question of whether the alliance with Russia required that France should commit its military forces in East Asia. On March 16, 1902, in response to the Anglo-Japanese Alliance, France and Russia had signed an additional agreement to their own treaty of alliance stating the necessity to maintain "the status quo and overall peace in the Far East," while reserving the right to take action in order to protect their interests in that region. With the opening of hostilities, rumor had it that the agreement contained a secret clause binding France to bring armed support to Russia wherever a conflict should take place. Under strong pressure from the deputies, Prime Minister Emile Combes and Foreign Minister Théophile Delcassé immediately devoted themselves to calming things down by assuring that no such clause existed. While a large majority of deputies and senators reiterated their support to the Franco-Russian Alliance, the government announced that France would maintain strict neutrality under all circumstances. It made it clear that the alliance, although it remained the immutable basis of French foreign policy, did not apply to East Asia as long as a third country did not get involved in the conflict. Moreover, Russia could not be given military assistance that it was not asking for, and France, in any case, would not embark on a war without the assent of the parliament. Were it only for the reason that Britain's neutrality in the conflict was implicitly conditional upon the non-intervention of France, no French politician, indeed, ever seriously considered sending troops to East Asia and risking British retaliations on French harbors or ships.

As a matter of fact, the constraints weighing on France's foreign policy did not leave its government much room for maneuver. On the one hand, the alliance with Russia had to be preserved at any cost. On the other, any incident that could harm the reconciliation with Britain had to be carefully avoided. The relations between Britain and France, often at odds on colonial issues, had been gradually warming up since the turn of the century, and the French government was now looking forward to reaching a conclusive settlement of all the contentious questions. Despite the war opposing their respective allies, the signing of the expected agreement, the Entente Cordiale, of no less importance for France than its alliance with Russia in the face of Germany's growing power, was actually to take place in Paris in April 1904.

A sentence from the daily *Le Temps* of February 12 may sum up the official position of France on the Russo-Japanese conflict: "The French nation unanimously wishes to loyally fulfill its obligations toward Russia without departing from an absolute neutrality." The financial and humanitarian aid that numerous French associations, trade-unions, or political groups from all over the country sent to the Russian wounded as early as March 1904 was not likely to test the inconsistency of such a position. But it was not to be the same for the request that St Petersburg addressed to Paris in September to assist the Russian Admiralty with the preparation of the route for the Baltic Fleet and to allow it to call at French overseas ports. Embarrassing though the request happened to be, too high were the stakes of the alliance with Russia to risk jeopardizing it by a flat refusal.

Preparations in Paris were carried out in relative secrecy, and it was intended that the assistance with the supply operations, merely a matter of "hospitality" diplomatically speaking, would be kept to a minimum; but of course the very presence of the Russian fleet in French ports could hardly pass unnoticed. Anyway, it did not take long before the Japanese government reacted. In early November its ambassador in Paris, Motono Ichirō, complained strongly about the assistance given to the Russian fleet in French waters—what his government considered a blatant breach of neutrality concerning "a vital question."[3] Meanwhile, Japanese newspapers such as *Mainichi* or *Nippon* published articles regretting France's alliance with Russia and contrasting the uncertain neutrality of its government with the expressions of sympathy addressed to Japan from Britain and the United States. The following year, when the Russian fleet put in successively at Madagascar and at Cam Ranh, in Vietnam, the Japanese government renewed its protestations. They were then accompanied by harsh anti-French attacks from the press and by popular demonstrations in front of the French embassy in Tokyo as well as in the streets of other cities.[4] With obvious embarrassment, the French government objected that helping to supply the Russian fleet with coal, water, and food was nothing else but ordinary humanitarian assistance.[5] On several occasions the relations between the two governments became so tense that the anxious Foreign Minister Théophile Delcassé was expecting an ultimatum from Tokyo at any moment.[6] Apart from those diplomatic incidents, the alliance of France with Russia also had the significant effect of depriving its industry of any Japanese order for the whole duration of the war.

Like the press of other Western countries, the French press gave a daily and extensive coverage of the Russo-Japanese War with special correspondents dispatched on the front. Widely read dailies such as *Le Petit Parisien*, *Le Petit Journal*, *Le Matin*, or *Le Siècle* sided straightaway with the Russian allies, often called "our friends," and showed little doubt about their final victory over a presumptuous Japan, guilty of having betrayed their sincere efforts to prevent the bloodshed. Every week or so the illustrated supplements of the most popular *Le Petit Parisien* and *Le Petit Journal* devoted at least one of their two full-page color pictures to the conflict. Those pictures usually showed dramatic episodes of the war underlining the fierce determination of the Japanese and the cunning means they could resort to. It would take months and an accumulation of Russian defeats before the Japanese soldiers were given due consideration for their courage and for their human attitude toward wounded enemies.

A commonly held opinion in the Russophile press was that the real blame for the war had to be laid on the American and British "imperialists" and "speculators." On the latter, especially, because the alliance that Britain had formed with Japan was regarded as having given Japan's expansionist drive a free rein, thus making impossible any peaceful settlement of its dispute with Russia.[7] To a public opinion easily moved to anti-British feelings, it seemed also that Japan had but followed Britain's example in making a surprise attack on Russian ships in Port Arthur and in Chemulpo on February 8 and 9 before any formal declaration of war.

Japan itself was accused of duplicity and dishonesty, of being a vain-glorious, bellicose, and brutally aggressive country, whose greed for conquests was threatening peace and the world order:

> Japan is a child people. Now that it has huge toys like battleships, it is not reasonable enough, not old enough not to try them. It wants to see how that works, like a "kid" who has been given a model railway.[8]

> Despite their borrowings from Western civilization, the Japanese remain barbarians.[9]

A most feared eventuality was that the victory of the "Mikado's soldiers" could lead to the "Japanization of China" and trigger off the "Yellow Peril," a notion combining ethnic or racial prejudice and economic protectionism. "For us," as one journalist puts it, "Russia is not only representing the white race contending with the Yellow race, it is the very soul of civilization fighting against the spirit of barbarism."[10] Another columnist writes: "We should be eager to see the victory of our ally for the two reasons that we are a European and a colonial nation."[11] By that time already, some even predicted that the Japanese expansion in neighboring countries would inevitably result in a conflict between Japan and the United States over the control of the Pacific.

However dominant pro-Russian feelings were, from the outset of the conflict the cause of Japan met also with some understanding, to a large extent inseparable from distrust if not abhorrence of its adversary. If one excepts a few liberals, such as the staunch advocates of free trade Yves Guyot and Anatole Leroy-Beaulieu, or a small elite of Japan experts, many of them gathering in the Société franco-japonaise de Paris founded in 1900, most supporters of Japan belonged to what may be called the republican and anti-Church (*laïque*) left and to the socialist movement, then divided into numerous groups professing a more or less radical rejection of parliamentary politics. They expressed their opinions in publications such as the socialist daily *L'Humanité*, launched in April 1904; the internationalist weekly *L'Européen*, where one can find articles of Russian opponents and of pro-governmental Japanese, among them the productive representative of Japan in Britain Suematsu Kenchō; the monthly *Annales de la jeunesse laïque* (Review of the Secular Youth), or the quite militant *Revue de l'enseignement primaire* (Review of Primary Education). Although seeming narrowly focused, the latter journals dealt with general politics and had a large readership, comprising in particular the teachers of *écoles laïques* or public schools—that is, state-run republican and non-denominational schools, as opposed to private and most often Catholic schools—who stood on the front line in the fight for *laïcité* and social progress.[12]

In an address given on February 13, Jean Jaurès, a member of the Chamber of Deputies and the leader of one of the two foremost socialist parties, the French Socialist Party, which was backing up the so-called "Bloc des gauches" (Union of the left-wing parties) government without taking part in it, demanded that "the alliance with Russia be loosened (*détendue*)." "Germany having no hostile intention toward France," he explained, the alliance had become an "unwise" provocation and an unnecessarily "exclusive" bond. It represented no longer a "safeguard" but a "danger." Accordingly, there was no justification for an intervention in East Asia, and any secret clause in the Franco-Russian agreement of 1902 had to be considered as "null and void."[13]

Jaurès' distrust of the alliance with Russia earned him severe criticism from right-wing politicians. Conversely, to revolutionary and antimilitarist hardliners, his statement was not strong enough. For instance, to Gustave Hervé, a very vocal pacifist and an uncompromising critic of parliamentary institutions, "loosening the alliance [was] insufficient," it should have been "broken off, and at once."[14] To Alfred Naquet, a well-known figure of the republican left-wing, then retired from active political life, and whose name remains attached to the introduction of the income tax and to the law on divorce, the alliance had to be "thoroughly denounced."[15]

Jules Guesde, the other leading figure of the socialist movement, strictly attached to the Marxist revolutionary line of action, and therefore an opponent of participation in the "bourgeois" system of representation, expressed a more downright commitment to the victory of Japan. It is with an unambiguous "*Vive le Japon!*" that he concluded his statement in *Le Mouvement socialiste* of March 15, 1904, an issue gathering the opinions on the war of European revolutionary leaders, who, for the most part, showed more concern about Japan's hegemonic aims.[16] For left-wing activists, it was neither from the Russian alliance, nor from war that redress for "the crime perpetrated against Alsace and Lorraine" should have been expected, but from the progress of pacifist, democratic, and socialist ideas in Germany and in other European countries.

Japan, a champion of progress and a liberator of the Russian people

Sympathy for Japan was feeding primarily on the hostility to the Russian autocracy that Naquet stigmatized as "the pivot of reaction in the world."[17] The war going on in East Asia, in its very brutality, appeared as the epitome of the class struggle that was taking place in France between the supporters of the secular republic and the conservative and nationalist camp linked to the Church and to the army. In contrast with the prevailing opinion, supporters of Japan saw the Russians as bearing full responsibility for the war as they refused, in the first place, to recognize Japan's interest in Korea. Never did they consider seriously backing down on any of their claims, it was said, and their diplomatic procrastination had no other aim than to allow the reinforcement of their defenses in East Asia. As to the surprise attack on their ships by the Japanese navy before the declaration of war, striking the first blow quicker was simply considered a matter of tactical smartness, especially with Russians who could easily be reminded of their treacherous destruction of the Ottoman fleet sheltered in Sinop, on the Black Sea, in 1853.[18]

For those actively committed to spreading democracy in the world, the prospect of a political and social change occurring in Russia was good enough reason to support Japan. Whatever the human cost, progress for Russia, as it appeared, had to go through Japan's victory, which could not but entail the rejection of the autocratic regime and the liberation of the Russian people. As the Russian opponent Nesvoy put it, "The campaign of Japan against Russia is one of civilization against barbarism, of the principle of representation against the principle of despotism. So organized a people as the Japanese is no danger for civilization."[19]

On the same grounds, the offer of mediation, which emerged in the fall of 1904, met with vigorous opposition from left-wing activists. On the one hand, stopping the war before its military conclusion would have deprived Japan of the benefits of its expected victory. It would have been like repeating the injustice of the Three-power Intervention after Japan's victory over China in 1895, and it was also to be feared that another conflict would occur again in the short term. On the other hand, a successful peace mediation would have predictably reinforced the tsarist regime, stigmatized as "the rule of the knout," and hindered any significant social reform in Russia for quite some time. It seemed obvious that the only reason why the Russian rulers were now looking for peace was that they realized that further military disasters would cause their authority to collapse. For Charles Paix-Séailles, a friend of Jaurès, the idea of mediation had to be rejected, for Japan's victory would be "the chastisement of a tyrannical rule" and would prevent "the consolidation of a heinous regime, the recurrence of massacres, the oppression of nationalities and of races." "The atrocities and the dead" of the Manchurian battlefields "were not to be made useless," and "[t]he liberation of Russia ought to compensate for them."[20] For Théodore Barth, "hopes of peace were premature," and Japan, as "an always improving representative of modern civilization, would fulfill a first-rate civilizing mission" if it could win over a "despotically ruled Russia" that has always been the "fulcrum of reaction."[21] In short, stopping the war now would spell "disaster for the Russian people." [22]

Anyway, the time for a peaceful solution was obviously long past, and the successive retreats and defeats inflicted on the Russians by the Japanese, with their share of sufferings for both armies, appeared as the high price to pay in order to move forward on the path of progress. Here is, for instance, how Gustave Hervé greets the fall of Mukden on March 10, 1905:

> Happy Russians! 150,000 soldiers lost in Manchuria, those are 150,000 guard dogs missing who can no longer bite them. The Japanese have been a great help to them by getting rid of those brutes who are responsible for shooting them down whenever they ask for some social security and some liberty![23]

The support lent to Japan in its war against Russia was not only motivated by considerations on the latter's political and social backwardness. It was also based on cultural, economic, and ethical arguments tending to assimilate Japan to Western nations, if not to make it a model for those nations. As regards culture in general, it is put forward that, unlike the Chinese, the Japanese are attracted to novelties. They evince that sense of curiosity that is deemed characteristic of modernity. There is no "mental slavery" among them, it is said: "they are free from the fetters of tradition."[24] The Japanese are not satisfied with being those skilful artists so widely praised in the West; they do value all the sciences. They have already translated and assimilated all the great Western thinkers to such an extent that "From the intellectual viewpoint, Japan is a country of Western civilization," with which "it is possible to establish an intellectual community."[25] As Duret, a former Communard, explains: "The Japanese were first forced to devote their energies to build a strong army, but behind the soldiers, educated men in every branch of scholarship are coming and will keep coming."[26]

"With their railways, telegraph and telephone lines, huge factories, banks, and strong army" the Japanese are perceived as being economically on a par with the West. "The evolution that the Slaves of Russia have laboriously accomplished in two centuries, since Peter-the-Great, the Malays of Japan have achieved it in one generation."[27] For its conspicuous capacity for self-organization, Japan has rightful claims to rank among the Great Powers. It has now become a "country of Western civilization." Duret again: "Within half-a-century the superior human culture that has formed in Europe will be rooted in Japan in such that it will develop a life of its own, free of servile imitation."[28]

Politically, too, Japan's constitution and legislation drew it close to Western nations, having nothing in common with Russia's immutable backwardness. The Japanese civil and penal codes are even said to be preferable to the French codes in some respects. Japan's political regime is described as relatively liberal, allowing the people to enjoy a complete freedom of expression through the press. Some activists, though, such as Longuet, would not fail to notice the paradox of a situation where the Japanese government was receiving the support of socialists, pacifists, or free-thinkers from abroad, while it was persecuting the socialist movement at home.[29]

Japan is also praised for the attitude of dignity and correctness of its troops in China during the Boxer Rebellion, whereas Western soldiers, brought up in a Christian culture, behaved, it is said, like ruffians. The quality of the medical aid provided to the injured, Russian as well as Japanese, is underlined with admiration as typifying a civilized behavior. For once, happily, as it is ironically pointed, the Japanese, so often mocked for aping Westerners, did not try to imitate them. In brief, Japan proved to have "no moral lesson to receive from us," a direct echo of Voltaire's appreciation of that country in his *Essais sur les mœurs et l'esprit des nations.*

The virtue of atheism

In the middle of the heated debate on the links between Church and State —the law on the separation of Church and State was to be passed on December 9, 1905—the issue of religion assumed great importance in the eyes of Japan's advocates.

The alleged absence of any sound religious feelings among the Japanese, as commonly reported by Western visitors to Japan, was no doubt quite laudable for many French socialists. Notwithstanding the numerous descriptions of temples, shrines, or religious festivals they contain, it is almost a commonplace of Western travel narratives of the Meiji era that most Japanese are foreign to any strong religious commitment, although the uneducated people can often be prey to superstitions, as is also reported. In the opinion of those visitors, only private, occasional, and selfish interests motivate religious practices among the Japanese. Here are the words of the fiery Gustave Hervé on that matter:

> What religion has become for such a people can easily be guessed. Among the ignorant masses that are slowly polished up by school education, there are still people who, like in China, practice ancestor worship, and some convinced Buddhists too, who are in fact as remote from Buddha's ethics as our Catholic bigots from the ethics of the Gospel. But there is probably no other less religious people in the world! Not even the French, whose lack of religiosity, however, is so noticeable within Europe. And, for sure, there is no other ruling class in the world, which professes so openly rationalism and atheism. Japan is not a place where Catholic or Protestant missionaries are persecuted, they are simply laughed at in their face.[30]

Félix Régamey—a well-known artist and a progressive who had visited Japan twice, and whose writings are quoted by Japan's advocates— also bears witness to the Japanese disregard for religion:

> Japanese are free from fanaticism. Their art and philosophy rely on the pure sources of life. They practice a smiling tolerance and an untiring

politeness. They are unwilling to accept religious speculations that would derive their strength from the fright of death and from the fear of eternal punishments. They give no handle for conversion. As our missionaries say: "These are bad pagans" [implying that they cannot be converted].[31]

For the economist and future socialist deputy Pierre Leroy-Beaulieu, who had spent several months in Japan, "that country affords the extraordinary sight of a people that has abandoned its twelve-century old civilization," apparently with great ease, "to adopt the civilization of another race."[32] According to him, however, there was one matter in which it had not followed the West: religion. If the Japanese had not adopted Christianity, he explained, it was because they had found it useless in solving their political and social problems. Consequently, they had rallied to "the fashionable ideas of the neutrality of the state and of the absolute freedom of consciousness."[33] Authors of socialist persuasion, such as the *normalien* Georges Weulersse, whose report appeared a year before the outbreak of the war, did not hesitate to underline what they considered as the "revolutionary affinities" between Meiji Japan and the France of the Third Republic, thus making the former some offspring of the French Revolution.[34]

Emperor worship itself, supposedly popular from antiquity, would have no longer been immune from skepticism. It would live on as a mere relic of the past, still necessary for the guidance of the insufficiently educated folk, but would be bound to dissolve sooner or later under the influence of Western political behavior and concepts. Ludovic Naudeau, a war correspondent of *Le Temps*, who spent many months in Japan after he had been captured by the Japanese at the fall of Mukden, envisaged its future in these terms: "The Mikado's divinity is a myth that will be taken away by the death of the present sovereign. The gods of the Shinto Olympus are moving off, they are already less visible, hidden by the smoke of factories."[35] In that respect, it was considered as certain that the very implementation of the constitution would lower the status of the monarch by prodding him into the management of current affairs.

With such representations in mind, it is no surprise that, for the socialist activists, the Manchurian battlefields had become like a stage, on a world scale, where "all the anticlerical democrats," represented by Japan, were fighting for real against all the reactionaries nurtured by the Church, represented by Russia.[36] Japan thus appeared as "the natural champion of socialism, reason and *laïcité*," an opinion severely criticized by the historian and journalist René Pinon.[37]

A newcomer among colonial powers, or Japan against the "white peril"

Supporters of Russia stirred up anti-Japanese feelings by laying stress on the fact that the victory of Japan over Russia in Manchuria would sooner or later result in its seizure of China, which, in turn, would directly endanger French Indo-China. At the beginning of 1905, the daily *L'Echo de Paris* published a confidential report, attributed to Marshall Kodama and addressed to Count Katsura, which outlined a plan of conquest of all East Asia, including French Indo-China. Because of contradictions and mistakes it apparently contained, the Japanese diplomats denounced it right away as a forgery made by the tsarist secret police.[38]

There were also rumors that the Indo-Chinese territories were swarming with Japanese spies fomenting sedition in order to prepare the ground for a Japanese occupation that should have taken place no later than in 1907.[39] Together with the Kodama Report, those rumors, disclosed by a bourgeois press notoriously bribed by Russian secret funds, were denounced by left-wing publications as mere incentives to invest more money in Indo-China and to take military action against Japan.

Socialist activists, most of them being naturally opposed to colonization, could not ignore Japan's aspiration to dominate Korea and Manchuria. As Naquet put it, "Capitalists, princes and kings are of the same kind everywhere in the world," and one could hardly expect Japanese capitalists to have more scruples about the exploitation of less advanced peoples than their Western counterparts.[40] Still, Naquet and other supporters of Japan considered that Japanese capitalism was first of all, in the context of the time, the manifestation of Japanese nationalism, itself a legitimate reaction to the way the Europeans had been treating the Asians for a century or more. In short, it was "a case of self-defense." Implicitly, Japan was acting in the name of all the Asians, and its nationalism was supposedly to serve as a model for all of them, especially for the peoples of Indo-China.

Among the authors who saw in Japan's rise on the international scene a blessing for the colonized peoples, one finds the very talented Anatole France, the winner of the Nobel Prize for Literature in 1921. His defense of Captain Dreyfus and of oppressed minorities had already won him a well-established reputation as a progressive when he published his book *Sur la Pierre blanche* (On the White Stone), which contains a most caustic, scathing, and hilarious criticism of the scientific and cultural arguments brought forward to predict that the Japanese were bound to be defeated. That work, a succession of "philosophical dialogues" about civilization and the history of humanity, first appeared as a series in *L'Humanité*, the organ of Jaurès' socialist party, which had just started to be published daily. It was thereafter completed to be published in a volume. On Japan's colonial ambition, answering to one of his characters who fears that, should the Japanese win the war, it would not take them long to seize Indo-China, the author writes:

> This is a great service that they would do to us ... Colonies are the scourge of the peoples ... In Asia, a small heroic people taught by Europe has been able to gain the respect of Europe. It is a great service that Japan has done to humanity in these barbarous times ... What the

Russians are now paying for in the seas of Japan and in Manchuria is not only their avid and brutal policy in the Orient, it is the colonial policy of the whole Europe. It is not only their crimes that they are expiating, but the crimes of the whole military and commercial Christendom . . . The Asians have been acquainted with the White Peril for a long time, . . . and the White Peril has created the Yellow Peril . . . We have taught the capitalist regime and war to the Japanese. They are frightening us for they are becoming similar to us.[41]

The first Russian defeats came as a surprise for many in France, but hopes still remained, as the readers of the popular press were made to believe, that the Russians could have the final word somehow. Yet, the succession of defeats and retreats that followed could no longer be put down to bad luck, and supporters of Russia gradually lost confidence in the competence of the Russian High Command. Some pinned their last hopes on the coming sea battle that could give the war a new turn, only to eventually learn of the crushing victory of the Japanese fleet in the Tsushima Straits.

After the Treaty of Portsmouth, the French government worked toward the reconciliation of the former adversaries. Along with Russia, France signed a general agreement with Japan in 1907, which was understood, at least on the French side, as the renewal of a so-called "traditional friendship" between the two countries. Both parties pledged to foster peace and security in East Asia, or, in other words, to preserve the possessions and interests of the foreign powers in the region. The agreement granted Japan the status of the most favored nation, but in Indo-China this applied only to the persons, not to the commercial exchanges. Although negotiations over a commercial convention between Japan and Indo-China were expected to follow soon, the protectionist bias of local French authorities prevented its conclusion until 1931.

Sequels

Notwithstanding the publication of books exploiting the fear caused by Japan's overwhelming victory, such as Léo Byram's essay *Petit Jap deviendra grand!* (1908) and Captain Danrit's saga *L'Invasion jaune*, while other authors were more reasonably foreseeing the risks of a confrontation between Japan and the United States over the domination of the Pacific,[42] relations between the two countries improved steadily to reach a climax during World War I with mutual declarations of friendship and solidarity. One issue of the *Cahiers de la guerre* even examined in detail the possibility of receiving direct support from the Japanese forces on the European front.[43] Thereafter, at least until 1937, French public opinion would remain sensibly less critical of Japan's activities in China than British and American public opinion. It is noticeable, in particular, that Japan's occupation of Manchuria and the creation of Manchukuo found quite a few supporters

among French lawyers and experts of Far Eastern questions, whose publications severely criticized the League of Nations for its adoption of the
Lytton Report.[44]

Compared to the period of the Russo-Japanese War, the 1930s are marked
by a reversal of the positions of left-wing and right-wing activists on Japan.
While the former, either communists or socialists, tried to mobilize public
opinion against Japan's murderous attacks on China, the latter, such as the
popular novelist and academician Claude Farrère, often unsatisfied with the
parliamentary régime, looked to Japan to find a champion of Western values
and a protector of order against the threat of communist expansion in China
and in Indo-China. As for governmental policy toward Japan, its professed
search of appeasement was in fact but another name for a fundamentally
ambivalent and hesitant attitude. Unable to mobilize enough strength to
seriously protect its interests in Indo-China and China and unwilling to side
with the United States and Britain in their leaning toward China, France
was nonetheless closely dependent on these two powers, especially on the
British ally, for its security in East Asia. Hence, the only card, if any, left
to play for successive French governments amounted to hardly more than
betting on Japan's goodwill and on the truth of its official statements.[45]

Notes

1 Tardieu, 1910: 25; Paléologue, 1934: 5.
2 Pinon, 1906: 223–4; Chun, 1970. The *Political Science Quarterly*, in its
   "Records of Political Events," gives evidence of this overwhelming sympathy
   of the French for Russia, which contrasted with the situation in other European
   countries: "In France pro-Russian sentiment was increasingly manifest and the
   expression of sympathy for Russia was so marked as to attract general European
   attention." In Garner, 1904: 334.
3 Paléologue, 1934: 174.
4 See the front-page illustration of *Le Petit Parisien*, May 14, 1905.
5 The coaling of the Russian fleet was to be provided all the way by the German
   company HAPAG (Hamburg-Amerikanische-Paketfahrt-Aktien-Gesellschaft),
   not without some legal complications and the implicit expectation of diplomatic
   benefits on the part of Kaiser Wilhelm. In Cecil, 1964.
6 Paléologue, 1934: 216, 285, 296–7.
7 See, for example, Pinon, 1906—a staunch opponent, among others, of London's
   Far Eastern policy.
8 De Lanessan in *Le Siècle*, February 8, 1904.
9 *Le Siècle*, February 10, 1904.
10 *Le Petit Parisien*, April 3, 1904.
11 Charles Dupuy in *La République française*, February 17, 1904.
12 The notion of *laïcité* resists any straightforward translation: it not only refers
   to a strict separation between the Church and the State, that is, a privatization
   of the Church, but also carries the idea of a struggle against the moral influence of all the clerics and, further, as openly claimed by some politicians,
   against any religious belief, contrary to contemporary interpretations that tend
   to reduce that notion to a shared tolerance.
13 *Le Temps*, February 16 and 18, 1904.

136   *Patrick Beillevaire*

14 Hervé, 1904b: 293.
15 Naquet, 1904a: 2.
16 Lévy, 1995: 132.
17 Naquet, 1904b: 300.
18 Naquet, 1904b: 299.
19 Nesvoy, 1904.
20 Paix-Séailles, 1904.
21 Barth, 1904.
22 Hervé, 1904d.
23 Hervé, 1905: 220.
24 Duret, 1904: 1.
25 Duret, 1904: 1; see also Hervé, 1904a.
26 Duret, 1904: 2.
27 Hervé, 1904a: 220.
28 Duret, 1904: 2.
29 Longuet, 1905.
30 Hervé, 1904a: 220.
31 Régamey, 1904: no pagination.
32 Leroy-Beaulieu, 1900: ix.
33 Leroy-Beaulieu, 1900: 309.
34 Weulersse, 1903: 347. After all, this was in line with the naive observation commonly made by more bourgeois visitors to Japan for whom its people appeared as "the French of the Far East."
35 Naudeau, 1909: 397.
36 Hervé, 1904c.
37 Pinon, 1906: 224–8.
38 Curiously, it would prove to be a sort of blueprint for Japan's future expansion in Asia. See Kerr, 1945.
39 Castex, 1904.
40 Naquet, 1904b: 301.
41 France, 1991: 1085–8.
42 For example, Aubert, 1906.
43 *Cahiers de la guerre*, 1916.
44 Beillevaire, 2005.
45 Dreifort, 1991; Laffey, 1989.

9 America's first cold war

The emergence of a new rivalry

Tal Tovy and Sharon Halevi

> There is raw human nature, irrepressible—like German trade and colonial jealousy toward you. So long as you and we have big navies, and Japan is in a financial hole, the Jap will do his best to keep his people in order; but weaken our navy, and fill the Jap treasury, and it will no longer [be] worthwhile for them to be unpopular with their own people. When the people of two nations are antagonistic, because of clashing interests, the peace can only be kept by force.
>
> (Alfred T. Mahan, Letter to Bouverie F. Clark, January 28, 1909)[1]

In this chapter we argue that the aftermath of the Russo-Japanese War can be viewed as the first modern instance of a "cold war," a precursor of its more famous counterpart, which existed between the United States and the Soviet Union from 1945 to 1990. We define a "cold war" as a period of intense antagonism between two powers that includes a military build-up accompanied by diplomatic and political maneuvers aimed at deterring the adversarial power from declaring open war. Such a period is often characterized by an arms race, by the concentrated development of war plans (during peacetime), by the increased polarization of domestic and international politics, and last by the seepage of this competition and conflict into contested economic regions.[2] Most of the literature on American military history suggests that such a cold war strategy was created, and fostered only in the aftermath of World War II.[3] We argue that an early version of a cold war came into being after the Russo-Japanese War and that this strategy informed American policy in the Pacific from the end of the Russo-Japanese War to the late 1930s.

In order to argue our case we first examine in detail the United States' attitude to Japan before the Russo-Japanese War and trace the immediate influence the war had on the United States as an emerging international power and point to the processes that lay at the base of America's antagonistic attitude toward Japan. We then proceed to examine several issues that were both directly and indirectly influenced by the outcome of the war, such as the United States' geo-strategic outlook on the Pacific region, the impact of the war on the US Navy's war plans, in particular "War Plan Orange," and finally domestic policy regarding immigration.

The American attitude to Japan before and during the Russo-Japanese War

Upon the end of the Spanish–American War (1898) and the conquest of the Philippines, the United States became firmly established as an international player with imperial ambitions. The United States' economic and strategic interests in the Pacific expanded and its involvement in the region deepened. A similar development occurred in Japan, and the two countries began to develop similar (though conflicting) interests in the region.[4] The Russo-Japanese conflict generated a significant change in the United States' military and diplomatic posture toward Japan. The traditional American support of Japan was abandoned from 1905 onward, and the United States began to regard Japan with growing unease. If in the past the United States had prepared itself for conventional military conflicts with potential enemies, the outcome of the Russo-Japanese War convinced it that it should invest more in military preparation and avoid an open conflict with Japan by means of a strategy of deterrence and containment. This change in outlook and policy and the slow deterioration of economic and diplomatic relations between the two powers would eventually lead to the open outbreak of hostilities between these two Pacific powers in the 1940s.

The Russo-Japanese War, in which Japan won a decisive victory on land and on sea over a European power, can be regarded therefore as a major watershed in the relations between the United States and Japan. From the political and military point of view, the United States viewed Japan from this point onward as a threat to American interests in East Asia and rapidly came to perceive Japan as its prime potential enemy in the region. From the economic standpoint, Japan threatened America's "Open Door" policy in China, while, on the domestic front, Americans (especially on the west coast) were growing increasingly anxious over the influx of immigrants from East Asia. More importantly, Japan now viewed itself as a major power in East Asia and began to assert its hegemony in China and Korea.

The prewar American support for Japan was a direct outcome of the strained relations between the United States and tsarist Russia. Since the end of the Boxer Rebellion (1901), relations between the two countries had slowly deteriorated. The main reasons for this deterioration were the Russian occupation of Manchuria, its continued refusal to withdraw its military forces from the region, and Russia's intention to act in violation of the American "Open Door" policy in Manchuria.[5] During Theodore Roosevelt's administration there were two prevailing (and opposing) positions regarding Russia and its occupation of Manchuria. Secretary of State John Hay contended that, if Russia would accept the principles of the "Open Door" policy, then the United States might tolerate the occupation of Manchuria. President Roosevelt, however, insisted that Russia withdraw from Manchuria and maintained that the occupation demonstrated Russia's aggressive stance. Roosevelt sought to strengthen the political standing of the Russian Minister of Finance, Sergei Witte, whom he viewed as a moderate and a person who could modernize Russia, which would accord with American political and economic interests. Roosevelt hoped that a Russian defeat in the battlefield could potentially accelerate political and economic changes in Russia, and would lead to its eventual withdrawal from Manchuria.

Roosevelt viewed Japan with a combination of apprehension and admiration, but between 1901 and 1905 admiration won out. As tensions between Japan and the United States eased after Japan's recognition of American sovereignty over Hawaii, the United States came to see Japan as a potential ally who could impede Russian imperial ambitions in East Asia. The upper echelons of the US Army, Navy, and State Department in particular shared the opinion that Russia could be contained only by means of military force,[6] and that, despite organizational changes in the US Navy (such as the creation of the Pacific Fleet) the United States was not prepared for an open outbreak of hostilities in East Asia.[7]

The United States' positive stance toward Japan solidified after Japan accepted the American "Open Door" policy in China;[8] the United States came to view Japan as a rising economic power and realized that Japan would become, within a few years, the most industrialized nation in East Asia. Once Japan did so, the United States hoped to find a prosperous market for its goods, just as it had done in the past with the industrialized European nations.[9] The complimentary descriptions of Japan's economic and military power were the outcome of a favorable view of Japan percolating from the highest levels of the American administration. According to this view, Japan's growing power was seen to work in favor of American interests in Asia.

During the Russo-Japanese War the United States was neutral but supportive of Japan.[10] This favorable disposition toward Japan was in part the result of the positive coverage of the war by American journalists, who portrayed the Japanese common soldier in a sympathetic and heroic manner.[11] The United States' pro-Japanese sentiments are also apparent from its behavior both before and immediately following the war. First, in 1905 the two countries signed an agreement in which the United States recognized Japan's special status in Korea and Japan reciprocated by recognizing American sovereignty in the Philippines. Second, the huge war expenses had forced Japan to seek out external loans, and almost half of the loans came from the United States. Third, during the peace talks, which culminated with the Treaty of Portsmouth, American support of Japanese interests was evident;[12] for example, despite sharp Japanese domestic criticism of the treaty, the treaty eventually did institute Korea as a Japanese protectorate and elevated Japan to the status of a regional power.

As noted, America's support of Japan was also very clearly a product of its political, strategic, and economic interests in East Asia. After 1898, Americans hoped to exploit the seemingly unlimited Chinese market and compete with other European powers. Roosevelt thought that the Russo-

Japanese War helped maintain American interests in the region, just as the balance of power and conflicts between the European powers helped maintain American interests in the Caribbean; a scenario in which both Japan and Russia exhausted their military and economic energies was not one toward which the Unites States was averse.[13] As Russia's crushing defeat by Japan resulted in its removal (albeit temporarily) from the Pacific theater, Roosevelt preferred not leave matters to chance; therefore, he took on the role of mediator, in order to ensure that the resulting peace treaty would be in America's best interests.[14]

The United States' main purpose during the talks was to shift Japan's attention away from China, where the United States had significant economic interests; as Japan's show of strength in the war raised doubts about the security of the Philippines, the United States hoped to divert Japan's attention elsewhere. During the negotiations preceding the Treaty of Portsmouth, the United States sought to preserve the hostility and tension between Russia and Japan (in part by supporting Japan). Despite Roosevelt's involvement in the negotiations, he was in no hurry to conclude a settlement. In a 1904 letter to his son, Roosevelt wrote:

> For several years Russia has behaved very badly in the far East [Far East], her attitude toward all nations, including us, but especially toward Japan, has been grossly overbearing. We had no sufficient cause for war with her . . . between ourselves—for you must not breathe that to anybody—I was thoroughly well pleased with the Japanese victory, for Japan is playing our game.

This is one of the clearest indications that, in the American view, as articulated by Roosevelt, Japan was acting in accord with the United States' interests.[15]

The main bone of contention during the talks was Sakhalin Island; both Russia and Japan claimed sovereignty over the island and both were not prepared to compromise over the issue. As a result of Roosevelt's mediation, the island was divided along the fiftieth latitude, with the northern part given to Russia and the southern to Japan; but, despite the island's demilitarization, it remained an unresolved issue. These events confirmed that the United States hoped that a continued Russian presence in the area would offset Japan's power.[16] However, even during this period, when the United States leaned toward Japan, the seeds of suspicion were already being sown.

The geo-strategic aspect: War Plan Orange

As a consequence of the war, a new era began in American–Japanese relations. The war had overturned the balance of power in East Asia and the

United States now stood alone against the rising military and economic power of Japan. The Japanese victory in the Russo-Japanese War spelled the collapse of the traditional American policy and interests. The United States did indeed wish for a Japanese victory in the war, but not for the complete and decisive defeat of Russia. The war drove Russia out of East Asia, both economically and politically, for the next four decades; Japan, on the other hand, emerged as a regional power strengthened economically and more importantly militarily. Japanese military confidence grew as both navy and army commanders gained crucial military experience in the course of the war.[17]

In the months following the war, the US Army and Navy had to redefine the balance of power in East Asia. While Britain was still regarded as a latent threat, Japan was increasingly becoming an overt one. The United States also faced new coalitions; the Anglo-Japanese Alliance was renewed in 1905 and again in 1911, and in 1907 the two former enemies, Japan and Russia, signed a treaty honoring each other's rights in Manchuria. Such coalitions and threats spurred the American military to commence drafting war plans in case of a future conflict with Japan; War Plan Orange was the key plan formulated during this period.[18] The history of Plan Orange confirms that the Unites States had begun to foresee Japan as an emerging threat even before the Russo-Japanese War, as the first version of the plan was put together in 1903. During that year, joint plans for the navy and army were drawn up in preparation for different scenarios; the main scenario concerned the repulse of a Japanese attack in the Pacific. This was the first strategic plan that the United States prepared in peacetime and, as the Japanese threat grew, the plan was augmented to address several different scenarios and outcomes.[19]

The goal of the war plan was to find the most appropriate way to defend American interests in East Asia, especially the Philippines, from Japanese attack. At this point in time, the navy and the army were debating issues concerning the defense of the Philippines, in particular the most suitable location for the construction of a large naval base, defendable from both land and sea. The army, after studying the battle of Port Arthur, concluded that defending a similar port in the Philippines would be impossible.[20] Instead, a decision was made to develop the existing port at Pearl Harbor and to establish it as the main American base in the western Pacific.[21]

Plan Orange included a set of directives for defending the Philippines and other American strongholds in the Pacific. The main assumption was that Japan would gain an initial, but temporary, military advantage in the area, as most of the American naval forces remained stationed in the Atlantic Ocean. Therefore, in case a Japanese attack was to occur, the American forces in the Philippines would execute a strategic retreat and barricade themselves in inland strongholds. The retreat's purpose was to avoid signifi- cant losses until the arrival of naval reinforcements from the Atlantic.

Eventually, the navy would arrive in the Pacific and Japanese forces would be destroyed. An early version of Plan Orange stated that certain strategic points in the Philippines and across the western Pacific (such as Hawaii and Guam) also need it to be defended, so that in an event of a Japanese attack they would join the American forces sailing in from the Atlantic via the Suez canal (or after 1914 via the Panama Canal).

As time passed the scenarios took on a more ominous tone. In 1907 the plan was updated; it now contended that Japan was capable of conquering Hawaii, blockading the Panama Canal (which was under construction) and even threatening the American west coast.[22] The military was to begin fortifying the Philippines and preparing its strongholds for sieges that would last from 90 to 120 days, until naval reinforcements would arrive.[23] The basic outline of Plan Orange— awaiting reinforcements while barricaded in strongholds within the Philippines—was to become the American defensive strategy in the Pacific up to 1941.[24] The Japanese war plan seems almost to mirror in reverse the American plan, as Japan's strategy in the western Pacific was also based on its naval forces. It stated that, with the outbreak of a war, Japan must move quickly to conquer the Philippines and Guam. Later, almost in a repeat of the Battle of Tsushima, the Japanese navy would lay in wait and destroy the American navy. Both Japan and the United States made use (albeit only up to a certain degree) of their respective strategic plans at the beginning of World War II in the Pacific.

Concomitant with the military planning, intense diplomatic activities with senior Japanese officials continued during 1908, resulting in several mutual agreements that stated that Japan would not instigate a war with the United States by attacking the Philippines, so long as in turn the United States did not thwart Japan's activities on the Asian mainland.[25] At that stage, as long as both countries honored these treaties war would be avoided. At the beginning of the second Sino-Japanese War (1937) and especially after the annexation of Indo-China (1941), when the United States attempted to check the Japanese military expansion into East Asia by applying economic sanctions, it became clear that these treaties were not honored and that both powers were headed toward an open military confrontation.

Thus, the United States' attitude toward Japan underwent a sea change during the Roosevelt administration (1901–9), during which Japan came to be identified as the United States' main adversary in the western Pacific. This position was the direct outcome of Japan's decisive victory in the Russo-Japanese War. While both countries tried to prevent or check the outbreak of open war between them, they succeeded only in postponing it. Roosevelt's strategy prompted Japan to concentrate on its territorial expansion; while appearing to uphold in principle the "Open Door" policy, Japan refrained from expanding into the eastern and southern Pacific (the Root–Takahira Agreement of 1908).

The impact the Russo-Japanese War on American policy toward Japan, 1909–21

The perception of Japan as the United States' major adversary in the Pacific lingered throughout the two following administrations of William Taft (1909–13) and Woodrow Wilson (1913–21). The Taft administration employed a more aggressive approach to its foreign policy toward Japan, known as the "Dollar Diplomacy,"[26] formulated by Secretary of State Philander Knox, and several other members of Taft's administration mostly in the State and Commerce departments. The main goal of the policy was to generate economic and political stability in regions with economic and strategic importance for the United States; the policy was employed in both Latin America and China, although Taft was not shy of using military force and his attitude did not undergo any change upon assuming office. Under the "Dollar Diplomacy" policy, the United States obliquely stated that, if economic stability in China (and Latin America) was not attained, and as a result American interests were harmed, it would contemplate military involvement.[27]

The "Dollar Diplomacy" policy was applied to China in response to the Russo-Japanese Alliance sealed in 1907; by signing this alliance two former enemies barred American companies who wished to expand their businesses into Manchuria.[28] The Taft administration deemed that the only option left to it was to employ economic measures against Japan; thus, the "Dollar Diplomacy" can definitely be seen as part of an economic strategy designed to contain Japan. The United States began lending significant sums of money to China mainly in the interest of preserving the "Open Door" policy. According to Taft, the industrialization of China was in America's best interests and would strengthen the ties between the United States and China. The policy deepened the United States' political involvement in China with the intention of limiting the other powers' involvement, especially Japan's.[29] Despite their aggressive stance, President Taft and the Secretary of State knew that the American public would not support going to war with Japan over Manchuria, as such a war would be perceived as serving Chinese, and not American, interests.[30]

The Wilson administration continued to implement this unyielding policy regarding Japan. In 1914, the outbreak of World War I recharged the tensions between the United States and Japan, specifically around issues such as Japan's involvement in the war, China's status, the involvement in the Russian Civil War, and the post-war agreements. Therefore, World War I and its outcome can be seen as a further step in the deterioration of relations between the United States and Japan. Japan soon came to see the war as an ideal opportunity to gain sovereignty over China and in the process complete its transformation into a leading world power. Some Japanese political leaders advocated entering the war as a means to capture the German colonies in East Asia. In August 1914, Japan declared war on

Germany and within a few months it had conquered all German Pacific colonies north of the equator. Japan took advantage of a significant European absence (or perhaps absent-mindedness) from Asia to issue China with a list of "Twenty-one Demands," in which Japan demanded in effect economic and political sovereignty over China, by threatening to conquer even more territories unless the Chinese government complied with these demands. Moreover, Japan wanted to install a shadow government that would actually run China, jeopardizing American interests there.

The United States made it clear that any treaty impairing the "Open Door" policy or harmful to its interests in China would not be accepted. Japan's declaration of the "Twenty-one Demands" and the United States' swift and aggressive rebuttal was a turning point in American–Japanese relations. From 1915 onward, Japan's every move in East Asia was noted, and there were constant attempts made to prevent it from increasing its political and economic involvement in China.[31] In 1917, the United States and Japan signed a treaty in which Japan accepted the Western powers' economic rights in China. On the other hand, the United States recognized Japan's special privileges in the Chinese areas under its control.[32] The haziness of the treaty enabled each country to interpret it according to its own economic, political, and strategic interests.

At the end of the war Japan was included with the other leading powers and invited to the Versailles talks; this inclusion in the summit testifies to the Western powers' increasing willingness (be it grudging at times) to treat Japan as a power with an equal stake in global policy debates, at least as these pertained to East Asia. From the American geo-strategic point of view, as Japan emerged as the major military power in East Asia it was now posed to threaten maritime shipping between the United States and the Philippines, capable of expanding its influence in China, and thus threatening American economic interests. Historian John Coogan argues that the American involvement in Siberia, during the Russian Civil War, was a result of the need to keep an eye on Japan in northern East Asia.[33]

The impact of the Russo-Japanese War on the US Navy

The Russo-Japanese War also had a major effect on the United States' naval thought and procedures. The lessons learned from this war fit in with the views of Alfred Thayer Mahan as articulated in his important and widely popular work *The Influence of Sea Power on History, 1660–1783* (1890), which had a lasting influence on the navy's long-term strategic planning. Mahan placed contemporary naval events within the context of a grand historical narrative and argued that in the modern era a nation's greatness and prosperity flowed from sea power, which had a fundamental economic importance. Mahan concluded that Britain's current naval superiority both ensured its safety and international status and provided the resources for its economic wealth by denying this advantage to its chief adversaries, mainly France (from the period of Louis XIV to Napoleon) by blockading the French ports. Britain's ensuing economic prosperity, which was derived in part from its control over maritime trade routes, enabled it to support Britain's allies on the European mainland and avoid having to display overtly its power in Europe.[34]

Mahan's conclusion was that a nation must develop its merchant fleet and acquire new territories that could provide it with access to raw materials. At the same time, a nation must establish a strong navy to protect these trade routes and its colonies. A navy's first priority was to ensure the total military defeat of the enemy's navy, by controlling the seas, and setting up the enemy fleet as its main strategic target. Thus, Mahan opposed the notion that a navy should be defense-orientated. If an "Open Door" policy toward China was to be implemented, then naval bases in the Pacific were necessary for the navy to support this policy with "Gunboat Diplomacy." According to Mahan, a large naval base had to be constructed in the Hawaii/ Guam area to protect American interests. The establishment of strong naval bases in those areas would alleviate the fear of a threat from Japan by enabling the navy to flank any Japanese invasion.

Margaret Sprout claims that evidence for Mahan's overwhelming influence on the shaping of naval thought can be found in the design of the world's largest battleships, especially those manufactured in Britain, Germany, and Japan. More importantly, several influential politicians adopted his theory.[35] When Theodore Roosevelt entered office as Undersecretary of the Navy during the McKinley administration (1897–1901), the US Navy was ranked eleventh in the world. By the time Roosevelt's presidential term ended in 1909, it ranked second (with the British Royal Navy ranking first), but most of the British vessels were old, and the US Navy was better equipped with newer and more modern battleships.[36] These developments were a direct outcome of the Russo-Japanese War, and the growing threat the Japanese navy posed to the United States.

After the Battle of Tsushima, President Roosevelt gave the Navy Department a direct order to study the reasons for the Japanese naval victory.[37] Some argue that the order held no particular political or military intent but stemmed from the professional curiosity of a man who had numerous dealings with naval affairs as well as a long-term interest in them.[38] Historian Stephen Howarth agrees with this view; however, he notes at the same time that Roosevelt was aware that Japan's complete victory over Russia would lead eventually to a struggle between the United States and Japan.[39] One of the navy's main conclusions in this study was that the core of the fleet, or its main strength, must consist of battleships. The battleships' return to the position of the navy's main platform lasted until their replacement by aircraft carriers during World War II.[40]

In 1907 growing antagonism toward Japan finally drove Roosevelt to state that only a strong and sizeable navy could ensure the United States' safety and protect its interests in East Asia. During that year, Congress approved the navy's request to build more battleships,[41] and in December of that year Roosevelt sent the "Great White Fleet" to show the flag around the world and display America's naval strength, especially in the Pacific Ocean. The cruise's main purpose was to demonstrate to Japan America's naval power and deter it from going to war. The second purpose was to position the navy closer to Japan in case of any Japanese attack.[42] An additional goal was to shore up public support for the construction of a new type of battleship, an American-made *Dreadnought* class, which Britain had already begun to deploy.[43] The "Great White Fleet" consisted of 16 battleships, escorted by destroyers and other auxiliary vessels. The fleet circumnavigated the globe between December 1907 and February 1909, visiting the major ports in Latin America, the western Pacific, the Indian Ocean, and the Mediterranean.[44] By 1908, the US Navy had 26 battleships and 15 armored cruisers, but Congress refused to support a long-term program of *Dreadnought* construction, although by the outbreak of World War I two ships were being built every year.[45]

The major strategic problem facing the American navy was how to offset Japan's geographic advantage or how to achieve decisive naval command of the western Pacific, when all its battleships were stationed in the Atlantic. Another problem was the issue of resupplying the ships with no secure naval bases available.[46] These questions emphasize that the US Navy viewed the Imperial Japanese Navy as the main threat to the American interests in the western Pacific. This defensive view solidified after the Japanese decisive victory in the Battle of Tsushima, especially since the US Navy had never participated in a maritime battle on such a scale. In order to resolve these problems it was decided to establish a fortified base in the western Pacific. After some discussion, the navy decided to establish its main naval base in Pearl Harbor. In addition, with the opening of the Panama Canal, the navy could now send for reinforcements from the east coast and the Atlantic.

In his inaugural address in 1909, President Taft stated that his administration would continue the build-up of the army and the navy.[47] Taft continued with the changes initiated by Roosevelt, but he never deployed a powerful military force in East Asia. By 1913, on the eve of World War I, the US Navy was strong and ranked second only to the Royal Navy. According to Taft, the US Navy was ready to meet the challenges from the United States' potential enemies, especially Japan.

Japanese immigration to the United States in the aftermath of the war

While Roosevelt did try to avoid an open war with Japan, it is impossible to ignore that other factors also played an important role in the deterioration of relations between the United States and Japan. Racial animosities on the west coast had soured relations between both countries, from as early as 1906. The last years of the Roosevelt administration and those of his successor, William Taft, were tainted by growing racism toward Japanese and other Asian immigrants (such as Chinese and Koreans) and attempts were made to limit their immigration to the United States.[48] Racial animosity toward Japanese immigrants, in particular, had emerged during the second half of the 1890s, when Asian immigrants were met with nativist hostility and discrimination. During this period, there was a massive wave of Japanese immigration to the Hawaiian Islands, where the Japanese constituted the largest Asian ethnic group. By the end of the nineteenth century, there were more than 26,000 Japanese in Hawaii (making up one-quarter of the total population). The United States feared that additional immigration would lead to a Japanese takeover of the islands.[49] Thus, the war did not instigate racial animosity, but accentuated it. Japan's military strength, coupled with its steady course of expansion in different regions in Asia and the growing population pressures in Japan itself, were defined as threatening the United States' domestic economic interests.

Tensions between the two countries escalated with the implementation of racist and xenophobic domestic policies, especially in California where the majority of Japanese immigrants ended up working on the railroads, as well as in canneries, mines, and logging camps. In 1906, the San Francisco school board, claiming that Japanese children were crowding white students out of the schools, segregated the former into separate schools and demanded that the US government persuade Japan to stop further emigration. The Japanese government sharply protested this show of prejudice. As neither President Roosevelt nor Secretary of State Elihu Root was interested in escalating the affair, they attempted to soothe Japanese policy makers for fear of further deteriorating relations with Japan, especially since both maintained that, as long as Japan's expansion was focused on the Asian mainland, Japan was in no position to pose an immediate threat to the United States.

As a result of President Roosevelt's intervention in California's state policies, the "Gentlemen's Agreement" was drawn up in February 1907. Roosevelt managed to talk the school board into changing its mind after making sure that the Japanese authorities would not issue passports to "laborers," excepting former residents of the United States, the parents, wives, or children of residents, or those who already possessed an interest in an American farming enterprise. The president requested that Congress and the city of San Francisco put an end to their discriminatory policies; Japan reciprocated by promising to limit the number of immigrants to the United States, an agreement that did slow down the influx of Japanese immigrants and brought some respite to racial agitations in California.[50]

Agitation against Japan and the Japanese continued, however, in a myriad of ways. In 1909, Homer Lea published his notorious *The Valor of Ignorance*, which described a Japanese surprise attack on Hawaii and the west coast.[51] The book was very popular, tapping into the American public's fear of Japan's military and economic expansion in East Asia. Anxieties such as these were renewed in 1913 when Japanese immigrants in California faced another wave of racial animosity, which in turn provoked another crisis between Japan and the United States. Japan perceived the renewed display of racial prejudice as a breach of the "Gentlemen's Agreement." In May 1913, President Wilson conveyed Japan's protest of American racism to his cabinet. Some military officials feared that the renewed exchanges of sharp protests could provoke a display of military power and the US military began preparations for such an outcome. Once again in the summer of 1913, the tense relations between the two countries were calmed down as a result of the Wilson administration's conciliatory approach toward Japan; one such step toward a compromise was the abandonment of the "Dollar Diplomacy" policy.[52] Japanese immigration to the United States came to a halt in 1924, when Congress passed the "Immigration Act"; although the act was directed mainly against immigration from eastern and southern Europe it did have a collateral impact on immigrants from Japan and other Asian countries.[53]

Concluding remarks: from coexistence to confrontation

To conclude our argument that a proto-cold war existed from the end of the Russo-Japanese War until the outbreak of World War II, we need to highlight key developments during the 1920s and the 1930s, a period during which impact of the Russo-Japanese War continued to resound. During this period the United States did maintain its hostile and suspicious stance toward Japan, which was now focused on its renewed territorial expansion in China. Historian Sadao Asada claims that American–Japanese rivalry resulted from different interpretations of the "Open Door" policy: while the United States viewed it as a tool to achieve equilibrium between the different powers' interests in China, Japan saw it as an opportunity to exploit China's resources for the benefit of Japan's growing economy and infrastructure.[54]

In November 1921, President Warren Harding convened a summit in Washington whose goal was to regulate the situation in East Asia and check the naval arms race.[55] The Washington Conference demonstrates that the United States was far from isolated from world affairs and testifies to America's intense involvement in East Asia and in the Pacific. At the Washington Conference, the Western powers presented a united front against Japanese expansionist intentions in East Asia. Under pressure from the United States and Britain, Japan was forced to retreat from Siberia and the Shantung Peninsula, conquered during World War I, and it had to acknowledge both China's independence and its borders (the Nine Powers Treaty).[56] The most important item, however, was the reduction in naval forces and the limitation of the naval arms race.

The Washington Conference was the first in history to deliberate arms limitations. With the destruction of the German and Russian navies, the

Japanese navy emerged the third largest in the world (after those of Britain and the United States). According to the Five Powers Treaty, all the signatory powers committed to cutting back their naval forces; according to the "5:5:3 Formula," Japan's navy was reduced to 60 percent of those of the United States and Britain. The United States recognized that the only possible way to defend its assets in the Pacific was if its navy maintained a sizeable advantage over the Japanese. The United States' main, and perhaps sole, interest during the Washington Conference was to check Japan's rising power in the Pacific,[57] for within less than a decade Japan had succeeded in defeating two major European powers (Russia and Germany), all the while demonstrating a high degree of operational capability both on land and at sea. From Japan's perspective, this formula would deal a death blow to any aspirations of supremacy in the Pacific. Japan estimated that, if its navy were to defeat the US Navy, it would need to be at least 70 percent of its size; unless this size was maintained any future conflict with the Unites States would be lost.[58]

The conference also marked a change in the texture of international relations. The Four Powers Treaty replaced the Anglo-Japanese Alliance, which was renewed in 1905 and in 1911. Both the United States and Britain were interested in terminating the Anglo-Japanese Alliance.[59] Britain feared in particular that Japan's eastern expansion may bring it closer to its "Crown jewel"—India.[60] The United States identified Japan's growing expansion in East Asia and its military force as a threat to American national security and interests and therefore for the first time openly attempted to impede Japan's expansion and limit its naval force. Therefore, almost as a precursor of its cold war strategy, the United States sought to consolidate a "block" of countries whose common goal would be to curb Japan's growing power. At the heart of the Four Powers Treaty lay the signatories' obligation to consult each other in matters pertaining to East Asia, thus counterbalancing Japan's hegemony in East Asia.[61]

The period between the Washington Conference and the late 1930s was characterized by a gradual but accelerating deterioration in American–Japanese relations. In the 1930s Japan's political life and its military were controlled by national and militant factions. As a result, Japan implemented a more aggressive policy toward China, until an all-out war with China broke out in 1937. The United States condemned this aggression and even supplied weapons to China; yet, the underlying assumption was that, as long as Japan was preoccupied by in China, Japan would not be able to assail American interests in Asia.

The outbreak of war in Europe (1939) shifted the balance of power in East Asia. European colonies in Southeast Asia were unprotected. Japan saw this as the ideal opportunity to conquer those territories and achieve economic self-sufficiency. The only power that could make Japan hesitate in expanding into Southeast Asia was the United States. In July 1940 the United States canceled its trade agreement with Japan and transferred its

Pacific Fleet to Pearl Harbor, sending in fighters and bombers to reinforce the forces in the Philippines. The harshest measure it took was the imposition of an embargo on the export of junk metal and petroleum (products critical to Japan's military industry) to Japan.[62] Japan, frantically yet unsuccessfully, attempted to rescind the ban. At the same time, the Japanese military began planning a combined military operation, intent on obtaining the petroleum resources in Indonesia and the iron mines and rubber plantations in Malaya, while neutralizing the American Pacific Fleet in Hawaii.[63]

Thus, from the outbreak of the Russo-Japanese War until the late 1930s American–Japanese relations retained an equivocal quality. Alongside diplomatic and economic relations there were increasing preparations for a future war with Japan. This was the first time in American history that the United States prepared war plans in peacetime directed at a specific adversary. Only after World War II do we find a similar pattern, this time between the United States and the Soviet Union, with all its associated characteristics: an arms race and attempts to limit it, local and global alliances and treaties whose aim was to limit the rival power, cultural and ideological rivalry, and an abiding fear of the other. Upon examination, all these characteristics can be found in American–Japanese relations from 1904 to 1941.

Despite diplomatic and economic ties, relations were strained and imbued with mutual suspicion, especially in the United States, which exhibited racial animosity toward Japanese immigrants. Both countries had conflicting interests in East Asia and the western Pacific; Japan's rise to the status of a world power in the aftermath of the Russo-Japanese War jeopardized American interests. As tensions increased, both militaries, especially their navies, made extensive preparations for war, which, almost like a self-fulfilling prophecy, did occur. The Japanese victory over Russia resulted in the United States' "discovery" of a new enemy. In its aftermath the United States treated Japan as a new and rising threat to its national security and economic interests in the Pacific. From this moment onward, the United States and Japan were bound for a collision.

Notes

1 Seager and Maguire, 1975, 277–8.
2 Mason, 1997; Painter, 1999.
3 Cronin, 1996; Mason, 1997; Painter, 1999.
4 Naster, 1996.
5 Pratt, 1965.
6 Challener, 1973.
7 Turk, 1978.
8 Naster, 1996.
9 Beale, 1956.
10 Esthus, 1988; Nish, 1985; Pratt, 1965.
11 Kowner, 2001.

12 Trani, 1969.
13 Naster, 1996.
14 Granville, 1985.
15 Combs, 1986; Morison, 1951–4, IV: 724.
16 Dennis, 1969.
17 Wilson, 1999; Wray and Conroy, 1983.
18 Miller, 1991.
19 Braisted, 1977; Morton, 1959.
20 Turk, 1978.
21 Granville, 1985.
22 Challener, 1973.
23 Major, 1978; Turk, 1978.
24 Miller, 1991.
25 Neu, 1987.
26 Combs, 1986.
27 LaFeber, 1993.
28 Pratt, 1965.
29 Iriye, 1977.
30 See Iriye, 1967. Many historians, including Scott Nearing, Charles Beard, and
    William Williams have argued in their studies that economic motives lay at the
    foundations of America's foreign policy during the 1920s. According to them,
    capitalism brought about American imperialism, which eventually led to the
    United States' involvement in World War I. Williams also claimed that Ameri-
    can capitalism brought about the United States' involvement in the Vietnam
    War. See, for example, Rosenberg 1994.
31 Kawamura, 2000.
32 Clements, 1987.
33 Coogan, 1994.
34 Rosinski, 1977.
35 Crowl, 1986; Sprout, 1943.
36 Cable, 1998.
37 Sondhaus, 2001.
38 Challener, 1973.
39 Howarth, 1999.
40 Sondhaus, 2001.
41 Baer, 1994; Howarth, 1999.
42 Naster, 1996.
43 Marks, 1981; Sondhaus, 2001.
44 Baer, 1994.
45 Sondhaus, 2001.
46 Baer, 1994.
47 Baer, 1994.
48 Bernard, 1998; Hunt, 1987.
49 Naster, 1996.
50 Neu, 1987.
51 Lea, 1909.
52 Naster, 1996.
53 Bernard, 1998; Tsuchida, 1998.
54 Asada, 1961.
55 Pratt, 1965.
56 In the course of the Washington Conference three treaties were signed: the Four
    Powers Treaty (the United States, Britain, Japan, and France); the Five Powers
    Treaty (the United States, Britain, Japan, Italy, and France); and the Nine Powers

Treaty (the United States, Britain, Japan, France, Portugal, Holland, Belgium, Italy, and China). See Iriye, 1967.
57 Naster, 1996.
58 Asada, 1961, 1993.
59 Rosen, 1978.
60 Bartlett, 1994.
61 Hall, 1987.
62 Sagan, 1988.
63 Sagan, 1988.

10 White Mongols?

The war and American discourses on race and religion

Joseph M. Henning

"Are the Japanese white?" This was the question posed to the United States Supreme Court in its 1922 case, *Takao Ozawa* v. *United States*. Ozawa, a Japanese immigrant who had lived in the United States since 1894, had applied for US citizenship in 1914 and was rejected because naturalized citizenship was limited by law to "free white persons" and those of African nativity or descent. In an earlier decision on the Ozawa case, a district court had ruled that Japanese immigrants were not eligible for naturalized citizenship because they were not white persons.

Ozawa appealed to the Supreme Court, arguing that the term "white persons" did not define a race, but dealt instead with the personal qualities that made a person fit for citizenship. The justices disagreed, concluding that "white" referred to someone of the Caucasian race. Recognizing the briefs filed on Ozawa's behalf, the Court wrote that it was not passing judgment on the "culture and enlightenment of the Japanese people," which it did not dispute. Moreover, it noted carefully that its decision did not imply "any suggestion of individual unworthiness or racial inferiority." Nevertheless, the Supreme Court concluded, Ozawa was "clearly of a race which is not Caucasian" and therefore not entitled to US citizenship.[1]

The Ozawa case had roots that stretched back to the turn of the twentieth century, when Japan defeated first China, then Russia, in wars that marked the culmination of the Meiji government's project of building a "rich nation, strong army" (*fukoku kyōhei*). These years marked an important shift in American–Japanese relations, which grew more strained as both nations embarked on imperial and commercial expansion in the Pacific.[2] When nineteenth-century Japan reshaped itself into a powerful modern state, it confounded American and European expectations. In the early years of American–Japanese relations, most Americans expected little of the Japanese. A "heathen" Asian people, they were considered to be spiritually and biologically ill-equipped for the task of national progress. Most American leaders believed firmly that Protestant Christians and Anglo-Saxons had a monopoly on modern civilization.[3]

Japan's defeat of white, Christian Russia posed an immense challenge to Western hierarchies of race and religion. In response, prominent American authorities on Japan—missionaries, journalists, and scholars—attempted to redefine the Japanese. The Russo-Japanese War provided a welcome opportunity for them to improve Japan's position in American public opinion. These experts depicted it as a conflict between East and West: Russia, however, represented the East, and Japan the West. They jettisoned the term "heathen" and argued instead that Japan better embodied Christian values and Anglo-Saxon institutions than did Russia. Pushing even further, some Americans presented evidence that the Japanese were, in fact, a white race— a claim that was intended to explain Japan's successes.

Ultimately, these claims did not convince American politicians who considered the Japanese to be undesirable immigrants to the United States. The campaign against Japanese immigration, which began just as the war was ending, relied on explicitly racist assumptions. Anti-Japanese activists warned that peace in Asia would bring a "Mongolian invasion" of Japanese laborers to the United States. Yet Japan's military triumph over Russia compelled American leaders to cloak their attacks on Japanese racial traits within respectful admiration for Japanese national achievements. While denouncing the Japanese as a race, they sought to avoid provoking Japan as a nation. The Russo-Japanese War thus opened a range of contradictory and competing discourses among those Americans sympathetic to Japan and those who were antagonistic. The questions raised by the war finally approached a resolution in the early 1920s with the Ozawa case. That decision and congressional legislation in 1924 prohibiting further Japanese immigration effectively closed the debate that the war had opened.

Classifying the Japanese, Russians, and Ainu

American friends of Japan crafted three different approaches to its racial and religious categorization. These explanations were not entirely consistent with each other, yet American missionaries, journalists, and scholars used each in attempts to improve the status of the Japanese in the accepted racial and religious hierarchies. Changing the common categorization of the Japanese as backward, heathen Asians required comparative analysis, in which the Russians and the Ainu, Japan's aboriginal people, played significant roles.

In the first explanation, American missionaries and journalists distinguished between Japan and Russia on the bases of both race and religion. Japanese reforms in the late nineteenth century already had compelled Americans to broaden the definition of "Christian." The Japanese government had effectively ended the centuries-old ban on Christianity in 1873, allowing missionaries to work freely among the Japanese. Even more significantly, Article 28 of the 1889 Constitution provided an important though limited guarantee of religious freedom; American missionaries, who earlier had been among the sharper critics of Japanese customs and beliefs, began to emerge as some of Japan's most sympathetic advocates.

In 1900, however, missionaries counted about 43,000 Protestant church members in a total population of about 45 million: less than 0.1 percent of Japan had converted.[4] By numerical standards, Japan was not a Christian nation. Yet many Americans considered freedom of religion to be a central component of Christian civilization—a component that Japan had decisively adopted. Furthermore, missionaries reported, Japan's military victories against China and Russia were opening new territory for religious freedom and Protestant evangelism. In Korea and Manchuria, Japan was opening the door for the Christian gospel.[5] Two generations of Americans had described the Japanese as "heathen"; but now, by its actions, Japan stood alongside the Christian nations of the West. To veteran clergymen like M.L. Gordon and William Elliot Griffis, Japan had become "Christian at heart," if not in name.[6]

Other prominent missionaries and journalists pushed these claims even further by contrasting Japan's achievements with Russia's stagnation. In the estimation of war correspondent George Kennan, the Japanese were more modern, civilized, and Christian than the Russians. Kennan's opinion was of particular significance: he first had become prominent in the late nineteenth century by writing and lecturing on the tyranny of tsarist Russia.[7] Clergymen also charged that Russia stood outside the fold of Christendom. They wrote that the Russian Orthodox Church bore no resemblance to the Christianity of progressive, Western nations. Medieval and oppressive, Russia's "sham Christianity" was plagued by superstition and the fetishism of icons. American observers pointed out that freedom of religion did not exist in Russia. A stark contrast with constitutional Japan, absolutist Russia encouraged religious persecution—an anti-Semitic pogrom in Kishinev in 1903 had provoked wide condemnation in the United States. According to American missionaries, Russia was "the least civilized nation of Europe" and an obstacle to "civilizing and Christianizing" East Asia. Because of Japan's constitutional commitment to religious toleration, they argued that it was, in fact, "more Christian" than "so-called Christian Russia."[8]

In a 1904 meeting with Presbyterian missionary William M. Imbrie, Prime Minister Katsura Tarō underscored these points, urging Americans to recognize that Japan was defending religious and political freedoms. In May, Imbrie conveyed Katsura's message to a crowd of 1,000 at a Tokyo meeting of religious organizations, and other missionaries reported the statement to journals in the United States. By the end of the Russo-Japanese War, many Americans agreed that the victor was Christian civilization as represented by Japan.[9]

Another variation of this approach focused on racially categorizing the Russians. At the May meeting in Tokyo, a Buddhist representative declared that the Russians, not the Japanese, were Mongols who constituted the true "Yellow Peril." In other venues, former cabinet minister Kaneko Kentarō and journalist Taguchi Ukichi made the same argument.[10] Other observers based their racial arguments on Russian social and political characteristics. Admitting that the Russians were members of the Caucasian race, American analysts divided it into two subcategories: Anglo-Saxon and Slav. In noting that Russians were a Slavic people, Americans identified them as an inferior group of whites. Anglo-Saxons, on the other hand, had proved their superiority by building the progressive nations of Great Britain and the United States. Because the Russians were Slavic, they were less capable than Anglo-Saxons and so remained mired in medieval autocracy. Consequently, wrote an American journalist, Russia stood for "methods, both social and political, precisely opposite to our own."[11]

Japan, on the other hand, was the only Asian nation to adopt Anglo-Saxon principles of government. According to missionary Sidney Gulick, Japan had "passed out of exclusively oriental life and is to-day, in important respects occidental," because it had adopted public education and constitutional government—the social and political hallmarks of "Anglo-Saxon civilization."[12] Thus, the military conflict between Japan and Russia was also political: democracy and progress were pitted against the "white peril" of autocracy and absolutism. American writers frequently noted that Japan had shed its Asiatic features to become "more European or generally Western" than its enemy.[13] Japan also was acting as an Anglo-Saxon proxy in the competition for imperial power in East Asia. Influential military strategist Alfred Mahan, who as a young naval officer had visited Japan in 1867–9, contended in his work *The Problem of Asia* that the Japanese were "racially Asiatic" but "adoptively European." As a sea power, Japan was a natural ally of the United States and Great Britain in the effort to thwart the expansion of Slavic Russia, a land power bent on establishing an exclusive commercial sphere in China.[14] Japan had successfully adopted those institutions and strategic interests that defined Christian, Anglo-Saxon nations.

The Japanese government deliberately encouraged such views, dispatching Kaneko to the United States in 1904 with the task of influencing American public opinion.[15] A graduate of Harvard Law School who had helped to draft Japan's 1889 constitution, Kaneko underscored similarities between American and Japanese interests in East Asia and warned of the differences between these and Russian interests. Along with Takahira Kogorō, Japan's Minister to the United States, and University of Chicago lecturer Ienaga Toyokichi, Kaneko published a stream of essays in American journals, arguing that the United States and Japan were working together to open the wealth of China to a fair commercial contest. Russia, however, hoped to absorb Manchuria and monopolize its trade. Russian victory in the war, the Japanese argued, would prevent the further spread of Western civilization in East Asia.[16] Kaneko reminded Americans that Japan steadily continued to introduce Western commerce and civilization to its less progressive continental neighbors, China and Korea. According to Kaneko:

[Japan], though Oriental, stands for modern Western civilization, and its success will mean ... the occidentalizing of the East. The other, though European, stands for an absolutism that is Oriental, and its success will mean the perpetuation of ignorance and the reign of force.[17]

These arguments convinced many Americans that Japan had earned a seat alongside the modern, constitutional powers of the West, while tsarist autocracy prevented Russia from progressing. Armed with this explanation, Americans were able to conclude that Japan's victory in 1905 did not undermine their belief in Christian, Anglo-Saxon superiority. Instead, the Russo-Japanese War supported that cherished principle: Japan had triumphed because it was more Christian, Western, and Anglo-Saxon than Russia.

The second American explanation for Japan's success focused on the Ainu. American interest in the Ainu grew in the last decades of the nineteenth century and resulted in a large number of popular and scholarly publications. These frequently emphasized similarities between the Ainu and Native Americans. Both were "lower types of human existence," according to Romyn Hitchcock, who collected Ainu artifacts in Hokkaido for the United States National Museum at the Smithsonian Institution.[18] Such conclusions were especially significant because, to many scholars, the Japanese conquest of the Ainu was a historical parallel to the United States' conquest of Native Americans.

In a paper first presented at the American Historical Association in 1893, Frederick Jackson Turner contended that American inventiveness and individualism had been forged by the nation's experience on its frontier: "the meeting point between savagery and civilization."[19] According to Turner's influential "frontier thesis," white settlers had relentlessly pushed the American frontier westward, extending the territory of civilization by conquering uncivilized Native Americans. Other Americans argued that Japan, too, had its own history of expansion: the prehistoric Yamato Japanese had moved northeastward as their civilization gradually swept aside the "primitive" Ainu.[20] "They are to the Japanese what the Indians are to the other people of America," claimed Congregational missionary Cyrus A. Clark.[21] He and his fellow American observers believed that, like themselves, the Japanese were a progressive and expansive people. In emphasizing these similarities, Americans thought that they had found a partial explanation for Meiji Japan's successes. The Japanese frontier experience had molded a nation able to fight for the advance of civilization.

The difficulty with this approach, however, was that the Ainu appeared to be white. Since the earliest scientific descriptions, Americans had emphasized the fairness of Ainu skin and the full beards of their men, which seemed to indicate that the Ainu were a Caucasian or Aryan people.[22] Scholarly authorities, such as anthropologists Frederick Starr and W.J. McGee, continued to back this hypothesis. (McGee himself did not use periods after his initials.) Starr, a University of Chicago professor, and

McGee, head of the Smithsonian Institution's Bureau of American Ethnology, brought a group of nine Ainu to the Louisiana Purchase Exposition in St Louis in 1904 as a living exhibit and concluded that the Ainu were Caucasian rather than Mongolian.[23] Also, John Batchelor, a long-serving British missionary to the Ainu and author of an Ainu–English–Japanese dictionary, determined that the Ainu language was Aryan and that the Ainu people were of Aryan stock.[24]

But in American racial ideology, how could superior whites—the Ainu—be a conquered people on the savage side of a frontier? Again, the answer lay in subdividing the white race: like the Russians, the Ainu were Slavic. Since the 1860s, when they first attracted the interest of American scholars, those who studied the Ainu had occasionally identified physical similarities between them and the Russians. The Ainu seemed to be from the Slavic branch of the Aryan family tree.[25] In 1904, scholar Paul Carus, accompanied by Starr, visited the Ainu in St Louis and later wrote in the journal *Open Court* that they, obviously white, were closest in blood to the Russians. In a conclusion similar to Kaneko's critique of Russian absolutism, he observed that the Ainu, much like Russian peasants, were "submissive" and "amenable to authority."[26] These characteristics stood in sharp contrast to the progressiveness and expansionism of the Japanese and Americans. To these American observers, categorizing both the Ainu and Russians as Slavic explained why they had failed when confronted by superior Japanese civilization. Although white, the Ainu and Russians were backward Slavs, not progressive and conquering Anglo-Saxons or Japanese. First in ancient history and then in modern times, Japan had indeed defeated two white peoples, but both were ostensibly less capable Slavic whites.

The third racial explanation of Meiji Japan's accomplishments focused on characteristics of the Japanese themselves. During the Russo-Japanese War, a writer joked in the *Nation* that the American Secretary of State should ceremonially adopt the Japanese into the white race,[27] but, in the decade following the war, some American experts on Japan argued that the Japanese were physically as well as adoptively white. Arthur May Knapp, a missionary and writer, pointed out that the Japanese complexion was as white as that of southern Europeans, another immigrant group facing nativism in the United States. Based on the Japanese capacity for progress, however, Knapp suggested that they were "Aryans to all intents and purposes."[28] His observation attracted the support of prominent *Outlook* correspondent Kennan and *Current Opinion*, which observed that Knapp provided an "ethnological basis" for explaining "why Japanese are white."[29]

In such efforts to recategorize the Japanese, William Elliot Griffis also attempted to focus American attention on the Ainu. Griffis, who served as pastor of Reformed and Congregational churches in the United States, had been a natural science teacher in Fukui and Tokyo in 1870–4 and became the most prolific and respected American writer on Japan in the late nineteenth and early twentieth centuries. (Komura Jutarō, Japan's Foreign

Minister during the Russo-Japanese War, had been one of Griffis' students at Kaisei Gakkō in Tokyo.) In addition to his writings, Griffis also lectured at churches, universities, and business associations. Because of his reputation as an authority on Japan, his pronouncements frequently attracted favorable attention in popular journals. Disregarding the theory that the Ainu were Slavic, Griffis emphasized instead their white characteristics. While discussing the intermixture of races in prehistoric Japan in his most influential work, *The Mikado's Empire*, he wrote that the primary racial stock of the Japanese was Ainu. (First published in 1876, *The Mikado's Empire* appeared in its eleventh edition in 1906.) In this popular work, he claimed that the prehistoric Ainu, who had lived throughout the archipelago, had been assimilated and had contributed the main component of the modern Japanese racial heritage. The Ainu remaining on Hokkaido were the descendants of those who had resisted Japanese expansion and had not been assimilated.[30]

After the Russo-Japanese War, Griffis emphasized the implications of the Japanese assimilation of the Ainu. The title page of his work *The Japanese Nation in Evolution* bore the epigraph "Race is the key to history."[31] Facing it was a portrait of Admiral Tōgō Heihachirō, who had commanded the victorious Japanese fleet at the Battle of Tsushima. In the book, Griffis contended that the aboriginal Ainu, who had provided the basic racial stock of the Japanese people, were white and their language Aryan. A photo of three Ainu men bore the title "Our Aryan Kinsmen in Japan."[32] Linguistics, archaeology, and history thus seemed to demonstrate ancestral links between the Japanese and Europeans. Having absorbed the Ainu, the Japanese were not Mongolian, Griffis claimed: the Japanese "at base are a 'white race'."[33] From this perspective, the Japanese were white because their basic racial and linguistic composition had included the white Ainu. A promotional pamphlet for *The Japanese Nation in Evolution* declared that it revealed for the first time the secret of Japan's success: "The White Blood in the Japanese."[34]

In the years following the Russo-Japanese War, Knapp, Kennan, and Griffis hoped that their efforts to promote the Japanese would influence US policy. From their expert perspectives, the Japanese were not an alien race but forgotten relatives, and so deserved to be treated as equals. Furthermore, Japan had successfully assimilated Anglo-Saxon political institutions. These national achievements supported the attempt to convince Americans that the Japanese were "free white persons" and thus statutorily fit for US citizenship. Doing so would undermine the growing movement to prohibit Japanese immigration.

Ultimately, such views did not sway policy, but neither were they unheard. Ozawa's attorney, George W. Wickersham, echoed these arguments. Addressing the Supreme Court in 1922, he referred to the Ainu as a Caucasian people and to the Japanese as free white persons. Wickersham concluded that the Japanese, "speaking an Aryan tongue and having Caucasian root stocks," were assimilable into American society.[35] The Court's decision against Ozawa would facilitate Congress's exclusion of Japanese immigrants two years later.

Racism and respect

Compared to the waves of immigration from southern and eastern Europe to the United States in the late nineteenth and early twentieth centuries, the flow of immigration from Japan was a trickle. While millions of European immigrants crossed the Atlantic, only 244,483 Japanese crossed the Pacific from 1901 to 1924.[36] Despite their relatively low numbers, Japanese immigrants encountered fierce racial hostility. In many ways, the campaign against Japanese immigration represented a continuation of the agitation against Chinese immigrants that culminated in the Chinese Exclusion Act of 1882. Anti-Japanese activists argued that Japanese immigrant laborers would undercut employment and wage opportunities for American workers. They contended that the Japanese were members of an "immoral" Asian race that would "contaminate" American whites and never assimilate into American society. Some members of Congress reminded the public that Japan's recent emergence from "barbarism" undermined any claim of the "wondrous superiority of this branch of the yellow race over the white races."[37] Although anti-Japanese activists recycled many of the racial arguments used against the Chinese, there were notable differences. As they racially castigated the Japanese, American politicians often simultaneously expressed admiration for Japan as a newly powerful and great nation. Japan's military triumphs led to public professions of respect, even from national anti-Japanese leaders who attacked its immigrants as members of an undesirable and unassimilable race.

As Washington and Tokyo worked to control the course of diplomacy in the last months of the Russo-Japanese War, America's Pacific coast provided unsettling diversions. In early 1905, the *San Francisco Chronicle* published a series of articles and editorials decrying the "invasion" of "little brown men" from Japan. The newspaper predicted that the number of immigrants would sharply increase when the war ended.[38] In May, the newly formed Japanese and Korean Exclusion League began campaigning against Japanese immigration and for segregation of Asian school children in San Francisco. The League realized its latter goal in October 1906, when the city's Board of Education ordered principals to send Asian children to a separate Oriental Public School. The board claimed its decision was a response to school overcrowding that had resulted from a devastating earthquake six months earlier and to the allegation that many Asian students were adults, whose attendance threatened the moral atmosphere of the schools. Few in San Francisco seemed to remember that Japan had contributed more in earthquake relief aid than all other countries combined.

In Washington, Congress considered Japanese immigration during hearings and floor debates on immigration legislation. Andrew Furuseth, a vice-president of the Japanese and Korean Exclusion League, offered a different perspective on the racial and political critique of Russia that American friends of Japan had introduced during the war. In congressional hearings, he referred to the thirteenth-century Mongol invasion of European Russia. Its soil, he observed, was soaked with Caucasian blood spilled by Mongolians. Furuseth instructed members of the House Committee on Foreign Affairs that the autocratic character of the Russian people had been forged in the fight to drive the Mongolians back over the Ural Mountains. He implicitly accepted Kaneko's censure of the Russian people's submission to autocratic authority but argued that it had developed only as the result of a "great race struggle," led by the tsar, to expel the alien Mongols. This was Turner's frontier thesis turned on its head: the struggle between savagery and civilization in Russia had produced an ingrained dependence, not individualism, in the Russian people. The political and social flaws of modern Russia thus were attributable to the Mongolian race, whose descendants, in Furuseth's view, were the Chinese and Japanese. The United States now faced a similar racial threat. "What is the West [the US Pacific region] going to be," he asked, "yellow or white?"[39] From this perspective, the racial struggle of the American frontier had not yet ended. It had simply shifted from the northern plains to the west coast.

The following year, Griffis again attempted to reverse these popular racial classifications. The Japanese were not members of the Mongolian race, he argued, despite the frequent use of the words "Mongol" and "Mongolian" in reference to the Japanese. Indeed, the Mongol invasion of Russia had infused Mongolian blood into the Slavic race. Japan, in contrast, had successfully resisted the Mongol onslaught when storms in the Tsushima Strait forced the invasion fleets to retreat. "Significantly enough in the same waters," Griffis wrote, "the semi-Mongol Russians, . . . in 1905, were checked by Admiral Tōgō Heihachirō."[40] In Griffis's racial framework, the Japanese were white, and the Russians were Mongolian. Such efforts failed to sway opponents of Japanese immigration.

At the heart of the anti-Japanese campaign, however, was a contradiction. While its national leaders declared their distaste for the Japanese as representatives of the Mongolian race, many also expressed respect for the Japanese nation. In a speech to the House of Representatives, Congressman Everis A. Hayes of California, citing his own personal contacts with Japanese, alleged that the vast majority were dishonest, immoral, and licentious. Because of such personal characteristics, he argued for the exclusion of Japanese immigrants, yet he encouraged his colleagues to "shout our bravos to the plucky little island nation," which had triumphantly overcome its geographical size disadvantage in the Russo-Japanese War by relying on courage and discipline. Hayes claimed to glory in the achievements of "our sister nation" and to oppose any efforts to slow Japan's progress.[41]

Other politicians attempted to mask their racism under the guise of the "separate but equal" doctrine that the Supreme Court had enshrined a decade earlier in its *Plessy* v. *Ferguson* decision. Senator John Gearin of Oregon, another opponent of Japanese immigration, argued that the white and yellow races were distinct and antagonistic. The history of Christendom was the history of the white race, which dominated other races because of centuries of superior mental and spiritual training. Thus, white men were "fitted for the duties and responsibilities of American citizenship." Japan was a friendly nation, but its civilization was utterly different. Asian and Christian civilizations had never successfully mixed, nor could the yellow and white races. "I do not say that they are inferior to us," said Gearin on the Senate floor. "[T]hey are different, that is all; and the difference is so striking—such a radical difference—that the two peoples can never become one people or become amalgamated at all."[42] As Hayes, Gearin, and their colleagues understood, Japan's military achievements posed a potential threat to the United States. The interests of the two nations could clash in the Pacific. Senator Francis G. Newlands of Nevada pointed out that the United States' possession of the Philippines now depended on good relations with Japan. "[W]e shall never be able to retain them if Japan says 'No'."[43] The anti-Japanese campaign thus threatened to undermine American interests if it appeared as unduly insulting to Japan. Racism had to be wrapped in respect.

Although Kennan and Griffis failed to convince American leaders that the Japanese were white, the Russo-Japanese War influenced American political rhetoric on Japan. It made clear to Americans that a new power and potential rival was on their Pacific doorstep. Even to those who viewed the Japanese as a flawed (if not inferior) race, Japan as a nation commanded respect by virtue of its rapid economic and military development. This same progress, however, was also cause for concern. America's newly won Pacific territories were now vulnerable to Japan. Opponents of Japanese immigration linked their racial attacks to the language of international respect to avoid outright provocation. Many leaders of the anti-Japanese movement thus praised the Japanese nation while denigrating its people.

President Theodore Roosevelt, a geo-strategic thinker who understood the risks posed by a powerful Japan and the anti-Japanese campaign, acted quickly to minimize them. In the Katsura–Taft Agreement of 1905, Roosevelt traded Japanese non-interference in the Philippines for the United States' non-interference in Korea, which Japan later annexed. In his annual message to Congress in December 1906, Roosevelt praised Japan as "one of the greatest of civilized nations" whose people were equal to "the foremost and most enlightened peoples of Europe and America." The San Francisco segregation order, the president observed, was a "wicked absurdity" representing "a confession of inferiority in our civilization." He then asked Congress to pass legislation offering naturalized citizenship to Japanese immigrants, a request that fell on deaf ears and which he pursued no further.[44] Accusing Roosevelt of favoring the Japanese over Americans,

California legislators and newspapers condemned his speech as a slap in the face. One congressman mocked the president's attempts to appease Japan by referring to his oft-cited motto, "speak softly and carry a big stick." Roosevelt's vaunted big stick, joked Anthony Michalek, himself an immigrant from Bohemia, had shrunk "to the magnificent dimensions of a toothpick."[45]

The president, however, continued to wield his formidable negotiating skills, with which he had mediated the Treaty of Portsmouth and won the 1906 Nobel Peace Prize. Conferring separately with the San Francisco Board of Education, the California congressional delegation, the congressional leadership, and the Japanese government, Roosevelt constructed a package of bargains to resolve the conflict. After White House meetings in February, the Board of Education rescinded the segregation order. In Congress, Speaker of the House Joseph Cannon attached an amendment to the immigration bill then under consideration that allowed the president to limit Japanese labor immigration from Hawaii, Canada, and Mexico. After Congress passed the bill in February, Roosevelt issued an executive order exercising this new power.

In diplomatic exchanges with Washington in early 1907, Tokyo indicated that it was willing to accept exclusion of Japanese immigrants if the United States granted naturalization rights. In effect, Japan suggested that Roosevelt put his money where his mouth had been in his address to Congress. Secretary of State Elihu Root, however, informed the Japanese that this was impossible: Congress would neither pass legislation nor ratify a treaty that offered naturalization to Japanese residents.[46] These talks eventually produced an exchange of diplomatic notes, the "Gentlemen's Agreement" of 1907–8, in which the Japanese vowed not to issue passports to laborers intending to go to the United States. Although Japan failed to win naturalization rights, it temporarily avoided the public humiliation of unilateral statutory exclusion. As Roosevelt had hoped, the "Gentlemen's Agreement" derailed congressional proposals for exclusion legislation.

As efforts to recategorize the Japanese as white sputtered, other tensions between the United States and Japan flared. In the late spring and summer of 1907, many newspapers in both countries predicted that war loomed on the horizon, even though Japan's military leadership continued to regard Russia, not the United States, as its most immediate concern. In May, mobs in San Francisco demonstrated outside Japanese restaurants and attacked customers, fueling the war scare. One American humorist imagined Roosevelt cowering under his bed with a dictionary learning to say "Spare us" in Japanese.[47] Instead, the president requested and received from the Joint Board of the Army and Navy contingency plans for war with Japan. The Board recommended that the American battleship fleet be sent to the Pacific, a conclusion with which Roosevelt concurred. In August, he announced that the fleet would sail. In addition to impressing the Japanese, he also intended the world cruise to bolster American support for his naval construction program and for the Republican Party's election prospects. In the fall, the war scare subsided in the midst of the warm reception afforded to Secretary of War William Taft during his visit to Japan. The American fleet was also well received when it visited Japan the following year. The racial animosities that had emerged since Japan's victory over Russia, however, did not disappear.

Conclusion

The Russo-Japanese War unleashed a variety of forces in American thought and politics. It opened new hopes for American friends of Japan, new fears and animosities among its adversaries, and new challenges for statesmen. For nearly two decades after the war, advocates like Griffis and Gulick attempted to promote the Japanese in American public opinion. Simultaneously, the anti-Japanese movement gained momentum on the Pacific coast. At the federal level, American statesmen attempted to preserve the American–Japanese friendship while also preparing for conflict.

In 1904, the fictitious character Mr Dooley reflected on the 50 years of American–Japanese relations that began with the Treaty of Kanagawa in 1854. Created by journalist Peter Finley Dunne, Mr Dooley was an Irish-American, Chicago saloon-keeper who philosophized about current events. Looking back over the half-century since Commodore Matthew C. Perry challenged Japan's seclusion, Mr Dooley observed, "We opened it up, . . . an' what did we find? . . . We didn't go in. There wasn't room. They come out."[48] Japan indeed had surprised many. A "heathen" Asian nation had accomplished in 50 years what had taken the United States and Europe some two centuries. Meiji Japan had transformed itself into an industrial-ized, militarily powerful, constitutional democracy. According to American assumptions about race and religion, this should have been impossible. Yet the evidence was incontrovertible. This gave Americans the chance to question the accuracy, indeed the very validity, of racial and religious hierarchies.

But Americans, even Japan's greatest friends, saw the matter differently. They declined to challenge their fundamental assumptions: "white" remained superior. Instead, they provided interpretations that reconciled the belief in white, Anglo-Saxon superiority with the seeming contradictions posed by Japan's stunning rise to power. Leading American authorities on Japan looked for and found various means to reposition the Japanese. Rather than question or abandon such hierarchies, these Americans preserved them, while promoting the Japanese within them.

Gulick was somewhat of an exception. Although he proposed establishing immigration quotas on the basis of race, he advocated removing all racial restrictions from the right to citizenship. According to Gulick, who taught at Dōshisha University in Kyoto from 1906 to 1913, the status of Japanese immigrants in the United States would remain precarious so long as they were ineligible to become naturalized citizens. Pointing out that the US Census Bureau included Mexicans, South Americans, Turks, and Arabs as "foreign-born white" persons, he argued that it was absurd for American courts to hold that "free white persons" included only Caucasians. Gulick concluded that Congress had the responsibility to correct this situation by redefining the qualifications for citizenship.[49]

Voices like those of Griffis and Gulick were heard by political leaders, but their calls for a reappraisal of the Japanese went largely unheeded. In fact, Congressman Hayes cited Gulick's work, *Evolution of the Japanese*, on the House floor. He did so, however, selectively and in defense of his claims that Japan was plagued by dishonesty and prostitution.[50] When Gulick testified before the Senate Committee on Immigration in 1914, one senator advised him to save his breath: "America has made up its mind as to what it is going to do with the Asiatic, and there is not a particle of use in your attempting to budge it."[51] Most Americans rejected not only the promotion of the Japanese to "white" status, but also the notion of removing racial restrictions on citizenship.

In the years following the Russo-Japanese War, the anti-Japanese movement outpaced the work of Japan's friends in the United States. California passed the Alien Land Law in 1913, prohibiting Japanese immigrants from owning land. The Supreme Court decided the Ozawa case in 1922, determining that Japanese immigrants were not white persons and therefore not entitled to naturalized citizenship. (Racial restrictions on citizenship remained in effect until 1952.) Also, Congress passed the National Origins Act in 1924, excluding Japanese immigrants and sharply reducing the numbers of southern and eastern European immigrants through the use of nationality quotas. Neither the Alien Land Law nor the National Origins Act mentioned the Japanese by name: instead, by legislative sleight of hand, they targeted Japanese immigrants by directing their legal prohibitions against "aliens ineligible to citizenship." By failing to question the validity of racial and religious hierarchies, most American friends of Meiji Japan indirectly assisted in ensuring their survival.

Notes

1 United States Supreme Court, 1922: 198.
2 Bailey, 1934; Esthus, 1966; Iriye, 1972; Neu, 1967.
3 Henning, 2000; Horsman, 1981; Hunt, 1987; Kowner, 2000b.
4 Cary, 1976: 296.
5 Hallock, 1905; Hulbert, 1904; Jones, 1895.
6 Gordon, 1899: 364; Griffis, 1906: 717; Harris, 1907: 39.
7 Kennan, 1904; Travis, 1990.
8 Griffis, 1905: 183; 1904: 185; *Missionary Review of the World*, 1904: 300; DeForest, 1905: 170.
9 Cosand, 1904: 573–4; Imbrie, 1906: 24–30; *Japan Weekly Mail*, 1904: 580.
10 *Japan Weekly Mail*, 1904: 580; Kimitada, 1974: 46; Stewart, 1904: 27.
11 Mahan, 1900: 41–4, 113–22, 150; Powell, 1904: 4.

12 Gulick, 1905: 88, 91–2.
13 Carus, 1904: 431.
14 Mahan, 1900: xix, 41–4, 113–22, 150; Reinsch, 1905.
15 Matsumura, 1987; Valliant, 1974: 422–5.
16 Ienaga, 1904; Kaneko, 1904; Takahira, 1904.
17 Kaneko, 1905: 5868–9.
18 Hitchcock, 1891: 442–3.
19 Turner, 1920: 3.
20 *Foreign Missionary*, 1877: 193–4; Todd, 1898: 350.
21 Clark, 1904: 63.
22 Bickmore, 1868a: 359–61; 1868b: 373–6; Brockett, 1888: 98.
23 McGee, 1904: vi; Starr, 1904: 107–10.
24 Batchelor, 1901: 11.
25 Bickmore, 1868a: 360; 1868b: 373–4.
26 Carus, 1905: 166, 168.
27 *Nation*, 1904: 255.
28 Knapp, 1912: 339–40; 1897: 5.
29 Kennan, 1912: 822; *Current Opinion*, 1913: 38–9.
30 Griffis, 1906: 34–5, 86–7.
31 Griffis, 1907a: i–ii.
32 Griffis, 1907a: facing 10.
33 Griffis, 1913: 723.
34 Griffis, 1907b.
35 United States Supreme Court, 1922: 179–86.
36 Daniels, 1977: 111.
37 United States Congress, 1905–7, February 18, 1907: 3229.
38 Daniels, 1977: 25.
39 Subcommittee on Chinese-Exclusion Bill, 1906: 166–8.
40 Griffis, 1907a: 209–14.
41 United States Congress, 1905–7, March 13, 1906: 3749–50.
42 United States Congress, 1905–7, January 7, 1907: 680.
43 United States Congress, 1905–7, February 16, 1907: 3098.
44 Roosevelt, 1906: 7054–5.
45 United States Congress, 1905–7, February 18, 1907: 3229.
46 Jessup, 1938: 19.
47 *Literary Digest*, 1907: 977.
48 Dunne, 1904: 1B.
49 Gulick, 1918: 24–5, 66–8.
50 United States Congress, 1905–7, March 13, 1906: 3749.
51 Gulick, 1918: 122.

Part III

East Asia and the colonial world

11 The impact of the war on China

Harold Z. Schiffrin

1905 was a decisive year in modern Chinese history. The imperial court authorized the study of foreign constitutions and appointed a commission to go abroad and study the subject. This was the first step toward establishing a constitutional monarchy. Next came the decision to abolish the traditional civil service examination system. This removed the main prop of the Confucian political system and weakened the incentive for studying the classics.[1] The result was a more rapid expansion of modern education, which was based largely upon the Japanese model, which also provided the example for the establishment of a Ministry of Education. More students were sent to study in Japan. The maximum number was estimated at between 8,000 and 9,000 in 1906.[2] Military modernization was accelerated, and, for the first time, many intellectuals and literati began enrolling in military academies and even enlisted as soldiers.[3] That same year, 1905, China's first modern-type political party, the Tongmenghui (United League), was formed under the leadership of Sun Yat-sen. Dedicated to the overthrow of the Qing (Manchu) dynasty, it advocated nationalism, democracy, and a form of socialism.[4] In addition, in 1905 the Chinese invoked an anti-American boycott because of discriminatory immigration laws that had been extended to include the Philippines. This was the first time that the boycott was used as a nationalist weapon, and the initiative came from public opinion, not from the throne. A Chinese historian called this "The best evidence of the birth of a national feeling in China."[5]

"The turning point in the world's history"

All these events that took place in China following the outbreak of the war in its northeastern territories can be subsumed under the heading "Nationalism and Modernization." Obviously, the Russo-Japanese War and Japan's victory were not directly responsible for all these developments. The first steps toward reform and modernization had already been undertaken by the throne in 1901, after the Boxer Rebellion and the invasion by the foreign powers.[6] Nationalist consciousness had been rising ever since the last decade of the nineteenth century, when both reformist and revolutionary organizations had made their appearance. Yet there can be no doubt that Japan's victory in 1905 served as a catalyst or accelerator that increased the pace and scope of all these developments. While the war invigorated the Indian and other Asian nationalist movements, the effect upon China was more immediate and intense.[7]

In support of this conclusion, it is worthwhile quoting the views of a contemporary Chinese historian who wrote about the war nine years later. Calling the conflict "The turning point in the world's history," he analyzed what he considered the "moral effect of the war in China":

> For the first time, a European power in carrying out her unrestrained aggression in Asia was obliged to own defeat at the hands of an Asiatic nation. The event was too instructive not to have its effect upon China, especially at a time when she was too weak either to participate in a war that was waged within her borders, or to compel the belligerents to respect her neutrality. Yesterday Japan was a semi-barbarous nation; today she beats Russia, becomes an ally of England, and is the only Asiatic nation that exercises jurisdiction over aliens within her borders. What may not China accomplish with her greater population, territory and resources, if only she follows in the footsteps of Japan? What will be her fate if she continues in her old ways? How can she face both Russia and Japan in Manchuria, if one of them has already proved to be more than a match for her? These are a few of the questions that suggested themselves to the mind of all thoughtful Chinese at the close of the Russo-Japanese War. Time and again has China been told what she should do; and now she knows what she can do as well as what she must do.[8]

There is no question that both the throne and the articulate public saw Japan's victory as the victory of constitutional government over autocracy. This became a common theme in the Chinese press. A Shanghai newspaper concluded that "The question of the relative merits of a constitutional monarchy and an autocratic monarchy would not have been answered had there not been this war."[9] Another paper wrote in a similar vein: "Russia's defeat is not a cause but a result; the result of her autocracy!"[10] The Japanese example also showed that modernization does not necessarily weaken central political power. And the Japanese victory gave additional influence to those who argued that domestic reform was ultimately the best defense against foreign pressures.[11] As an example, in 1906 the government began the elimination of opium-smoking, perhaps the most successful and popular of all reforms. The throne authorized political reform and began planning financial reform. And in 1907–8 it authorized the establishment of provincial assemblies, which was the most important of constitutional reforms after the war.

After the signing of the Portsmouth Treaty in September 1905, the Northeast, of course, attracted immediate attention because Japan's acquisition of Russian rights and concessions there created the major source of friction between the two countries. Instead of the term "Manchuria," which is a "modern creation, used mainly by Westerners and Japanese," I will refer to the "Northeast," which is the shorter form of the Chinese term, "Three Northeast Provinces—*Dongbei Sansheng*."[12] How the Chinese government tried to deal with this new situation will be discussed later.

Chinese attitudes to the war

First, it is worth noting how the Chinese public, in particular the more articulate sector—students, and reformist and revolutionary leaders like Liang Qichao and Sun Yat-sen—reacted to the war. Before the war, Chinese students in Tokyo organized a "Resist Russia" movement in order to force the government to compel the Russians to remove the troops they had sent to the Northeast during the Boxer Rebellion. In 1903 they formed a student army with several hundred members. They volunteered to return to China to help defend the Northeast, and sent a telegram to Yuan Shikai, the most important official in North China, and urged that he resist Russia. Naturally, the Chinese government was in no position to fight Russia, and, in any case, it was suspicious of the students' motives, since they did not hide their anti-Manchu feelings. Pressure from the Chinese government, with assistance from the Japanese authorities, caused the dissolution of the student army.[13]

In February 1904, when the war began, there were rumors that a number of students contributed to the Japanese war fund, and that they had even requested permission to join the Imperial Japanese Army as volunteers. Students in Zhejiang province agitated for military training.[14] The general opinion among the students was that Japan would win, but, in any case, China would be the loser. Still, better to be on the side of the winners instead of being passive neutrals. The overseas Chinese (*huaqiao*) were also concerned. On February 16, a week after the war began, Chinese from America, Australia, Asia, and Africa sent telegrams to the Chinese Foreign Office, asking that China join Japan against Russia in order to protect the Northeast. But a few days earlier, February 12, China had declared neutrality, and that same day the United States requested both Japan and Russia to honor Chinese neutrality.[15] But, as expected, both belligerents ignored these statements. Meanwhile, the declaration of neutrality further inflamed anti-Manchu sentiments among students in China and abroad. As an alien, and not ethnic Chinese dynasty, the Manchus were vulnerable to the charge of not being fully committed to protecting the nation's honor and sovereignty. The suspicion, of course, was baseless, as demonstrated by the government's attempts to resist imperialist incursions in the past and by its efforts to defend the Northeast.

The war naturally aroused tremendous interest in China. This was the period of the flowering of modern Chinese journalism and the growing power of public opinion. In 1904 the Commercial Press of Shanghai began publishing a special magazine, *Ri-E Zhanji* (Japanese–Russian War Chronicle), which was devoted solely to the course of the conflict.[16] The unique characteristic of the war was that the battlefield was the territory of a third, neutral, sovereign nation. This was unprecedented in modern international relations.[17] More than anything else, it exposed the weakness of the Qing dynasty and China's inferior status in the international community. In attacking the government's neutral stand, some students stressed that common cultural and ethnic ties obligated China to join Japan in the war. Not only the students but public opinion in general favored Japan. But these feelings were not sufficient to dispel distrust of Japan's ultimate motives. When the war broke out, a Shanghai newspaper that had been formed in 1903 to sound the alarm against Russia now warned that ultimately Japan would be as predatory as Russia.[18] Even those students who called for joint Sino-Japanese action against Russia and who spoke about Yellow-race solidarity against the White race, did not subscribe to Sun Yat-sen's dream of a Pan-Asian alliance. Actually, after Japan's victory, this new evidence of its power soon contributed to fear of Japanese imperialist designs. Added to this was the students' resentment of Japanese arrogant and discriminatory behavior.

The experience of Lu Xun, who was studying medicine in Sendai during the war, exemplifies the demeaning attitude toward Chinese students. But Lu's experience also shows that decent and solicitous feelings toward Chinese students were not absent. When Lu, who was the only Chinese enrolled, received a passing grade in the first-year anatomy course, some of his Japanese classmates accused him of getting the questions beforehand from the instructor. Why were they suspicious? Lu explained it sarcastically: "China is a weak country, therefore the Chinese must be an inferior people, and for a Chinese to get more than sixty marks could not be due to his own efforts." Then, in his second year, when the class was treated to a magic lantern show, he had to join the cheering and clapping when slides of Japanese victories were shown. But when his classmates cheered and shouted "Banzai" at the sight of Chinese being executed as Russian spies while other Chinese looked on, he was deeply affected by what he saw as the tragic apathy of the Chinese people. "At that time and in that place," he wrote, "it made me change my mind," and soon afterward he gave up the study of medicine and left Sendai. However, it is worth noting that the main theme of his reminiscent essay was to pay tribute to his Japanese teacher, Mr Fujino, who treated him kindly, corrected his notes and took pains to make sure that he had learned the material. Thus, it was not so much resentment of Japan as it was pity for his own people and his determination to "change their spirit" that motivated his decision to leave

Japan and pursue a literary career that would make him one of the greatest writers of modern China.[19]

In addition to increased anti-Manchu feelings, the post-war period saw a rise in anti-imperialist sentiments and a growing distrust of all foreign powers. Nationalism became the dominant mood, infecting Chinese students, intellectuals, and the literate public, which was becoming larger. Yet, despite growing suspicions of Japan, there is no doubt that Chinese students were impressed by Japanese patriotism. The stories of General Nogi, who had lost two sons in the war "won universal admiration." This example of Japanese patriotism had a positive effect on Chinese nationalism.[20] Japanese chauvinism, which grew throughout the decade, reached new heights with the victory over Russia, while contempt for the Chinese grew. If the war strengthened Chinese nationalism and anti-Manchuism, however, the 1905 Russian Revolution and accounts of Russian dissidents—Nihilists and Social Revolutionaries, which were vividly portrayed in the Chinese press, probably contributed more directly to reinforcing revolutionary tendencies among students and intellectuals. Japan served as a meeting-ground for Russian and Chinese émigré revolutionaries.[21]

The reformist leader, Liang Qichao, who had formerly been optimistic concerning Japan's role, changed his mind when the war broke out. Now he was more realistic and felt that, no matter who won, China would be the loser. If Japan won, it would merely replace Russia.[22] Sun Yat-sen, however, continued to believe in Pan-Asianism based upon Sino-Japanese friendship and mutual interests.[23] The war, he said later, was a triumph of morale over superior numbers. To him, Japan's victory was above all a triumph for all Asian people, especially those who were victims of European imperialism.[24] Twenty years after the war, he told a Japanese audience that he had been in London when news arrived of Admiral Tōgō's victory in the naval battle of Tsushima Straits. Europeans, he said, were surprised, and the British, ostensibly Japan's ally, were not too happy. In their eyes, he said, Japan's victory over Russia was certainly not a blessing for the White race. In the final analysis, he concluded, "Blood is thicker than water." Later, on his way back to Asia, when his ship passed through the Suez Canal, Arab port workers told him how happy they were when they saw Russian hospital ships carrying the wounded back to Russia. This had proved to them that Japan had won the war.[25] In 1913 he argued that Japan had merely fought Russia to protect its rights in Korea, and that Russia posed a greater danger to China.[26] But Sun's optimistic view of Japan's intentions toward China was not typical of Chinese public opinion. Liang Qichao's more realistic attitude has already been noted. The thousands of students in Japan did not enjoy the special treatment that Sun received from his Japanese hosts.[27] Sun was on close terms with members of the Japanese elite, such as Inukai Tsuyoshi and Kodama Gentarō. He did not suffer from the insults and humiliation so many students experienced in their day-to-day contact with Japanese.[28]

Japanese imperialism in the Northeast

Not long after the signing of the Portsmouth Treaty of September 5, 1905, Japanese policies and behavior in the Northeast vindicated the more realistic and pessimistic views of Chinese observers. Initially, the treaty provisions relating to China did not seem to weaken but actually to strengthen China's position in the Northeast. The Russians were now evicted from the south, and, while Japan took over the Russian lease in southern Liaotung (Kwantung peninsula), including Lushun (Port Arthur) and Dairen, and the southern section of the Chinese Eastern Railway—from Lushun to Changchun (South Manchurian Railway), Japan also recognized Chinese sovereignty and administration in the entire Northeast. On December 22 China signed a treaty with Japan (the Komura Treaty) agreeing to the Portsmouth transfers, and, in return, Japan agreed not to obstruct measures that China might take for developing the area and promoting its commerce.

Instead, after 1905 Japan expanded its claims, and the entire post-war period was characterized by Sino-Japanese disputes involving competing railroad, industrial, and commercial interests. Moreover, Russia still threatened Chinese sovereignty in the north. Its position there was strengthened in July 1907 when it signed an agreement with Japan to cooperate in the Northeast: "each to support the other within its respective sphere."[29] The Manchu government, despite is declining power and popularity, tried to respond to the Japanese threat in the south as well as to the continued Russian pressure in the north. Actually, since the closing years of the nineteenth century the throne had seen the necessity of strengthening the Chinese presence in the Northeast in response to Russian advances, and had eased restrictions to Chinese immigration to what had been considered an exclusive Manchu preserve. By the turn of the century the population there was about 14 million, 80 percent of which was Chinese, most of whom were immigrants from Ho-pei (Hebei) and Shantung. However, the region had been generally neglected and, given its size (almost as large as Germany and France combined) and its resources, it was underpopulated. The Russo-Japanese War gave further impetus to the policy of strengthening the Northeast, and the government took steps to defend what was now seen as a double threat to the original Manchu homeland. More than that, the Northeast was considered vital to China's security and its future economic development. After 1905 the Manchu government could not be accused of being indifferent to the fate of the Northeast.

In 1906 it sent two leading officials, Zai Zhen and Xu Shichang, to survey the situation and propose measures to strengthen Chinese influence. Their report of January 1907 and subsequent proposals throughout the year by local officials called for the reorganization of regional finances, reorganization of civil and military administrations, spread of education, modernization of the military forces, official encouragement of Chinese settlement, including areas that had been reserved solely for Manchus, construction of railroads to compete with Japanese and Russian interests, and the opening of the Northeast to investment by foreign nations other than Japan and Russia. In short, the government was urged to take any measure that could counteract Japanese and Russian influence.[30]

In line with these recommendations, in April the government carried out a comprehensive reorganization of the region. Until then, the administration of the Northeast had been organized on a purely military basis. Now a governor-general was appointed to head the administration instead of the former Manchu General-in-Chief or Tartar General (Jiang Jun) and the military governors who had served in the three provinces—Fengtien, Kirin, and Heilungkiang—were replaced by civil governors. In other words, the Northeast was now administered in the same manner as the Chinese interior. The appointments to crucial positions reflect the seriousness of the government's intentions. Xu Shichang, an outstanding official who had held several high positions, and who would later be president of the Republic, became governor-general, and another highly qualified civil servant, the American-educated Tang Shaoyi, who later served as the first premier of the Republic, became governor of Fengtien. Both would act vigorously to protect and promote Chinese interests in the Northeast, and would frequently protest against Japanese violations of Chinese sovereignty.[31]

Despite the government's efforts to maintain Chinese sovereignty over the Northeast and develop its economy for the benefit of the entire country, it could not match the political, financial, and military superiority of the Japanese. The main Japanese instrument for exploiting its acquisitions was the South Manchurian Railway Company—usually known by its abbreviated Japanese name, Mantetsu. The Japanese invested heavily in developing the rich natural resources of the region, including coal, iron, and timber, and in the production of soybeans and in the domination of foreign trade.[32]

One explanation for Japan's policies is that it was determined to dominate the Northeast because it lacked the money to break into the European financial monopoly in the rest of China, while Britain and France were only too happy to let Japan indulge in its imperialist ambitions in the Northeast rather than threaten their own political and economic interests in China, Southeast Asia, and India.[33] Actually, it could be argued that, after 1905, the Northeast was hardly different from European colonial possessions, such as India, Java, or Indo-China.[34] The Japanese were able to achieve this not only because China did not have the power to resist, but because the European powers and the United States would not offer political assistance, despite Japanese violations of treaty obligations.

Though the American railroad magnate, Edward H. Harriman, and the American Consul General in Mukden, Willard Straight, had hoped to penetrate the Russo-Japanese domination of Northeast railroads, their plans never got off the ground because neither their government nor American financial capitalists were sufficiently interested to make this a major policy issue. After Harriman's death in September 1909, Secretary of State Knox did attempt to internationalize Northeast railways, but his so-called "neutral-ization" scheme not only met with Russian and Japanese opposition but failed to obtain British and French support. What Knox and President Taft should have realized was that these powers gave higher priority to their strategic interests in Europe, and were reluctant to antagonize their allies—Japan and Russia—who were needed in the impending conflict in Europe. In any case, in the 1908 Root–Takahira Agreement the United States had implicitly recognized Japan's special rights in the Northeast in return for a Japanese pledge to respect the security of the Philippines.[35] The American position was aptly summarized by ex-President Theodore Roosevelt, who in 1910 wrote:

> as regards Manchuria, if the Japanese choose to follow a course of conduct to which we are adverse, we cannot stop it unless we are to go to war, and a successful war about Manchuria would require a fleet as good as that of England, plus an army as good as that of Germany.[36]

So China was on its own, and its attempts to secure foreign funding to compete with the Japanese were thwarted. The fate of the proposed Hsinmintun–Fakumen railroad in Fengtien province illustrates China's isolation. When the government turned to foreign sources—first American and then British—for financing the project, the Japanese immediately began filing protests. The basis of their objection was an alleged secret clause in the 1905 Komura Treaty in which China undertook not to construct any railway parallel to the South Manchurian line or any branch line that would prejudice the interests of the Japanese railway. Tang Shaoyi, who had signed the 1905 agreement, denied the existence of this clause and argued that it had merely been discussed. Whatever the case, in November 1907 the Chinese concluded an agreement with a British firm for financing and building the railway.[37] Japanese pressure was unremitting for the next two years, and the project was dropped after the British government refused to support it, despite the fact that a British firm and British commercial interests were involved. Political, rather than economic, considerations dictated policy.

Similarly, both Britain and France catered to Russian interests and refused to support China's proposed Chinchou–Aigun railway, which would have crossed the Northeast from the south and reached the Russian border. As Foreign Secretary Grey informed parliament in June 1910, the terms of the Anglo-Russian agreement required that China first "come to terms with Russia about it" before Britain could participate in the project.[38] The Anglo-Russian agreement (1899) to which he referred had been a trade-off: Russia would not compete with the British in the Yangtze basin, and Britain would not interfere with Russian concessions "north of the Great Wall of China."[39]

Thus, despite pro forma respect for Chinese sovereignty and the "Open Door" principle, there was no effective challenge to the Japanese and

Russian claims that their strategic and economic interests gave them veto power over China's railway projects in the Northeast. These two foreign countries could determine where China could build railways and which countries could participate in the financing, construction, and operation of the lines. In effect, Japan and Russia denied China's right to develop the Northeast according to its own economic and strategic interests. Because of their own interests, the other major powers did not resist the Japanese and Russian demands. In this post-1905 period the Chinese were learning that interests, and not international agreements and commitments, dictated the foreign policies of the major powers.

Chinese resistance

This was precisely the period, however, when a new awareness of its own economic and strategic interests animated Chinese policy. The strategic danger to the Northeast was seen as especially critical because of Japanese and Russian cooperation. Leading officials warned Beijing that Japan and Russia were "strangling the Northeast."[40] Though foreigners had been extracting economic rights and infringing upon Chinese sovereignty for over 50 years since the first of the "unequal treaties" (Nanking Treaty of 1842), by 1905 Chinese resistance to imperialism had not only hardened but had assumed a more sophisticated and multifaceted form. Chinese diplomats elaborated on the time-honored technique of delaying and prolonging negotiations with stronger parties, utilized modern legal concepts, and contested every Japanese demand concerning railways, mining and forestry rights, deployment of railway guards, and other issues. In February 1909, Ijuin, the Japanese minister, protested to the Chinese Foreign Ministry that there were still six unresolved issues.[41] At the same time, Chinese diplomats kept foreign nations informed of their difficult negotiations with the Japanese and sought international assistance to finance their own projects in the region.

Though these efforts were thwarted, as already mentioned, what is particularly important is the new Chinese approach to the entire subject of economic development. In 1909 and especially in 1910 after Japan annexed Korea, Chinese officials recognized the need for major policy changes to save the Northeast. In order to create countervailing forces, there were proposals to open tax-free trading ports for a ten-year period, to revise trade agreements to encourage commerce, to allow foreigners from all countries to have mining and forestry rights and establish public companies, to borrow money to establish an industrial bank and to invest in land reclamation and increased immigration, and to develop Hulutao port.[42] In essence, these and other suggestions to eliminate trade barriers, invest in development, and institute administrative reforms almost appear to anticipate the "Reform and Open Door" policies that have changed the face of China in recent decades.

It is, of course, true that nationalist fervor had propelled a "rights recovery" movement throughout China during the post-Boxer decade,[43] but the situation in the Northeast was different in three respects. First, it was not just a matter of "recovering" rights but of defending against new and more ominous threats to Chinese territory. There was a genuine fear that the Northeast, rich in economic resources and so close to the all-important area of Beijing and the northern plain, was threatened by an aggressive neighbor. Second, by virtue of its annexation of Korea, Japan now had a common border with China. This made the threat more visible. Third, nationalist sentiments had intensified, motivating officials and exciting the public-at-large. Japan's heavy-handed methods elicited unprecedented resistance—foreshadowing the reaction to the "Twenty-one Demands" of 1915.[44]

Among the numerous points of contention, it is worth mentioning the Antung–Mukden railroad, a narrow gauge (2ft 6in) line that Japan had built to facilitate movement to the northern front during the war. The 1905 Komura Treaty had given Japan the right to improve this line. By converting the railway to standard gauge (4ft 8½in), Japan would have a railway linking the Sinuiju–Pusan line of Korea with the South Manchurian Railway at Mukden. The linkage was strategically important for Japan: it would give it the fastest route between Japan and Europe and, of course, would be a convenient military supply route to the Northeast.[45] However, what was strategically advantageous to Japan posed a threat to China, and its diplomats fiercely resisted the plan. They argued that the "improvements" authorized by the 1905 treaty did not include changing the gauge.[46] In 1909 it was still on the list of unresolved issues between the two countries as Chinese officials applied their usual delaying tactics. In the meantime, Chinese public opinion was aroused. The Antung–Mukden railway became a matter of national concern, and in August 1909 provoked anti-Japanese boycotts in Beijing, Tientsin, and the Northeast provinces.[47] Protests were sounded in far away Canton.[48] Finally, in September 1909 a Japanese ultimatum forced China to yield, and the government suppressed the anti-Japanese protest movements.[49] This additional evidence of the government's inability to resist Japanese pressure was another blow to its prestige and strengthened dissident movements, both reformist and revolutionary.

Yet China was able to score at least one victory in its contests with the Japanese. This was the Chientao dispute, which concerned the border between Kirin and Korea, which in 1905 had become a Japanese protectorate. Chientao had also been included in the list of unresolved issues submitted by Minister Ijuin in 1909. The territory is located at the source of the Yalu and north of the T'umen, the two rivers that form the border, and was settled by many Koreans. After 1905 Chinese officials protested against border violations, and in the following years there were bloody clashes with Japanese military police (*kempeitai*). In 1907 the Japanese demanded that the border be extended to all land north of the T'umen that had come under Korean cultivation. In the ensuing dispute the Chinese government received help from an unexpected source. Song Jiaoren, a major leader of the Tongmenghui, which was committed to overthrowing the Manchu dynasty, had been exploring ways to establish a revolutionary base in the Northeast but, when the border dispute arose, he switched his attention to defending the nation's sovereignty. Using geographical and historical evidence, in 1908 he wrote a monograph, *Jiandao Wenti* (The Chientao Question), which strengthened the Chinese case for retaining the T'umen river border. Although the Japanese tried to convince him that it was not in the interests of the revolutionary movement to help the Manchu government, Song gave higher priority to the need to defend territorial integrity. His monograph was published in Shanghai and helped the Chinese negotiators. Beijing was so impressed, it even offered Song a position in the Foreign Ministry, which he rejected. He had proved his patriotism but was still a revolutionary. On September 4, 1909 the dispute was settled in China's favor, with the border being fixed as the middle of the T'umen. Song had argued that Chientao was the "back gate to the Northeast, and that its loss would open the Northeast to greater Japanese pressure."[50] However, despite the settlement, in 1910 there were still reports of Japanese military police causing trouble and loss of life at Yenchi in the Chientao region.[51]

Song Jiaoren soon realized that some of the so-called Japanese "friends" of the Chinese Revolution were involved in Japan's aggressive plans for the Northeast. By 1911 he was seeing Japan not so much as a model for China, but as the major threat.[52] Except for Sun Yat-sen and some of his close associates, these anti-Japanese sentiments were widely shared among revolutionaries and the general public. Indicative of this mood was a rumor that circulated in China in the spring of 1911. Probably originating in revolutionary circles and given wide press coverage, this fictitious report charged that Japan had initiated a meeting of the world powers in Paris to plan the dismemberment of China. The rumor was circulated at a time when the public was worried about Russian, and especially Japanese, aggressive ambitions.[53] The Russo-Japanese Agreement (1907) and the Russo-Japanese Treaty (1910), in which the two powers recognized their respective spheres and provided for joint action, could not fail to intensify these fears.[54]

The question arises as to why Japan bore the brunt of anti-imperialist agitation. Russia, it could be argued, posed an even greater threat to China, not only in the Northeast but in Mongolia and Sinkiang as well. The Russians were hardly less demanding and arrogant in their dealings with Chinese officials in the Northeast, where Governor General Xiliang warned that Russia was "wildly ambitious."[55] Japan posed the greater economic challenge, however, and her proximity to China "and her intrusions into Chinese politics in defense of her sphere of influence made her a more tangible and immediate threat to the integrity of China than the distant" Western powers.[56] Hence, Chinese sources record more disputes with the Japanese.

Furthermore, an important cause of Chinese resentment may have been the feeling of betrayal. Japan had ostensibly fought the war to neutralize the Russian danger to China as well as to itself. Instead, Japan was co-operating with Russia and other imperialist powers to victimize China. Forgotten were high-sounding declarations of common cultural ties, shared values, and so on. Western arrogance and predatory ambitions were nothing new to the Chinese. But this kind of treatment from their "younger brothers" was particularly galling. In 1906 Dr George Morrison, the London *Times* correspondent who had previously championed Japan's cause against Russia, wrote that "[i]n Manchuria the Japanese are hated with a fervor that you can hardly imagine." His opinion was shared by a British doctor who claimed that the Japanese had been "received with open arms by the Chinese who remembered how well they had comported themselves in 1894–95," but "now there is not a Chinese who would not rejoice to have back the Russians.[57]

At the same time, the Japanese were enraged by Chinese defiance and what seemed like quibbling over matters like railway gauges when for the preceding 50 years China had granted wholesale concessions to Europeans. Of course, what Japan failed to realize was that China had changed. Here I might add parenthetically that there was at least one area of cooperation in the Northeast: the outbreak of plague in Harbin in 1910–11, which threatened to spread as far as northern China, led to the formation of a Sino-Japanese plague prevention conference.[58] By further exposing the inability of the government to resist Japanese demands after 1905, it can be concluded that the war had at least an indirect effect on the revolution of 1911. Chinese nationalists wanted a strong, centralized state that could mobilize the nation and roll back the imperialist tide, and the Manchu dynasty was deemed incapable of achieving this goal. Though based on its attempts to resist the Japanese after 1905, blaming the government for incompetence in foreign relations, as Song Jiaoren did, was not entirely justified.[59] When the revolution did erupt in October 1911, the Northeast remained conservative. The revolutionary movement had not been well organized there. Though anti-Japanese and anti-imperialist feelings were not lacking, anti-dynastic sentiments were subordinated to the concern for stability.[60]

Finally, the Japanese subsequently did exert the "greater pressure" Song Jiaoren had feared, and in 1931 invaded the entire Northeast. For 1905 was not only a decisive year in Chinese history, it was a turning point in Japanese history.[61] Victory in 1905 inflated Japanese ambitions and sense of destiny as a power on the Asian continent precisely at a time when Chinese nationalism and resistance to imperialism were on the rise. Antagonism was inevitable, and the potential for armed conflict increased. In a sense, this was ironic. The early years of the century had been distinguished by unprecedented Sino-Japanese cooperation. The entire Chinese reform movement of the post-Boxer era had benefited from Japanese assistance in education and in various administrative fields,[62] but by 1908 this "Golden Decade" of Sino-Japanese relations had ended and the two nations were on a collision course.

Notes

1 Schiffrin, 1970: 344–7.
2 Harrell, 1992: 2.
3 Hatano, 1968: 375.
4 Schiffrin, 1970: 361–2.
5 Li, 1914: 617.
6 Cameron, 1931: 56–180.
7 Cameron, 1931: 78; Garraty and Gay, 1972: 1037.
8 Li, 1914: 617.
9 Rhoads, 1975: 97.
10 Ch'en, 1961: 95.
11 Rhoads, 1975: 72.
12 McCormack, 1977: 4.
13 Schiffrin, 1970: 260–2.
14 Rankin, 1971: 166.
15 Guo, 1963: 1197–8.
16 Lin, 1936: 111.
17 Ch'en, 1961: 94.
18 Rankin, 1971: 99.
19 Harrell, 1992: 82; Lu, 1956: iv, v, 402–9.
20 Jansen, 1975: 153.
21 Price, 1974: 153–4, 160.
22 Price, 1974: 178–9.
23 Jansen, 1954: 210–12; Schiffrin, 1980: 172.
24 Sun, 1921: 481.
25 Sun, 1924: 164.
26 Sun, 1913: 347.
27 Harrell, 1992: 211.
28 Jansen, 1954.
29 Willoughby, 1927: 173; Griswold, 1938: 146–7.
30 Cameron, 1931: 108; Guo, 1963: 1273, 1277, 1283.
31 Brunnert and Hagelstrom, 1912: 384–6; Guo, 1963: 1273.
32 McCormack, 1977: 5–8; Myers, 1989: 101–32.
33 Griswold, 1938: 151.
34 Murphey, 1970: 48.
35 Griswold, 1938: 129.
36 Griswold, 1938: 132.
37 Guo, 1963: 1292
38 Willoughby, 1927: 186.
39 Willoughby, 1927: 146.
40 Guo, 1963: 1352.
41 Guo, 1963: 1324.
42 Guo, 1963: 1365, 1368.
43 Wright, 1968: 11–19.
44 Chow, 1960: 21–5.
45 Eto, 1986: 91.

182   *Harold Z. Schiffrin*

46 Chirol, 1976: 491.
47 Guo, 1963: 1335.
48 Wright, 1968: 9.
49 Eto, 1986: 91; Ono, 1994: 36.
50 Liew, 1971: 66–7; Price, 1984: 74; Guo, 1963: 1337.
51 Guo, 1963: 1354, 1356.
52 Price, 1984: 76.
53 Ono, 1994: 25–39.
54 Willoughby, 1927: 173, 187.
55 Guo, 1963: 1361.
56 Duus, 1983: 157.
57 Morrison, 1976: 370.
58 Guo, 1963: 1378, 1384.
59 Price, 1984: 74–8.
60 Bergere, 1968: 261; Li, 1994: 41–51; McCormack, 1977: 21, 33–4.
61 Duus, 1983: 153–7; Banno, 1983: 164.
62 Reynolds, 1993.

12 On the confluence of history and memory

The significance of the war for Korea

Guy Podoler and Michael Robinson

In the Korean traditional calendar, which is based on the Chinese 60-year cycle, the name of each year is composed of two Chinese characters. The year 1905, which happened to be the forty-second year of the cycle, is called *ŭlsa*, and in that year Japan coerced Korea into signing the Protectorate Treaty in the aftermath of its victory over Russia. Decades later, with the completion of a full cycle, historian C.I. Eugene Kim pondered over the 1965 normalization treaty with Japan and asked, "Was 1965 to be another 1905 for Korea?" "It is, indeed, paradoxical," he observed, "that, in this age when the concepts of progress and modernization have held such sway over the minds of Koreans, this cyclic notion from the cultural past still receives major attention."[1]

These reflections on the symbolic historical and cultural freight borne by the year of *ŭlsa* epitomize the impact that the Russo-Japanese War has had on Korea. In what follows we attempt to show that, however the roots and consequences of the war might be interpreted, the narrative of the war and ultimate slide into colonial rule itself is the source of an important repository of national images that have become enshrined in a central place in national memory. The war deeply influenced Korea and Koreans of the early twentieth century, and these repercussions have kept resonating throughout the postcolonial divided peninsula, playing a key role in the process of recollecting the past in the face of needs of the present and visions for the future. Accordingly, we explore the influences of the war on Korea by looking through an historical zoom lens that allows varying temporal focal points. Through this we survey the effects of the war and we show how these effects were perceived later in time.

Under this framework, our discussion relies on various agents and forms that both construct and reflect historical memory; namely, we deal with (postcolonial) historians, memorial sites, governments, and popular responses.[2] We begin with an overview of the events pertaining to Japan's takeover of Korea; although most of these have been widely examined in relevant scholarship, their presentation is nevertheless required as an historical backbone for our discussion.[3]

A colony in the making

In 1905 Japan emerged triumphant from among the countries that had been vying with each other for supremacy in Korea since the 1870s. In 1876 Japan mimicked the "gunboat diplomacy" of the Western powers to impose on Korea the unequal Kanghwa Treaty, which signaled the "opening" of the "Hermit Kingdom." Four years later Japan also became the first country to open a legation in Seoul; however, it did not proceed to strengthen its hold on Korea. Although the Kanghwa Treaty established Korea as an independent nation in the eyes of Japan, it took a war with China (1895) to eliminate the special "tributary" ties that Korea had had with that country; and another decade would pass before Japan could independently assert its unchallenged suzerainty over Korea in the aftermath of the defeat of Russia in 1905.

Disturbed by Japan's and Russia's ambitions in the 1880s, China encouraged the Korean court to sign a series of treaties with other Western countries so that Korea would "lodge itself in the web of the new diplomacy by allying with the less attentive spiders."[4] Also, after the Soldiers' Mutiny of 1882 (*Imo kullan*), during which the Japanese legation was burned down, the Japanese minister returned to Seoul with an armed force, an act to which the Chinese responded by dispatching a much larger force. They then swiftly moved on to mold the Korean political scene in line with their interests. This was especially significant following the ill-fated *Kapsin* Coup of December 1884, which was an attempt by reform-minded Koreans—with some Japanese assistance—to bring Korea's independence into effect by ending Chinese influence and implementing reforms inspired by the Meiji Restoration. The Chinese force quelled the mutiny and order was restored. Japan then proposed that both Japanese and Chinese forces withdraw from Korea, and the matter was settled in the Convention of Tientsin in April 1885. During the decade that followed, China became heavily involved in Korea's diplomatic, domestic, and economic affairs and secured its stance as the dominant foreign power on the peninsula.

In the spring of 1894 the Korean Tonghak peasant movement protested against the corrupt government by initiating a large-scale armed uprising. At the request of Queen Min, Chinese forces entered Korea to assist in putting down the rebellion, an act to which Japan quickly responded by sending an armed force of its own. After the outbreak of the Sino-Japanese War in July, the Tonghak fought to expel the Japanese that were strengthening their hold over Korea; however, their "righteous armies" (*ŭibyŏng*) were overwhelmed by government and Japanese troops. During the war with China, the Japanese took control over the Korean palace and they set up a pro-Japanese government that replaced Queen Min's pro-Chinese one. Between July 1894 and February 1896 this government launched a full-scale reform program known as the *Kabo* Reforms. It aimed to completely transform Korean traditional political, financial, and social order in accordance with modern models. It is probable that this reform effort infuriated the public much more than did the murder of Queen Min in October 1895. The elimination of the queen was an initiative by the Japanese minister in Seoul, Miura Gorō, who was worried about the growing rapprochement between the Korean court and the Russians. Russia proved its strength, while exposing Japan's weakness, when it had led the Three-power Intervention, which ended in the Japanese concession of major loots of war.[5] Thus, despite the fact that Japan had defeated China, the rising opposition against the *Kabo* Reforms and the murder of the queen were both symptomatic of temporary decline in Japanese supremacy in Korea.

In February 1896 King Kojong managed to escape from the palace to the Russian legation, where he stayed for a year, and a new government that was dominated by pro-Russian officials was formed in place of the Japanese-backed cabinet. Although the king, in an act that intended to symbolize independence, moved out of the Russian legation following pressure from the public, and announced that his country was now the "Great Han Empire"—making himself "emperor"—the following years saw the balance of dominance in Korea shift from the Japanese to the Russians. As tensions between Russia and Japan mounted, the latter was far from impressed by Korea's January 1904 declaration about its neutral stance in the conflict. Immediately after the attack in Port Arthur, a large Japanese force was sent to Korea and a first coerced agreement was signed on February 23. Two more "agreements" then followed, in August and in April 1905, and through these three protocols Japan gradually acquired control over Korea's affairs. The almost fatal blow to Korea's sovereignty came after Japan's defeat of Russia, when, in November 1905, a Japanese force headed by prominent statesman Itō Hirobumi forced the Protectorate (*ŭlsa*) Treaty on a divided Korean government. Japan was now in charge of Korea's foreign affairs, and a Japanese resident general oversaw Korea's domestic matters.

In July–August 1907 the Japanese tightened their hold. After Kojong had appealed to the foreign powers for help by opposing the Protectorate Treaty in a letter that was publicized in the *Taehan Maeil Sinbo* newspaper, and by sending messengers to the Second Hague Peace Conference, the Japanese orchestrated his dethronement. Shortly after, they forced the cabinet to sign an agreement that stipulated the installation of Japanese vice-ministers in the government, and the Japanese resident general was given, in effect, official authority to meddle in all of Korea's internal affairs. Shortly thereafter the Korean army was disbanded and, finally, on August 22, 1910 Korean Prime Minister Yi Wan-yong signed a treaty of annexation. A week later Kojong's son, King (or Emperor) Sunjong, had no choice but to relinquish his throne, hence the longest dynasty in East Asian history, the Chosŏn dynasty (1392–1910), came to an end. Korea was now officially a colony of imperial Japan.

Writing on the eve of the Russo-Japanese War, Basil H. Chamberlain —an important early Western scholar of Japan who was also decidedly pro-Japanese—asserted: "Having absorbed all the useful elements of our culture, young Japan's eager is to communicate these to her neighbours. To act as broker between West and East is her self-imposed mission. Korea's regeneration was Japan's work until Russia stepped in."[6] Koreans have commonly rejected Chamberlain's "white man's burden" thinking (or "yellow man's burden" in this case) with regard to Japan's role in Korea. Also, Chamberlain's romanticism with regard to Japan was expressed by his view that, in the case of a future perilous commercial struggle in the region, "Who could help falling in love with so fair an enemy?"[7] It goes without saying that this approach, too, was spurned by the Koreans at the time and even more so after liberation in 1945.

The historian Kang Man-gil summarized the annexation as the result of a combination of factors: the policies of imperial Japan, the recognition and support that the foreign powers had given to Japan, the declining incompetent government of the "Great Han Empire," the Korean people who were incapable of replacing their government with a sovereign one, and the nation's failure to make the best use of its geopolitical location.[8] Without entering the debate as to whether Japanese imperialism in general and Korea's annexation in particular resulted from well-advanced planning or from pragmatic accommodation to changing circumstances, it must be noted that the common notion among Koreans is that control over their country had been a long-time aim in Japan.[9] This notion has been crucial in shaping the contents of the mainstream Korean historical narrative, which spins the story of the country's loss of sovereignty.

"National spirit" of resistance

At the exhibition halls that are situated in the grounds of South Korea's two national cemeteries, in Seoul and in Taejŏn, the following text stands out in the sections dedicated to the 1905–10 period:

> Alas! How mortifying it is.
> Our twenty million fellow countrymen
> who became slaves of others!
> Are we to live? Are we to die?
> Has the national spirit [*kukmin chŏngsin*],
> which had existed for four thousand years since Tan'gun,
> suddenly perished in a single night?[10]
> How mortifying, mortifying.
> Fellow countrymen! Fellow countrymen!

This paragraph has been extracted for purposes of display at the halls from one of the more commonly cited Korean nationalist texts. Several days after the signing of the Protectorate Treaty, Chang Chi-yŏn, then editor of the *Hwangsŏng sinmun* (Capital Gazette), wrote and published in his newspaper a highly emotional reaction to his nation's predicament, concluding it with the lines above.[11] Thus, by highlighting this text in the exhibition, present-day curators, in their capacity as memory agents, follow the footsteps of postcolonial nationalist writers and, at the same time, further anchor this text in the historical memory of the collective. Most importantly, in assuming that there is such a thing as "a spirit of a nation," they pose before contemporary visitors the vexing, though quite abstract, problem regarding the nature of their nation's spirit.

It is possible to find the key for defining the "spirit of the Korean nation" in another one of the better-known documents associated with the nation-alist ethos of the late Chosŏn dynasty—the testament of Min Yŏng-hwan, who was a respected official and military aide-de-camp to the Korean emperor. After the signing of the Protectorate Treaty, Min committed suicide, leaving an impassioned entreaty for the nation's independence, an act that was soon followed by other officials. With the use of the word "sorrowful/mournful" (*sŭlp'ŭda*) Min opened his testament—which appears, among other places, on a carved stone monument on the grounds of the Independ-ence Hall in Ch'ŏnan-si, the country's largest memorial site—by lamenting over the nation's fate. He then addressed his 20 million compatriots, promising them that even after his death he would assist them from the afterworld (*hwangch'on* and *chiha*). As Andre Schmid has shown, Min's suicide and the related idea of "life" after death in connection with the nationalist struggle have greatly influenced "the shift toward a more spiritual vision of the nation" at the aftermath of the Russo-Japanese War, signaling as it did the loss of state and territory.[12] It is thus no coincidence that, adjacent to the above-mentioned text, under the theme of loss of inde-pendence, exhibits are dedicated to the struggle that evolved after 1904. Korea was dead in body but alive through the spirit of resistance, a message that secures an unbroken line of existence. While for early twentieth-century Koreans this was a message of hope, in postcolonial divided Korea this message has been conflated with new meanings. Thus, the 1904–10 period witnessed a transformation of the terms of national struggle even as the cause of independence was lost in the short term.

South Korean historians commonly typify the form that the Korean resist-ance took during this period by distinguishing between two main currents. One is the armed struggle of the "righteous armies," the *ŭibyŏng*, and the second is the unarmed resistance manifested by the activities of the "patri-otic enlightenment movement" (*aegukkyemong undong*). A third venerated form of resistance, which will be discussed in the following section, was heroic acts of individuals. (Kojong's letter to protest the Protectorate Treaty and the mission he sent to The Hague are also mentioned as manifestations of resistance.)

As with the Tonghak guerrillas in the summer of 1894, the armed resistance that sprouted in 1904 aimed at expelling the Japanese invaders from Korea. Judging from a message sent on July 1 to instigate the armed fight, the initiators believed that the war between Russia and Japan not only kept the Japanese busy but had also sown schisms and confusion in their homeland; thus, Koreans should grab the opportunity and rise.[13] During the Russo-Japanese War, as well as later in 1906, *ŭibyŏng* fighters—mostly led by literati elites—clashed with Japanese forces in different places; however, a dramatic shift in the armed struggle occurred after professional soldiers from the disbanded Korean army had joined the guerrillas in 1907. Since then, more and more commoners joined in as well. According to Japanese sources, a total of 141,815 insurgents took part in 2,852 collisions from August 1907, until the Japanese crushed this wave of resistance in June 1911. The most turbulent year was 1908, with 69,832 insurgents and 1,451 clashes.[14] Targets for those attacks, it should be noted, were not only Japanese garrisons and infrastructure, but also Japanese settlers and pro-Japanese Koreans.

The "patriotic enlightenment movement" is the name given to the political, social, cultural, and educational societies and scholarship, as well as the press, that were active from 1904 until Korea's annexation. The aim of this movement was to strengthen the Korean people by edifying them.[15] In this regard, inspiration for the movement came in no small measure from its most significant predecessor—the Independence Club; yet, although such activity existed before 1904, South Korean historians[16] tend to distinguish between stages in the enlightenment and reform movement, and to specifically highlight the 1904–10 period.[17]

The first organization of the "patriotic enlightenment movement," the Poanhoe (Korea Preservation Society), was founded in mid-1904 to launch a campaign against the Nagamori plan, which aimed at transferring all uncultivated land in Korea to Japanese hands. By organizing public protests and utilizing the press, the society managed to create a significant stir that had much impact on the Japanese decision to finally withdraw from the plan in late 1904. In the following years many more organizations were founded, e.g. Taehan chaganghoe (Korea Self-strengthening Society), Sinminhoe (New People's Association), and Taehan hyŏphoe (Korea Association); numerous Korean private schools were set up, new trends in literature and in the study of the Korean language appeared, and new newspapers acted as a vital platform for writers to publish and spread their thought.

Furthermore, postcolonial southern historians regard the period as a milestone in the development of Korean historiography. Historian Lee Ki-baik explains that historians of that time "strove above all to foster a sense of national pride and self respect,"[18] and, although it is common to refer to Sin Ch'ae-ho's "Toksa sillon" (A New Reading of History) (1908) as the work that had founded modern—and as Shin Yong-ha stresses "nationalist"—Korean historiography,[19] Cho Tong-gŏl identifies also Hwang Ŭi-don's *Taedong ch'ŏngsa* (History of Korea) (1909) as an equally important co-founder of Korean modern historical science.[20] In any case, historians of the 1904–10 period wrote new histories and spun the biographies of old Korean heroes in an attempt to establish a meaningful and proud history of a nation that had lost its sovereignty. Later, postcolonial historians have grounded those writers in the postcolonial historical national narrative, "using" them as protagonists to cement it; thus, they assigned them the same role as those "founding historians" had assigned to their own subjects of research.

What was the significance of the armed and the unarmed struggles, which, in the final analysis, had failed to save Korea from annexation? Nationalist historian Shin Yong-ha asserts that, besides being "a shining symbol of Korea's patriotic spirit,"[21] the struggle of the *ŭibyŏng* postponed the annexation of Korea by three years, hence allowing the "patriotic enlightenment movement" to firmly establish itself.[22] Emphasis is then given in the narrative to the direct impact that those struggles had on post-1910 resistance.[23] Moreover, South Korean historians commonly refer to the pre-1910 struggle as the resistance of the *people*.[24] The two currents of struggle constitute in the master narrative a crucial link in the history of the Korean people's struggle, leading, most importantly, to the legitimization of the southern state. One way for historians to make this link is by claiming that, specifically between 1905 and 1910, the notion of a republican form of government had been adopted and advocated.[25] This claim suggests the existence of a historical continuum between the struggle of that time, the Korean Provisional Government that was established in Shanghai in April 1919, and the postcolonial Republic of Korea (South Korea).

For North Korean historians, in comparison, these forms of struggle belonged to the bourgeois nationalist movement,[26] a movement that proceeded with its poor performance in the 1910–20 period as well.[27] In the northern narrative the lack of a significant leadership was critical in those years. For example, by depicting the members of the Korean Provisional Government as "embarking on a pilgrimage to beg for independence," and as "gathering funds for independence from patriotic-fellow-countrymen and then squandering it,"[28] they belittle the role of that organ. Instead, the North's narrative of valor and legitimacy centers on the appearance in the 1930s of the person who later became the country's "Great Leader," Kim Il Sung, and his guerrillas.

In sum, South Korean historian Pak Hwan opined that one flaw in the research of the nationalist movement in his country has been the excessive concentration on the history of the struggle, at the expense of other themes.[29] Thus, while North Korea treats the period of 1904–10 as one more link in the history of bourgeois nationalism, in the South it is underscored as an exceptional time; it is interpreted as a convergence of different forms of conduct, into a heroic display that later influenced and inspired Korean resistance under colonial rule. And, as we explain below, a clear-cut dichotomy between the contemporaneous patriots and traitors has been an important theme in this regard in South Korean historical memory.

Patriots and traitors

As Itō Hirobumi and the Japanese minister in Seoul Hayashi Gonsuke marched with their soldiers into the palace of the Korean emperor to coerce the Korean government into signing the Protectorate Treaty on November 17, a dramatic event occurred. According to Korean sources, Prime Minister Han Kyu-sŏl displayed such an ardent opposition to signing the treaty, that he was finally dragged from the room by the Japanese troops.[30] This act earned him the status of a revered patriot, as is exemplified by the display of his official uniform inside a glass case at the Kŭndae minjok undonggwan (Modern Nationalist Movement Hall), the second exhibition room of the Independence Hall.

The selection of patriots such as Han is a way for creators of national histories to concretize their narratives. Patriots provide this historiography with human faces that both encapsulate and demonstrate the "spirit of the nation," thus making these narratives easier to identify with. The above-mentioned Min Yŏng-hwan is another case in point as is Pak Sŏng-hwan—the commander who committed suicide after bringing his unit into Seoul for disbandment in the summer of 1907. The fact that the soldiers had refused to disband and rose to rebel furthers the image of Pak's suicide, enhancing its role as a transmitter of national spirit.

In addition, a different heroic type, that of the patriotic-assassin, has also been lauded in conjunction with that period. In March 1908, Chŏn Myŏng-un and Chang In-hwan killed Durham W. Stevens in San Francisco. Stevens was an American employee of the Japanese Foreign Minister, who acted as a foreign adviser to the Korean government following one of the protocols that Japan had imposed on Korea during its war against Russia. Contemporaneous Koreans regarded Stevens as an agent who "spied for the Japanese and worked against the Koreans during the critical year of 1905."[31] Another celebrated hero is Yi Chae-myŏng, and it is no coincidence that, in the Photographic Exhibition Hall in Seoul National Cemetery, his photograph is placed next to the pictures of Chŏn and Chang. In December 1909 Yi attempted to kill Yi Wan-yong, who had signed all three of the crucial treaties that both formalized and gave substance to Korea's colonization (in 1905 as Minister of Education, and in 1907 and 1910 as the prime minister). For Koreans, Yi Wan-yong has thus become "the darkest name in Korean history."[32]

There is no doubt that, among all those who attacked traitors, collaborators, or Japanese before, during, or after Korea's annexation, the most famous is An Chung-gŭn. On the morning of October 26, 1909, An shot Itō Hirobumi to death at Harbin station in Manchuria, and he was executed exactly five months later. An has become one of the most revered national heroes in South Korea, and he is highly appreciated in North Korea as well. One example of the place he occupies in Korean national memory is the naming of a *hyŏng*—a form in T'aekwŏndo, Korea's most noted martial art—after him, which is a rare honor reserved only for Korea's greatest.[33]

It is important to notice that An's assassination is often described not as an individualist act, but as an operation executed in the context of the strategy of the *ŭibyŏng*, which attacked Japanese infrastructure and interests.[34] This notion grounds both An's heroic sacrifice and the death of a Japanese who is considered to have been at the pinnacle of Japan's aggression within the broader historical context of resistance. This is a tangibly represented conspicuous image at the Tongnip chŏnjaenggwan (Independence War Hall), the fifth exhibition room of Independence Hall. Three bronze statues placed side by side on pedestals dominate half the space of this hall. They are dedicated to Yun Pong-gil, who threw a bomb at Japanese dignitaries in Shanghai in 1932; Kim Chwa-jin, a famous military commander who was involved in battles against Japanese forces; and An Chung-gŭn. This form of representation, together with the theme title of the hall under which it is exhibited, overcomes the notion that An's act was simply an individual act of political assassination.

The role of An as a carrier and transmitter of Korea's national spirit is expressed by the stone that stands at the entrance to Patriot An Chung-gŭn Memorial Hall in Namsan Park, Seoul. It is carved with the inscription "Minjok chŏnggi ŭi chŏndang"—"a shrine of righteous national spirit." Moreover, as the whereabouts of An's body are still unknown, an opportunity is presented before South Korea to convey a clear message pertaining to the issue of legitimacy. At Hyoch'ang Park in Seoul there is a burial plot called "Sam ŭisa myo" (Tombs of the three martyrs), where three patriots from the colonial period are buried. In the same line as these graves there is an additional empty tomb without a gravestone that waits for the time An's body will be recovered. This setting conveys the idea that the soil of postliberation South Korea is the proper and legitimate place for absorbing this important patriot. In Confucian ritual standards this placement implies that the South has assumed the role of the elder son, the one who bears the responsibilities associated with filial piety. By appropriating An Chung-gŭn's fictive grave site the South represents itself as the legitimate heir of the pre-divided Korean nation in competition with North Korea, which also venerates An's memory.

On the opposite side from the patriotic martyrs, southern nationalist history highlights the denounced traitors. Traitors related to the colonial period are branded in Korean as *ch'inilp'a*, "pro-Japanese faction," which is a derogatory term that lumps together diverse and more complicated motives, thoughts, and forms of human behavior. In this regard we should note the thoughts of Korean writers on the issue of race.[35] At the time of the Russo-Japanese War, for example, Ch'oe Kyŏng-hwan, in his *Taedong yŏksa* (History of Korea) (1905), described his country as having a very tight connection with Japan, as the two are similar in their race and their writing.[36] Of course, this observation does not make Ch'oe a traitor, but a similar notion leads another writer, Yun Ch'i-ho, to the following frankness: after the Russian defeat at the Battle of Tsushima, Yun, a former prominent figure in the Independence Club, lamented over Korea's loss of independence, while at the same time expressing how proud he was of Japan for vindicating the honor of the yellow race.[37] In February 2002, when a group of South Korean lawmakers, which called itself the Korea Parliamentary League on National Spirit (Minjokchŏnggi rŭl paroseu nŭn kukhoeŭiwŏn moim), published in an unprecedented act a list of 708 names of people who they defined as pro-Japanese collaborators, Yun's name appeared on it because he had accepted functions in Japanese councils after Korea's annexation.

An interesting impression by a Western eyewitness to the events in Korea at the turn of the century further illustrates the complexity of this issue. Frederick A. McKenzie was a Canadian reporter for the London's *Daily Mail*. He wrote that in his travels in the country during the first weeks of the war he had met more than a few Koreans from whom he heard "nothing but expressions of friendship to the Japanese." Those Koreans disliked the Russians "because of their lack of discipline and want of restraint" and because of the soldiers' "occasional interference with Korean women." McKenzie wrote that coolies and farmers, as well as better-educated people, each out of his own interest, held their hopes that Japan would advance reforms in Korea's traditional system.[38]

In any event, the years 1904–10 have supplied postcolonial Korea with many more obvious villains—perhaps its most despised. The traitors include people such as Song Pyŏng-jun, leader of the Ilchinhoe (United Advancement Society)—an organization that supported and cooperated with Japan during its war against Russia and until it was dissolved in 1910, and the cabinet members who signed the humiliating treaties. In fact, the two types of historical figures (patriots and traitors) used in contrast to each other reciprocally intensify their polarized images. And exhibition halls that excel in being able to construct and convey strong, immediate visual images exploit the juxtaposition of such images. In Sŏdaemun Prison History Hall, for example, under the title "Ŭlsa 5 choyak" (The *Ŭlsa* Treaty of 5), there is a juxtaposition of photographs of the ministers who signed the 1905 treaty with a photograph of Min Yŏng-hwan.[39] At another site, the Photographic Exhibition Hall in Seoul National Cemetery, the photographs of Min and his testament dominate the section dedicated to the Protectorate Treaty. Here, there are no photographs of traitors; the traitors are brought into the narrative only through the titles of the photographs of patriots. The photograph of Yi Chae-myŏng is accompanied by the title: "Martyr Yi

Chae-myŏng who stabbed the traitor Yi Wan-yong (1909)," and Chŏn Myŏng-un and Chang In-hwan are described as martyrs who "killed the pro-Japanese [*ch'inil*] diplomat Stevens (1908)."

These arrangements operate on two levels. First, as mentioned, they make the heroic patriot more admirable and the traitor more despicable. On a second level they marginalize the phenomenon of collaboration. The exhibitions are tangible manifestations of a trend that was dominant in South Korea for decades: to minimize collaboration, in the words of De Ceuster, to a few "useful scapegoats," and to "hardly more than a footnote in the history of the nation."[40] While North Korea purged those it had regarded as collaborators during its early stages of development, for South Korea, whose first administrations were heavily based on personnel that had cooperated with colonial authorities, the issue has been an ongoing challenge to the legitimacy of the state.[41] In sum, by the parallel that is created between the foreigner Stevens and the defined group of Korean traitors, and by the emphasized dichotomy between the "pro-Japanese" and their contemporary patriots, the Korean traitor is eliminated from the nation and South Korea relieves itself from the onus of collaboration.

An islet in a sea of passions

So far we have explored the nexus between the historical period that was dominated by the Russo-Japanese War and postcolonial interpretations of this era in the context of nationalist narratives of resistance. In the present section we do not treat resistance in its strict sense, nor do we center on historical figures. Rather, the last part of our discussion focuses on a tiny territory, which, as Koreans see it, was basically the first Korean land that Japan took over prior to the official annexation of 1910. Although this territory was returned to (South) Korea after colonial rule had ended, it still remains a cause of painful memories from the time of Korea's demise and of the resultant high passions. Koreans call this territory Tokdo (獨島 "lonely island"), while the Japanese name it Takeshima (竹島 "bamboo island"). It is beyond the scope of our discussion to delve into the place Tokdo had occupied in the histories of Korea and Japan prior to the year 1904, and we shall also leave the views regarding the legality of the claims for sovereignty over the territory to others.[42] Instead, our attention is on the conspicuous disproportion between the size and the practical importance of Tokdo, and the effect that this territory is having on Japan–South Korea relations.

Tokdo consists of two barren and uninhibited islets with some 30 reefs around them. It covers an area of approximately 0.2 square kilometers, and is located in the East Sea (or Sea of Japan), about 90 kilometers (56 miles) from the South Korean island of Ullŭngdo and 160 kilometers (100 miles) from Japan's Okinoshima. In late September 1904, a Japanese by the name of Nakai Yozaburō wrote a letter to several ministries requesting that Japan incorporate the islets into its territory and then lease them to him for fishing rights and the hunting of sea lions. Despite the opposition of the Ministry of Home Affairs, the Foreign Ministry and the government as a whole supported the appeal because the islets were seen as strategically important for the war against Russia.[43] In January 1905 the government reached a decision to annex Tokdo, and it gave jurisdiction over the islets to Shimane prefecture. On February 22, Shimane prefecture published a public notice to that effect, using the name Takeshima. During the war, the Japanese erected there an observation tower, and later, in July 1906, Tokdo was leased to Nakai's fishing and hunting company. It should be noticed that it was only in March of that year that Korea first became aware of Tokdo's seizure.[44]

After the colonial period, the subject of Tokdo surfaced again on different occasions. In 1954, for example, Japan urged that the Tokdo dispute would be brought before the International Court of Justice, but South Korea objected. In that same year, and in the face of Japanese protest, the South Korean government issued stamps of Tokdo, an act it has repeated several times since. When in January 2004 South Korea again produced Tokdo postage stamps, the Japanese Foreign Minister summoned the South Korean ambassador to Tokyo, while the Japanese ambassador to South Korea paid a visit to the South Korean Vice Foreign Minister, both to lodge Japan's protest. In February 1996, furious anti-Japanese demonstrations broke out in Seoul after Japanese Foreign Minister Ikeda reaffirmed his country's claim to the islets. That year, the heightened emotions regarding Tokdo influenced the already rising tensions associated with the World Cup bidding competition between the two countries.[45] In any case, we should keep in mind that the Tokdo problem was left unresolved by the 1965 normalization treaty between the two countries.

When the Tokdo issue captured headlines in early 2005, the passionate reactions that were expressed underscored the irony involved: the two governments designated the year 2005 as "Year of Korea–Japan Friendship" to mark the fortieth anniversary of the normalization treaty. South Korea was outraged when the assembly of Shimane prefecture announced its decision to designate February 22 as "Takeshima Day" to commemorate the centenary of the prefecture's official announcement regarding its jurisdiction over the territory. An overwhelming majority at the assembly voted in support of this ordinance. In an instant, the event provoked a variety of reactions that rained on the parade of the "friendship year" between the former colonizer and its former victim.

On the governmental level, the standing committee of the National Security Council issued a statement on March 17 condemning the Japanese move. It specified that South Korea intended, first, to take measures to safeguard the country's territorial right over Tokdo; second, to utilize all possible means to emend any distorted understanding of history; third, to urge Japan to compensate victims of the colonial period; fourth, to closely follow

Japan's move toward becoming a leading figure in the international community—a move that depended on earning the trust of its neighbors; and, lastly, to not abandon the belief that the two countries could keep working together for peace and stability in the region; thus, South Korea would continue with operative measures in this regard. South Korea also announced that it would establish a special parliamentary committee for Tokdo. Several weeks later, it made strong official protests after the Japanese government approved controversial textbooks in which, among other things, Tokdo was depicted as Japanese territory.

As for immediate symbolic responses, measures were taken to double the 70-people quota that was allowed to visit Tokdo every day (limitations are imposed, so it is explained, out of security and environmental concerns). Then, on April 23, on a boat that carried the new number of 140 daily visitors, was a couple that made history: they married in the first wedding ever to take place on the islets. In an act of protest against the Japanese recent claim to the territory, the couple married in a traditional Korean ceremony after receiving special approval from the authorities. And, finally, on the popular level, impassioned anti-Japanese demonstrations took place in Seoul in front of the Japanese embassy. Japanese flags were burnt, demonstrators cut off their fingers, and one protestor even set himself on fire.[46]

Given the fact that in the end the Tokdo islets are far from being a significantly beneficial territory in economic, strategic, or any other terms, it is obvious from the intensity of the reactions that the problem of Tokdo is representative of the problem of the colonial past as a whole. Responses to Japanese actions or declarations in connection to this past, as well as raising this past independently, are motivated by factors such as: truly deep emotions of sorrow, rage, humiliation, and so on, which are associated with the memory of the painful past; political interests of individuals who capitalize on the issue to earn popular support; and, also, the state's strategy in the bilateral and international arenas.[47]

The issue of Tokdo is unique in this context, for it is the only territorial vestige associated with the occupation period. For South Korea it symbolizes the initial actual seizure of Korean land, an act that was but one more measure in the process of Japan's takeover of Korea during the critical time of its war against Russia. One sort of South Korean reaction to Tokdo, and to declarations such as those made by the assembly of Shimane prefecture, could be to brush aside Japanese claims in a firm laconic manner and to avoid the passionate fuss; however, South Korea cannot do this because colonial memory is heavily dominant on both popular and official levels. This means that the fierce display of resistance and the repetitive assertions over sovereignty, which were manifested during the Tokdo crisis, stem more from the recollection of a difficult past than they do from confidence in a tightly secured present.

Conclusion

During the Russo-Japanese War Japan succeeded in furthering its hold over Korea. The victory over the last contender for influence in Korea cleared the way to the annexation of 1910. For Koreans this period signifies the dark dawn of colonial rule—a problematic historical link that binds the crumbling of the Chosŏn dynasty in the late nineteenth century with the 35-year oppression of colonial rule. At the same time it is recollected as a meaningful piece of the past in which the "spirit of the nation"—defined in terms of a heroic struggle—has not died and must be maintained as an important mainstay of collective memory.

As North Korea sees it, the people of that period displayed their bravery, but, in the final analysis, their fight remained hopeless due to a lack of true leadership. For South Korea, the diverse forms of resistance that had developed kept inspiring Koreans under colonial rule as well as their post-colonial descendants. In this narrative, the commonly mentioned weakness of the Chosŏn dynasty rulers is contrasted to this heroic image in order to enhance the national patriotism of Korea's pantheon of patriots. The assertion that one reason for the fall of the dynasty was its continuous search for the protection of a foreign power makes the 1904–10 struggle far more admirable because the elimination of Russia in the war meant that Korea was on its own. The image of the ability to rise and resist at this darkest moment of national history enunciates a message of hope and reassurance for both the present and the future.

Notes

1 Kim, 1966: 34.
2 History writing in postcolonial Korea has known various trends and schools. For our purposes, we relate to representative notions that demonstrate the dominating narratives.
3 For commonly cited English-language works that expound the dynamics of the Japanese penetration of Korea before, during, and in the aftermath of the Russo-Japanese War, see Conroy, 1960; Duus, 1995; and Kim and Kim, 1967.
4 Cumings, 1997: 103.
5 Lee, 1965: 42–8.
6 Chamberlain, 1902: 9.
7 Chamberlain, 1902: 9.
8 Kang, 1999: 28.
9 See, for example, Eckert *et al.*, 1990: 240–1; Lee 1984: 313. For various approaches and discussions regarding the nature of Japanese imperialism, see Beasley, 1987; Calman, 1992; Conroy, 1960; Duus, 1995; and Wray and Conroy, 1983: 121–48.
10 Tan'gun is the mythical progenitor of the Korean nation.
11 For other translations of this text, see Duus, 1995: 195; and Lee, 1984: 330.
12 Schmid, 2002: 142–4, 142.
13 Shin, 2000: 155.
14 Lee, 1965: 81.

15 Lee, 1984: 327.
16 For example, Cho, 1994: 14; and Shin, 2000: 195.
17 Established by Sŏ Chae-p'il (Philip Jaisohn), the Independence Club (Tongnip hyŏphoe) was active in the years 1896–8. It called for an independent foreign policy that would not lean toward any foreign power; it adopted the Western model of the nation-state, including popular participation in politics; and it launched projects aimed at evoking patriotism among Koreans. The club published *The Independent* (*Tongnip sinmun*), a modern newspaper printed in *han'gŭl* (the Korean native script), and it led a campaign for the construction of two concrete national symbols, Independence Gate and Independence Hall (not the Independence Hall that is the monumental memorial site near Ch'ŏnan). Although the king supported the club's activities for a while, he finally ordered it to dissolve in late 1898 under the pretext that it was striving to replace the monarchy with a republic.
18 Lee, 1984: 337.
19 Shin, 2000: 211.
20 Cho, 1994: 19, 22.
21 Shin, 2000: 190.
22 Shin, 2000: 191.
23 Lee, 1984: 339–40; Shin, 2000: 218–20.
24 See, for example, Hong, 2001; Lew, 1985: 49; and Shin, 2000: 191, 198.
25 Hong, 2001: 153; Shin, 1994: 17.
26 Kang, 1990: 10–14.
27 Hwang, 1998: 51–7.
28 Hwang, 1998: 56.
29 Pak, 1998: 30.
30 Lee, 1984: 310.
31 Nahm, 1988: 217.
32 Cumings, 1997: 145.
33 The "Chung-gŏn pattern" is practiced by the International T'aekwŏndo Federation, which is one of T'aekwŏndo's two major schools and the one that is favored by the north. Also, it is interesting to mention that Frederick A. McKenzie—whose books *The Tragedy of Korea* (1908) and *Korea's Fight for Freedom* (1920) were highly sympathetic toward Korea and present details about Japan's harsh oppression—believed that the killing of Itō was counter-productive. He enumerates both practical and moral reasons to explain this view (see McKenzie, 1969 [1920]: 171–4), and regrets that "some Koreans stooped to the favourite Oriental weapon of assassination" (McKenzie, 1969 [1920]: 172).
34 See, for example, Kang *et al.*, 1994: 226; and Shin, 1995: Preface; 2001: 127.
35 For a good discussion on this issue, see Schmid, 2002: 86–100.
36 Song, 1994: 318.
37 Lone, 1988: 122.
38 McKenzie, 1969 [1920]: 80.
39 The Japanese started the construction of Sŏdaemun Prison in 1907 to house Korean prisoners. They opened it in October 1908, and used it throughout the colonial period. After liberation, South Korea continued to use the facility for its own purposes, and closed it in November 1987. During the late 1980s and throughout the 1990s the place and its vicinity—Sŏdaemun Independence Park—were refurbished, and Sŏdaemun Prison History Hall opened in 1998.
40 De Ceuster, 2002: 217. This trend to marginalize the issue of collaboration is gradually undergoing a shift. As manifested by the list of 708 collaborators, the issue is receiving growing attention in public discourse, in a trend that sets to "come to terms" with this poignant part of the past.

41 De Ceuster, 2002.
42 For a focus on the Korean side on these matters, see the *Korea Observer*'s two special issues on Tokdo: vol. 28, no. 3 (autumn 1997) and vol. 29, no. 1 (spring 1998).
43 Park and Bae, 1998: 145–6.
44 Park and Bae, 1998: 156; Sato, 1998: 171.
45 Butler, 2002: 52.
46 Takahashi, 2005.
47 For example, South Korea heavily employed the colonial past for earning support during its bid for the 2002 World Cup in the 1990s. See Butler, 2002: 45–6.

13 Ironies of history
The war and the origins of East Asian radicalism

Yitzhak Shichor

By the early twenty-first century, East Asian socialist (or "communist") regimes that had been established some 50 years earlier still survive. In a retrospective view, this is one of the most intriguing phenomena of the post-World War II world, for at that time—and to a certain extent even today—continental East Asia did not have the fully developed infrastructures needed according to Marx to build socialism. These include urbanization, industrialization, advanced capitalism, and a sophisticated bourgeois society, not to mention an exploited proletariat—all typical of Western Europe as early as the nineteenth century. Soviet and East European socialist regimes that had been built on less advanced socio-economic foundations (supposed to be more solid and stable) collapsed by the early 1990s. On the other hand, East Asian socialism, which has diverged from the Marxist model and even contradicted it both in theory and in practice, has still managed to survive and to preserve—albeit with many modifications—communist party rule. The reasons for the initial absorption of socialism in East Asia, the later consolidation of Marxism-Leninism (communism), and its heretofore survivability are diverse and complex, and fall beyond the scope of this chapter—save one. It relates to the role of Japan and to the implications of its 1905 victory over Russia. This victory has ended the era of moderation and reformism in East Asian political activism and paved the way for radical and revolutionary modes of thinking and acting. This is true of the main East Asian countries that were later to become communist, namely Vietnam and China, as well as of Russia and—primarily and paradoxically—of Japan, though it has never become communist.

East Asian socialism: the Japanese connection

Ostensibly, there was no reason why Japan would play any role in the emergence of East Asian communism. On the contrary, in its social and especially economic features Japan conforms much more to the Western European countries where no socialist or communist regimes have been established. Nonetheless, Japan, the first East Asian country that had opened to the West and later swallowed large parts of East Asia, has unwillingly enabled in a dialectical way the emergence of nationalist movements. Some of these movements had relied from the very beginning on Marxist-Leninist ideologies and also enjoyed the support of the Soviet Union and international revolutionary organizations. This process, whose main stage ended with the establishment of East Asian communist regimes in the middle of the twentieth century, had begun in the late nineteenth century.

Although communism has finally settled in mainland northeast Asia (China, Vietnam, and North Korea), part of its origins could be traced to Japan. The Meiji Restoration, modernization and industrialization, and the opening to the West, had paved the way for the introduction of socialist ideas and the creation of a new terminology. These affected not only Japanese intellectuals but also thousands of Chinese, Korean, and Vietnamese students, reformers, and revolutionaries who studied or stayed in Japan in the late nineteenth and early twentieth century. The absorption of socialist thought in Japan was determined by a process of selection—conscious or unconscious—from the rich reservoir of ideas that had gradually aggregated in the West during many decades, but that reached Japan almost instantly.

This selection was governed by Japan's cultural and intellectual legacy as well as by its economic and social realities. To begin with, though essentially aristocratic, Japan had adopted Confucian and Buddhist traditions that considered society to be a humane, harmonious, and organic framework and consistently ignored and rejected the concept of class struggle. Rugged capitalism, which involved individualism, egoism, and competition, was instinctively regarded as a dangerous threat to collectivist familial values. Indeed, the political reality still reflected the predominance and centrality of the state and the government. At the same time, the social and economic reality had not yet created serious class tensions and gaps that could feed radicalism. It is the adjusted combination of these legacies that affected the early selection of doctrines adopted in late nineteenth-century Japan. They included first and foremost moderate state socialism, human Christian socialism, and social democracy, which underlined the accomplishment of social and economic justice by legitimate and parliamentarian means, under the auspices of and through the state, and without violence.[1]

Apparently, there was no intrinsic contradiction between socialism and the fundamental values of Japanese society. Consequently, the early socialists did not consider themselves external to the society but an integral part of it. Nevertheless, the government (and to a considerable extent also the community) perceived even this minimalist self-determination as exceptional. Therefore, what became known as "Japanese socialism" has never crystallized into a wide-ranging movement of inner or outer significance (such as in Western Europe). Historically, it was no more than a marginal intellectual exercise whose political, social, and economic contribution has been marginal. It is doubtful whether the Japanese "socialists" had really understood the principles of Marxism and its social, economic, and especially political implications. Indeed, in these respects Japan's contribution to the emergence of Asian communism later on has been rather limited, despite the fact that it has provided revolutionaries with conceptual infra-structures for the variety of their socialist manifestations. Put differently, when the vibrations of the 1917 Russian Revolution reached East Asia, socialism had already become familiar to intellectuals and activists— primarily thanks to Japan. And it was the 1904–5 war against Russia that had led socialist fermentation in Japan to its climax.

Socialism or nationalism: the roots of Japanese radicalism

The moderate tendencies of Japanese socialism began to radicalize in the first decade of the twentieth century. First and foremost, this radicaliza-tion was an outcome of the disproportion between the moderate and weak nature of Japanese socialism, and the tough and uncompromising reaction of the state, which instinctively treated socialism as radical from the very beginning. At this point it should be made clear that radicalism is a rela-tive rather than an absolute concept and could vary from place to place and from time to time. An ideology that is considered radical in one political environment could be considered moderate in another. Similarly, an ideology could be considered moderate at the present but could deteriorate into radicalism in the future. Therefore, the Japanese (and also the Chinese) governments have often reacted to the *potential* implications of moderate socialism that could materialize in the future rather than to its *actual* and limited significance at the present. This policy led to a self-fulfilling prophecy. Some social-democratic leaders concluded that, under contem-porary political circumstances, moderate and gradual means to promote socio-economic justice could never succeed and therefore, radical, violent, and even revolutionary measures should be adopted and directed against the government. While this realization was beginning to take shape, Tokyo decided to grant asylum to refugees and exiles primarily from Russia— now regarded, after China's defeat in 1895, as its main and immediate enemy in East Asia. These refugees and exiles imported with them radical, anarchist, and communist ideas as well as experience that—given the dis-appointment with moderate socialism—fell on attentive ears.

Most importantly, "the Russo-Japanese War marked the takeoff point of Japanese imperialism—the historical moment when a position on the Asian mainland and hegemony in East Asia became a fundamental national commitment."[2] In this respect, the Russo-Japanese War (and the conse-quent 1905 revolution) had far-reaching implications for Japan in two senses that concerned the introduction, consolidation, and, no less important, survivability of Asian communism. For one, the war contributed to the radicalization of the moderate East Asian socialist movements toward anarchism and syndicalism, the use of violence, and the illegitimacy and discredit of democratic parliamentarianism, social democracy, and state socialism. For another, it contributed to underlining nationalism—on both sides of the political map. On the right, it triggered the development of proto-fascist chauvinism, militarism, and imperialism. On the left, the same chauvinism and imperialism reflexively led to the assimilation of nationalism among East Asian leftist revolutionary movements long before Lenin was to develop and advertise these concepts. These implications have been evident primarily in Japan itself but also in China, Vietnam, and the Russian Far East.

The war against Russia fed two contradictory tendencies in the Japanese public, and especially among the youth: on the one hand, a belief in "success," progress, and power and, on the other hand, primarily among those who had expressed concern and doubts about the state before the war, frustration, desperation, and individualistic self-concentration. To the government's disappointment, the students did not manifest particular enthusiasm for the war. On the contrary, they remained apathetic, restrained, and passive. Paradoxically, it had been the victory over Russia that had enabled the emergence of more radical trends. Until then, Japanese society had reflected, and to a great extent had also fed, the government's concern about the threats to Japan's independence and most of the energy had been mobilized toward the consolidation of the state and the nation and toward achieving "wealth and power." Now it seemed that one goal, power, had been achieved—and apparently quite easily. Consequently, a sense of ease and relaxation of tension prevailed. Yet the second goal, wealth, was not yet achieved. Moreover, according to "public opinion" (which had been more activist than the leaders from the very beginning), Japan had managed to win the war but lose the peace. Thus, criticism of the war was not limited to the left. Rightist groups criticized the Katsura government for its concessions during the negotiations that had led to the Portsmouth Treaty and urged the public to reject the treaty. After the treaty turned down Japan's expectation for Russian territories and primarily for Russian reparations, violent demonstrations erupted in Tokyo by the masses that had carried the heavy burden of the war.[3]

Following clashes with the police the military was called to intervene and on September 6, 1905, one day after the treaty was signed, martial law was declared—the first time for the suppression of riots.[4] Some consider these riots (the Hibiya riots) as evidence of the beginning of an urban mass movement that played an active role in Japanese politics, a first expression of civil society, and an initial political participation that led to the Taisho Democracy. Some even regard them as one of the earlier roots of the Japanese hostility that began to develop against the United States (which forced Japan to make the concession in the Treaty of Portsmouth).[5] Although Japan was still mostly agrarian after the war, industrialization, which was given a push following the victory, formed the first step that transferred Japan to the capitalist age at the beginning of which it was necessary to bridge between the individual's pursuit of wealth, and that of the state.

One outcome was a growing sympathy for the socialist movement and later for anarchism, a process that was taken as a threat to the Japanese bourgeoisie—which had never really upheld liberalism—and that had put it on a reactionary course as an imperialist bourgeoisie.[6]

The early Japanese socialist movement not only emphasized moderate socialism, which, following the German model, regarded the state as a central agency in applying a social justice that could be achieved only by legitimate means, elections, and parliamentary votes. It was also affiliated with Christianity. Consequently, the share of Christians among Japanese socialists in general, and among their leaders in particular, was relatively high, leading to a clear convergence between Christianity and socialism not only in view of values but also in view of the legacy of the persecution of Christianity in the past and official suspicions at the present. This convergence is also one of the reasons for the relatively harsh governmental reaction to Japanese socialism. In all these respects, the years 1904–5 were a turning point.

It is commonly assumed that the Russo-Japanese confrontation unified the socialists in their opposition to the war.[7] Yet, despite its theoretical logic, such a conclusion does not conform to the outcome of recent research. As a matter of fact, the Russo-Japanese War had foreshadowed World War I, which took place ten years later, in demonstrating that national identity overshadows class identity and undermines revolutionary solidarity. As we shall see below, this tendency was articulated not only in the imported Japanese socialism but also in genuine European socialism. The Russo-Japanese War weakened the center, exposed a breach in the socialist movement, and led to radicalization in both directions—to the right toward militarism, fascism, and chauvinism, and to the left toward revolutionary anarchism, primarily in relation to the link between nationalism and socialism.[8] It is the war that pushed the Japanese socialists (or at least those who continued to reject national patriotism and refused to "convert") outside the social frame. As mentioned above, until the war the Japanese socialists had never doubted the connection between nationalism, the national essence, and the national polity (*kokutai*), on the one hand, and socialism, on the other. They had not only failed to recognize the contradiction between these two concepts but, on the contrary, had perceived the conformity, combination, and interdependence between them (as in Germany). In their view, the main threat to the *kokutai* derived primarily from Western capitalism, which, being based on exploitation and individualism, seemed to negate the Japanese tradition.

Such dilemmas had not emerged during the Sino-Japanese War (1894–5) because Japanese socialism was still in its infancy, because China—unlike Russia—had not been considered the embodiment of authoritarianism, and because Europe had not been interested in the war. Moreover, the socio-economic burden involved in the Sino-Japanese War had been substantially smaller compared to the costs Japan was to pay ten years later. The Russo-

Japanese War already led to a rift between those who—on behalf of universalistic values—criticized the aggressive policy of the Japanese government, and those who—on behalf of particularistic values—exposed their patriotic nationalism, justified Japanese imperialist policy, and stood to defend the *kokutai*. Faced by the war, the Japanese socialists could not compromise between supra-national socialism and imperialist socialism. As a result of this dilemma and predicament, the Japanese socialist movement split into a number of groups, leading to conflicts and factionalism.[9]

The war and the emergence of Japanese radicalism

In August 1905 a group of rightist radicals led by Yamaji Aizan established the National-Socialist Party, or the State-Socialist Party, known as Kokka Shakaitō. A Christian influenced by both Confucianism and historical materialism, Yamaji considered the state a supra-class entity situated above society whose survival was more fundamentally important than upholding individual rights and liberties. Already articulated before the war, his ideas merged afterward into an integrated and logical world outlook. He regarded the war as a stage in Japan's inevitable facing of an ongoing threat that had accelerated within a few years, right at the end of the nineteenth century. This threat included the American occupation of Hawaii and the Philippines, the German presence in Shantung, the Russian foothold in Dalian (Dalny, southern Manchuria), the French deployment at the Bay of Canton (Guangzhou), and the Boxer Rebellion, during which foreign powers fought on Chinese soil.

Another figure who failed to perceive any contradiction between socialism and nationalism was Kita Ikki, who was 21 at the beginning of the Russo-Japanese War. Already as a young man he was inclined to Japanese socialism, whose leaders considered him a promising addition to their movement, despite the fact that, unlike them, he supported the war. His first book, *Theory of the State and Pure Socialism*, published in May 1906, had been considerably influenced by the Russo-Japanese War and especially by the Hibiya riots, which to him demonstrated the "people's power." The book's main idea is that Japan was ripe for social democracy in the "legal" sense but not yet in the economic sense. The election to the House of Representatives of socialists who represent the people would symbolize the end of class struggle and the overthrow of the aristocratic stratum, thereby laying the basis for economic development. In this respect there is full convergence between the interests of the state and those of society. Kita Ikki acknowledged the mission of Japanese imperialism and ultimately became the leader of the radical right.[10]

In an apparently surprising move, many of the Christian socialists who had earlier contributed to Japanese socialism its humanity, compassion, and rejection of violence now chose to stand alongside this group. As mentioned above, before the war a substantial number of Japanese socialists considered Christianity (which cares for the soul) as perfectly compatible with socialism (which cares for the body). Yet, the Christians' behavior throughout the war shocked many of the Japanese socialists. The support and legitimization provided by the Christians to the Japanese government in its war against Russia not only caused a split in the socialist movement but also, and inevitably, transformed the government's attitude. Christianity had been perceived until the Meiji Restoration as a fifth column that represented the Western imperialist powers—leading to a brutal suppression and persecution of Christians. Although the government regarded the West as a model, its concern about possible subversion underlined and may have aggravated its suspicious attitude toward Christians even after the Restoration. However, the Christians' support of Japan's war against Russia transformed the government's policy not only (positively) toward them but also, and by necessity, (negatively) toward their former socialist colleagues, who continued to oppose the war. The Christians' about-face in fact provided Tokyo with ammunition to further crack down on the socialist opposition.

Those socialists who had adopted a pacifist stand and opposed the war long before it erupted (and were now perceived by the government as radical) used harsh words to criticize the Christian socialists. They accused them of considering the tens of thousands of victims and the suppression of the working class as a result of the war a reasonable price to win political and social legitimization. Kōtoku Shūsui, who soon became one of the radicals' leaders, said: "Japanese Christianity, which was before the war the religion of [the] poor, [has] literally now changed within only two years to a great bourgeois religion and a machine of the State and militarism!"[11] Consequently, in October 1905, immediately as the war was over, the Christian socialists withdrew from the socialist movement and set up a new monthly called *Shin kigen* (The New Age). The split became official.

Furthermore, it soon became evident that the attitudes of Japan's Christian socialists conformed to those of European socialism, so that a split was created not only within the Japanese socialist movement but also between part of it and European socialism. As mentioned above, initially the Japanese socialist movement and its different currents had opposed the war. Yet, its later breakdown derived, among other things, from the stand of the European social democracy, which, based on its hostility to Russia (or, in other words, for nationalist considerations), had openly welcomed, anticipated, and encouraged a Japanese victory. The European socialist parties were unaware of the heavy cost the Japanese proletariat was paying for the war, not to mention other sacrifices. This was an unexpected source of support for the Japanese government against the domestic opposition, so much so that the emperor himself expressed satisfaction with "the splendid attitude of the European socialist parties' newspapers" toward the war.[12]

No wonder that under these circumstances some of the most prominent leaders of Japanese socialism, such as Katayama Sen, who was a social democrat and a Christian, could and would no longer hide their patriotism.

He, the Japanese who in the Sixth Socialist International Congress held in Amsterdam in August 1904—during the Russo-Japanese War—publicly shook the Russian Plekhanov's hand, failed to see the fundamental contradiction between his support of the government and the traditional orientation of Japanese socialism that favored parliamentarism and that he continued to represent. Although he rejected war, in principle he supported the Japanese victory as a lesser evil. His position, and that of the leaders of European socialism, further contributed to the split and drew criticism (initially moderate and restrained) from a pacifist (though small and isolated) group of Japanese socialists. While the war was still going on, these pacifists radicalized their attitudes, first and foremost Kōtoku Shūsui and his partner Sakai Toshihiko, who was later the first to introduce Lenin's works to Japan.[13]

The war and the emergence of leftist radicalism in Japan

The principled opposition of these socialists to war and imperialism had begun as early as 1900, long before the eruption of the Russo-Japanese War. Throughout the war they tried to preserve their moderate and parliamentarian socialist identity. However, they gradually realized that it was impossible to compromise with Japan's existing political system. It is against this background that they formed a group called in the literature "political" or "materialistic," which later emerged as an anti-parliamentarian and anarcho-syndicalist faction. They used wartime to cement the connection with socialist parties that had been part of the Second International (an organization formed in 1889 by socialist and labour parties who wished to work together for international socialism) and to intensively publish "radical" literature that included Marxist works, among them the first Japanese translation of the Communist Manifesto (November 1904), which appeared in the *Heimin Shimbun* (Common People's News). Issued for the first time on November 15, 1903, the newspaper became the leading radical organ in Tokyo. In its 64 issues (distributed in 3,500 to 4,500 copies until it closed down in January 1905), the newspaper urged the Russian Social Democratic Party to unite with the Japanese socialists in their opposition to "patriotism and militarism" throughout the war. Both parties categorically rejected war on behalf of universalistic principles according to which war is but a struggle among capitalist class interests. It is not important who wins—the working class always loses. For the radicals, opposition to war was, therefore, not only a moral obligation, it was also a social and economic issue of supreme importance.[14]

In March 1904 the newspaper published an open letter to the Russian Socialist Party, which rejected the war and emphasized a socialist class solidarity that ignores race, territory, or nation. Winning wide international resonance, the letter called for the struggle to be directed against the "real" enemies—militarism and patriotism. Published in its organ *Iskra* (Spark), the Russian reply, perhaps written by Lenin himself (or by Trotsky), praised the Japanese socialist approach but urged the use of "force against force, violence against violence." While this exchange of letters formed the first meaningful contact between the Russian revolutionaries led by Lenin and the Japanese socialists, Kōtoku was alarmed by the radical message. He was quick to distinguish between the Japanese socialists and the Russians:

> We are neither Nihilists nor Terrorists, but Social Democrats, and are always fighting for peace. We object absolutely to using military force in our fighting. We have to fight by peaceful means; by reason and speech ... Those who are fighting for humanity must remember that the end does not justify the means.[15]

In another article published at the end of that month Kōtoku attacked military service and the high taxes imposed to finance the war. Although he did not call for desertion and remained committed to parliamentarianism, his criticism of the war was inevitably perceived as heresy and treason. Moreover, although in his works and speeches he deliberately underlined moderation, his image was perceived as radical both by his supporters and by the public. In his case, as in the decision to go to war, it was the public that triggered the government. In April 1904 Sakai Toshihiko was sentenced to three months' imprisonment and the continued publication of the news-paper was forbidden (following an appeal his sentence was reduced to two months and he was allowed to continue publishing the newspaper). Still, the police increased its watch over his supporters and the newspaper, harassed its sellers, and warned their families. On May 27, 1904, all of Tokyo's correspondents were called to the police. They were told that the nation was at war and that the socialists' activities caused danger, under-mined the emperor's position, and confused the people. Any contact with the socialists and their works was forbidden. In November both Kōtoku and Sakai were accused of disturbing public peace and were sentenced to five months' imprisonment. While appealing to the court they realized that the police were determined to close down the newspaper and therefore decided to make the first step. At the end of January 1905 they closed down the paper on their own initiative and then began to serve their sentence.

Leaderless, the Japanese pacifist movement began to splinter in various directions. Furthermore, Japan's military successes, which had ended in such an impressive victory, undermined the remnants of opposition to the war. The socialists' attempt to introduce their own candidate in the parlia-mentary election in May 1906 failed miserably. The anti-war campaign did not stand a chance, certainly at that stage, especially when the lower classes had no access to the election and the police prohibited any propaganda activity. Kinsohita, the socialist candidate, received 32 votes out of a possible 16,000, which was another proof, and a clear-cut one, that the democratic-parliamentarian course was but a dead end for the socialists.

Instead of the closed-down *Heimin Shimbun*, a new monthly was launched, *Chokugen* (Straight Talk). Before it too closed down, due to the split with the Christians, it went on with the policy of publishing "radical" articles till the end of the war. Among others, these included the works of Russian revolutionaries and a long series on Marx's theory. *Chokugen* also provided information about the *narodniki* (and especially about Tolstoy who had been admired by Japanese intellectuals and socialists since the 1880s) and, with a barely hidden sense of satisfaction and identification, about the terrorist activities of their successors, the Social Revolutionary Party. At the end of 1905, after his release from prison, Kōtoku founded a new newspaper called *Hikari* (Light), precisely five years after Lenin began publishing *Iskra*.

Kōtoku was one of those prominent Japanese socialists who, during the war and in its wake, underwent a "conversion" process. His apparently lasted five months, from February to July 1905. In February, when he began to serve his sentence, and against the background of the 1905 revolution in Russia, Kōtoku published two sympathetic articles that dealt with the Russian Social Revolutionary Party and its nihilist legacy, while criticizing for the first time the Russian Social Democratic Party and its disappointing policy. Yet this process, derived also from his Samurai origins and from his unqualified attitude to violence, had begun to take shape already in March 1904, when his letter to the Russian socialists had been published. In the summer of 1904 he had already begun to question the need for the state and external authority at large. As his disapproval of the government grew stronger, Tokyo reacted accordingly to further clip his wings. In his words: "Indeed, I had gone [to prison] as a Marxian Socialist and returned a radical Anarchist."[16]

This definition is perhaps correct in a retrospective view, but there is doubt as to whether it was so clear-cut at the time. Kōtoku's interest in anarchism formed part of a general interest in intellectual and socialist contemporary currents. His emphasis on his anarchist identity was directed toward a foreign audience. During the war he began to correspond with Albert Johnson, an anarchist activist from San Francisco, who laid before him the anarchist doctrine. Even before Kōtoku's imprisonment Johnson sent him Kropotkin's 1898 book *Fields, Factories and Workshops* and other books from which Kōtoku claimed to have learned "the evil of government and the good of anarchy" as well as the defects in Christianity. His prison letters by no means supply concrete evidence that his conversion to anarchism was taking place in those months, but the seeds sown earlier undoubtedly began to sprout during his imprisonment. In fact, his conversion may have ripened in the first few months *after* his release. Depressed by the situation in Japan, which, according to him, had deteriorated into a police state, Kōtoku began to question not only its authority but also that of the emperor and finally *any* authority. To the surprise of his friends, this process was completed on the eve of his departure to the United States on November 14, 1905, as a voluntary exile. By the time of his return in June

1906 he had already become clearly disillusioned by the social-democratic model created by the German Socialist Party (SPD) that had guided Japanese socialism since the late nineteenth century. Kōtoku became an anarcho-syndicalist who upheld "direct action," which included not only strikes but also terrorist activity.

The radicalization in Kōtoku's stand conformed to the changes in Japan. During the war Japanese socialism tended to support more and more terrorist activity and the influence of the Russian radical left, such as the populists (*narodniki*) and the Social Revolutionaries (SRs). The revival of populist radicalism in Japan was an outcome of the war and especially of the 1905 revolution. For those socialists (such as Kōtoku) who heretofore had rejected the use of violence for the promotion of socialist ends, the revolution proved the advantages of violence as compared to more moderate means. Moreover, the Japanese socialists who had perceived pre-1905 revolution Russia as backward and barbaric (compared to the Western model), now considered post-1905 revolution Russia, for a while, as a source of inspiration and a model in itself. Until the 1917 Bolshevik Revolution Kōtoku's style of anarchism and syndicalism had an overwhelming influence on the Japanese socialist movement.[17] Violence as a political and revolutionary means was no longer a theoretical issue for the Japanese socialists. During the war and in its wake many Russian refugees arrived in Japan from Siberia and set up a community in Nagasaki. The Japanese government identified a common interest in fighting Russian autocracy between itself and this community that could help in the war effort.[18] Yet these refugees brought with them a tendency for political terrorism and also supplied explosives and training for revolutionaries in China. Noteworthy among them was Russel, whose real name was Nikolai Sudzilovskii and who settled in Japan during the war. Another colorful figure was Grigorii Gershuni, who was the head of the Social Revolutionary Party's infamous "military organization" and who escaped from Siberia to Japan in November 1906. In Japan he met many revolutionaries, including Sun Yat-sen. Kōtoku, who by that time had already begun to reject the illusion of constitutional socialist politics, admired him. Ultimately, Kōtoku was accused for conspiring against the emperor and was executed in 1911.

There are a number of examples of moderate Japanese socialists who were encouraged by the war to become radical leftists and who adopted "materialistic" orientations of anarchism and "direct action." And there are examples of the opposite. Takabatake Motoyuki, for instance, who had been a Christian, first tended to the left but then strayed to the right in the direction of the state, a course taken by some of the most prominent European anarchists. After the war, he abandoned Christianity and joined the "materialist" faction of Japanese socialism. Although he failed to recognize the contradiction between Marxism and nationalism, he supported, from 1907, Kōtoku's "direct action" anarchist policy. Ōsugi Sakai could be added to this list. He had been Kōtoku's friend and partner in his anti-militarist policy well before the war (he was then only 19). Under his influence he later became one of the anarchists' leaders, yet in the end remained a Japanese patriot. He, like Takabatake, supported Tokyo in the war against Russia. Already then, and certainly after the Bolshevik Revolution, he distinguished between the universalistic, theoretical, and ideal socialist agenda (which he still upheld) and the particularistic, practical, and actual nationalist agenda (where he was concerned about Russian, and later Soviet, expansionist ambitions).[19] Therefore, the Russo-Japanese War did not necessarily contribute to the rejection of socialist ideology but did contribute a good deal, and for many years, to the rejection of Russia and then the Soviet Union, as its propelling power. The war highlighted the Russian threat to Japan, giving, therefore, the highest priority, above all other considerations, to the defense of the people and the nation.[20] At the same time, the war laid the infrastructure for a radical activism in the Russian Far East that ultimately made a decisive contribution to the promotion and consolidation of Asian communism.

The implications of the war for Russian radicalism

Although one tends to forget that it is an integral part of Asia, Russia itself had undergone revolutionary processes that created the infrastructure for the "export" and promotion of revolutions and radicalism in the entire region. Hardly any revolutionary conditions had existed in the Russian Far East prior to the war with Japan. The proportion of poor peasants in the society was relatively low (less than 20 percent), and the proletariat was small and spread among modest family enterprises, workshops, railroads, and ports. While many soldiers were deployed everywhere, they were disciplined and loyal to the government. Also, the proportion of urban population in the region was higher than in any other Russian province. Two parties had been competing there at the turn of the nineteenth century. Active primarily among the elites, teachers, officials, and engineers, the SRs upheld freedom, agrarian socialism, and an improvement in the peasants' and workers' standard of living. The Russian Social Democratic Party was active at the beginning of the twentieth century especially among the railroad workers and the students.[21]

It is the Russo-Japanese War that created conditions for revolutionary activity. In 1904 martial law was imposed on the Maritime District, which was close to the war zone, and in 1905 was extended to the Amur District. The war entailed inflation, hunger, shortages, and low morale. The frustration erupted after the peace treaty was signed at Portsmouth on September 5, 1905. Some 900,000 reserve troops, which remained in the region but could not return (the Russians had only one 7,500-kilometer railroad), revolted. Postal, telegraph, and railroad workers and gold miners joined them. They temporarily seized power in Vladivostok and Chita and briefly took over the Russian-owned China Eastern Railway. It is this unrest that had fed those leaders and revolutionaries who later provided assistance to the first East Asian communist movements, based on Lenin's doctrines.

As evident in his article "The Fall of Port Arthur," Lenin was pleased with the Japanese victory that defeated "Russian absolutism, but not the people." For him, the war, together with the 1905 revolution and the revolutions in Persia and Turkey, was evidence of a revolutionary change or (as implied by the title of his 1908 article) "Inflammable Materials in World Politics." Later, during World War I, he urged the proletariat to rejoice in Russia's defeat, as did the popular masses in 1905 after Japan had beaten the rule of the tsar. At that time, Lenin ignored the national-patriotic stand (unlike Stalin, who celebrated in his victory speech of September 1945 the revenge the Japanese finally received 40 years after tsarist Russia's shameful submission). Nationalism, which did not play a major role among Russian revolutionaries, did play a major role for Vietnamese revolutionaries.

The implications of the war for Vietnamese radicalism

At the beginning of the twentieth century the leaders of the Vietnamese national movement were looking for help in their struggle against French colonialism. China, which in the past had been the most influential power in Vietnam, could no longer provide assistance following its defeat in the war with France in 1884–5, and was preoccupied with resolving its own problems, both internal and external. Apparently, post-Meiji Restoration Japan had become an alternative. Soon, however, Vietnamese nationalists became distrustful of Japan, especially when Tokyo exposed its imperialist policy by its victory over China in 1895, followed by a takeover of Taiwan and the Ryukyu Islands and a penetration of Korea. Under these circumstances, Japan's readiness to help Vietnamese nationalism raised suspicions about its motives. Yet, 15 years later the Russo-Japanese War, and especially Japan's victory, had deeply affected the younger and educated layer of Vietnamese society. These events provided another opportunity for a re-evaluation of the meanings and outcomes of Japanese modernization and thereby contributed toward stiffening the Vietnamese nationalist attitude against France. Although Japanese modernization had been launched 30 years earlier, it stood the test of time only when it defeated Russia— a Western power. Even in today's perspective this should be regarded as a great achievement but in those days it had tremendous and unprecedented significance.

Japan's victory taught Vietnam's nationalist leaders two main lessons. The first was that the only way in which the East could cope with the West was by acquiring Western scientific, technological, and general knowledge (like Japan). The second was that such modernization is possible only in the framework of an independent entity (such as Japan). Consequently, Vietnam (and other Asian colonies or semi-colonies) should seek national liberation even by force. Although Japan had never been subject to colonial rule, it still provided the model. One of Hanoi's most prestigious private classical education institutions, the Dong Kinh Nghia Thuc (Eastern Capital [namely China] No Tuition School), which combined Confucian orthodoxy with modern subjects, regarded pre-modern China as *thien-trieu* (celestial court), or the center of civilization. At the same time it regarded modern China (as well as Vietnam) as a backward country compared to the superiority of modern Japan. The discussion reaches its climax in the description of the Russo-Japanese War and especially of the crucial Tsushima battle. Given these events, Japan is now pronounced *thien-trieu* and thereby replaces China as the center of civilization.[22] These views were shared by many of Vietnam's modern leaders.

A well-known one was Phan Boi Chau, a Vietnamese scholar who set up in 1904 the Duy Tan Hoi (Reformation, or Modernization, Society), which was engaged in sending students to Japan, upheld the restoration of the legitimate dynasty (Nguyen), and urged the expulsion of the French. In early 1905 he traveled to Japan to ask for Japanese (military) aid. His trip had been motivated by the "common" racial features, by the Meiji Restoration model, by the Japanese example of constitutional monarchy, and by the concentration in Japan of Chinese intellectual expatriates. Phan had been influenced by Kang Yuwei (K'ang Yu-wei) and Liang Qichao (Liang Ch'i-ch'ao), who were reformists rather than revolutionaries. But it was primarily Japan's success in its war against Russia that governed Phan's decision to seek Tokyo's support. The Vietnamese would have not turned to Japan had it not been for this victory, which shifted the movement from moderate reformism to revolutionary radicalism. Phan believed that Japan had been interested in expelling France, and the West, from Asia. In his memoirs *Prison Notes* (1913), Phan wrote:

> The Japanese victory has opened an entirely new world to us . . . Before the French invasion, we knew only China. After the French came, France was the only country we knew, besides China. The Vietnamese never dreamed of the changing world and new trends . . . Japan's victory greatly influences us and changes our thinking.
>
> The problem of arms (in the struggle against France) will not be resolved without foreign assistance. In the light of history, geography, and race, China seems the best choice. But China has already conceded its sovereignty [in Vietnam] to France under the Tianjin [Tientsin] Treaty following the war of 1884. Those who fled to China, expecting help after the anti-French rising of 1885–86 had failed, were disappointed.[23]

The outcome of the war produced experiments, in which the Vietnamese became involved, to set up pan-Asian solidarity organizations. The League of East Asian Peoples was established in Singapore. In the summer of 1905 two Chinese scholars, Zhang Binlin (Chang Pin-lin) and Zhang Ji (Chang Chi), set up the Association for Asian Solidarity, which was an anarchist organization. In 1908 the East Asian Alliance was formed in Japan. A great irony (which also reflected the attitude of the powers) had been hidden in these moves under Japanese auspices—not only in a retrospective view but also in those days. The turn to the Japanese was made precisely when they themselves joined the imperialist "club." In 1905 Japan took over Korea, making it a protectorate—a first stage toward a complete annexation of Korea in 1910. In 1931 Japan occupied Manchuria and in 1937 invaded China. In fact, the prospect that Japan would support liberal or republican elements in Asia became inconceivable—although at that time it was difficult to see. Yet, within a few years, before the end of the decade, Japan's direction became evident to the Vietnamese national movement. In a retrospective view Phan mentions his impossible stand, but it is doubtful if he had realized it in 1905. China was facing a similar dilemma, though much more serious.

The implications of the war for Chinese radicalism

The impact of the Meiji Restoration on China was slow, primarily because of the conservative nature of the Manchu administration, which considered itself more Confucian than Confucius. While the reform attempts that reached their climax in 1898 had failed, reality did not leave any choice and the court began, reluctantly and sluggishly, to initiate reform in education and the military as early as 1901. These and other moves gathered momentum in 1905, to a great extent (but not exclusively), because of the Russo-Japanese War. Michael Gasster counts four key events that made the year 1905 a turning point in Chinese history. They include the abolition of the traditional examination system, the decision to investigate external models of constitutional monarchy, the foundation of Sun Yat-sen's Revolutionary Alliance, and Japan's victory over Russia (together with the October Manifesto of the 1905 revolution in Russia, which promised, for the first time, a constitution).[24]

Even before the outbreak of the war, the deployment of Russian troops in Manchuria (following the Boxer Protocol) had created an anti-Russian as well as a pro-Japanese climate among Chinese students and intellectuals that was articulated in publications and associations, mostly in Shanghai. Later to become the Republic's Education Minister and Rector of Beijing University, Cai Yuanpei (Ts'ai Yuan-p'ei) and his colleagues began to publish a newspaper in December 1903 called *Eshi Jingwen* (*E-shih ching-wen*, Important News about Russia). It was intended not only to warn against Russian expansionism but also to promote radical, especially nihilist, revolutionary sentiments. As the first news about Russia's defeat by Japan began to arrive, an editorial published on February 11, 1904 exulted:

An autocratic country which has violated every principle of justice, has sent its people, whose resentment has accumulated to breaking point, into war against a constitutional country. They retreated at the first encounter and suffered defeat. This is nothing other than a stirring demonstration of the law that autocracies lose. Highly gratifying! Highly gratifying![25]

Soon after the outbreak of the war the newspaper's name was changed and from late February 1904 it was published as *Jingzhong Ribao* (*Ching-chung jih-pao*, Alarm Bell Daily News). Its contents have also changed. In addition to reporting the course of the war the newspaper adopted a strong nationalist stand, not only anti-Russian (that had been evident heretofore) but also anti-Japanese. While initially it called for a Sino-Japanese alliance directed against Russia, it soon became disillusioned about Japan's ultimate intentions toward China. Other journals reached a similar conclusion that, ultimately, Japan would become no less aggressive than Russia, especially at China's expense, and therefore denounced all kinds of imperialism. Following Cai's resignation, Liu Shipei (Liu Shih-p'ei), soon to become the leading Chinese anarchist in Japan, took over the paper. It was closed down by the Shanghai Municipality in January 1905.[26]

Liang Qichao was among the few Chinese intellectuals who were in Japan and who shared the anti-imperialist stand. As early as March 1904 his journal, *Xinmin Congbao* (*Hsin-min ts'ung-pao*, New People Magazine), warned that the belief that Japan would act magnanimously and would return Manchuria to China was but a dream. Japan would strive to increase its control over this region and would behave in the same way the other powers behaved. He rejected the idea that China should rely on Japan for its defense (along the Monroe Doctrine lines, which guaranteed the security of South America). Liang was a consistent partner to the radicals in his criticism of the different kinds of imperialism, a view that conflicted with Sun Yat-sen's.[27] Sun, on the contrary, exploited the Western feelings of shock and amazement at the Japanese victory in order to mobilize support for China (for example, in France) as a counterweight to the emergence of Japan. While his efforts failed he still considered Japan as the major base of the Chinese revolutionary movement. This was but one of the dialectical and paradoxical implications of the war for China.

First, there is little doubt that it was because of the war (which had created a model for a victory of a constitutional monarchy over an autocracy) that the Qing (Ch'ing) court began to seriously consider transforming its political system. Chinese reformists (mostly expatriates in Japan) had theoretically favored a constitutional regime at the expense of an absolutist monarchy already in late nineteenth-century and early twentieth-century forums, but practical measures in this direction were directly motivated by Russia's defeat. In December 1905, immediately after the war, a Chinese delegation of five ministers was sent to Japan, Britain, the United States,

Germany, and France, to explore their ruling systems and the possibility of formulating a constitution for China. The departure of the delegation was delayed by four months following an attempt by radical terrorists to blow up the train that would have taken the delegation out of Beijing in September. This attempt reflected the radicals' concern that the delegation's conclusions would only reinforce the foreign dynastic regime. Indeed, the delegation returned in July 1906 and recommended unanimously that a constitution be adopted. Preparations began in early September. China's attitude toward Japan was ambivalent. Despite (and perhaps because of) the humiliation in the 1894–5 Sino-Japanese War and the territorial price that China had to pay in the 1904–5 Russo-Japanese War, the Chinese still regarded Japan as a model.

Second, the Russo-Japanese War was actually fought on Chinese soil. Yet China was not directly involved nor could determine, or even influence, which foreign power would ultimately govern Manchuria—a Chinese territory—let alone engineer the return of this region to Chinese sovereignty. Japan's victory harmed not only Russia but also (and first of all) China (as well as Korea), and stirred a good deal of agitation among Chinese students and intellectuals. The admiration for Japan's victory, on the one hand, and the frustration about the helplessness of the Chinese government, on the other hand, together contributed to the strengthening and consolidation of Chinese nationalism. In August 1905, following a decade of uncoordinated and disunited activity, one national-political organization was established, the Revolutionary Alliance chaired by Sun Yat-sen, which, six years later, led to the so-called Republican Revolution.

Third, Japan's victory paradoxically underlined the Western threat to Asia and had shaped its anti-imperialist orientation long before Lenin turned it into a policy aimed at triggering the revolution in those countries under foreign domination, either fully or partly. Revolutionary publications in Shanghai firmly protested against Russia's takeover of Manchuria. At the same time they condemned the Manchus for allowing the violation of Chinese territory or, at least, for not reacting properly. Russia's defeat pointed to the danger from the foreign powers that was facing China's independence. Only a few Chinese intellectuals regarded Japan, for that matter and at that time, as a "foreign power." On the contrary, it represented a model—primarily of military power—that totally contradicted the Manchu weakness. Japan's victory over Russia encouraged Japanese-led experimentation with pan-Asian organizations directed against the West. Only a few, if any, of those who praised Japan's superiority (including Sun Yat-sen) realized at that time that the threat implied in Japan's pan-Asian policy was an expression of the drive toward imperialist domination. Attention was centered on the West. Fed by the war, the emergence of Chinese nationalist consciousness stimulated local cooperation between the government and the traditional elites in an effort to claim and retrieve the mines and railroad concessions handed to the West in previous years. Beginning in

1905, a number of provinces tried, and to a great extent also succeeded, to abolish or modify contracts with foreign companies or acquire the concessions often at a cost that was greater than the sum that had already been invested in the project. In this policy, economic considerations of profitability were secondary to nationalist considerations and to feelings of pride and independence.

Finally, the number of Chinese cadets in military academies (both in China and in Japan) increased substantially after Japan's victory. As noted by Hatano:

> In the year after the Russo-Japanese War, many literati and intellectuals enrolled in military schools and even enlisted as soldiers. Some of them remained in the rank and file to encourage revolutionary activity among the troops; others were sent to military schools and were promoted to lower officer rank. These soldiers, noncommissioned officers, and lower commissioned officers became the core of the expanding revolutionary activity in the army.[28]

Conclusion

There is no need to exaggerate the implications of the Russo-Japanese War for East Asian radicalism. On the one hand, in many parts of Asia, and outside, activities, both conventional and radical, routinely continued and seemed completely detached from the course of the war. On the other hand, the long-term implications of the war were mainly symbolic and conceptual, while the concrete and practical implications were short term (the real impact on radicalism was related to the 1917 Russian Revolution, the growing familiarity with Lenin's doctrines, and the foundation of the Comintern as an organization dedicated to the promotion of revolution in Asia). Set up in early 1906, a relatively moderate Japanese government, led by Saionji Kimmochi, enabled a certain degree of freedom of association. Some of the Christian socialists and the "political" or "materialistic" group were reunited and founded (again) the Japanese Socialist Party. It should be recalled that the dimensions of this phenomenon were very modest. In 1904 the police estimated the number of socialists in Japan at approximately 3,000. In fact, there were only about 200, mostly students and some journalists. They were too few to exploit the hardships that the war caused to workers, while playing on their patriotic feelings. The end of the war was accompanied by a serious recession and unemployment (many demobilized soldiers became redundant). In 1906 the number and scale of industrial conflicts and violent incidents multiplied four and five times, but the government used the wartime to consolidate capitalism and the banks, to nationalize the railroads, and to develop the economy. Apparently, conditions were created for radical activism, but Japanese socialism has never managed to take off and become a significant component in

Japanese politics. In this respect, the Russo-Japanese War was but a passing cloud. Moreover, the Asian enthusiasm about the Japanese model quickly subsided. Those few who had seen the writing on the wall well before the war were now joined by many others who became concerned about Japanese imperialism. Japan's victory had first been perceived as a massive encouraging injection to the non-Western nations in their belief in, and ability to bring about, the eradication of Western domination in a global context (East against West). Japan was regarded as an ally, a model, a means. Yet, within a few years, the meaning of its victory had been transformed, now focusing more on the Asian context and regarded as a first step in Japan's overall strategy, which had originated in the late nineteenth century, to dominate the entire region. Thus, Japan, which was now turned into an adversary, an enemy, and a target, sowed in its amazing victory over Russia the seeds of its defeat 40 years later.

Notes

1 Powles, 1961: 89–129.
2 Duus, 1983.
3 More than 60,000 were killed and nearly 22,000 died of disease. War expenses were 8.5 times higher than the cost of the Sino-Japanese War (1894–5); 6.6 times the regular state income in 1903; and 11.7 times more than the tax income. Wage-freezing and a drastic price rise caused the population a great deal of suffering.
4 Mitchell, 1983: 134–9.
5 Okamoto, 1982: 262–70.
6 Some argue that Japan's war against Russia (and certainly that against China) were not imperialist wars in the Leninist sense of representing monopolistic capital and economic goals, but rather a reflection of domestic and international political considerations. Economic considerations began to play a central role only after the Russo-Japanese War, as evident in the annexation of Korea and the subsequent Japanese expansion. Hoston, 1986: 260–4.
7 Kublin, 1950.
8 Crump, 1983.
9 Hoston, 1994: 184–5.
10 Wilson, 1969.
11 Letter, December 1906. In Crump, 1983: 291–2.
12 Crump, 1983: 74.
13 Notehelfer, 1971.
14 Wilson, 1999: 168–75. It is important to note that ten years earlier Kōtoku supported Japan's war against China. As an idealist he considered the war as Japan's mission, as the most advanced nation in Asia, to bring "progress" to the backward countries and to save the entire continent from Western penetration. At that time he, along with his socialist colleagues, failed to see the contradiction between socialism and nationalism. What changed his mind was the outcome of the war, which expanded Japanese control of East Asia, which, in his view, was useless. Kōtoku approved of the Japanese contribution to Asia but disapproved of Japanese imperialism. For a more detailed analysis of Kōtoku's opposition to the Russo-Japanese War, see Wilson, 1999: 168–75.
15 Quoted in Notehelfer, 1971: 99.

16 A letter to Albert Johnson, August 10, 1905, quoted in Notehelfer, 1971: 113.
17 Hoston, 1986: 21–3.
18 Akashi, 1988.
19 Stanley, 1982.
20 Hoston, 1994: 327–8, 416–17.
21 This section is based on Stephan, 1994: 99–107.
22 Marr, 1971: 164–5.
23 Quoted in Kawamoto, 1984: 120, 121.
24 Gasster, 1969: 59–60.
25 Quoted in Price, 1974: 178.
26 Duiker, 1977: 12; Rankin, 1971: 99; Price, 1974: 179.
27 Scalapino and Yu, 1985: 115–16.
28 Hatano, 1968: 375.

14 Tokyo as a shared Mecca of modernity

War echoes in the colonial Malay world

Michael Laffan[1]

Writing for a Dutch audience in 1901, a Sumatran medical student living in Holland, Abdul Rivai (b. 1877), remarked that, if the Dutch were to attend to their colonial population with justice, then they would:

> turn their face in prayer no longer to the *ka'bah* but to The Hague, where they know the Queen of the Netherlands, dearly beloved by . . . all, and to whose subjects they are indebted for their happiness and prosperity, to be enthroned.[2]

Written three years prior to the Russo-Japanese War, the words of Abdul Rivai make direct reference to the faith of the majority of the Indies by specific reference to the *qibla*, that is, the direction of prayer focused on the locus of the Ka'ba in Mecca. However, his explicit replacement of Mecca by The Hague also demonstrates that he was an imbiber of the Dutch policy of "association." This was a policy guided to a large degree by the renowned orientalist C. Snouck Hurgronje (1857–1936), who argued that Islam had to be privatized by its adherents, and who advocated the development of an elite class of subjects enamored of a Dutch model for progress and modernity. In this relationship, Islam was to be confined to the realm of family and personal life, and all thoughts of political independence were to be deferred until such time that the Indonesians (as they would one day be called) had achieved the rank of junior partners in a world where East and West could meet as bride and groom.

On the other hand, in the aftermath of the war an Egyptian visitor to Southeast Asia en route for Japan, who presented himself as a voice of an equally modern but Muslim nation using the pen-name of Ali Ahmad al-Jarjawi, lays out an entirely different future orientation for its peoples—peoples whom he elides with those of Asia in general and specifically derides as being Muslim brothers in name only and bedevilled by superstition and lassitude. This orientation was predicated on the widespread hopes that the Japanese would soon convert to Islam:

> [There are those that] say that the conversion of Japan will bring back the past glory of [Islam] ... [It will] revive its lost marks of power and greatness and it will implant in the hearts of all the nations the love for Islam that existed in those bygone ages. And they adorn this by saying that the Japanese nation is the Eastern state marked out for position and greatness in the eyes of every state and government throughout the East and the West. And if it converts, then there would be no stopping it from organizing the Muslims of China and India together as one in order to create a tripartite Islamic power on land and sea. Thus the whole Muslim word will be empowered, and the Mikado will be like Saladin. Then all the independent Islamic kingdoms will unite completely in the name of religion ... with Tokyo as the *qibla* of the Muslims in the Far East as the Sublime Porte [Istanbul] is to the Muslims of the Near East.[3]

As we shall see later, such a view was shared to a degree by the publishers of a Singaporean journal for Islamic reform, *al-Imam* (1906–8), who were also captivated by the news of an ascendant Japan. And, like al-Jarjawi, they too looked to Japan for certain answers and voiced what now seem to be rather prosaic hopes about the future religious orientation of the Meiji emperor.

Whereas the above juxtaposition of the statements of a Netherlands-oriented Sumatran and a Japanophile Egyptian seems to lay out two distinct trajectories, I argue that their expressions were closely entwined and, more importantly, read together in island Southeast Asia, with its largely Muslim population adjudged to be in need of a new focal point for their political affections. Through close attention to two journals that encapsulated these variant trajectories in Batavia and Singapore, in addition to brief comparisons of other statements from the region, this chapter will explore how this intersection, and therefore the *amplification* of their respective messages, hinged upon Japan's success in the war. I will also suggest that such an examination shows how the war had crucial implications for the globally agreed opposition of East and West to be elided with that of Islam and colonizer, in addition to proving the global applicability of modern methods of education and reform.

Finally, I should pay tribute here to a now classic article by Barbara Andaya, who first wrote of the shift in orientation in Muslim Southeast Asia, and among the court elite of Riau in particular, from the Ottoman Empire to Tokyo as an alternative savior from Dutch colonialism.[4] While much of my earlier work on this topic was first inspired by her article, I shall suggest here that it is perhaps better to see that Tokyo featured as one of several lodestars in the firmament of what C.A. Bayly has called "hybrid modernity."[5] Certainly, it is clear that Japan's light glimmered somewhat indirectly in Southeast Asia, and through refractive lenses in The Hague and Cairo, well before becoming an alternative to Istanbul, or yet what

Benedict Anderson once called "the light of Asia."[6] And the Japanese in turn knew well how to filter that light for local conditions when they came to Indonesia.

Southeast Asia and the Japanese image before the war

Maritime Southeast Asia has long occupied a crucial place on the trade route linking China with India and the West. Positioned as an archipelago off the coast of mainland Asia, Japan was also a participant in this international network. By the fourth century, both it and the lands that would one day be known as Malaysia and Indonesia were links in a continuous chain of Buddhist study centers; one scholar has even suggested that the origins of one Javanese script may be found in the handwriting of an Indian scholar resident in Japan.[7] A thousand years later again, much of this global trade had come to be handled by Muslim merchants, though it was still a maritime world that encompassed diversity. In the fifteenth century, one of the four harbormasters of the leading Malayo-Muslim entrepôt of Malacca had the specific task of dealing with the trade of Champa, China, and the kingdom of Ryukyu (in which Japanese trade must have figured), while Japanese trade with the entire archipelago would expand markedly after 1570 and until its prohibition by the Tokugawa Shogunate in 1635.[8]

Such a regional presence of Japanese in the sixteenth century is also attested in contemporary Thai accounts, but it was increasingly a corollary of the widespread displacements of soldiers of fortune caused by the wars at home and then the policies of the Tokugawa. The Dutch merchant Jeremie van Vliet (1602–63) reported that King Prasat Thong (r. 1629–56) had seized the throne with the aid of some 800 Japanese mercenaries whose services he retained as his elite bodyguard.[9] Such killers were there for the hiring by all. The notorious governor general of Batavia, Jan Pieterszoon Coen (1586–1629), had already employed Japanese mercenaries for his suppression of the population of the island of Banda in 1621.[10]

Even so, clear references to the Japanese or Japanese products in Malay literature are rare beyond the occasional mention in texts like the Ambonese *Hikayat Tanah Hitu* (c. 1650) and then a very gory incident in the popular adventures of the Malaccan hero Hang Tuah. In this account Hang Tuah travels to Siam to purchase elephants for the Sultan and meets with a band of famous "swashbucklers" (*pendekar*) of *Jepun*.[11]

Beyond perhaps being regarded as a source of swordsmen for hire, by the end of the nineteenth century Japan figured largely in Indies' imaginations as a source of cheap goods and exoticism. Japanese women were particularly sought after as prostitutes. One Malay ruler, Abu Bakar of Johore, was well known for his penchant in this regard, and the account of his tour of Japan in 1883 features the regular (but probably temporary) conversion of local women to satisfy that predilection.[12] Certainly, the stereotype was powerful enough for the great Indonesian novelist Pramoedya

Ananta Toer to have one of his characters bewitched by the beauty of a Japanese prostitute in the first of his four novels based on the life of the Javanese journalist Tirtoadhisuryo.[13]

The unflattering images of slashing swords and costly charms would change, but slowly, and well before the struggles at Port Arthur and in the Straits of Tsushima. The first direct shift in awareness may be noted as a by-product of the voyage of an Ottoman warship, the *Ertugrul*, sent by Sultan Abdülhamid to Japan with the declared purpose of conveying a congratulatory medal to his Meiji contemporary. Although its story was ultimately tinged by tragedy—the vessel sank in a typhoon with great loss of life—the mission may well have already been a success if we accept Selim Deringil's contention that the real motive for its dispatch was the raising of the Ottoman banner in Southeast Asian waters.[14] The *Ertugrul* was certainly the object of widespread attention when it docked in Singapore in 1889–90. According to Anthony Reid, members of the Acehnese resistance, already locked in a war with the Dutch for some 17 years, hoped to pass appeals for aid from either Tokyo or Istanbul to the ship's captain.[15]

More tangible recognition came in the wake of the Sino-Japanese conflict of 1894–5. Quite against global expectations, Japan defeated China. This led directly to Japan being seen as a model for reformers in Korea and more especially in China, where there was both a rethinking of the style of modernizations required and a retrospective casting of the very real innovations that had taken place under the Qing as a grand failure.[16] Equally, there was interest shown in Japan among the sizeable Chinese communities of the Netherlands Indies. In 1895, the Malay language newspaper *Bintang Barat* reported on the success of Japan, first detailing their exemplary emotional attachment to their homeland (*tanah ajar*), which facilitated their occupation of Formosa, and then reporting on a group of Japanese touring in Sumatra with pictures of the war that were apparently in great demand among local Chinese who were paying ten cents per head to view them.[17]

Changes were also engendered in Europe. Perhaps mindful of their special history of diplomatic relations with the Tokugawa, but most certainly following strong diplomatic pressure from an assertive Japan when the bilateral treaty was revised in 1896, the Dutch parliament decreed (through the Japannerwet of 1899) that Japanese subjects were henceforth "made equal" (*gelijkgesteld*). That is, they were granted European status with all its attendant privileges. Incidentally, this was also the year in which the young Queen Wilhelmina made her speech announcing that the Dutch had an "ethical" concern for their Asian charges, and were henceforth endeavoring to provide more for their moral and physical uplift. It was also a policy that dovetailed neatly with Snouck's ideas of "association."

Despite their coincidental debuts, the Japannerwet and the ethical policy were not seen as related, at least in Holland. Certainly, the former policy was not imagined to have much impact in the Indies, where barely a thousand Japanese were registered as living in 1905, 80 percent of whom were women engaged as prostitutes and hairdressers.[18] Nevertheless, the elevation, seemingly confirmed by the signing of a military pact with Great Britain in 1902, directly stimulated the sizeable Chinese minority to press— and press hard—for the same status. Their call was all the louder given that the Japanese were previously fellow "Foreign Orientals" (*vreemde ooster-lingen*) of the second, and most ambiguous, tier of the Dutch colonial system, which lay between the Dutch and the indigenous populations of Malays, Javanese, and other Austronesian peoples with whom they were now supposedly most concerned.

This realignment of ethnic fortunes on the ascending ladder of civiliza-tion in both Europe and Asia was raised in the early issues of the first of the periodicals to be examined here. This was *Bintang Hindia* (Indies Star), a broadsheet co-produced in Weltevreden by a Dutch veteran of the Aceh War, Lieutenant Clockener Brousson, and in The Hague by his Indonesian partner, Abdul Rivai, who had moved there in 1899 after marriage to a Dutch widow—an act that caused his parents to accuse him of apostasy.[19] The paper itself presented didactic articles in Malay, Dutch, and Javanese and was lavishly illustrated with large photographs showing both the colony and the metropolitan *qibla* to which its population—or at least its administrators—were intended to aspire. Certainly, the newly elevated Governor General Joannes Benedictus van Heutsz, who had risen to his post in 1904 on the back of his apparent success in finally quelling the Acehnese insurgency, realized the propaganda value of *Bintang Hindia* (his portrait had already graced the cover in April 1903) and agreed to subsidize it handsomely.[20]

Bintang Hindia was in many ways the primary organ communicating the Dutch government's newfound ethical interest in educational uplift for the peoples of the Indies. But it also reflected the specific interests of the expatriate Rivai, in particular his desire that others follow in his foot-steps to Europe, for which he had once nominated a rather un-Dutch example for his own colonizers:

> Taking as my cue my own investigations and good impressions here in Holland, I hereby take the opportunity to bring Japan to the attention of the colonial master, [a country] whose current progress is all thanks to the many Japanese youngsters sent to Europe. Imagine [if you will, the implications if] so many natives who, having spent some years in native society developing some promise and having a demonstrable aptitude for study, might be able to expand their knowledge here in Holland.[21]

Once he was in a position to disseminate his views from Holland, Rivai hoped that the eyes of his fellow "natives" would also be directed to the Japanese. In any event, Japan was often discussed in the *Bintang Hindia*, an interest no doubt given Dutch sanction as that nation had clearly followed the Western prescription of industrialization and imperialism, even having acquired a colony of its own in Formosa. The May edition of 1903, for example, included a portrait of Marquis Itō Hirobumi in his dress uniform.[22] As such, the Japanese stood shoulder-to-shoulder on the great, and gloriously militaristic, stage of the world—a situation that must have created strange encounters in the Indies if a Japanese hairdresser ever did assert her right to ride in the same carriage of a tram as one of the many Dutch women now arriving from the metropole in ever greater numbers.

War and on . . .

A reading of *Bintang Hindia* shows that Japan was presented as being of interest to Dutch citizen and Indies subject alike because of its people's ability to emulate Western-defined modernity while maintaining their distinct national culture. A feature article appearing shortly before the war spoke admiringly of the heightened aesthetic sensibilities of the Japanese, explaining how Europeans were drawn to Japanese art because of the underlying high quality of its culture.[23] When war did break out, Clockener and Rivai went to press with no small degree of enthusiasm for Japan, and predicted victory over the Russians, though not without some soul-searching as to the blow dealt to the "modern" ideals to which their paper spoke.

> At the time of writing—8 February—the cables bring us news that war has broken out in East Asia. From this day forth the blood of humankind will soak a part of the world. Whatever the meaning of a war is [understood to be] between two kingdoms that have long readied their land and sea forces, that have long sharpened their swords, while loading their rifles and cannon—the [defining] act of this twentieth age . . . the meaning of this war is well known to all readers: "Mass Slaughter" (*"Pemboenoehan Raja"*). This is the name of war. Mass slaughter in this century . . . the "century of progress" (*"abad kemadjoean"*). And all the while one nation assails the other with the word *peace*.[24]

Certainly, blame for the war was firmly assigned to Russia, whose emperor it was that had first called for the establishment of an international arbiter. Not without irony did Abdul Rivai note that there was a so-called "Peace Palace" near his office. From here, though, the article outlines the cause of the war as the expansion of Russian interest in Manchuria on the pretext of protecting its railway and unseating the Japanese from their (natural?) interests in China. Even so, with the Russian build-up there had been a corresponding Japanese build-up, and its armada was declared more than equal to the task, bolstered as it was by the support of the Anglo-Japanese Alliance. The editors also speculated on the broader ramifications of the conflict if it were to last more than a few months:

We the Indies people are also reminded of our land (*tanah kita*). The question that comes to mind is: "Won't the Indies (Tanah Hindia) be drawn into the troubles of the Russo-Japanese conflict?" Such a question gives us cause to think of the Russian warships that will come to East Asia. Even if our Government has declared that the Indies will not intervene on the side of Japan or Russia, what if Russian warships were to pass through our lands short of coal and [being] unable to procure it, must take it by force from Emmahaven, Sabang or Deli? ... What then of the Indies? Shall we resist? And with what? The Indies has no armada to counter those of the European nations. In short: the Russo-Japanese War is not without meaning for our land.[25]

Certainly, this second Japanese war would prove of even greater meaning for the Indies and the wider colonial world. It is worth noting here that the explicit reference above to "our land," the world, and progress was actually quite novel in the Indies—or at least it was in a paper with an explicitly shared constituency of Dutch and native alike. But it would become a constant feature in the papers of the day and those to come, when peoples of Southeast Asia would, in large part through the medium of print capitalism, conceive of the modern world assembled in the states mapped out for them by their colonial masters, or—as in the case of Thailand— left to them in part as a result of mapping elsewhere.[26] Of course, *Bintang Hindia* differed from later nationalist periodicals in that its concept of "ours" included the metropole, with a government in The Hague, its use of the Dutch name Emmahaven (now Teluk Bayur), and explicitly Dutch-defined notions of progress.

Despite the obvious sympathies of the editors in the war, the coverage was not relentlessly partisan. Keeping with the didactic aims of the journal, readers were given background information on both parties. These included potted geographies, battlefield maps (with the caveat that readers were to understand that the ships represented—white for Russia, black for Japan— had since moved), statistics on troops and equipment, and the respective national anthems—the latter being accompanied by a bilingual note on the power of such hymns to move and galvanize a people. After all, "a song too is a weapon."[27]

Further details would appear in the following weeks as the Baltic Fleet under the command of Vice Admiral Rozhestvenskii made its pioneering voyage around the Cape of Good Hope with decks overloaded with coal to avoid calling at hostile (or yet neutral) ports. Photos sourced from contemporary European periodicals tracked the vessels and land campaign and speculated on the respective fighting qualities of the combatants. The Japanese were declared to be willing national heroes and thus more than a match for wretched conscripts of a moribund empire. And once the clashes did take place, artists' impressions gave Indies readers the same message that their colonizers would experience—or indeed anyone who has ever perused a copy of Cassell's *History of the Russo-Japanese War*. There were images of the Meiji emperor on horseback, impressions of the Dogger Bank debacle (when the Russian fleet fired on English fishermen in the mistaken belief that Japanese torpedo boats were lying in wait in the English Channel), and of General Nogi Maresuke standing amid the ruins of Port Arthur.[28]

But, while the following months gave the chance for feature pieces on the (victorious) royal family as much as its Western-equipped men, there could be a hard edge to the use of Japan as a model; and well after the treaty had been signed and Japan began its inexorable intervention in Korea, it remained foregrounded in the minds of many in the press. In March 1907, Abdul Rivai penned an essay that appeared under the now standard portrait of the Meiji emperor and briefly visited the geography, history, and religion of Japan, though he used the exercise as a not-too-subtle foil against his own patrons, with whom he was then having arguments. For, whereas he quoted material concerning the allegedly hybrid Sino-Ainu origins of the Japanese—origins that his sources said the Japanese did their best to obscure, it was clear to Rivai that they represented the greatest example of an Asian nation that had done well on the unequal global playing field.

Rivai also made sure to attribute any misplaced feelings of cultural inferiority to one race in particular:

> This [preceding passage] is information that tells us that the Japanese people is now embarrassed about the form of its origins. And given that the white-skinned people are the most elevated on the face of the earth, then the Japanese must therefore wish to obscure their origins (*menghilangkan asal-oesolnya*). This must have been written by a white-skinned person. Such [attribution] reminds us that even if there are people of the Indies that have already been made equal by law with the peoples of Europe (*gelijkstelling*), it is impossible for ink and paper to change flesh and blood!!![29]

Rivai then wrote with some indignation that the American government still refused to acknowledge Japanese equivalence in the way that the Dutch had. He even ventured that, if such recognition was not forthcoming, then Admiral Tōgō Heihachirō would take his own (black) ships to threaten America; inverting the conventional opening scene of the story of Japan's modernization. For Rivai, then, Japan could be Asian and ascendant, modern and militant. For the editors of *al-Imam*, connected to a rival intellectual *qibla*, Japan needed something else.

Al-Imam: the East as Islam ascendant

Compared to the explicitly Dutch-oriented *Bintang Hindia*, Singapore's *al-Imam* seems on first impression to be an exact opposite. It announced that its purpose was religious reform, not emulation of a colonial master;

its script was Arabic, whereas that of *Bintang Hindia* was roman (aside from the orthographic inclusion of the Arabic glottal stop ء); it had few images, whereas *Bintang Hindia* was in many respects a photo-journal; it drew heavily on Arabic for national and technical terms, not Dutch; and its constituents were declared to be the many Muslim peoples of "our side" of the Muslim world rather than the loyal protégés of distant colonizers.

It was also the function of a different partnership. Whereas Clockener Brousson and Rivai were linked across the seas as veteran hand of the Dutch Indies and eager Sumatran pupil in Holland, the founders of *al-Imam* consisted of an alliance between Malays affiliated to the emasculated court of Riau Lingga and the sons of mixed marriages between local mothers and expatriate Arabs. The vast majority of these Arabs came from Hadramaut, now a province of the modern Republic of Yemen, who, like the Chinese, faced harassment in the Netherlands Indies as Foreign Orientals. From the beginning, their orientation toward fellow Muslims in the archipelago was made clear, with the editorial by Salim al-Kalali—whom the Dutch suspected of having been involved in the Aceh War—declaiming:

> Indeed we are not of the same lineage as the people of this place, nonetheless as those who are locally born we have become attached to their country as our homeland (*watan*) for we have drunk its milk, grown up on its flesh and blood and enjoyed all its benefits. Should we not therefore feel indebted to its country and people?[30]

Whereas this was also an orientation that was presented in terms of seemingly natural leadership grounded in their (Arab) links to the Middle East, it was not conceived solely in terms of ancient history.[31] *Al-Imam* stressed the very newness of their intellectual connections and the universal utility of seeing the modern in action, whether in the great Ottoman fleet (described as "the Islamic Fleet"), or in the new ways of thinking about Islam, and especially Islamic education, as voiced by religious reformers in Cairo such as the late Muhammad Abduh (1849–1905) and Rashid Rida (1865–1935).

As Natalie Mobini-Kesheh has argued, Chinese mobilization to found welfare organizations and societies in the neighboring Dutch territories and spurred, as we have seen, by the successes and elevation of the Japanese was also an important element in the early activities of the Hadrami diaspora, and especially their own attempt to break loose of the strictures imposed by being Foreign Orientals.[32] While they had trouble defining their constituents in a sometimes confusing deployment of language about "we Easterners," "we Muslims," or "fellow-siders," respectively, there was a clear orientation to the utility of Japan—after all, had not the Ottomans, whom they admired, long been interested in the rise of this state?

Indeed, there had long been an interest in Japan shown in the Ottoman lands (and the nominally Ottoman lands such as Egypt) even before the Ertugrul voyage. The first evidence for this seems to be found in didactic papers like Beirut's *al-Jinan* or Cairo's *al-Muqtataf* in the 1870s and 1880s.[33] Then, in the aftermath of the sinking of the Ertugrul, there were haphazard attempts at making contact—more often than not initiated by the Japanese, whose unofficial embassy in Istanbul had attempted to spy on the Black Sea Fleet as it slipped southward in 1904. Still, Japan was certainly popular among Muslims globally, a phenomenon that is now attracting increasing scholarly interest.[34]

As a part of this globalizing Muslim curiosity, the editors of *al-Imam* showed genuine interest in Japan, and all the more so because of the fact that this victory had resonated with their interests on at least three levels: first, it was a victory against the state that had done more than any other to weaken the Ottoman Empire; second, it was a victory of an "Eastern" nation over a Western empire; and, third, it was a victory for national independence over colonial ambition (even if the nation in question had colonial designs of its own). There was also a personal connection, in that one of its editors, Muhammad bin Aqil (1863–1931), had made a visit to Japan in 1898–9 together with his close friend and perhaps spiritual mentor, Sayyid Abd Allah al-Zawawi (1850–1924).[35]

The central problem, though, was the very lack of the final link to cement Japan's fate to that of the Islamic world, namely Islam itself. In some parts of the world ingenious arguments were formulated. In Bukhara, for example, a court scribe to the Manghit dynasty (1753–1921) explained the success of the Japanese against the Russians as a result of the secret conversion of the emperor, which he said had been predicted by prophetic tradition;[36] and, whereas *al-Imam* made no such claim, it was a much hoped for possibility that was seemingly in train.

In its maiden issue of July 1906, and under the banner of "Islam and Japan," *al-Imam* announced that the Japanese were establishing a commission to consider the question of the future national religion, to which the Ottoman Empire had allegedly dispatched three of its leading scholars. It was also reported, on the authority of a Tokyo resident called Abd al-Rahman Thomson, that the "Mikado" had thanked the Ottoman emperor for the mission, advising that the commission would sit for two months.[37] Here the journal pondered the reasoning for and ramifications of Japan's conversion. It was argued that, as the Japanese were now conversant with Western technology, they recognized that their nation needed to convert to one of the four truly revealed religions to complete the transition to modernity. The choice as to which faith to adopt, according to the editors, would then be made clear by the degree to which its exponents accepted the Japanese as equals of themselves (and of Britain for good measure). Here the argument was made that only Muslims would accept the Japanese as true equals (if not benevolent superiors), and once they had embraced the faith it would only be a short time before they would join their brothers in China, Siam, Malaya, and the Netherlands Indies, further adding that it "would come as no surprise" if Japan were to emerge as the leader of all the peoples east of the entrance to the Red Sea.

The British authorities in Singapore were aware of these enthusiasms, but were dismissive rather than anxious. As one official wrote:

> Much of this is sheer bombastic nonsense. It is almost impossible to conceive of a people in the forefront of civilization like the Japanese adopting a religion so hopelessly out of touch with the modern world as that amalgam of Judaism and Christianity which Mohamed planted in the mind of the seventh-century Arab . . . The outcome of the Russo-Japanese War has certainly been a check to the eastern progress of Russia; but it may result equally, though the fact is not yet patent, as a check to European aggression in other parts of Asia.[38]

It also seems that the Tokyo event announced in *al-Imam* was the very same occasion purportedly attended by the Egyptian whose comments on Tokyo's pan-Asian *qibla*-potential I cited above. Furthermore, it is possible that al-Jarjawi may prove to be a retired Egyptian army officer, Ahmad Affandi Fadli, whom *al-Imam* reported to be returning from a two-month inspection tour of Japan's schools full of praise for its people's industry in elevating their homeland (Ar. *watan*) and nation (Ar. *umma*)—though with little to say, at that point, of its religion.[39]

In any case, more was hoped for, and after the first announcement of the Japanese commission—which al-Jarjawi would represent as a congress to choose a new state religion, with Islam the obvious, but ultimately stymied front-runner—reactions were soon elicited from excited readers. One penned a short poem framing East and West as dormant and active respectively:

Tanyalah umat timur yang mulya	The noble people of the East enquire
Apakah penyakit didalam dunya?	What illness ails the world?
Kami mencita fursa dan peluang	We seek chance and opportunity
Angin yang baik jangan terbuang!	Let not a good wind be wasted!
Umat timur tidur cendera	The people of the East sleep soundly
Umat barat bertambah mara	The people of the West advance steadily

This was followed by the same writer's call for "the religious scholars of the East" to awake from their negligence so as to activate for their own people, and a long review article on Japan and Islam discussing the merits of "civilization" (Ar. *tamaddun*). Here he pointed out that there were nations that were more advanced than Japan and that perhaps these—and the ones occupying Muslim countries in particular—should be converted first. Even so, he admitted that the whole world had now heard of the victory over Russia, implying that if there was a nation on the global stage worth gaining for Islam, then Japan was it.[40]

Muslim or not, Japan was to be emulated. As such, it was frequently cited in *al-Imam* as an "Eastern" model, a view no doubt bolstered by Rashid Rida's initial enthusiasm for the conversion of the Japanese, which he had voiced in 1906.[41] In this respect it is worth noting that there were more articles in *al-Imam* sourced from the Cairo-based paper *al-Liwa'*— the organ of the nationalist Mustafa Kamil (1874–1908)—than from Rashid Rida's *al-Manar*. In his own quest for Egyptian independence from Britain, Kamil often used Japan as the best example for modern "Easterners" (*shar-qiyyin*), and even predicted that one day the Japanese would expand their empire to the cost of the Dutch and would be warmly welcomed by their fellow Easterners of "Jawa."[42]

Even so, the Malay readership was certainly aware that *al-Manar* was the primary source of *al-Imam*'s authority to speak on matters of religion and progress. In another letter, a correspondent commenced by thanking both Cairo's *al-Manar* and *al-Imam* for showing "the way of improvement and benefit in elevating our people of this eastern side."[43] He argued that "we peoples of the East on this side" are "the people of Islam," and then equated Cairo as the natural destination for Malays seeking to better themselves with the intellectual pilgrimages of the many Japanese who had been sent to Europe. As we have seen, such an exemplary pilgrimage was also admired by Rivai, who had been the first indigenous Indonesian enrolled in the medical program at the University of Amsterdam.[44] The difference for the correspondent to *al-Imam*, though, and one enunciated in his article, was that the Japanese were able to *safely* venture to the West as they *already had* a sound understanding of their *own* religion and history, something Rivai seems to have abandoned as a client of the Ethici.

This piece was followed by a discussion of the tensions between Japan and America, much in the way that Abdul Rivai had been concerned by the inconsistency shown by the Western nations toward their "yellow-skinned" equals. Later issues followed the question of the Japanese in California. Still, such was of minor interest compared with the constant Islam–Japan comparison that was also wedded to *al-Imam*'s stated purpose of translating the modern vocabulary of the Arab lands, and Egypt in particular. It was no mere typesetter's coincidence when, in May 1907, a long feature article that explained the meaning of key terms in vogue in Cairo such as "nation" (*umma*), "homeland" (*watan*), "government" (*hukuma*), and "independence" (*hurriyya*) was immediately followed by an advertisement for a recent Malay translation of Mustafa Kamil's *The Radiant Sun*. The work was described as a "history" of Japan but was in effect an ode to its Meiji reformers, their industry, and their development, with frequent emphasis on the power of patriotism (*wataniyya*) as the engine of success.[45]

The translation itself, being written in Arabic script and completed by an associate of *al-Imam* on its own press, would be frequently commended to readers. And, whereas the translator, Encik Abdullah bin Abdul Rahman of Muar, encountered a degree of difficulty in his own word choice regarding Kamil's avowedly secular enthusiasm for *wataniyya* (which he usually rendered as "love for fellow [Muslim] countrymen" rather than "love of homeland" per se), he was able to effectively communicate the important lesson that it was one's defense of one's own culture (and therefore the Malays' Islam) that guaranteed national advancement and ultimately would deliver independence.[46] Despite issues of translation and the occasionally turgid style of the original, the book was very well received. According to Za'ba, "it helped stimulate among its readers a feeling of pride and hope for the renascence of Oriental peoples, even the Malays" and, together with another of Encik Abdullah's translations, "earned a recognized place in Malay literature."[47]

Whereas Japan was so clearly being read about by the men of *al-Imam* through Egyptian papers—both religious and secular—before tailoring the lesson for a more explicitly Muslim local audience, it is worth noting that Cairo was to some extent presented in *al-Imam* as an interim destination. Assuming that a soundly modern religious education had been instilled there, a Malay could then safely journey on to France, the ultimate source of modernity itself, and most especially ideas of patriotism and nation that Egyptians like Mustafa Kamil had found in the nineteenth century. Indeed, this was the very argument put forward among the Malay student body at al-Azhar University in the 1910s, and again in the 1920s, when the readers of *al-Imam*, and then their sons, could disseminate its message from modern Cairo itself.[48] After the Hajj to Mecca, Cairo had everything one could want it seems, except for that final diploma . . . which was still to be had from Paris.[49]

Distinct views and separate concerns?

Al-Imam has been identified previously as an Islamic "response" to the "bourgeois" interventions of avowedly non-religious Malay papers like *Utusan Melayu*.[50] But this is an anachronistic oversimplification of how ostensibly secular and religious papers were supposedly read against each other in Singapore as much as in Cairo. Not only did the editors of *al-Imam* source their material from the reformist writings of Abduh and Rida, they engaged—as did contemporary Egyptians—with non-religious movements and their papers, as is evidenced by their usage of what was originally an explicitly nationalist reading of the meaning of the rise of Meiji Japan given added credence by its prediction of victory over Russia. It is also curious to see how the modular axes of *qibla* are less than straight, with Muslim Japanophiles journeying to both The Hague and Cairo, and yet thinking of Mecca and Paris at the same time.

Of course there were differences. *Utusan Melayu* was far less concerned with the importance of Arabic terminology in its pages, or yet the teaching of Arabic in Malay schools *if* it was to be to the detriment of other languages. Still, it made space for the Arabic script, featuring a page in that format with stories that crossed over, but did not absolutely replicate, the roman script front page. In this sense it was rather like the first "Arab" paper of Indonesia, *al-Bashir* (commenced 1914), which had pages in Arabic and Malay with intersecting rather than identical content. Whereas the Arab pages addressed "Arab" concerns and talked of Hadramaut, the Malay pages were concerned with reform and religion in general. In either rubric Japan could have served as a model.

Furthermore, Arabic script was not necessarily any ideological boundary to the readers of journals like *Bintang Hindia*. As one Sumatran later wrote—and in the Arabic script—the Malay writings of Abdul Rivai, with his "lively" prose and "sharp pen," had been crucial to his intellectual awakening; but, alongside this, he emphasized with great enthusiasm the very pictorial nature of the journal, with its "beautiful pictures, of kings and great men from all over the world," not to mention its "attractive young women," never before seen in the Indies in such a way.[51] Whether the editors of *al-Imam* would have been so enthusiastic about the young ladies is another matter, and by comparison too they were less than fulsome in their praise of the Dutch—even if occasional contributions could speak, as Rivai would have hoped, of the just rule of the Dutch Queen. The *Utusan Melayu* also evinced a more obviously cooperative attitude to the British than *al-Imam* when discussing the activities of Mustafa Kamil in Egypt. Even so, both *al-Imam* and *Utusan Melayu* (which *al-Imam* warmly welcomed in October 1907) featured readers' letters addressing comments in the other paper, while *Bintang Hindia* featured short articles—sometimes complete with portraits— on the guiding hands of the *Utusan* and *al-Imam*, and indeed many other newly founded papers.

Again, too, there was Japan to unite them. All three papers paid attention to Japan's diplomatic problems with the United States, and all three were interested in globally dominant notions of education and national progress for which Japan served as a model. *Utusan Melayu* frequently listed Japan among lists of successful modern nations, and described how it had replaced Germany as the (very military) model nation for Asians:

> In the beginning Germans were employed [to teach Chinese soldiers drill], however since the war between Russia and Japan, Japanese have begun to replace Germans because at this time they are able to teach Chinese in far better ways.[52]

One wonders, though, what exactly made them better. Were they better because of the recent proven success against Russia or better because they came from fellow Asians (or yet "Easterners")? Either way, both would be points in Japan's initial favor right until 1941, and a little beyond too.

Regional impact

Much as their readerships and messages intersected in the region, the real legacy of these papers is also shared, with tracings felt in the journals to come as much as among readers at the courts of Bali or in the highlands of Sumatra. For example, the editors of *al-Munir*, a west Sumatran journal that was the local heir to *al-Imam*, reflected in 1911 how everyone now knew that "the land of the rising sun had opened the eyes of many," although they bewailed the enormity of their own task: "if only we could instill the same sense of unity and purpose in our nation!"[53]

Again, in the Javanese paper *Kaoem Moeda*, a certain S.G. could remark in 1918 that the Russo-Japanese War had shown that people of all colors could become "first class people," and could cite a relatively new organization, the Boedi Oetomo (Noble Endeavour), as an example of how the Javanese could emulate the Japanese.[54] Certainly, there was a link between the two. Its founder, Wahidin Soedirohoesodo, was a Javanese aristocrat who had once shared a flat with Abdul Rivai in Amsterdam, who was indebted to his writings on progress in the *Bintang Hindia*, and shared his admiration for Japan.[55] Adam furthermore links both *Bintang Hindia* and Boedi Oetomo to the example set by the Indies Chinese association Tiong Hoa Hwee Koan, established in the wake of Japanese gains in status in the Indies.[56]

It would be relatively easy here to catalogue the many references to Japan in the public utterances and papers of the years to come, from Singapore to Surabaya, or from Ahmad Surkati to "Achmad" Sukarno, but it is worth noting too that not all the echoes of Japan were in print, even if they clearly emanated from expanding print culture, or were at least started among the circles of "readers" drawn to the photographic images of Japan popularized in *Bintang Hindia*.

There is, for example, at least one manuscript account of the war in the form of an epic poem (*syair*) drawn from newspapers, the *Syair Perang Ruslan Jepun*. Now held in St Petersburg, this was completed on January 2, 1906;[57] and, at about the same time, a courtier from Puri Kawan, in non-Muslim Bali, began a thinly disguised pornographic novel, entitled *Awi-Awian Payudan Rus-Jepang* (The Tale of the Russo-Japanese War), with a certain "Mr Penis" sitting on his bed and turning the pages of a contemporary newspaper showing pictures of the war.[58] Based on the images he described, and in order or appearance, of balloons and warships, the paper was none other than the *Bintang Hindia*, leading one to wonder if his primary enthusiasm was more for the young ladies noticed by Zain than the clashes of Russians and Japanese, which he would use as metaphors for sexual congress.[59]

Somewhat more earnest examples of the rising image of Japan may be found further to the west. Around 1919, the pro-Dutch traditionalist Datoek Sanggoeno Di Radjo—an opponent of the local heirs to *al-Imam*'s message—rephrased a traditional Minangkabau verse that places the historic kingdom as an equal to Turkey and China (by virtue of their common lineage from Alexander the Great), replacing the latter with Japan.[60] Further inland, the local Dutch Resident, Daniel van der Meulen, reported how the Christian Batak people repeated rumors of "a great ship that would sail through the clouds with a Japanese army that would overthrow the Dutch."[61] Others were not content to wait for a Japanese fleet, water-borne or otherwise. As I mentioned earlier, Barbara Andaya has written about the various missions—mostly covert—sent to Tokyo from the courts of East Sumatra and the Riau archipelago.[62] Also, the papers of Java in the 1910s frequently alluded to the presence of a large Indonesian community of students in Japan, even citing numbers that would lead one to believe that there were more Indonesians there than in Cairo.[63]

When war broke out in Europe in 1914, the Dutch were concerned about the repercussions in the South China Sea if Holland were to be drawn in on the side of Germany, thus leaving the Indies—still without any naval force to speak of—open to Japanese invasion. According to Harry Poeze, the first formal incarnation of a formally constituted Indies intelligence service in the Indies, the Kantoor Inlichtingen, was founded in that year "to document and counteract Japanese activities."[64] The specter of Japan or Japanese agents, who indeed seemed to be active in some parts of the archipelago, was also the cause for the inclusion of a special secret section of the fortnightly reports sent from Batavia to The Hague.[65]

Meanwhile, in the Netherlands there was debate as to whether Indonesians should be entrusted with arms to defend their (Dutch) archipelago. As it happened, and not by any dint of special planning on the Dutch side, the projected disaster was averted by 1917, and discussions of arming the indigenous population for self-defense were once more shelved. Throughout this period, more and more Indonesians evinced an interest in Japan. These included the Dutch-educated nationalist, Mohammad Hatta, who would visit in 1933, and the founder of the Parindra party, Soetomo, who went in 1936. For Hatta, who had been greeted as "the Gandhi of Java," the visit confirmed doubts about Japan that had already been implanted after the 1931 annexation of Manchuria;[66] and when he later collaborated with Sukarno under the Japanese, both he and his new patrons were mutually suspicious.[67]

Soetomo, on the other hand, was captivated by the pan-Asian potential of Japan for the largest Muslim people of Asia. As he wrote home to his party members using language that seems appropriate here:

> It may be that in later days, the flow of children of Indonesia who journey to Japan will increase to the point that Japan becomes a "Second Mecca." I hope that this may be the case as it has been in the holy land, the land of our great and holy prophet Mohammad. Is it not so that among the Asian races who journey there, it is Indonesians who are the most numerous?![68]

As Ethan Mark also notes, such a view was echoed by other Indonesians. A contributor to *Soeara Oemoem* observed that, just as Mecca had been the holy land for Muslims, then Tokyo would be the "magnet" for future intellectuals, while the nationalist comrade of Hatta, Sjahrir, had also remarked that the middle classes were looking fondly toward Japan.[69] Despite the earlier debates and a great deal of hand-wringing by the Dutch, when Japan did invade in March 1942, Mustafa Kamil's prediction was posthumously proven. In Medan, for example, Japanese troops were greeted by a large crowd in front of the main mosque shouting *Banzai!*[70] It was also clear that the shared legacy of modernity, Islam, and Asian power would be played upon by the Japanese very effectively. In the early weeks of the occupation, worshipers in major mosques in Jakarta found themselves joined by a small number of Japanese converts under the direction of Colonel Hori, soon to be head of the Religious Affairs Office, led four decades beforehand by Snouck Hurgronje.[71]

However, over the course of the occupation with the planned reorientation of the Muslim population to Tokyo as the hub of the new Greater East Asian Co-prosperity Sphere, serious tensions emerged between the Japanese and a number of non-cooperative Muslim leaders. Hamka has claimed that this hinged on a certain incident involving his father, Haji Rasul, a former contributor to *al-Munir*, who had nonetheless neither welcomed nor challenged the arriving Japanese. Hamka asserts that Haji Rasul was the first Muslim scholar to actively protest against the forced practice of bowing in the direction of the emperor (*saikeirei*) as it conflicted with the Muslim obligation of prostration toward Mecca alone.[72] As he paints it, his father wrote an epistle on the matter for Colonel Hori, disputing the compatibility of teachings about the emperor's divinity and Islam. Hori then leaves for Tokyo—never to return—leaving behind a number of Japanese "with Muslim names," of whom Hamka remarks: "Whether they were real Muslims or not, God only knows!"[73]

This account is an exaggeration of Rasul's influence among the Indonesian population at large. As Ethan Mark notes, the ritual was only suspended in certain sensitive areas and did not become a general point of resentment until late in the occupation.[74] Nevertheless, the sensitivity of *qibla*—spiritual or political—need not be doubted, nor should its usage in the literature of national advancement among Indonesians at home and abroad. One expatriate of long-standing residence in Cairo, Fu'ad Fakhr al-Din (b. 1918), wrote in his own history of Indonesia—a work composed in Arabic and yet resting ultimately on Dutch scholarship—that Indonesians had once erroneously believed that Holland had been "the source of light," "the Ka'ba of learning," and "the *qibla* of culture."[75]

However, whereas Fakhr al-Din would have located these foci in the international setting of Cairo, by 1965 a great many other Muslim Southeast Asians were to find them within the boundaries of their now recognizable homeland—whether in the former colonial gulag of Boven Digul, to which the Dutch had consigned its political prisoners (including Hatta, Sjahrir, and Sukarno), in the new papers of their nation written in a language now marked as their own (i.e. "Indonesian" rather than "Malay"), or in the fiery speeches of Sukarno. Or at least they did before the turmoil of September 30 that year, which saw the communist putsch and General Suharto's countercoup, whose subsequent echoes have long since displaced memories of the direct encounter with Indonesia's last radiant colonizers. The Dutch and Japanese may be gone, but, as the ongoing tension between Islamists and their opponents demonstrates, the search for a shared national *qibla* goes on, even as both sides look on occasion northward for Asian inspiration.

Notes

1 The author thanks Ian Proudfoot, Amir Ryad, and colleagues at the Department of History, Princeton University, for reacting to an earlier draft of this contribution, in particular Sheldon Garon and Ben Elman.

   For research on this topic I used the National Archives, The Hague, Series 2.05.03, A.190, box 451, as well as the following serials: *Bintang Barat*, Batavia; *al-Imam*, Singapore; *Bintang Hindia*, Amsterdam/Weltevreden; *al-Jinan*, Beirut; and *al-Munir*, Padang.

2 Cited in Poeze, 1989: 91.

3 Al-Jarjawi, 1908: 159–60.

4 Andaya, 1977.

5 See Bayly, 2004.

6 Anderson, 1966.

7 Sundberg, 2004: 110–16.

8 Reid, 1993: 15–16.

9 Van der Kraan, 2000: 8.

10 Milton, 1999: 317; Reid, 1993: 274.

11 For mentions of the Japanese in the *Hikayat Hang Tuah*, see the edition of Kassim Ahmad (1975: 418–23). For the *Hikayat Tanah Hitu*, see Straver *et al.* (2004: 45 XXII; 55 XXIV; 61 XXV). There is also a very brief mention of a Japanese sword conferred as a gift in the *Hikayat Banjar*. See Ras 1968: 258–9. All the instances cited here were found using the Malay Concordance Project (MCP); see http://www.anu.edu.au/asianstudies/ahcen/proudfoot/MCP/ (accessed April 13, 2005).

12 Sweeney, 1980: 120–1.

13 Pramoedya, 1982: 150–60.

14 Deringil, 2003: 44.

15 Reid, 1969: 258.

16 In this regard, see Elman 2004. I would also like to thank Professor Elman for his comments on this draft and reminding me of the place of China and the Chinese in this broader story.

17 See "Kebranijan bangsa Djepang," *Bintang Barat*, no. 169, 1895 and *Bintang Barat*, no.182, 1895. With many thanks to Ian Proudfoot for bringing this to my attention.

18 Fasseur, 1994: 37.

19 Poeze *et al.*, 1986: 33.

20 Poeze, 1989.

21 Translation of passage cited in Poeze *et al.*, 1986: 34.
22 *Bintang Hindia*, 1 (9), May 1903.
23 *Bintang Hindia*, 2 (2), February 1, 1904
24 *Bintang Hindia*, 2 (5), February 1904: 47.
25 *Bintang Hindia*, 2 (5), February 1904: 47.
26 This is not to say that the Thais were not also engaged in the cartography of empire. See Thongchai, 1994.
27 *Bintang Hindia*, 2 (5), February 1904: 51.
28 See *Bintang Hindia*, 2 (6) and (7), 1904.
29 *Bintang Hindia*, 4 (24), March 1907: 294.
30 *Al-Imam*, 1 (1), July 23, 1906.
31 See Mandal, 1997; and Roff, 1967.
32 Mobini-Kesheh, 1999.
33 *Al-Jinan*, 3 (7), 1872: 221; Kenny, 1976: 153.
34 Esenbel, 2004; Worringer, forthcoming.
35 Roff, 2002: 100.
36 Adhami, 1999.
37 *Al-Imam*, 1 (1), July 1906: 30–1. Abd al-Rahman Thomson was a New Zealand businessman active in Tokyo who had converted in about 1900. He is also said to have sponsored the translation into English of a work by the Dutch-backed *mufti* of Batavia, Sayyid Uthman bin Aqil. Thomas Eich, personal communication, March 8, 2002.
38 "Japan and Islam; Eastern's Wish for Militant Over-lord," Nationaal Archief, The Hague, Series 2.05.03, A.190, box 451: 59.
39 See *al-Imam*, 1 (3), September 1906: 93–4. This information seems to fit the profile and interests of al-Jarjawi, whose travelogue I have discussed elsewhere. See Laffan, 2001.
40 *Al-Imam*, 1 (2), August 1906: 52–64.
41 Rida started expressing his enthusiasm for the conversion of Japan in 1905. See his articles: "Da'wat al-yaban ila 'l-islam," *al-Manar*, 8 (18), 16 Ramadan 1323 (November 13, 1905): 705–12, and "Da'wat al-islam fi 'l-yaban," *al-Manar*, 9 (1), 30 Dhu 'l-qa'da 1324 (February 24, 1906): 75–8. See also Adams 1968: 196. It should be noted that Rida was concerned that the spreading of Islamic propaganda in Japan should be inspired by religious intentions alone and supported by a properly prepared mission from al-Azhar. He was certainly unimpressed by the more political motives underlying the calls of his contemporaries, such as Mustafa Kamil. With thanks to Umar Ryad of Leiden University.
42 See, for example, "Return the light to the East," *al-Imam*, 1 (6), December 1906: 190–1, as quoted from *al-Liwa'*. For an example of Kamil's patronizing view of the peoples of Southeast Asia, see *al-Liwa'*, November 6, 1904.
43 *Al-Imam*, 1 (7), January 1907: 245–53.
44 Coté, 1996: 13.
45 Kamil, 1904, 1906.
46 Laffan, 1996.
47 Za'ba, 1940: 148.
48 Laffan, 2003: 140, 219.
49 In a sense too, this both supports and inverts Benedict Anderson's point related to cartography and the modern, when he observes that "Cairo and Mecca were beginning to be visualized in a strange new way, no longer simply as sites in a sacred Muslim geography, but also as dots on paper sheets which included dots for Paris, Moscow, Manila and Caracas." Anderson, 1991: 170–1.
50 Milner, 1995.
51 Zain, 1948: 48.

52 *Utusan Melayu*, 22, December 26, 1907.
53 *Al-Munir*, 1 (12), August 8, 1911.
54 *Kaoem Moeda*, 195, October 28, 1918.
55 See Poeze *et al.*, 1986: 35; Nagazumi, 1969.
56 Adam, 1995: 105–6.
57 Braginsky and Boldyareva, 1990: 176.
58 Creese, 2004.
59 See Creese, 2004.
60 Hadler, 2005.
61 Van der Meulen, 1981: 45.
62 Andaya, 1977.
63 *Neratja*, 1 (7), July 10, 1917, claimed that Raden Soemarsono, the former judge of Purworejo, planned to travel to Tokyo to found a hall of residence for 100 Indies students living there.
64 Poeze, 1994: 230.
65 Among such activities one can point to the contacts made between the Tatar Japanophile Abduresid Ibrahim (1857–1944) and Muhammad bin Muhammad Ali of Sambas. By late 1911, the latter is reported to have assisted the Japanese in purchasing tracts of coastal land (Ucar, 1995: 15–17). Ucar also referred to an earlier visit to Tokyo by a certain Sayyid Uthman Alawi with the intent of spreading Islam in Japan, but this may actually be a reference either to Abd al-Rahman Thomson's plans to translate one of his works for the Japanese market (see note 37 above), or else the 1898–9 visit of Uthman's son-in-law, Muhammad bin Aqil. I am grateful to Renee Worringer for having brought Ucar's article to my attention and for providing me with a synopsis of its contents.
66 Mark, 2003: 130–1.
67 Goto, 2003: 86–9.
68 Soetomo, April 22, 1936, as quoted in Mark, 2003: 143.
69 Mark, 2003: 144.
70 Benda, 1958: 106.
71 Benda, 1958: 111.
72 Hamka, 1958: 183–7.
73 Hamka, 1958: 186.
74 See Mark, 2003: 536–7.
75 Fakhr al-Din, 1965: 61.

15 India and the war

T.R. Sareen

Historical events are not seen in isolation. An event that takes place in one region of the world almost invariably transcends its physical dimensions and produces repercussions in other areas. One such important event was the Russo-Japanese War of 1904–5, which ushered in new forces in world history. India also could not have remained isolated from the main currents of world events, especially from developments on the Asian continent in which it had itself played a dominant role since the dawn of history.

For the past hundred years, historians have assessed this event from different perspectives. For some, it was the beginning of a racial war between the Asians and the West; for others, it was the beginning of the end of European domination in the world.[1] Asian historians have looked at the Russo-Japanese War as a "symbol of the regeneration of the East."[2] In their opinion, the signal defeat of a great European nation by a small eastern nation had created a stir all over Asia, and may be taken as "the real beginning of nationalism in Asia." Some historians, while conceding its impact on nationalism in India, have argued that it was of a very "short duration."[3] and all the admiration shown for Japan in India was not "spontaneous" but artificial, and was "fed to the Indians by their British colonial masters."[4] The study of British official papers, however, gives us a different picture of the impact this event produced on India. In this chapter an attempt is made to examine how the Russo-Japanese War had provided a powerful stimulus to Indian people then living under the colonial rule of Britain and how it had given a new turn to the concept of nationalism in India. When the war occurred the nationalist movement in India, originating in the nineteenth century, had grown in strength and volume. As is known, many factors were responsible for this development, and their cumulative effect was that, by the beginning of the twentieth century, Indian nationalism was seeking a radical change.[5]

More than a hundred years of political subjugation had reduced India to a state of stark backwardness and an acceptance of slavery as almost inevitable. The British had failed to solve the economic and political problems of the people. Political organizations, though allowed to function under British patronage, had failed to produce any significant positive results. The Indian National Congress (INC), formed in 1885, had been aiming at good government, a wider employment of educated Indians in higher services, and the introduction of representative institutions. The leaders of the INC had been trying to achieve these objectives through constitutional means, but in vain.

Toward the closing years of the nineteenth century, dissatisfaction with the rate of progress achieved or attempted by the INC began to grow and many political leaders felt the need for the adoption of methods that it was hoped would produce more tangible results. Conditions had worsened further by various acts of blazing indiscrimination introduced during Lord Curzon's viceroyalty. Curzon had no respect for the political aspirations of the people and even at times refused to receive the leaders of the INC when they wanted to hand over to him their resolutions for political concessions.[6]

Public response

While a nationwide resentment against the Curzonian rule was developing in India, one of the most dramatic events took place in East Asia, where the two Great Powers Russia and Japan became locked in a war over Korea. The news of the first Japanese victories over Russia came as an agreeable surprise to India and aroused immense enthusiasm among the people. The nationalist press, while expressing surprise at the war, observed that the "sympathy of India goes to Japan and it is the universal wish of our country that she may succeed in inflicting the severest possible blow on her military adversary."[7]

However, confidence in the final victory of Japan was not entertained until General Aleksei Kuropatkin was routed and Admiral Tōgō Heihachirō inflicted a defeat on the Russian fleet. The display of solidarity with Japan found further expression by raising funds in aid of wounded Japanese soldiers and war widows. It is also recorded that, when Japan was giving blows to Russia and making history on the plains of Manchuria, all Indians from the lowest to the highest, young and old, were following the course of the war with a glow of pride and satisfaction. As Asians they were entitled to share in the victories of Japan.[8] An English observer noticed the stir of excitement that was passing through the country and wrote that "even in the remote villages people talked about the victories of Japan, as they sat in their circle and passed around the *huqqa* at night."[9]

To counter the public interest in the Japanese victory, the pro-British press began to draw attention to the serious consequences of the war. References were made to the new dangers of "Russo-phobia" and the "Yellow Peril." It was stated by the pro-government press that, since Russia had lost Manchuria, it would now turn its eyes to India. The Russian invasion of India was considered as neither "chimerical nor impractical." Even before the defeat of Russia one paper warned that "if Russia was ousted from Manchuria, she would turn her attention toward India," and "even if

Russia was successful in the war, then she would seriously threaten the Indian Empire." In either case, the paper concluded, the war was "an unmitigated evil for India."[10] The nationalist press hardly gave any credence to such views, which had been circulated, first, to warn the people of the false danger from the Russian side and, second, to justify the large military expenditure being incurred by the government, which would, in turn, be shouldered by the Indians. In the opinion of these papers, after the defeat of Russia any fears of danger from that quarter were absolutely "groundless."[11] It was believed that Lord Curzon was trying to revive the fear of the "Russian bogey." Indeed, we find that, in a secret dispatch to London from Lord Kitchener, the Commander in Chief, it was stated that there was no "immediate danger of an attack by Russia."[12]

As regards the "Yellow Peril," while London was very pleased with the success of its ally, and on the growing friendly relations between Japan and Britain, especially after the renewal of the Anglo-Japanese Alliance, the Indian government had begun to feel uneasy about the emergence of all-round praise in Indian political circles for Japan on its victories and the Japanese interest in Indian nationalism. The real significance for India in the outcome of the Russo-Japanese War was not so much the concern over "Russo-phobia" or the "Yellow Peril," but the apprehension that the Japanese success had touched the imagination of the people. They looked at war as a struggle "between Europe and Asia," and the latter's victory demonstrated that European superiority was a myth. The nationalist press hailed it as a "glorious victory," saying that the "Asiatic race has broken the pride of the greatest power in Europe so thoroughly that not even hope of retrieval is left."[13]

Political impact

The influence of Japanese success had a tremendous psychological impact on India, as it electrified the atmosphere and stirred the country with enthusiasm and hope for its own future. Thirty years later Jawaharlal Nehru recalled the excitement he had felt as a young man at the Japanese victories. He wrote that in India they "lessened the feeling of inferiority from which most of us suffered." He wrote further that a great European power had been defeated and, therefore, Asia could still defeat Europe as it had done in the past. Nationalism spread more rapidly over the Eastern countries and cries of "Asia for the Asians" were heard. But nationalism was not merely clinging to the old customs or beliefs. "Japan's victory," Nehru concluded, "was seen to be due to the adoption of the industrial methods of the West and these ideas and methods became more popular all over the East."[14]

Though the end of the British Empire was not yet in sight, Nehru was said to have become absolute confident that the independence of India was not far away.[15] In other words, besides correcting the illusion that the West was invincible, the victory of Japan infused "[much-]needed confidence among the peoples"; it helped them "to clear away illusions and signs . . . [were] . . . visible of the awakening of a new life."[16] Relying on the pro-British press, some writers, however, tried to project that all the admiration for Japan was not a spontaneous outpouring, "but rather a large part of it was manufactured and fed to the Indians by the colonial masters." In their opinion, there were no fellow feelings in India for the Japanese and their jubilation over Japan's success was due to the fact that Japan was an ally of Britain.[17]

This argument is not convincing in view of the strong agitation that had started against the British in India and in view of subsequent developments. It is also contradicted by the secret report of the Director of Criminal Intelligence (DCI), who wrote that the victory of Japan over Russia had filled the entire Oriental world with new hope and ambition and proved to be a most potent stimulus to Indian nationalism. In his view, the Japanese success "inspired India to the realization that it would only be a matter of time before its people would also be able to hold their own as free people in their own country."[18] It was from this time onward that a feeling began to spread that, if the Japanese could defeat the Russians, there was no power on earth that could stop the Indians from throwing the British out. The feeling began to be voiced by every nationalist leader that India could triumph over Britain if its people studied and emulated Japan. The opinion expressed by the DCI above is further confirmed by another contemporary observer, who recorded that:

> officially the Anglo-Saxon people were in sympathy with the Japanese, but the individual British in India looked upon Japan with suspicion. It was a question of prestige. A European power like the Russian being whipped by a small Asiatic nation like the Japanese. Why, that was unthinkable. It was a prelude to a revolution in Asia. The Anglo-Indian imperialist was uneasy at its impact on India and he was not wrong. The Japanese success over Russia materially contributed to the development of [the] nationalist movement in India.[19]

Even Gandhi at that time in South Africa was impressed by Japan and told the people that, besides praising the Japanese victories, they should learn the secrets of Japanese success. He wrote that everyone, Indians in particular, had much to learn from Japan and that they should imbibe the spirit of unity, patriotism, and sacrifice that had made Japan great and was the secret of its success. He added:

> When everyone in Japan, the rich and the poor, came to believe in self respect, the country became free. She could give Russia a slap in the face and today Japan's flag flies very high in the world. In the same way, we must, too, need to feel the spirit of self respect. Having

remained in bondage for a long time like a caged parrot, we cannot realize what honor and freedom are.

"Our reading of this account of the Japanese war," he concluded, "would be fruitful only if we emulate to some extent the example of Japan."[20]

In India the nationalist leadership, which was mostly drawn from the urban educated class, found in the Japanese example a convenient model for intensifying its struggle against British domination and raised its voice for political freedom. Nationalist leaders began to associate their country's poverty with British exploitation and regarded the British view of their own importance as a part of wider Western belief. When this was realized, "the nature of Japan's success over Russia became clear" and the Indian political leaders began "to see the Russo-Japanese war as the first battle in the struggle of Asia for freedom from foreign domination."[21] They started to spread the idea of a united self-governing India. They had lost faith in the British.

Japanese nationalism: a lesson for Indians

All shades of political leaders saw in Japan the most telling example of a country meeting the West with weapons borrowed from the West and began a systematic campaign to inculcate in the people the Japanese ideals. While presenting the Japanese model before the people, every national leader chose to emphasize those aspects of the Japanese character that appealed to him the most and he thought were most suitable for the people here. For instance, Dadabhai Naoroji, the grand old man of Indian politics, told them that the secret of Japanese success lay in the spirit of sacrifice both individual and collective. He exhorted the people to develop that spirit and emphasized that without it the political freedom of India would remain a distant goal.[22] G.K. Gokhale, another moderate leader, urged the people to learn lessons from Japan and to cultivate the sense of national pride, patriotism, discipline, and obedience. He advised them to show devotion to the motherland as was done in Japan. "Loyalty and obedience," Gokhale said, were "the invaluable lessons by which we could advance forward."[23] Sister Nivadita (Margaret Noble, a disciple of Swami Vivekananda) pointed out self-help as the most important Japanese lesson for the Indian people to follow. Yet others looked upon the Japanese spirit of self-reliance as worthy of adoption as it had contributed to the material and industrial progress of that country.[24] As a matter of fact, in the minds of the educated people words like patriotism, nationalism, discipline, and self-help became synonymous with Japan.

From the British point of view, there was nothing objectionable in this preaching of the ideals of Japan, but they were disturbed at the impact it was producing on the course of the national movement. From this point onward, it practically changed the very basis of the national movement in

India. There was division in the political ideology of the nationalist leadership. Some of the INC leaders now began to emphasize that India should be governed in the interest of Indians themselves. From good government they started demanding self-government. *"Swaraj"* (meaning "independence" or "freedom") became the new slogan. The INC resolutions passed during 1905–6 at its annual sessions were the expressions of the legitimate demands of the people, which the example of Japan had helped in projecting in clear terms. The Benares session of the INC, held toward the end of 1905, especially referred to how the rise of Japan had produced a great moral impression. The leaders mentioned that the services for the motherland would become as great and overmastering a passion as in Japan.

On the other hand, the success of Japan also gave rise to the emergence of a new group of leaders. The INC had so far followed the policy of moderation and cooperation with the British, but the new leadership started advocating more aggressive methods for achieving the goal of freedom. Bal Gangadhar Tilak, who assumed the leadership of this faction, cited the example of Ireland and Japan for the Indians to follow. He said that protests alone were of no use. Recommending radical methods, Tilak made pointed references to Japan and asked the people to follow "her methods." He laid emphasis on their efficiency, and on their spirit of "self sacrifice and ardent devotion," which were the main reasons for Japanese success and which were necessary for the attainment of India's political aspirations.[25]

With the growing admiration of Japan there was a quickening of political unrest in India. This new spirit, no doubt, had been fostered by the example of Japan, but it also received further impetus from an act of government. This was the announcement on July 19, 1905 that the partition of Bengal was to be carried out, despite the fact that there had been strong opposition from the people when the scheme was first announced by the government. The announcement fell like a bombshell upon the people, who had of late become accustomed to the news of victories of the East over the West. The success of Japan gave edge to the voices that were raised against the partition. The slogans of "Boycott" and "Swadeshi" were raised by Indian political leaders. The former aimed for a general boycott of foreign goods and British goods, in particular. The latter was its counterpart.[26]

The aim of the *Swadeshi* movement was to boycott all foreign goods, particularly of British manufacture, and to encourage the use of home-made goods. Japanese goods were excluded from this boycott, which upset the British because of their commercial rivalry with Japan. Supporting the resolution of boycott, Tilak asked the people to "show preference above all to native and next to Japanese manufacturers." If the *Swadeshi* movement hurt British commercial interests, the *Swaraj* slogan threatened the foundation of British rule in India. The boycott of British goods was used as a political weapon to put pressure on the government. The movement soon spread to the schools, the courts, and the administration. The boycott gave stimulus to the indigenous industry. This movement made a tremendous appeal to the common people who came forward to participate in political meetings and demonstrations.[27]

At the same time there was a section of the youth who started advocating a different political ideology inspired by the example of Japan. Frustrated and exasperated by the negative policies of the British in India, including their refusal to consider the demand for self-rule, they resorted to direct action and the use of violence to achieve the desired results. In the estimate of the DCI it was only after the Russo-Japanese War that the revolutionary ideals that had remained virtually dormant since 1857 were revived and the Indians began their violent activities and organized conspiracies to overthrow British rule. Under the impact of the new ideology, a number of associations for the promotion of physical culture sprang up all over the country. The revolutionaries had a following that comprised mostly educated young men. What had struck them about Japan was that the Western nations had come to recognize Japan on an equal basis only when they came to know that Japan also possessed the key to opening the flood gates of "hell fire." Surprisingly, even the nationalist press not only began to preach the revolutionary ideas but even started lauding those who were promoting them. They were equally impressed by the Japanese notion of dying for one's country. The revolutionary spirit was fostered by leaders such as Aurobindo Ghose, B.C. Pal, and Har Dayal.[28]

British officials were taken by surprise at the rapid growth of revolutionary activities and tried to curb them by a number of repressive measures. Consequently, many young revolutionaries either went underground or left for foreign lands. Many chose to go to Japan to seek support in their fight for liberation from the British.[29] Neither the *Swadeshi* movement nor the demand for *Swaraj* had as yet received any direct material assistance from Japan. And yet the mere fact that Japan had shown the path was enough to inspire the nationalist opinion to spell out its demands clearly before the British. However, British officials began to admit that the victory of Japan had a very unsettling effect on the minds of the nationalist leaders, some of whom were beginning to hail Japan as the defender and champion of Asia. The home member, R.H. Craddock lamented: "I believe that things would have been much quieter in India, had Japan met defeat from Russia." "It was Japan's victory," he commented further, that started the idea of "*Swaraj* in India."[30] Valentine Chirol, a perceptive British journalist, observed that the emergence of Japan had made a powerful impact on India, and added that it would not be surprising if Indian nationalists were to seek Japanese "guidance and assistance," for the liberation of their motherland.[31]

Chirol was not wrong. Thereafter, there began to grow a close cooperation between Indian nationalists and Japan. As a mark of admiration for Japan, Indian students went to Japanese universities in large numbers apparently for the purpose of technical education. Earlier, the British had tried to put a stop to the flow of students on account of the reports they had received about Japanese interest in them. Along with students from other Asian countries, they had formed an Oriental Young Men's Association with the object of facilitating the cultivation of friendship between the Japanese and Indians and other Asian students studying in Japan. The association had on its membership a number of influential Japanese who were friendly toward India. Although they "attributed very little political significance to this association," the Indian government took serious note of the anti-British writings of some of the students. A report in the London *Spectator* had warned that much harm might be done "if the government of India does not take steps to stop the dispatching of Indian students to Japan." The cordial relations between the Japanese and the Indians were not to the liking of diehard imperialists like Lord Curzon. He strongly objected to the practice of students going to Japan where, in his view, they were likely to be influenced by sentiments tending toward "discontent and disloyalty." It was then decided that, in the future, students going to Japan should produce a "certificate of identity signed by a responsible officer."[32]

At the same time it was expected in London that the renewal of the Anglo-Japanese Alliance would create better relations between the Indian government and Japan. On the other hand, the Indian government had never shared the confidence with which Britain had viewed the growth of Japanese power within the Anglo-Japanese Alliance. They had not been happy about the provisions made for Japanese assistance in the defense of India, which had been included in the alliance without reference to them. Naturally,

> [the prevalent] attitude towards Japan in India was that the alliance was from the viewpoint of the empire, a disagreeable necessity and from the Indian side unfortunate that Britain had to rely on an Asian power to help defend her interests, for this diminished British prestige in the eyes of the Indians.[33]

Whether the renewal of the alliance was made to stem the heightened political feelings encouraged by the Russo-Japanese War, it is difficult to say. But the fact remains that the alliance definitely made it difficult for Japan to express sympathy openly for the cause of Indian independence at least for some time. Still, the officials watched with apprehension the growing admiration for Japan and the friendly attitude of the Japanese toward the Indians. It is recorded that Curzon was so much perturbed at the growing intimacy between Japan and India that he refused to see the Japanese consul in India, who had gone to Simla to express the sympathy of his government over India's sufferings in the recent earthquake.[34] The *Hitvadi*, an Indian journal, explaining the reasons for Curzon's refusal to see the Japanese consul, pointed out that he was afraid of Japan becoming closer to India and felt that the Indian national movement might be strengthened by this growing intimacy between these two Asiatic peoples.[35]

Japan's interest in Indian nationalism

Despite the restrictions, large numbers of students left for Japan after the Russo-Japanese War. They went there not merely to promote their academic interests, but also to spread news about the Indian nationalist movement and to mobilize Japanese public opinion in support of it. Their political activity gained wide support when they were given facilities to celebrate the Shiviji festival.[36] The opportunity was used to invite the prominent Japanese political leader Count Okuma and Chinese activists like Thang Ziang to address the students. It appears that Okuma was greatly impressed by the Indian students. Denouncing British rule in India, he said that the three hundred million Indians who were suppressed by the Europeans were looking for the protection of Japan. He requested the Japanese businessmen to take more interest in trade with India and make *Swadeshi* a success.[37]

The Indian government was not expecting such a condemnation of their rule from the Japanese side and promptly sent a note of protest to the Japanese government. The British ambassador drew the attention of Viscount Hayashi to the above speech of Okuma. Calcutta, however, was assured by London that it was an isolated speech and, despite the expression of sympathy, Japan was subject to the Anglo-Japanese Alliance and it was not expected that it would support the cause of the Indian nationalists.[38] In spite of these assurances, the Indian government began to regard Japan as a menace to their rule. At this stage, there was, of course, no direct involvement of Japan in Indian nationalism for the attainment of self-rule or *Swaraj*, but the encouragement that the Indian students and subsequently the Indian revolutionaries received for carrying on their anti-British activities and their "links with pan-Asian circles in Japan was sufficient to increase the anxiety in India."[39]

From the study of the official papers it is now known that the Japanese support of Indian revolutionaries increased to such an extent within a few years that it was cited as one of the charges against Japan by the Indian government at the time of the renewal of the Anglo-Japanese Alliance in 1921. I have dealt with the alliance of Indian revolutionaries with Japan for weakening the British hold over India elsewhere.[40] Suffice to say here that preventing Japanese assistance from reaching the Indian nationalists became a matter of top priority for the British in India. However, within a few years after the Russo-Japanese War they were informed by their agent in Japan that the Japanese were "casting covetous eyes on much of what England now holds." The Japanese had also realized that "the strength of England's position in the East is closely bound up with her possession of India," and "any weakening of England's hold on India would therefore bring Japan closer to the goal of paramount political power in the East." The agent concluded that the Japanese were likely to "impart vigor and life to the Indian revolutionary movement" and it was "bound to impose a serious strain on the relations between England and Japan," in future.[41] Gradually, it began to be held in London and Calcutta that the defeat of Russia would inevitably encourage Asian nationalism and it would become difficult for Britain to hold the Indian Empire. Japanese interest in Indian nationalism, it was suspected, was based on the hope that it would embarrass Britain and increase their own influence in Asia. As to the fear of the British in India that Japan was likely to become the champion of the East against the West, this was not shared by Britain.

Surprisingly, the fact that Japan by its victories was itself becoming a colonial power was not considered seriously by the Indian nationalist leaders at that time. What mattered to them was that the success of Japan had shattered the illusion of European invincibility, and raised the self-esteem and self-confidence of the people. All leaders were deeply inclined toward Japan, and the INC was even toying with the idea of going along with Japan in the pursuit of a pan-Asian ideal. However, very soon they were disillusioned with Japan on account of its aggressive policy in China. On the other hand, the Indian revolutionaries remained tied to Japan till the end of World War II and their alliance, despite the Japanese defeat, sounded the death knell of the British Empire in India.[42]

The prevalent official opinion in India, however, was that the Indian nationalists as yet were not ready to purchase freedom from the British at the cost of subjugation to Japan. But, at the same time, it would be detrimental to the British interest if the government was going to ignore the legitimate demands of the Indians for a greater share in governing themselves. The DCI warned:

> the glowing eulogies of Japan indulged in by the politicians with the object of making blacker by contrasts their tales of British misgovernment in India might lead one to imagine that the substitution of Japanese rule for British would be welcome but the educated Indian is still more inclined to appeal to [the] British against Japan than Japan against the British. It is argued that the increasing power of Japan is a menace to British rule in India which can only be defeated by the establishment of a contented self-governing India with a strong national army and navy.[43]

Conclusion

Naturally, under the circumstances the question before the British was whether they should submit to the new spirit of nationalism that had arisen in the wake of the Russo-Japanese war or ignore it as they had been doing earlier. The indications are that the British were now willing to admit the fitness of the oriental people for self-government and to initiate the gradual introduction of reforms to some extent. After the departure of Curzon, the new viceroy, Lord Minto, who arrived in the fall of 1905, was quick to recognize the aspirations that were stirring the hearts of the people and recommended to London that it was "necessary to satisfy them to a reasonable extent by giving the Indians larger share in the administration." Consequently, soon after two Indians were appointed to the viceroy's council. While extending support to the viceroy, even John Morley, the secretary of state for India, encouraged him to "make a good start in the way of reforms in the popular direction."[44]

The success of Japan thus gave a new impulse to Indian nationalism and its impact was not short-lived, rather Indian nationalism under the guidance of the revolutionaries remained tied to Japan till the end of World War II. Of course, another section of the Indian political elite of the INC was disillusioned with Japan when it came to light within a few years that it was likely to exploit the other Asian countries quite as much as the Europeans had been doing. But at that time the moderate leaders of the INC were deeply impressed and frequently cited the example of Japan to inspire the people with a sense of patriotism and self-sacrifice—the two secrets of Japanese success. The new turn in Indian nationalism also introduced the spirit of extremism and the use of violent methods to attain the goal of freedom. Indian nationalism now began to run on the lines of claiming legitimate rights rather than the attitude of seeking concessions, as was the case before the Russo-Japanese War. The nationalists of the moderate school still believed that the British position was unshakeable, but they were less sure of its indefinite continuance. War had taught the people that the greatness of a nation does not depend upon its size and population, but mainly on qualities like self-reliance, patriotism, and self-sacrifice. More important was the lesson that good government was no substitute for self-government under a foreign power and freedom was necessary for the social and economic development of a nation.

Notes

1 Wells and Wilson, 1999: 20.
2 Prasad, 1979: 41–2.
3 Friedman, 1940: 19.
4 Narasimha Murthy, 1986: 21–2.
5 Lajapat Rai, 1918: 30.
6 *Native Newspaper Reports*, Bengal, 1905. These reports were prepared by the Home Department and contained comments of the newspapers in vernacular on men and events. They provided the information that the British officers used to guide them in their day-to-day affairs. The majority of the original newspapers and periodicals in regional languages have not survived, so one has to rely on the translations reproduced in these reports, which are available in the National Archive of India, New Delhi, and the British Library, London.
7 Native newspaper, Bengal, 1905.
8 Native newspaper, Bengal, 1905.
9 Andrews, 1912: 4.
10 Native newspaper, Bengal, 1905.
11 Native newspaper, Madras, 1905.

12 Arthur, 1920: 152.
13 Native newspaper, Bengal, 1905.
14 Nehru, 1949: 401–2.
15 Cortazzi and Daniels, 2002: 203.
16 Native newspaper, Bengal, 1905.
17 Narasimha Murthy, 1986: 21–2.
18 Foreign Office No. 371/3424/1918 for D. Petrie's Memorandum on the Impact of Russo-Japanese War on India (Public Record Office, London)
19 Foreign Department Proceedings, External B, Confidential B, 1917, nos. 1–42 (National Archive of India, New Delhi).
20 Gandhi, 1967: 456–7.
21 Edwardes, 1967: 185.
22 Dadabhai, 1917: 41.
23 Gokhale, 1918: 102–3.
24 Narasimha Murthy, 1977: 32.
25 Tilak, 1920: 204–5.
26 Sitaramayya, 1946: 84.
27 Pal, 1910: 43.
28 Ker, 1973: 20–30.
29 Sareen, 1979: 16–21.
30 Home Department Proceedings, Political A, August 1917, nos. 7–16 (National Archive of India, New Delhi).
31 Chirol, 1910: 111–12.
32 Foreign Department Proceedings, Internal B, August 1910, no. 420 (National Archive of India, New Delhi).
33 Lowe, 1969: 43.
34 Native newspaper, Bengal, 1905.
35 Native newspaper, Bengal, 1905.
36 Foreign Department Proceedings, Secret External, March 1908, no. 179 (National Archive of India, New Delhi).
37 Foreign Department Proceedings, Secret External, March 1908, no. 179 (National Archive of India, New Delhi).
38 Foreign Department Proceedings, External A, October 1921, nos. 218–49 (National Archive of India, New Delhi.
39 Lowe, 1969: 43.
40 Sareen, 1993: 10–12.
41 Foreign Department Proceedings, Secret External, 1917, nos. 1–42 (National Archive of India, New Delhi).
42 Sareen, 1986: 228–36.
43 Foreign Department Proceedings Secret External, 1918, nos. 29–34 (National Archive of India, New Delhi).
44 Morley to Minto, June 15, 1906, Morley Papers (India Office Library and Records, UK).

Part IV
The military arena

16 A model not to follow

The European armies and the lessons of the war

Yigal Sheffy

A year after the termination of the Russo-Japanese War, General Sir John French, then commander of the Aldershot Military District, commented on a lecture he presented on the lessons of the war. Advocating meticulous study of this conflict and basing his judgment on its lessons, he anticipated a future war to be stationary and firepower oriented, with maneuverability possible only under the cover of darkness.[1]

Eight years later, however, when the battlefields on the Western Front did indeed vindicate this anticipation in World War I by turning mobile fighting into fully positional trench warfare, French, now a field marshal commanding the British Expeditionary Force in France and Belgium, admitted being utterly surprised by the new reality of warfare, radically revolutionized by modern weaponry and field defenses.[2] Sebastian Dobson, in his illuminating introduction to a volume of reports from British officers attached to the Imperial Japanese Army during the Russo-Japanese War, further showed French's profound bewilderment, quoting from the latter's post-war memoirs:

> No previous experience, no conclusion I had been able to draw from campaigns in which I had taken part, or from a close study of the new conditions in which the war of today is waged, has led me to antici- pate a war of positions. All my thoughts, all my prospective plans, all my possible alternatives of action, were concentrated upon a war of movement and manoeuvre.[3]

There is nothing like the gap between French's early observations and his later revelations to demonstrate the truth that lies in another British officer's dictum regarding the relationship between observation and absorp- tion of war's lessons. Lieutenant-General Ian Hamilton, known best for his role as commander-in-chief of the ill-fated Mediterranean Expedition- ary Force on Gallipoli in 1915, served during the Russo-Japanese War as the highest-ranking British observer attached to the Imperial Japanese Army. Upon his return he summed up his impressions and the lessons of the war in two thick volumes, where he also discussed the impact of modern weapons systems and field defenses on the combat in 1904–5, implicitly referring to their effects on the future battlefield. Hamilton began with a methodological warning, as if foreseeing the future: the study of military history is always slightly misleading. The facts discovered during a given event are often imbalanced and not exhaustive, making the narrative susceptible to "national and regimental vainglory ... On the actual day of battle naked truths may be picked up for the asking; by the following morning they have already begun to get into their uniform."[4] The British intellectual and officer put his finger on one of the major flaws of military learning: the process in which real lessons, pure and isolated at the beginning, will eventually be affected by an unrelated, incorrect, or biased input, consequently losing their validity.[5]

Hamilton's rather pessimistic warning regarding human inaptitude at drawing lessons from wars, as well as the apparent gap between cognition and reality demonstrated by French's words, provide an appropriate starting point for discussing the military lessons of the Russo-Japanese War and the dynamics in which they were in fact learned and assimilated by the European armies. This discussion has not yet ended, as the century-old argument over the essence of the lessons and the way European armies adopted or rejected them still continues.[6]

In the short period of nine years between the end of the Russo-Japanese War and the outbreak of World War I, the discussion proceeded on the practical level, involving mainly practitioners (the military, the arms industry, and R&D entrepreneurs) and military theoreticians. It revolved primarily around what the last war might teach about future conflicts, and if its lessons were similar to those of the other recent wars, in South Africa, Europe, and America. But World War I soon put the Russo-Japanese War lessons to practical test, and the effects of the latter on the former were soon referred to in the past tense, on both sides of the equation. The practitioners lost interest (some probably evaded the subject, concerned that such a comparison may cast a negative shadow on their own conduct during the Great War) and the discussion shifted to the historians' domain.

Examining the lessons and their implementation in retrospect, the historians naturally adopted comparative approaches, assessing each lesson according to its compatibility with what actually took place during World War I. The discussion no longer centered on the potential significance of any given lesson for an unknown future, but made value judgments about the lesson: right or wrong. Did the war in 1904–5 indicate future events of 1914–18? Were those indications recognized by contemporaries, and if so did they accept or reject them and for what reasons? In other words, examination of the military lessons of the Russo-Japanese War suffered from the application of hindsight (read: biased judgment), where later events determined the historiographic approach to an earlier phenomenon, occasionally leading a historian's verdict astray.

The quantity and range of lessons examined during the pre-World War I era were enormous: from the color of uniforms, day-to-day provisions, and medical treatment at the individual level; through the effect of machine guns and quick-firing guns on the battlefield at the tactical level; and of logistics and transportation on campaigns at the operational level; and through relations between naval power and land warfare at the strategic level; to the formation of national security policy at the grand-strategy level. One doctrinal matter ran through all levels: the European armies' lessons with regard to the correlation between offense and defense, and their relative significance for future combat. The practical implications of this core issue greatly occupied the armies' attention between 1905 and 1914, while its retrospective interpretation still occupies historians' attention to this day.[7]

All the Great Powers in Europe entered World War I with a distinctly offensive military doctrine and security strategy. They all paid a terrible price after the offensives they launched not only failed to obtain their objectives, but indeed backfired in a matter of months. The German "Schlieffen Plan," whose implementation violated Belgian neutrality, was one of the major factors causing Great Britain to enter the war in Europe. The French "Plan 17," which preferred to attack in Alsace, Lorraine, and Luxembourg, instead of deploying opposite the attacking German army, allowed the Germans to occupy large parts of French territory. The Russian "Plan A" resulted in the destruction of a major part of the Russian army in East Prussia, while the plans conceived in Vienna were extremely harmful to the Austro-Hungarian army in Galicia.

In hindsight, this almost blind adoption of the offensive strategies was without doubt far from rational, giving credence to the hypothesis that had they opted for a defensive strategy the Great War would not only have shrunk into a local, limited, and short engagement, it might not have occurred at all.[8] As the circumstances in which the European offensive doctrine was formulated have been extensively discussed, this chapter will focus primarily on its connection to the Russo-Japanese War. Structurally, the argument here is that a distinct correlation existed between the lessons adopted and implemented or rejected by European armies and the basic perception that already dominated military doctrines, and that these lessons were utilized to strengthen those doctrines, marking a target around the arrow. Conceptually, the contribution made by the Russo-Japanese War to the preservation of the existing beliefs and prevailing doctrines regarding the supremacy of offence over defense is pointed out, although, in retrospect, the real lessons should have challenged such notions.

The Europeans' sources of information

The main source of information for the European armies about the events taking place on the battlefields of Manchuria were the military observers sent to follow the conflict. The war broke out at a time of a widespread faith among the armies of the industrialized world in the possibility of understanding modern warfare without taking an active part in it, by observing the wars of others. The Crimean War in the mid-nineteenth century was the first in which the position of military observer was formulated, and the American Civil War (1861–5) and the Franco-Prussian War (1870–1) were the first in which many observers from non-combatant countries closely followed the protagonists. Their lessons were documented and became part of military studies at the beginning of the twentieth century. The Boer War in South Africa (1899–1902) also attracted many observers, and together with the Russo-Japanese War became the focal point of discussion and doctrinal deliberation on the eve of World War I.[9]

The war in Manchuria and Korea was one of the most observed non-European wars prior to 1914. Eighty-three officers from 15 countries were specially sent to reinforce the military attachés already serving in Tokyo and St Petersburg. The majority of them covered the war from the Japanese side, reporting home at length about their experiences, findings, and conclusions (the British alone sent over 240 reports of that nature). The list of observers included officers who later played key roles in their armies and were therefore in positions in which they were able to implement their lessons of the Russo-Japanese War in practice. Among the more prominent among them were Lieutenant-General Ian Hamilton, already mentioned; Lieutenant-General William Nicholson, Chief of the British Imperial General Staff from 1908 to 1912; General (then Colonel) John Pershing, commander-in-chief of the American Expeditionary Force in France during World War I; and General (then Captain) Max Hoffman, the famed chief operations officer of the German Eighth Army on the Eastern Front in 1914. Also on the list were French, Italian, Austrian, American, and British officers who served during the world war as commanders of armies, corps, divisions, and fleets, as well as senior staff officers of those armies.[10]

In addition to the observers, European military correspondents were present in the warring countries, providing ongoing reports to their newspapers on the war. Many were far from understanding the military profession or the local languages, and in fact were kept away from the actual battlefields by the authorities (who regarded them as a menace) and therefore they based much of the content of their reports on information obtained by talking to the observers.[11] It is therefore not at all surprising that the information and opinions published in European media were similar in content to the official reports of the observers, read in the war ministries and general staffs. Considered of independent origin, the former ostensibly verified the latter reports, thus strengthening the tendency to adopt their conclusions.

All the Western armies saw the war as a testing ground for modern warfare, the lessons of which should be meticulously examined. Judging solely by the quantity of official publications appearing in Europe after the war, the data, analysis, and assessments sent home during the war or brought back at the end of it by the observers and attachés were undoubtedly taken very seriously by the military. Between 1906 and 1914, at least five of the observing powers published official multi-volume series about the war, based on the observers' reports and sometimes written by them, in the sense of an "official history" of a war that the writer was not part of. The British War Office published a series of five volumes describing the unfolding of the war on land and sea, and a three-volume second series, containing the observers' reports, among them a volume dedicated to the medical dimension. The German publication consisted of 13 volumes (and was immediately translated into English and published in London in seven volumes), and further series appeared in Paris, Vienna, and Washington.[12] The enormous number of articles published in professional military journals all over Europe on the war and its lessons, and the many lectures given by the observers, journalists, and various specialists in the military clubs of the European capitals, all indicate the importance ascribed by the old continent to the understanding of the testing ground in the east.

The dilemma of offense and defense

When the Russo-Japanese War broke out, Europe was deeply engaged in a fundamental discourse over the changing nature of future warfare, pursuant to the changes the continent had experienced since the Napoleonic era. During the crystallization period of the nation-states, their armies were reshaped as well, following hitherto unfamiliar lines. The most substantial—and salient—were, first, the creation of mass armies, as a result of introducing compulsory and reserve service, and, second, the ideological cohesion molded by new national identity. The military implications of the mass army were twofold: on the one hand it provided longer strategic breathing space and facilitated the operational concentration of force for the decisive strike. On the other hand, however, it made it difficult to achieve surprise due to the necessity to mobilize, move, and maneuver large formations, and it was harder to maintain the armed forces logistically and support a protracted war financially.

Moreover, the emergence of national ideology changed war aims: no longer a mere victory over the opposing army, but a more total resolution, perhaps even to the point of the latter's annihilation. Finally, national cohesion and shared purpose directly affected soldiers' motivation and willingness to fight. Armies and wars were also influenced by the technological revolution of the nineteenth century, whose contribution to land warfare was expressed primarily in the fields of firepower and mobility. The former showed constant improvement in volume, accuracy, and effectiveness, represented by the magazine-loaded rifle, the machine gun, the quick-firing gun, and better ammunition. In the latter, improved transport and maneuverability, first and foremost the ever expanding railroad system, made their appearance, facilitating faster shifts between centers of gravity, both strategic and operational.

These changes gradually led the European armies to wide-ranging deliberations on the nature of future warfare, including the relationship between offensive and defensive forms of warfare. In essence, the discourse turned to validation or refutation of a leading principle of the military profession and a major cornerstone of traditional military education, namely the initiated attack as the preferred type of combat. The question asked was whether this was still valid, or whether recent developments caused the battlefield's supremacy to shift from attack to defense. This was less a matter of evolving pure military theory and more a practical realization of the growing difficulty in attaining the military and national aims of war by means of offensives and attacks in the face of increasingly powerful defenders. On the eve of the Russo-Japanese War the traditional offensive school of thought still had the upper hand.

Outwardly, the discourse was confined to the narrow context of the military profession alone; in fact, however, it was part of a greater social and cultural subtext, examining the function of the army in a nation-state, the standing of the military system in a mobilized society, and the role of war in Europe's new environment. Within this context, the European agenda tackled key questions: Would the army continue to hoist the flag for the state? Would the officer corps continue fulfilling its role as protector of the existing traditional order and retain its power and prestige? Or would new forces arise to invalidate the army's centrality, thus threatening its privileged socio-economic status? And so on.

In the French Republic, for example, a fundamental motive behind the offensive bias was to be found in the organizational interest of the officer class in preventing the standing army from becoming a mere training cadre for a mass civilian army of conscripts and reservists, so as not to diminish the officer corps' high standing. From the Franco-Prussian War onward a prevalent approach among the French military argued that defense did not necessitate the high proficiency and morale that were required for attack. Defensive action, therefore, seemed the type of combat more appropriate for reservists, and this primacy of offense over defense would, by implication, leave the military establishment intact.[13] In Germany the circumstances were different, but there too they were contingent on the army's traditional prestige resting on a history of offensive victories—against Austria in 1866 and France in 1870. Any challenge to that outlook could be harmful to the standing and prestige of officers of the Second Reich.[14]

The British army also persisted with the offensive doctrine, but from a completely different angle. As a naval power, Britain did not see itself becoming involved in large-scale continental operations against other European armies, and therefore had not been obliged to adapt to the evolving changes in land warfare since the Napoleonic Wars. However, Britain's military perception was rooted in its imperial-colonial being, where the offensive mode was assumed a necessity behind unwavering British commitment to its imperial standing. It was also one of the effective means to protect the country's image and prestige in the eyes of subjects and neighbors alike, without investing in vast human resources of soldiers and administrators, who were always in short supply.[15]

At the beginning of the twentieth century, then, the European armies expected to conduct the next war using mobile, mostly offensive, action. The model to shape the offensive doctrine was based on the successful wars in the eras of Napoleon and German unification. True, the tacticians realized that firepower achieved lethality more than ever, but they expected that its effects would, if anything, change the face of battle in favor of attack, which would then become more efficient, providing advantage to rapid, prompt, and decisive maneuvers. The history of recent wars had shown that the initiator won, as proven by Frederick the Great and Napoleon, who achieved their most impressive victories by aggressive maneuvering that neutralized their foes time after time. The wars between Austria and France, and Austria and Prussia, and the Franco-Prussian War were all examples of fast offensive action defeating hesitant opponents. The Russians' advance against the slow Ottomans in the Balkans (1877–8) was also taken as evidence that attack could overcome fortified positions even in mountainous regions. European commentators were inclined to disregard the lessons of the American Civil War as an exception, fought between hastily drafted civilian masses and hence not indicative of any future European conflict. Conversely, the Boer War received much more attention and it was difficult to ignore the direction it pointed at: the British failed in their attempts to advance in the face of the rapid rate of fire produced by the German Mauser rifles in the hands of the Boers. However, once again this war too was labeled by many a colonial war, with very few and limited implications.

The Russo-Japanese War was viewed in an entirely different light, as the largest army in Europe faced an army whose abilities were still an enigma, but which was known for its modern armament, training, and organization. From the very first moment the war in East Asia was perceived as more balanced, therefore more relevant than the above-mentioned wars, providing lessons worth learning. Wide consensus prevailed among the military observers, and accordingly among the armies in which they served, that on the techno-tactical level, modern firepower had achieved mastery of the battlefield and that the tactical area in front of the defensive line had become an impassable "zone of death." The weapon that made its most impressive and influential debut was the machine gun. In South Africa the British and the Boers had rarely used machine guns, and it was the same at the start of the war in Manchuria. But toward its end both sides had sent every machine gun they could get their hands on to the front (the Russians ended the war with approximately 800 machine guns), and both Russian and Japanese front-line officers who had experienced its action recommended that this automatic weapon be introduced at the lower levels of battalion and company. The observers' unanimous verdict emphasized the devastating effect of machine guns, and after 1905 all armies concluded that they had become essential, especially in a fight with an enemy who already had them in its arsenal. The importance of introducing this weapon into the infantry was now undoubted.[16]

By the end of the first decade of the twentieth century all the great European armies had progressed from the phase of trial and error (existing on the eve of the war), to the phase of procurement and equipment of an average of two machine guns per infantry brigade (or regiment) or independent battalion, the objective being a section of two to four machine guns for every infantry battalion.[17] At this stage experience of the machine gun's action represented Hamilton's object lesson in "naked truth," as most observers pointed out the advantages of the machine gun to the defenders as a counterweight to the numerically superior attacking troops, hitting them from behind covered emplacements. On the basis of its observer's reports, French intelligence established that:

> The Manchurian war has shown the incontestable value of machine guns. Opinions are unanimous concerning the great material and moral effects, which they produce . . . It was above all in the defensive that these weapons displayed their terrible effectiveness . . . literally mow down the attackers.[18]

The observers clearly identified the overwhelming advantages modern firepower provided for the defense by rifles, machine guns, and artillery. They understood, for example, that the nature of this fire prescribed a different form of defenses from the familiar large fortress, and that it would include mostly field entrenchment. They reported, accurately, that the lengthening of the front line was an inevitable result of the growing defensive firepower and pointed out the necessity of digging in, in both attack and defense (a tactic that both the Russians and the Japanese used extensively). A French summary established that the experience of the war in the east proved that "it is almost impossible for a front protected by really powerful weapons and field defenses to be broken through even by troops of undaunted courage willing to sacrifice any number of lives."[19]

However, as the observational findings developed into analytical conclusions the consensus between observers and armies began to fade, as the opinions of the former were apparently not those that the general staffs were interested in hearing. Instead of adopting the self-evident conclusions from the finding that the new firepower created severe difficulties for the attackers, and eroded, or even cancelled out, the traditional advantage of the attack, the military attempted to bend the lessons to the ruling offensive doctrinal line. Supporters of the "cult of offensive" disparaged the use of machine guns in Korea and Manchuria for defense alone as a tactical mistake. To their mind, the Japanese and the Russians alike failed to exploit the true advantages of this weapon for attack, and therefore the ensuing ruling for the defense was too simplistic; instead, an offensive doctrine had to be developed to offset the supremacy of the defensive firepower. Consequently, after the Russo-Japanese War most armies restored the emphasis on the offensive and tried to integrate the machine gun into training, maneuvers, and doctrine to support the assaulting infantry in the attack. Soon World War I was to prove once again the terrible effect of the machine gun in breaking attacks, just as it had done in the Russo-Japanese War; but in 1914 this dreadful lesson came as a surprise for most armies. Having rejected it a few years earlier, they insisted on clinging to their offensive bias.[20]

That same biased perception affected lessons learned about the artillery as well. The limited use of heavy guns on both sides (mostly by the Japanese in the bombardment of Port Arthur) let every observer interpret it differently, according to his own outlook. The French, whose battle drill unmistakably relied on quick-firing field guns, dismissed the value of heavy artillery, pointing out its limited use during the war and the difficulties of mobility. The Germans, on the other hand, whose heavy artillery technology was far advanced already by the end of the nineteenth century, came to a contrary conclusion, arguing that the poor performance of heavy artillery in the Russo-Japanese War was a result of misuse, and therefore did not reflect reality. For them, the Japanese experience at Port Arthur served to reinforce their conviction that only heavy artillery was able to destroy the strong fortifications and defenses that had become the rule in modern warfare.[21] Other armies chose not to follow this line, preferring to invest their limited resources in other weapons systems. The British observers were of mixed opinion. Those who were attached to the Russian army were much more impressed by the Japanese artillery than their compatriots reporting from the Japanese side, perhaps because they were on the receiving end; but in London the overwhelming opinion was that their conclusions were exaggerated.[22] In practice the British army also refrained from arming itself with howitzers and high explosive shells, which had been used so impressively during the war (unlike old-style shrapnel and cast-iron shells), and like the French army it paid dearly for this at the beginning of the Great War.

As for field defenses, the German general staff was the only one to translate the observers' findings into practical doctrinal lessons, after being persuaded that they were essential for defending occupied ground against counter-attacks. From 1906, foreign observers of German army maneuvers reported the appearance of defensive positions built out of several lines of trenches deep enough for troops to stand upright, interconnected by communications trenches and protected by barbed wire, just as in Manchuria. Some argue that it was the adoption of this very lesson that facilitated the shift of the German army from offense to defense at the end of 1914 faster than any other army on the Western Front.[23] This case, however, is the exception to the rule. Knowing in retrospect the frustration and even breaking of infantry attacks in France and Flanders by machine guns and heavy artillery during World War I, one can trace this effect back to the Russo-Japanese War. At the time, however, the contribution of these weapons systems to defense failed to shake the general confidence in the ethos of the offensive. The voices of its critics were hushed by its advocates, who determined that the growing destructive power of weaponry had no bearing on the traditional maxim that only attack could achieve results, that only an offensive would secure victory, and that those two were achievable even under the new conditions.

The results of the Russo-Japanese War proved, according to the supporters of the offensive doctrine, that inter-arm coordination, especially between infantry and artillery, which took full advantage of the new firepower in attack, had become the key to overcoming the modern firepower of defense. Although the new armament had improved the efficiency of defense, and could potentially even block the offensive advance by causing many casualties, by the same token it would increase the attackers' capabilities. Proper employment of firepower in attack, and especially the efficient handling of modern artillery, with its continuous quick-fire capability, long range, accuracy of indirect fire, and effective payload of the shells, were seen as enough to force defenders to seek cover and neutralize their guns, to prevent them from holding the trenches, and to pave the way for an uninterrupted infantry advance.[24] All observers were greatly impressed by the Japanese tactics of supporting gunfire, by which the artillery barrage laid down on the enemy's frontline continued until the attacking infantry stood practically right over the Russian trenches. Before then, armies had customarily stopped the covering fire earlier, allowing a safety range for their own assaulting troops. The offensive school argued further that the war had proven that tactically the infantry would be able to overcome the defensive fire wall by employing fire and movement, manifesting both combat mobility and the efficiency of modern weapons.

A major lesson of the new fire effect already adopted by most European armies after the Boer War was the necessity to loosen up the rigid structure of units on the attack. Traditionally, such a force advanced in tight battle formation, closely controlled by its commanders and firing concentrated volleys. The French were the first to introduce the tactical change, and by 1904 their military doctrine stressed the necessity of encouraging both soldiers and junior officers to show initiative on the battlefield and the importance of maneuver, dispersed movement, use of terrain for cover, flexibility in formations, and offensive motivation. The French saw the Russo-Japanese War as vindication of their offensive tactics and the importance of initiative "inherent in our race," and stressed the positive lesson they took from the dispersed movement of the Japanese units.[25]

This spreading out by the Japanese, claimed the French, had kept the enemy occupied at many points of contact and firing along the front and flanks, had baffled him, had thrown him off balance, and had prevented the Russian tactical reserve from acting in time to decide the battle. The Germans understood this concept even earlier, and in the period between the end of the war in South Africa and the start of the war in Manchuria they had tried what they labeled "Boer tactics" in the annual imperial maneuvers, using dispersed formations that took advantage of the terrain for cover and concealment. Impressed by the vulnerability of tight formations employed on the Russian attacks in comparison with the sustainability of the spread-out Japanese formations in 1905, Kaiser Wilhelm himself called for more spacing in infantry movement.[26] Those two wars led the British army as well to an emphasis on field-craft and the importance of inter-arm coordination.[27]

The conclusions drawn from the Russo-Japanese War, however, pointing to the problematic elements in the ethos of offensive, were too overreaching for its adherents, and they were quick to sound a warning against an overall embracing of the lessons. Much like their caution regarding the "inapt" lessons of the Boer War, they repeatedly maintained that several of the failures and successes were the result of mistakes made on both sides, and that the war in Manchuria was therefore far from rendering the traditional principles and previous doctrine irrelevant. The French and the Germans, for example, claimed that the initial failures sustained by the British during their attacks on Boer positions were less a result of an enhanced defensive capability and more a consequence of abandonment of the offensive doctrine. To their minds, the British gunfire on the Boer's defenses ceased before the assaulting infantry crossed their start line (unlike the use of artillery by the Japanese), thus allowing the enemy to regain its tactical balance; they failed to act decisively (for example, by restraining the cavalry from pursuing the retreating enemy) and also made little use of quick-firing guns in their attacks. The Russo-Japanese War served to strengthen these lessons; this time the British concurred with views expressed by the French and German general staffs that both protagonists misused their field guns in attack, and that the inadequate artillery preparation of the battlefield contributed to the slow movement and protracted multi-casualty attacks of them both.[28]

Accordingly, French observers were able to report that the war was further proof of the supremacy of offense and maneuver over passive defense. Even the Russians' numerical supremacy and its incorporation with field fortifications did not save their defensive strategy, in the opinion of those observers, who chose to ignore the fact that the Russians suffered more when they attacked then when they were on the defensive. By contrast, the British commanders, although they indeed interpreted the Russo-Japanese War as expressing an increase in the tactical importance of defense, pointed to effective measures of offensive compensation, such as concentration of firepower and closer coordination.[29] In that spirit a British account concluded:

The [Manchurian] war has certainly not demonstrated that frontal attacks are a sheer impossibility ... Where very large modern armies are concerned, attacks must be frontal, and that part the enemy's front will be selected for the main attack, before which a large force can be concentrated quickly and secretly, and the attack of the infantry will be covered and supported by artillery and cavalry. No weak screen of quick firing guns will breach the line, and against the breach will be sent a mess of infantry to break the line. Through the break in the line will pour the cavalry divisions, to complete the victory and hamper the reserves from coming up to stop the breach by an offensive return, or to restore the battle by a counterstroke.[30]

The importance of morale

While the professional techno-tactical lessons remained open to commentary, the observers pointed out the lessons in the realm of morale as sharp and clear. The Japanese may have lost approximately 50,000 men in their repeated storming of Port Arthur, compared with approximately 28,000 Russians, but eventually they achieved their goal and took the fortress. Despite the extending range of contact between the two sides, despite the Japanese infantry's exposure to the modern fire storm, despite the lack of sufficient artillery cover, and despite the terrible losses they sustained with their assault tactics, they were able, finally, to push on with the attack, proving the supremacy of the offensive. The assumption that every attack would inevitably include heavy losses was accepted in the Western armies as a given fact. The British army, for example, calculated on the basis of the lessons of the Russo-Japanese War that any expeditionary force they sent to Europe would suffer losses of 75 percent in the first six months of fighting.[31] Placing the emphasis on the merit of combatants, the observers determined that the lessons of the war chosen for the guidance of the officer corps should be less about technological innovations and more about military spirit and national ethos. From the officers' perspective the key to success lay in excellence of command, a high degree of morale, and strength of determination, through which one could overcome the material power of the modern weaponry of defense.[32]

The Russo-Japanese War was fought in an environment in which General Alfred von Schlieffen, the German chief of the general staff, facing the possibility of a two-front war, emphasized the national necessity of a rapid short annihilation campaign on one front, since only the immediate removal of one of its opponents could give Germany a chance to overcome the other. It was an environment in which Lieutenant-Colonel Ferdinand Foch (later marshall and supreme commander of allied armies on the Western Front) preached as early as 1903 the need to increase the offensive character of the army and promote élan. The majority of French officers rejected the lessons implied by the use of the new weapons in South Africa, claiming that they were misemployed and in small quantities. To their mind, the Boers' early successes in the face of the British were caused by the superior morale of the former and the reluctance of the latter to take losses. However, the Boers finally lost precisely because they stuck to defensive tactics. For the Europeans, the Boer War was a further demonstration that an army whose military doctrine was based on *offensive à outrance*, would gain the upper hand.[33]

Depending on such a military ethos, French observers of the Russo-Japanese War naturally looked for the traits that the French officer corps expected of itself, as well as of the men, specifically high morale, determination, firmness, leadership, discipline, precision, and political loyalty. Based on this perspective, it was easy for the observers to be convinced that the victors displayed those precise qualities, and their reports were indeed full of praise for the Japanese soldiers who had shown constant initiative, who had attacked at any price despite heavy losses with unbending discipline, and who had demonstrated high standards of aggressiveness, sacrifice, and patriotism. In such an ambience it was easy to interpret the Japanese victory as confirming the efficacy of offensive tactics. In the eyes of the French, even if the war had introduced the might of modern defensive firepower and shown that it could no longer be ignored, it also demonstrated that it succumbed to the strategic and morale advantages of offense. In accordance with this view, the war substantiated yet again that attack and maneuver were superior to passive defense; the observers ignored the fact that the adoption of defensive tactics by the Russians was precisely the act that saved them from a much worse defeat, or possibly even annihilation. Indeed, at least in that respect, the Russo-Japanese War undid the defensive lessons left over from the Boer War. Small wonder that the French military theoretician Colonel Louis Grandmaison had no hesitation in attributing the Japanese victories to "the absolute and unreserved offensive spirit, animating officers and men alike,"[34] and French Regulations for the Conduct of Major Formations decreed in 1913 that "the French Army, returning to its tradition, recognizes no other law save that of the offensive."[35]

A similar approach emerged also in Germany, where Alfred von Schlieffen rejected the defensive lessons implied by the recent wars, except on the lowest tactical level. Even more, the Russian achievements in defense stimulated his urge to increase the tempo and persistence of the attack to prevent it being halted, "as was the case in the east." The armament may have changed, von Schlieffen believed, but the basic laws of warfare remained firm: it was impossible to defeat an enemy without attacking and annihilating him. The German observers of the Russo-Japanese War were extremely critical of the passivity, in their opinion, that typified the Russian officers, and of their reluctance to sustain casualties; the Germans pointed to what they called the Russians' inferior morale in the face of the aggressive determination motivating the Japanese. In their mind, the source of Russian defeat stemmed from inert commanders rather than from material inferiority. "The will to conquer, conquered," the official German history of the war stated.[36]

The British were not far from their continental colleagues. Their official history of the Russo-Japanese War emphasized the conclusion that Japanese determination was the one crucial factor enabling them to overcome the operational hardships of terrain and firepower. Senior British observers also pointed out the spirit of Bushido and Shintoism, which in their view were the embodiment of the Japanese national characteristics, elevating the human factor to its superior position over firepower.[37] In fact, this was a mirror image of the traditional values of the Victorian-Edwardian army. Any adoption of a tactical or technological solution in overcoming the lethal wall of defensive fire might promote an unacceptable, perhaps even dangerous, approach among the British officers at the beginning of the twentieth century, which would imply the preference for professional merit over social status.[38]

Epilogue

Four decades after the Russo-Japanese War, and toward the end of World War II, the eminent military historian Basil Henry Liddell Hart stated:

> If the study of war in the past has so often proved fallible as a guide to the course and conduct of the next war, it implies not that war is unsuited to scientific study but that the study has not been scientific enough in spirit and method.[39]

The main "lesson" drawn by the European armies from the Russo-Japanese War, namely the continued superiority of attack over defense, was wrong, and it was indeed discarded ten years later. It seems therefore appropriate to apply Liddell Hart's conclusion to the subject discussed here.

After the Boer and the Russo-Japanese Wars, no one disputed the destructive power of the new weaponry, or ignored the concrete lessons that pointed to the difficulties it caused to the attack. However, the more abstract meanings of the subject remained vague to contemporaries. The implications of themes like protracted war, continuous undecided battles, long periods of deadlock on the front, and the different character of the two armies were inconclusive and could be read in more than one way. They therefore received contradictory interpretations, while observers from the same army reached completely different conclusions on the same specific subject. An example is the intense discussion in the Europeans armies over the role of cavalry in the modern battle and its position in relation to the new firepower on the one hand and traditional shock tactics on the other.[40] In such circumstances it was easy to channel the lessons toward narrow military self-interests and insist on the validity of the traditional outlook. Accordingly, Major-General (later Lieutenant General) Edward Altham could state in 1914 that the "Manchurian campaign has wiped out the mistaken inference from South African experiences that bayonet fighting belonged to the past."[41] To a great extent, observers and armies alike found whatever they were seeking in the war, and they used it to further establish their approach: validation of the European emphasis that it was still possible to preach the strategic and tactical advantages of offense over defense as the key to military victory, and as a result to preserve the status of the modern army in its relations with state and society.

Notes

1 Dobson, 2000: 13.
2 Neilson, 1991: 17.
3 Dobson, 2000: 13.
4 Hamilton, 1905, I: v.
5 For further discussion on Hamilton's view on this point, see Lee, 2000: 91.
6 For example, Beckett, 2001: 44–7; Cox, 1992: 389–401; and Mackenzie, 1999: 30–40. On lessons adopted, see Black, 2002: 36–9; Gilbert, 1997: xx; and Herrmann 1996: 22ff.
7 Herwig, 1997; Philips, 2002; Snyder, 1984a; van Evera, 1984; Wesseling, 2000.
8 I owe this reflection to Professor Michael Howard. See Howard, 1997: 22.
9 On the formulation and evolvement of the institution of military observers, see Vagts, 1967.
10 On the observers, see Dobson, 2000; Greenwood, 1971: 96–119; and Towle, 1999: 158–68;
11 Knightly, 1975: 44, 61–2; Mathews, 1957: 141–57; Slattery, 2004; and Towle, 1998: 20–1;
12 Austria-Hungary General Staff, 1910–14; German General Staff, 1908–14; Great Britain, War Office, General Staff, 1906–8; United States War Department, 1906–7; Corbett, 1914; Dobson, 2000.
13 Wesseling, 2000: 170–8.
14 Snyder, 1984b: 119–21.
15 On the importance of prestige in British imperial thinking, see French, 1987: 45–59; and Sheffy, 1998: 109–13.
16 Ellis, 1975: 65–8.
17 Travers, 1978: 532–7.
18 Herrmann, 1996: 68.
19 Connaughton, 1988: 275.
20 Graham, 1982: 190–3.
21 Herrmann, 1996: 90–2; Zabecki, 1994: 11.
22 Bidwell and Graham, 1982: 7–58; Towle, 1999: 165.
23 Graham, 1982: 90.
24 Towle, 1971: 65.
25 Herrmann, 1996: 82.
26 Herrmann, 1996: 87.
27 Griffith, 1994: 48–9.
28 Herrmann, 1996: 27.

29 Johnson, 1994: 182.
30 Connaughton, 1988: 275–6.
31 Strachen, 2001: 200.
32 Towle, 1998: 27; Travers, 1987: 87 and *passim*.
33 Porch 1975, 1981: 213–41, 232–45.
34 Wesseling, 2000: 167.
35 Howard, 1986: 520.
36 Mackenzie, 1999: 33.
37 Travers, 1979: 271–7; 1987: 64–8; Howard, 1984: 14–19.
38 For a discussion on British military values, see Spiers, 1994.
39 Liddell Hart, 1944: 25.
40 Bond, 1965: 113–14.
41 Travers, 1987: 45.

17 The impact of the war on naval warfare

Rotem Kowner[1]

From a naval point of view, the Russo-Japanese War was the most important campaign since the Napoleonic Wars, and had a marked influence, albeit brief, on the development of warfare at sea. Its greatest impact was obviously on the fleets of Russia and Japan. Whereas the former, the world's third largest, declined substantially after the war, the latter burgeoned into one of the world's mightiest. In addition, it was primarily the British Royal Navy, the leading naval force at that time, that showed great interest in the naval engagement of the war. The lessons learnt in the war played a significant role in the minor revolution in naval development and the subsequent naval race that took place among the powers, Britain and Germany in particular, in the decade before World War I.

The naval dimension had extreme importance in the Russo-Japanese War. Several years before its outbreak, both Japan and Russia concluded that domination of the seas in their vicinity would be crucial to any future conflict between them. As soon as the war began the two combatants vied fiercely for the control of the waters in the vicinity of Korea and Manchuria, knowing that it would determine the conflict. They were absolutely right. Other naval powers, however, expressed much interest in this naval struggle for other reasons. Both navies were equipped with numerous modern warships, and their unprecedented clash was supposed to yield invaluable information on naval tactics and construction, as well as on subsequent weapon development. For this purpose, they dispatched scores of observers who impatiently followed the great drama and sought to learn its lessons.

Since the Russo-Turkish War of 1877–8 and the battle of the Yalu River in 1894, the world had not witnessed any major naval engagement, and in this interval the warship had undergone tremendous evolution. Accordingly, avid observers had much to report on any naval engagement from the first day of the war. The drama reached its climax with the epic voyage of the Baltic Fleet and its ultimate demise at the battle of Tsushima. For many months before the battle the fleet drew the attention of the entire world. Not only were its position and objectives no secret, but also throughout the journey the press reported on its progress and predicaments. As in a Greek tragedy, the Russian armada slowly progressed toward its inevitable clash with the entire Japanese fleet. In the aftermath of the battle the expectation of significant lessons was entirely fulfilled. The war served as an overture to the great naval battles of World War I, and the strategic circumstances at the outbreak of war even bring to mind the later fierce American–Japanese clash during the Pacific War (1941–5). In technology the naval campaign of the Russo-Japanese War signaled the end of an era in naval evolution, yet it served as a precursor for the weapons systems and tactics that major navies would adopt and the dilemmas they would face during the following 40 years.

The war and the fate of the battleship

The most immediate contribution of the war to naval warfare was its impact on the development and virtually the destiny of the battleship in the following decades. Following several radical developments, if not revolutions, in naval technology during the nineteenth century, the status of the capital ship, a large steel-built vessel protected by thick armor and armed with large guns, lay in doubt.[2] During the 1880s the leading navies held heated debates as to the role of this warship in the future naval arena. Some of them, notably the French group known as *La jeune école* and headed by Vice Admiral Théophile Aube, argued that the battleship was an outdated and expensive vessel that had lost its advantage in view of the technological developments of the time. In the future, asserted the adherents of that school, only relatively small and fast vessels such as the cruiser at most, and perhaps just the small torpedo boat, would be able to cope with the new threats such as the torpedo, rapid guns, and mines. Concerned by their inability to compete with the accelerated pace of expansion of the Royal Navy, other large fleets were drawn to this approach and began to equip themselves with small torpedo boats and destroyers (which were intended to combat torpedo boats) in ever growing numbers.[3]

Opposing this school were the proponents of the large battleship, arguing that it had not lost its hegemony. Prominent among them was the leading American naval historian and theorist Alfred Thayer Mahan. In two major works published in 1890–2, Mahan asserted that naval power was a key to international success and that whoever ruled the sea and seaborne commerce would win the war.[4] Mahan's views did not contain much that was new, but they sounded the bell at the right time and reinforced widespread tendencies that were already prevalent. His books won high acclaim from naval circles of all the powers, as well as from advocates of imperialist expansion, and were soon translated into German, following the personal initiative of Kaiser Wilhelm II, Russian, and Japanese. They marked the beginning of a 15-year period known today as the pre-modern age in the development of naval warfare (1890–1905). It was a brief but intensive spell, which ended abruptly soon after the Russo-Japanese War. It witnessed the introduction of smokeless gunpowder, armor-piercing shells, and rapid-firing guns; significant improvements in torpedo engines that turned them into efficient weapons; and slight improvements in firing control that doubled the effective range of the big guns.

The most significant naval transformation in this short period, however, took place in the construction of the battleship itself. In 1889, a year prior to the publication of Mahan's first book, the keel of the first ship of the *Royal Sovereign* class was laid in Britain. Naval experts considered this class the first of a new type of battleship that would be labeled 17 years later as the Pre-Dreadnought. Compared with earlier battleships, it was characterized by a high turret in its prow that made it easier to withstand a high sea and facilitated sailing at higher speeds. In addition, the use of steel and nickel plates improved protection and saved weight. The outcome was a stronger ship that became the prototype for most battleships built throughout the world until the end of the Russo-Japanese War. The new battleship also marked the beginning of a renewed naval arms race in Europe, mainly between the Royal Navy and the French and Russian navies, with the Imperial German Navy trailing behind them. In view of the impressive build-up of French naval power in the early 1880s, Britain declared a "two-power standard" (in the 1889 Naval Defence Act) and adopted greater expansion programs, with the intention of being able to face any combination of two of the other largest fleets. For this purpose Britain appropriated large budgets that allowed the rapid construction of additional battleships, ending by late 1905 with an unmatched force of 47 Pre-Dreadnought battleships. They all shared a similar design and had a primary battery placed on two turrets, each with two barrels of the same caliber.[5]

On the eve of the Russo-Japanese War more than a hundred battleships of Pre-Dreadnought design were sailing the seas, flying the flags of nine navies.[6] The construction of these warships involved enormous expenditure, which placed a heavy burden on the defense budgets of their countries. This financial burden was accompanied by serious doubts, for both military and economic reasons. Without any naval battle since the onset of the Pre-Dreadnought age, and with the constant improvements in the quality of the torpedo, naval experts had strong reasons to question the ability of the ever growing battleship to cope with the new threats in the naval arena. Quite a few thought therefore that, like dinosaurs, they would become extinct at the first encounter with smaller, cheaper, and more efficient warships.

The emergence of the *Dreadnought*

Doubts about the use of the battleship in general, and its primary armament in particular, vanished altogether as a consequence of the battle of Tsushima. In the eyes of the major navies, the outcome of this battle confirmed Mahan's theses regarding the decisive importance of the battleship. At the same time, the battle left no doubt about the necessity for further improvements that would make the battleship more resistant and powerful. First and foremost, the lessons of the naval engagements of the Russo-Japanese War concerned the armament of the battleship. Until 1905 the leading navies equipped their battleships with a primary and a secondary battery. The purpose of the primary battery was to engage primarily other battleships and it usually relied on four guns in two turrets, front and rear—usually 305-millimeter caliber (12 inches in bore diameter).[7] The secondary battery was intended for assisting the primary battery against capital ships, but also for engaging smaller warships, mostly torpedo boats and destroyers, and included scores of guns with calibers ranging between 76 and 152 millimeters (3–6 inches).[8]

Analyses of the battle of Tsushima emphasized the decisive, but not necessarily exclusive, importance of the primary battery in an engagement between battleships. In Tsushima, and even more so in the battle in the Yellow Sea nine months earlier, fire was opened at distances previously unknown.[9] The fact that only guns of large caliber were used in such a long-distance engagement had dramatic repercussions. First, the development of armor, in thickness and quality, made it possible only for guns of especially large caliber to cause any significant damage and even to sink battleships or armored cruisers; second, only ships with especially thick armor were able to withstand a hit by those guns. The logical outcome was evident. A well-protected battleship with eight or even a dozen big guns could be equivalent to two or even three existing Pre-Dreadnought battleships of the size of the Japanese flagship *Mikasa*.

One reason for the need for an efficient and drastic solution to the problem of firepower was the wide variety of firing systems that had been created over the years. This variety prevented the possibility of control and complicated the necessary uniformity.[10] The other reason was the availability of proper technology. The idea of arming a battleship with numerous big guns and stripping it of its secondary battery began to take form even prior to Tsushima. Already in 1903 the Royal Navy had conducted several successful experiments in long-range fire and improved fire control. The promising results induced experts such as Edward Harding to contend that additional improvement in fire control and fire rate of the heavy guns, in several years' time, might put engagement between battleships beyond the range of small caliber guns and would keep them at a distance even beyond the efficient range of torpedoes.[11]

The last but not least important reason for the need for a new type of battleship was economic. At the outbreak of the Russo-Japanese War the budget of the Royal Navy was double its budget 15 years earlier, bringing the burden on the empire to new limits.[12] Appointed as First Sea Lord in October 1904, Admiral John Fisher expressed his readiness for budget cuts. Actually, he had no intention of either reducing the fleet's firepower or overstraining its budget, but he was willing to decommission over 150 obsolete vessels. At the same time, he was aware of the necessity to provide high-quality replacements for the quantitative loss and to increase the fleet's firepower against the rising German competition. Fisher had in fact voiced his readiness to cut the number of warships but not the firepower a few years earlier, but the reports that the British naval observers sent from East Asia left him no further room for doubt.[13]

In March 1905, two months before the battle of Tsushima, the Admiralty approved plans for a revolutionary all-big-gun battleship. It was to be armed with ten 305-millimeter (12-inch) guns, all capable of simultaneously aiming at a single target under a central firing control. The decision did not require the lessons of Tsushima, since already at the end of the battle in the Yellow Sea in August 1904 the senior British naval observer, Captain William Pakenham, composed an encomium to long-range fire. Stationed aboard the Japanese battleship *Asahi* throughout most of the war, Pakenham suggested it was possible to open fire at a distance of 20,000 meters (about 22,000 yards) and to consider a firing range of 10,000 meters as being at close quarters. In the following months other British naval observers added their support to this view and quoted the opinions of Japanese officers that heavy guns were much more efficient than medium guns at the long ranges that were expected in future naval battles. Pakenham himself wrote:

> the effect of the fire of every gun is so much less than that of the next larger size, that when 12-inch guns are firing, shots from 10-inch pass unnoticed, while, for all the respect they instill, 8-inch or 6-inch guns might then just as well be pea-shooters, and the 12 pr. [pounder guns] simply does not count.[14]

The reports of the British naval observers soon reached the Admiralty, and for years afterwards their conclusions were used in discussions within the Royal Navy regarding the absorption of new technologies.[15] In the fall of 1905 Fisher conducted a new gunnery exercise in which the firing ranges were from 4,500 to 6,300 meters (5,000 to 7,000 yards) instead of the 2,000 yards until then. The greater number of guns in the primary battery was not the only factor in the firepower of the battleship, and in the following years the Royal Navy sought also to increase the caliber of the guns and improve the firing control system. Within a few years it increased the caliber of the primary battery from 305 millimeters (12 inches) to 343 millimeters (13.5 inches), and in 1912 it ordered the first class to be armed with 381-millimeter (15-inch) guns. The Americans and the Japanese did not sit idly by, but armed their own new capital ships with 356-millimeter (14-inch) guns. Three decades later the gunnery race reached its peak, when the Imperial Japanese Navy armed a pair of battleships, the *Yamato* and her sister ship the *Musashi*, with 460-millimeter (18.1-inch) guns.

The conclusions derived from the battle of Tsushima supported greater reliance on big guns but did not entirely solve the issue of the secondary battery. Was it necessary at all? In 1905 some believed it was useless, and supported the construction of an all-big-gun ship without a secondary battery. The idea of such a battleship had emerged before the war,[16] and even Fisher considered it earlier, but now the time was ripe.[17] From then on, British shipbuilders faithfully followed this conception, and eliminated completely the use of the secondary battery in their subsequent designs. It remained doubtful, however, to what extent the battle of Tsushima confirmed this idea. Mahan, for example, was among those who stated that the battle proved exactly the opposite. Except for certain decisive hits by the primary battery, he argued, the victory was due to the rain of shells from medium guns that, although they could not sink the ships, did cause critical damage to human life and equipment. British opponents of the all-big-gun ship also regarded the outcome of Tsushima as contradicting that concept. Admiral Edmund Fremantle, for example, believed that the firing distances in the battle in the Yellow Sea were an exception, and urged that the idea of avoiding close range was alien to British naval traditions.[18] The pressure was fruitful, gradually eroding the intention of having a battleship with virtually no secondary battery. From 1910 onward, new battleships were rearmed with a secondary battery.[19]

The thickness and the quality of the ship's armor became another important target for improvement in the wake of the battle of Tsushima. In the traditional duel between armor and armament, it seemed that the armor had the upper hand in the Russo-Japanese War. After the battle of Tsushima, for example, the Japanese counted about 40 hits by 305-millimeter gun shells to their ships, similar to the number of hits they inflicted on Russian ships.[20] Yet not a single Japanese battleship was sunk in this engagement. True, the Russian shells were of lesser power and some of them did not explode, but the main reason that no Japanese ship was sunk was the quality of British shipbuilding, the armor in particular. The Japanese ships were built to the finest metallurgical technology of the time, were well compartmented, and were designed in the sturdiest fashion so that their resistance to Russian shells was relatively high. Still, the Japanese gunnery too failed in most cases to breach the armor of its rival's battleships, even though it did cause extensive damage that effectively put the ships out of action, and often facilitated *coups de grace* delivered by torpedoes fired at close range.[21] These testimonies were unequivocal proof that thicker armor plating amidships, but also on the decks and around the turrets, could provide better defense against any type of shell, and ultimately might guarantee the battleship's survival.

The importance of speed for battleship action also gained significant support during the war. Admiral Tōgō Heihachirō's ability to execute his famous maneuvers at Tsushima, allowing him to move parallel with the Russian main force, was attributed to his ships' advantage of speed. By contrast, the lack of such an advantage in the Battle of the Yellow Sea prevented Tōgō from bridging the gap with its opponent, and, were it not for a lucky strike at the Russian flagship *Tsesarevich*, the battle would have been lost. British observers emphasized in their reports the speed factor and saw it as second in importance only to firepower. They argued that greater speed would allow not only a quick entry into an effective firing range against enemy ships but also a quick exit from the danger range. It could also enable the battleship to avoid torpedo attacks and contact with submarines. Fisher himself used to say that speed "is armor," but the question was at what price.[22] Even a small increase in the speed of the battleship required bigger engines, bigger fuel tanks, and consequently heavier armor to protect them. In turn, they increased the weight of the ship and lowered its speed. Thus, the balance between thick armor and higher speed demanded vast resources in a period of budgetary cutbacks. Only a new propulsion system, the steam turbine, was able to break this vicious circle, but this technology had never been used to propel a warship on the scale of a capital ship. Its eventual utilization in the new British battleship soon after the war increased its speed drastically as compared with other naval vessels of similar displacement.[23]

Overall, the naval battles of the Russo-Japanese War confirmed the convictions of British supporters for a future all-big-gun battleship with stronger armor and higher speed. In October 1905, four months after the battle of Tsushima, the Royal Navy started constructing a battleship that included substantial improvements in armament, armor, and speed. The project was completed with great effort in exactly a year, and the new ship, named *Dreadnought*, was an immediate sensation. It was superior to any contemporary battleship in each of the three cardinal yardsticks for battleships. Its ten 305-millimeter guns constituted an unprecedented primary battery; it had an extremely thick armor plating of 280 millimeters (11 inches) under the water line; and its maximum speed was 39 kilometers an hour (21 knots), almost 4 kilometers an hour (2 knots) faster than its fastest competitor.[24] Until the *Dreadnought*, the 15-year period of rapid development of the battleship had witnessed a gradual improvement in all these features, but no ship could claim a significant improvement in all three at once. Hence, the *Dreadnought* was nothing short of a revolution, at least in the short evolution of the modern battleship. It was, however, a conceptual rather than a technological revolution, since by and large the technology already existed and the Admiralty merely required Fisher's forceful leadership to utilize it in concert.

Taking place after the decision to build the *Dreadnought*, the battle of Tsushima served as a catalyst for the construction, but not as its underlying cause. Paradoxically, with the launching of the *Dreadnought* the following year, all battleships that had taken part in the battle became outdated at one fell swoop, along, of course, with over 100 battleships of seven other navies. The Royal Navy, which had led naval technology throughout the nineteenth century, won a new edge, and forced other major fleets to reconsider their expansion programs. In this sense, British lessons learned from the Russo-Japanese War had a lingering effect on the construction of capital ships at least until the end of World War II. The *Dreadnought* itself soon became a generic name for all new battleships with large numbers of heavy guns, and the enormous sums invested in the construction of the latest Pre-Dreadnought classes were virtually wasted.

The development of battleships did not end with the birth of the *Dreadnought*. By 1911 the Royal Navy completed ten new battleships of five consecutive classes, each bigger than its predecessor, and within five years from the completion of the *Dreadnought* it developed a second generation of battleships known as Super-Dreadnought. Every new class boasted a slight improvement in armament, armor, and speed, at a rate that astonished the naval experts. World War I accelerated the rapid evolution of the battleship and, during the 1930s, when the International Conferences on Naval Limitation lost their influence, the pace of development increased even further.

Together with the *Dreadnought*, the Russo-Japanese War was associated also with the birth of the battlecruiser. This mutation between the battleship and the cruiser was born in the fading pre-war debate over the fate of the battleship. Unlike the *Dreadnought*, however, it did not fit the new naval circumstances Britain faced after the war and proved less successful and more short-lived. The battlecruiser was entirely the brainchild of Fisher. Although his term as First Sea Lord coincided with the golden age of the battleship, he himself was an enthusiastic supporter of fast vessels, and envisioned the development of a new capital ship similar to the *Dreadnought* in firepower, but with much greater speed as a result of more powerful engines and thinner armor.[25] His vision was based on a pre-war scenario that emphasized defense of imperial trade routes and engagements against inferior Russian and French cruisers.[26] Fisher's new warship was supposed to be fast enough to avoid torpedo attacks and to use its heavy guns against enemy warships of any size. His vision did not alter much during the Russo-Japanese War. He believed that greater firing range and improved armor-piercing shells would ensure that the difference between the armament of the battleship and of the battlecruiser would prove insignificant. Moreover, Fisher estimated that a fleet composed of battlecruisers would be more economical and efficient than a fleet combining battleships and ordinary cruisers.[27] Consistent with this approach, he authorized in 1905 the first three British battlecruisers of the *Invincible* class, which were completed three years later.[28]

Nevertheless, the Russo-Japanese War was detrimental to the concept of the battlecruiser. More than anything, it was the change in Britain's naval adversaries that affected the destiny of this warship. As Russia ceased to be a genuine menace, and France became an ally, German naval aspirations and expansion programs suddenly seemed much more threatening than before. Concern with the nearby German threat required solid battleships rather than fast long-range cruisers. The rude awakening from Fisher's dream did not take long. The Royal Navy's original plan had been for only one battleship of the *Dreadnought* class and three battlecruisers of the *Invincible* class, but at the outbreak of World War I it had three times more battleships than battlecruisers. Furthermore, as a result of the lessons of the Russo-Japanese War and the strong support for the *Dreadnought*, the *Invincible* class bore ultimately greater resemblance to a battleship than to a cruiser. During the construction of the *Dreadnought* Fisher fought against the widespread tendencies in the Royal Navy to prefer this warship over battlecruisers, but was unsuccessful. In this case, at least, his opponents proved right.[29]

Repercussions on the major fleets

For a few years after the Russo-Japanese War, the Royal Navy stood in an unprecedented position. With the demise of two of Russia's fleets, and with the emergence of the *Dreadnought* and the *Invincible* classes, it gained the both qualitative and quantitative lead it had not had during the previous two decades. Still, Britain followed the naval campaign off Manchuria closely not only for technological reasons.[30] The rapprochement with France, the world's second naval power, and notably the massive losses of the Russian navy, allowed Britain to reconsider the need for the costly two-power standard it had set since 1889. By late 1905, Britain maintained, in fact, a three-power standard in Europe![31]

The alliance with Japan signed in 1902, and subsequently the diminished Russian threat as a result of the war, allowed the Royal Navy to accelerate the process of replacing most of its outdated cruisers and gunboats, and concentrate its build-up on the German threat in the Atlantic.[32] The British choice of a lean, high-standard fleet rather than a multi-vessel one was sharply criticized at home.[33] Critics too pointed to the war and its lessons to prove that old vessels could be useful. In particular, they argued, the inability of Japan to stop assaults on its shipping lanes by Russian cruisers during the first half of the war proved that a limited number of British battlecruisers, however superb, were insufficient to defend the shipping lanes of the vast empire and locate enemy warships. Old cruisers, they further maintained, were better than no cruisers at all. Another warship that the war proved to be useful, in their eyes, was the slow gunboat that used to guard diplomatic missions in foreign ports. The sinking of the Russian-protected cruiser *Variag* and the gunship *Koreets* in Chemulpo at the outbreak of the war was an example of the risk such vessels faced, resulting in the British decision to reduce their presence. On the other hand, the assistance two British gunships provided during the riots in Shanghai in December 1905 demonstrated that the decision was appropriate perhaps in times of war, but in times of peace and for "police duties" in colonial ports there was still room even for such obsolete vessels.[34]

The minor revolution Fisher initiated was followed closely by the other major navies. With the completion of the *Dreadnought* they were forced to reconsider their plans and even to halt actual construction of their suddenly outdated battleships and large cruisers. The Imperial German Navy, under the dynamic command of Admiral Alfred von Tirpitz, was the first to be affected. While starting its expansion program (the first *Flottengesetz*) in 1898, during the decade of 1904–14 it shot up meteorically from being the world's sixth largest navy to being second only to the Royal Navy. With the enthusiastic encouragement of the kaiser, it responded to the *Dreadnought* challenge with an interval of two years. Initially, the development of the *Dreadnought* was a significant blow, as Germany was forced to stop the construction of the new *Nassau* class for a year and to widen the Kiel Canal to allow the passage of larger warships.[35] German industrial capability, however, could face the challenge, and its accelerated pace of warship construction caused great concern (known as the "naval crisis") in Britain during 1908–9, but less in the Admiralty. In turn, Britain reacted by increasing its own naval allocations and accelerating naval construction while simultaneously proposing means to win the naval race.[36]

After the Russo-Japanese War Britain identified the Imperial German Navy as its main rival. In October 1906 Fisher acknowledged that Germany was the only plausible foe, and to deter it Britain should maintain a fleet double Germany's in power.[37] Fisher did all he could to maintain this lead by keeping control over the navy budgets. To this end he overstated the power of the German navy and emphasized only the shrinking gap between the two navies regarding the *Dreadnought*-class battleship, while disregarding the enormous surplus of Pre-Dreadnought ships at the disposal of the Royal Navy. Accordingly, the official announcement of the cancellation of the two-power standard was postponed until 1912, two years after the replacement of Fisher, when the standard was altered to an advantage of 60 percent in the number of *Dreadnought*-class battleships over those of Germany.[38]

In the naval race that began between the two navies, the British had a slight edge for constructing the first *Dreadnought* battleship, but they virtually lost the enormous advantage they had held in Pre-Dreadnought classes before the war.[39] The confrontation turned into a two-headed race between Britain and Germany because the battleship had become the pinnacle of technological capability, and only extremely wealthy nations could afford to finance its construction. By the time World War I broke out Germany had 15 *Dreadnought*-class battleships, only seven less than Britain.[40] Still, the inability of the German navy to compete with its British rival in both quantitative and qualitative terms in the first two years of the war pushed Germany into accelerated construction of submarines in an attempt to compromise the blockade and disrupt the Allies' supply lines.

After 1904, the French navy witnessed a rapid decline, notably in relative terms. With the conclusion of the Entente Cordiale, France literally abandoned the naval race with Britain and started appropriating a greater portion of its defense budget to the development of massive land forces to face the German menace.[41] With diminished allocations and changing priorities (starting partly in 1902), the French navy did not counteract aptly the challenge set by the emergence of HMS *Dreadnought*.[42] This inability notwithstanding, in the aftermath of Tsushima, the French navy abandoned completely its attraction to the warfare of small vessels, and in 1909 became committed to a battleship navy.[43] This move was too late and indecisive. Within two years of the war, not only did the French navy lose its position as the world's second naval power, but its ships were increasingly regarded as obsolete.[44] The new runner-up was momentarily the US Navy. Completing the expansion program envisioned by President Theodore Roosevelt, the US Navy posed a challenge but not a genuine threat to the hegemony of the Royal Navy. Roosevelt wanted a stong navy that could deter and face any threat, and after the war he regarded the Japanese navy as the foremost likely opponent. While attempting to calm the tensions with Japan, he acted vigorously to obtain greater budgets for naval construction. In spite of Mahan's opposition, the navy entered the *Dreadnought* age aggressively, but without the full support of Congress. When Roosevelt left office in 1909, the US Navy remained with neither a close friend in the Oval Office nor an accepted policy, and it gradually lost it strength, one it would regain only after World War I.[45]

In terms of sheer size and motivation, the Russo-Japanese War most affected the Russians' naval power, the world's third largest force before the war. It marked its eclipse, dropping to sixth place and virtual marginality. The Imperial Japanese Navy was affected less adversely, and retained the fifth place it held before the war.[46] In absolute terms, however, the Japanese navy increased its size substantially by incorporating several Russian battleships, and newly built capital ships, whereas the Russian navy was the only naval force among the powers that dwindled considerably. Moreover, the Russian navy not only lost a great part of its able officer cadre but also the remnants of its credibility faded with the decision makers in St Petersburg. The Japanese navy, by contrast, gained much combat experience and self-confidence, which affected its ambitions overseas and its conduct in subsequent interservice competition at home.[47]

For the Russian navy, indeed, the war was a total disaster. It lost about two-thirds of its capital ships, but also much of its fighting spirit and self-confidence.[48] Thereafter, it experienced a continuous decline that reached its nadir in the 1920s. In the intervening years naval officers who returned from Japanese captivity underwent a series of interrogations and court-martials, and until 1907 the Duma objected to granting the navy any construction budgets. It was only five years after the war that the Russian navy began building battleships again, and two more years passed until its construction budget showed any significant shift upward. After the war the Russian naval presence in the Pacific Ocean became symbolic, and the Baltic Fleet began its reorganization only a few years before World War I, although as a combat unit it never regained its former strength. The Black Sea Fleet was the only naval force to remain intact, and during World War I it played an inglorious role in the war against Turkish and German forces. Another factor in the decline of the Russian navy was the revolutionary activity among its men. During the revolution of 1905 the navy had become an ideological hotbed, manifested in local mutinies, the most famous of them being the mutiny aboard the battleship *Kniaz Potemkin Tavritcheskii*. This radical activity did not cease even after the Bolshevik Revolution, and in March 1921 it culminated in a large-scale mutiny at the naval base of Kronstadt. The suppression of the mutiny and the execution of thousands of navy personnel caused serious damage to the navy as a whole and the Baltic Fleet in particular, resulting in a lingering distrust and limited allocations for many years to come. After 1921, the Soviet navy entered into an extended period of relative paralysis and decline, from which it re-emerged as a considerable naval power only in the 1960s and 1970s.[49]

For the Japanese navy, the experience of the war had a conspicuous effect in four spheres that lingered until its disbanding in 1945. These were the view of the decisive naval battle as a single engagement determined by large capital ships armed with heavy guns; the preference for high-quality ships and armament over quantity; the emphasis on night torpedo strikes; and the concept of a war of attrition against an enemy with numerical advantage.[50] The perception of a huge decisive naval battle was undoubtedly the main legacy from the battle of Tsushima. Thereafter, all naval plans for war against a future enemy, the US Navy in particular, anticipated a decisive battle near the shores of Japan. According to this conception, one large engagement such as the battle of Tsushima could determine the naval campaign, but also the entire war. Even in December 1941, on the eve of the attack on Pearl Harbor, large surface battles still held a central place in the strategic plans of the Japanese navy and its construction plans. The attack on Pearl Harbor was not a refutation of this view, but a gamble intended to realize it. Anticipating American recovery and the regrouping of its naval forces, the principal Japanese scenario for the Pacific War foresaw a decisive naval battle that would lead to the final victory.[51]

The impact on the development of naval weaponry

The insights and experience of the Russo-Japanese War led to further technological development in virtually every naval weapon, such as the gun, the torpedo, and the naval mine. The impact of this development on naval warfare was felt throughout the first half of the twentieth century. The first field in which significant innovations were made was naval artillery. Despite the relatively short fire range of the primary battery in the battle of Tsushima, the accuracy rate of both belligerents remained low—less than 10 percent, and probably far less.[52] Moreover, the need to keep battleships out of range of medium- or small-caliber guns resulted in the increased use of long-range fire, hence even lower accuracy. The deficiencies of naval artillery revealed at Tsushima called for urgent improvements. In the next decade all major navies made considerable efforts to improve fire control. Still in the lead, the Royal Navy had begun to put greater emphasis on naval artillery before the turn of the century, but in the post-war years it made a special effort in this realm. Improvements in fire control kept the heavy guns as the main naval weapon and led to a rapid increase in the effective fire range and weight of the shell.[53]

As a promising naval weapon, the torpedo was perhaps the greatest technological disappointment of the war, due to its very low accuracy.[54] Nonetheless, the fear of an enemy using torpedoes shaped to some extent the style of combat on both sides. They avoided approaching each other and were afraid of night warfare, in which small torpedo boats could gain the upper hand. Other navies did not underestimate the torpedo, and, despite its limited effectiveness in the war, the pre-war momentum of its development was not checked. An ardent advocate of torpedo use, Fisher regarded it as a weapon of the future. In May 1904 he received a report about another technical improvement that increased the range of the torpedo to about 2,700 meters (about 3,000 yards). With such progress it was obvious that in a short time the range of the torpedo could be longer than the effective range of gunfire from the ships against which it was to be launched. Fisher's forecast was correct, and was realized probably sooner than he imagined. Within a decade the torpedo range, which stood at about 4,000 meters (about 4,400 yards) in 1905, increased to about 10,000 meters (about 11,000 yards), while its speed more than doubled.[55] Ten years later the torpedo emerged as a reliable weapon, and during World War I it proved to be relatively accurate, especially when launched at close range from submarines.[56]

Another naval weapon that made its virtual debut in the Russo-Japanese War was the naval mine. Mines were used unsuccessfully against warships as early as the seventeenth century, but the spring of 1904 marked the beginning of massive use of this inexpensive and unsophisticated weapon, which was nevertheless far more efficient than the torpedo. Both sides used mines extensively, and both lacked suitable means to counter them. In those circumstances their effect was highly destructive. Mining of the coastal area off Port Arthur caused the sinking of three battleships, five cruisers, and three destroyers, and the loss of thousands of crewmen on both sides.[57] All the Japanese capital ships lost in the war were sunk by mines. Critically, mines had strategic significance as evident from the sinking of the two Japanese battleships *Hatsuse* and *Yashima*—a third of Japan's battleships— in one day. For Russia, mines had even greater repercussions because of the loss of the charismatic commander of the Pacific Fleet, Vice Admiral Stepan Makarov, aboard the battleship *Petropavlovsk*. His death due to a mine hit brought the Russian naval initiative to a halt, and condemned the Port Arthur squadron to a slow death in the harbor.

In the aftermath of the war the naval powers recognized the threat of the mine and attempted to ban its use at the Hague Convention of 1907. Rather than being atrocious it was simply a novel weapon, and the world, to paraphrase Basil Henry Liddell Hart's view on the introduction of chlorine gas in warfare a decade later, condones abuses but abhors novelty.[58] Eventually, the mine's murderous effectiveness kept it operational, and instead of banning it all major navies endeavored to develop minesweepers to locate and neutralize it.[59] It comes as no surprise that the Russian navy was the first to recognize this need, and in 1910 it built a vessel intended specifically for minesweeping. Initially, the Royal Navy did not regard the mine as a valid weapon, but due to Fisher's strong impressions of its effect in the war it was finally included in the war plans of 1913 with the support of the First Lord of the Admiralty, Winston Churchill.[60] During World War I, mines continued to be the primary means of sinking warships, as the German navy demonstrated with the sinking of the British battleship *Odysseus* at the onset of hostilities.[61]

The epic voyage of the Baltic Fleet, and the inconvenient use of coal in particular, provided much food for thought in the field of logistics. Compared with the lengthy and precious time it required to coal ships at sea, oil seemed promising. Fueling with it was relatively quick and could be done in motion. Eventually, it was the success in obtaining reliable sources of oil in the years after the war, rather than the ordeal of the Baltic Fleet, that spurred a gradual shift to using it for military purposes. In 1909 the Royal Navy decided that all its future destroyers would be powered by oil, and within three years this decision was implemented also in regard to the new class of battleships, the *Queen Elizabeth*.[62] The transition to the use of oil by the major navies was also associated with the development of naval diesel engines, but nonetheless the ability to utilize this relatively new source of energy was more geopolitical than technical.[63] European powers went in quest of it to distant locations such as the Middle East and the Persian Gulf, and so began a bitter struggle for influence over those areas that has never ceased since. Similarly, the Russo-Japanese War did not result in the construction of auxiliary and coaling ships specifically built for supply and refueling. For the British the logistic constraints that hampered the Russian navy were less problematic, since Britain controlled many ports along the main routes of its empire. Eventually, only the vast and continuous needs of World War I speeded up the development and the use of special navy ships for these purposes.[64]

The war and the advent of a true naval revolution

While heralding a new age in the development of the battleship, the Russo-Japanese War missed out on the submarine and the airplane, the two most crucial developments in naval warfare in the twentieth century. Their absence does not necessarily mean that the war did not assist in promoting their development. On the contrary, operational requirements during the war increased awareness of these new technologies and the pressure to further develop them for full operational use.

The submarine missed the war by several months. In late 1904 both belligerents had submarines, but they did not regard them as ready for operational deployment. By the end of the war the Russian navy transferred 14 small submarines to Vladivostok by means of the Trans-Siberian Railway, too late for any effective use. All the major navies shared their distrust of the submarine, even though it had a relatively long history. Beginning with David Bushnell's famous *Turtle*, which failed to sink a British warship during the American War of Independence, the subsequent century witnessed numerous attempts to construct submarines for military purposes.[65] Significant steps toward this objective were made only in the last decade of the nineteenth century. In 1892 a submarine was armed for the first time with a tube for launching torpedoes, and six years later this new weapon was launched successfully under water.[66] The Royal Navy began the construction of submarines in 1901, and a year later the Russian navy followed suit.[67] By the outbreak of the Russo-Japanese War all the large navies except the German had acquired submarines. Nevertheless, in 1904 all still defined the submarine as an experimental vessel and did not put it into operational use.[68]

The difficulties the Japanese navy faced in sinking the Russian warships hiding in the safe haven of Port Arthur aroused special interest in submarines. Believing a submarine could penetrate the port and sink the Russian ships, Fisher began to view it as a plausible offensive weapon. Two months after the war broke out, he wrote to a friend: "my beloved submarines . . . are not only going to increase the naval power of England seven times more than present . . . but they are going to bring the income tax down."[69] A month later he referred to the submarine in a longer letter, lamenting its absence in the fleets of the two belligerents. This time Fisher proved almost prophetic, stating that submarines on offensive missions would revolutionize the war at sea.[70]

On January 24, 1905, three weeks after the fall of Port Arthur, Fisher sent Prime Minister Arthur Balfour two "rough papers" (entitled "Submarines Used Defensively" and "Submarines Used Offensively"), in which he formulated his concept of "flotilla defense."[71] Fisher proposed to abandon the traditional dependence on battleships for deterrence and defense of the British Isles, and rely instead on the flotilla, that is destroyers and submarines, which can also be used offensively in the Channel and the Mediterranean. This vision of the submarine faced great opposition at the Admiralty, but Fisher's foresight was realized within a decade. Unfortunately, in his case, it was grasped by Britain's arch rival, the German navy. Fisher, however, was reacting to, rather than causing, a change. While the war provided him with the strategic insights, certain technological improvements at the same time enabled the submarine to play the role it was intended to. During the war the French navy, followed by the Royal Navy, developed diesel engines that replaced gasoline engines for surface power, and in 1908 the Royal Navy completed the first submarine that could sail relatively long distances.[72] Fisher's vision of the submarine, however, won firm opposition, and after his retirement, and more so between 1912 and 1914, the production of submarines for operational purposes in Britain was reduced to a trickle.[73] The first submarines were used for intelligence gathering and for assault on merchant shipping, but with further development of the torpedo they soon emerged as an efficient weapon against warships as well. In 1912 a Greek submarine conducted an instructive demonstration of the submarine's offensive capacity when it attacked a Turkish cruiser with torpedoes. It missed its target, but during the first months of World War I German submarines did sink a number of capital ships, thereby displaying painfully the extent to which this vessel had advanced since the Russo-Japanese War.[74]

The airplane was totally absent from naval use in 1904–5, for the simple reason that the first flight of a powered machine took place less than two months before the outbreak of the war.[75] The Russo-Japanese War was the first military conflict after the pioneering flight of the Wright brothers, and it demonstrated the necessity of adopting such a technology for military use. On land, improvements in artillery range required means to locate enemy positions. Both the Russians and the Japanese solved the problem by flying balloons tied to the ground for lookout purposes. In the naval arena too, gunnery range had more than doubled compared with previous wars, but both sides continued to depend on observation posts on ships. Two years after the war the Wright brothers approached the Royal Navy with an offer to sell them a plane. The British rejected the offer, but the US Navy showed some interest in the new technology. By late 1910, the Americans had taken the lead in the development of the airplane for military use, as Eugene Ely took off from an inclined platform on the deck of the cruiser *Birmingham*; in a subsequent exercise two months later he landed on similar platform at sea.[76] Another direction in the development of naval aviation in the decade after the Russo-Japanese War was the transformation of merchant ships into mother ships for amphibious seaplanes. During the two years that preceded World War I the French, the British, and the Japanese began to make use of such airplanes for scouting and naval assault, and in September 1914 Japanese amphibian airplanes executed the first ground assault from the sea as they bombed the German base in Tsingtao, China.[77] In the following decade the specifically designed aircraft carrier emerged, to begin its long evolution via Taranto, Pearl Harbor, and Midway until it wholly succeeded the battleship as the centerpiece of the fleets of the foremost naval powers.

Conclusions

Twelve years after the Russo-Japanese War the submarine became an effective weapon of strategic value, although the battleship with its multiple heavy guns still epitomized naval power. Three decades later there was no longer any doubt that the battleship had become an anachronism. German U-boats in the Atlantic Ocean almost choked Britain, and airplanes taking off from Japanese carriers struck at American battleships in Pearl Harbor and sank in minutes the imposing British battleship *Prince of Wales* and its battlecruiser consort *Repulse* on their way to Singapore. The lessons of the naval campaign during the Russo-Japanese War gave no inkling of that outcome, nor a model for future naval engagements. Instead, it served as a catalyst for developing ever larger capital ships. The example of the battle of Tsushima did not recur, however. The battle of Jutland in 1916 was momentous and demonstrated the ultimate failure of Tirpitz's strategic concept, but in terms of losses it was far from decisive. Without a dramatic climax, World War I was characterized, especially after Jutland, by a long war of attrition and a struggle over supply routes, where the submarines, destroyers, and even Q-ships enjoyed unprecedented importance.[78]

Although the Royal Navy under the command of the charismatic and visionary Admiral Fisher seemed to draw the most forthright conclusions from the Russo-Japanese War, it was these conclusions that contained the seeds of its downfall. In the short run, the war intensified the need for a revolutionary battleship, and the Royal Navy was able to apply the data its observers faithfully gathered and construct a ship of unmatched quality. Mahan, however, was aware of the risks inherent in too simplistic conclusions regarding the war. A year after the battle of Tsushima he argued against concentrating the resources of a navy around a small number of warships of massive power, and warned that the construction of ships of ever increasing size would be financially destructive.[79]

Initially, the *Dreadnought* yielded a significant advantage for the Royal Navy over its German rival; but it sparked a naval race that forced Fisher to allocate much of his resources to the construction of ever bigger capital ships. Other navies that were less aware of the lessons of the war, or unable to compete with the British, devoted a more significant portion of their budgets to more revolutionary solutions, such as the submarine and subsequently the aircraft carrier. Within a decade after the Russo-Japanese War Germany began to depend on submarines, and a decade later still, the American and Japanese navies started constructing modern aircraft carriers, which were to transform warfare at sea. The Russo-Japanese War preceded the onset of this new era by a few years. It nonetheless marked the sudden death of the pre-modern stage and served as a preface to a brief but fascinating period in which the modern battleship ruled the waves.

Notes

1 The author thanks Cord Eberspaecher, Felix Brenner, and Yigal Sheffy for their insightful comments on early drafts of this chapter.
2 These revolutions included the introduction of the steam engine, the screw propeller, armor, shell guns, and rifle ordnance. See Hobson, 2002: 24–57.

3 On the French school, see Bueb, 1971; Ropp, 1987: 155–80; and Walser, 1992: 58–90, 180–200. On the German attraction to the French school during the 1880s, see Lambi, 1984: 7–9.
4 See Mahan, 1890, 1892. On Mahan's influence on naval thought at the end of the nineteenth century, see Gough, 1988; and St John, 1971. Mahan's dictum was echoed, for example, in two speeches Kaiser Wilhelm II delivered in 1895 before members of the *Reichstag* and officers of the Prussian Royal Military Academy. See Lambi, 1984: 34.
5 On the European naval race in the 1880–90s, see Kennedy, 1983: 165–71.
6 During this 15-year period, other European navies also built a large number of battleships with similar features. France had twenty battleships of the first line, Germany twenty-five, Italy nine, Austria three, and Spain one. On the other side of the Atlantic the US Navy had twenty-four ships of five different classes before the end of the Russo-Japanese War; Russia and Japan also joined this exclusive club. The Imperial Russian Navy began building a Pre-Dreadnought battleship in 1892 and completed the construction of twenty ships during this period. The Imperial Japanese Navy ordered two of its first battleships from Britain based on the *Royal Sovereign* class in 1893, and three years later another four based on the *Majestic* class. See George, 1998: 78; and Neudeck and Schröder, 1904.
7 The caliber of the main battery ranged between 280 and 343 millimeters (11–13.5 inches), although 305-millimeter (12-inch) caliber was nearly the standard for most of the Pre-Dreadnought classes.
8 Completed in Britain in 1902, the Japanese flagship *Mikasa*, for example, was armed with four 305-millimeter (12-inch) guns, fourteen 152-millimeter (6-inch) guns, and twenty 76.2-millimeter (3-inch) guns.
9 The range for opening fire at the battle of Tsushima was approximately 6,400 meters (about 7,000 yards).
10 For example, *King Edward the Seventh*, the last class of battleship constructed in Britain before the war, was armed with four 305-millimeter (12-inch) guns, four 234-millimeter (9.2-inch) guns, and ten 152 millimeter (6-inch) guns.
11 On the British experiments in long-range fire, see Marder, 1961: 35.
12 On the governmental pressures to cut naval budgets in Britain, see Fairbanks, 1991: 262.
13 On Fisher's decision, see Grove, 1995: 47.
14 Cited in Marder, 1940: 531.
15 The observers' reports served as a reference for Corbett's classified book on the naval campaign during the Russo-Japanese War. See Corbett and Slade, 1914. Fisher himself mentioned Pakenham's report in a letter to Edward Grey in 1908; in Marder, 1956: 156.
16 In an article published in *Jane's Fighting Ships* in 1903 entitled "An Ideal Battleship for the British Fleet," the chief constructor of the Royal Italian Navy, Vittorio Emanuel Cuniberti, proposed a battleship of 17,000 tons armed with a dozen 305-millimeter (12-inch) guns and entirely without a secondary battery. In 1904 it was announced that the US Navy was planning a battleship (the *South Carolina* class) with eight 12-inch guns. On Cuniberti's article, see George, 1998: 91.
17 Fisher himself stated years later that the idea of a ship with guns of uniform caliber had been on his mind as far back as 1900 in Malta in a discussion with the chief engineer of the Royal Navy. Some attribute the idea of a battleship based on a primary battery alone to a conversation Fisher held as early as 1882. See, for example, Houge, 1964: 15–16.
18 Admiral Fremantle is quoted in Towle, 1977: 69.

19 Completed in Britain in 1910, the *Orion* class was armed with sixteen 102-millimeter (4-inch) guns, and five years later the *Queen Elizabeth* class was armed with a dozen 152-millimeter (6-inch) guns.

20 The number of hits suffered by Japanese ships should come as no surprise since the Russians had 41 guns of 254-millimeter (10-inch) and larger caliber, compared with only 17 guns of similar caliber on the Japanese side.

21 On the invulnerability of Russian battleship armor in Tsushima, see Evans and Peattie, 1997: 125.

22 Fisher's view on speed is quoted in Marder, 1961: 59.

23 For the discussion on the importance of speed in the Royal Navy, see Towle, 1977: 72–3.

24 For the *Dreadnought*'s specifications, see Parkes, 1990: 447.

25 On Fisher's support of the battlecruiser, see Sumida, 1993: 37–61.

26 For Fisher's warning against a Russo-French combined threat and surprise attack on Malta and Egypt during 1900–1, see Chapman, 2004.

27 Fisher's attraction to the battlecruiser concept is relevant to a current thesis suggesting that, when he was appointed First Sea Lord in 1904, he was not concerned with the German navy. Most elements of his reform plan, this thesis holds, emerged when France and Russia were still perceived as the major threat to Britain and even later on his early plans did not alter much. Fisher's persistence in viewing the battlecruiser as a main element in any future struggle was therefore related to identifying Britain's chief adversaries. See, for example, Lambert, 1999; 2001a: 70–2.

28 Having 96 percent of the displacement of the *Dreadnought*, the *Invincible* class was armed with eight 305-millimeter (12-inch) guns, and enjoyed an exceptionally long operational range and an unprecedented speed of 50 kilometers per hour (27 knots). These performances were obtained at the cost of having one turret less than the *Dreadnought*, and armor whose maximum thickness was only 152 millimeters (6 inches), half that of the *Dreadnought*.

29 Other navies did not overlook the gamble involved in the investment in this type of warship. Until World War I only three navies (of Britain, Germany, and Japan) were equipped with battlecruisers. Fear of the battlecruiser's inability to face battleships was confirmed a decade later in the battle of Jutland (1916) when the Royal Navy lost three battlecruisers and only one battleship, even though most of the warships in that clash were battleships.

30 On Fisher's interest in the war, see Mackay, 1973: 307.

31 In terms of battleships, for example, Britain had 47, whereas Germany had 17, France 18, and Russia 5. (O'Brien mentions 46 battleships.) In O'Brien, 1998: 31.

32 Following Fisher's decision, 90 obsolete and small ships were sold off and a further 64 were put into reserve.

33 Oblivious to Fisher's intentions, some of the British observers, Captain Pakenham in particular, emphasized the role of older vessels and the need to preserve them, thereby providing ammunition for Fisher's critics. Fisher, however, considered these reports to support his idea of an all-big-gun ship on which he was working at the time. See Towle, 1977: 74–5.

34 On the debate over the size of the Royal Navy during and following the war, see Towle, 1977: 75–7.

35 On the effects of the war and the *Dreadnought* revolution on the German navy, see Herwig, 1980: 33–68, 1991; Steltzer, 1989: 238–55; Weir, 1992; and Woodward, 1935: 100–20.

36 On the naval crisis in Britain in 1908–9, see O'Brien, 1998: 33–44, 73–97.

37 Fisher's position on the German fleet is presented in Herwig, 1980: 50.

38 On the change of standard in the Royal Navy, see Marder, 1961: 182–3; and O'Brien, 1998: 25–46.
39 On the British–German naval race after the war, see Goldrick, 1995.
40 On the eve of World War I, France had ten *Dreadnoughts* (as well as 21 Pre-Dreadnoughts), Italy had three (15), Austro-Hungary had six (6), Russia had four (11), Japan had two (8), and the United States had ten (25). In George, 1998: 99; Hough, 1998: 55.
41 Whereas the French defense expenditure reduced slightly in 1905, its army expenditure increased. For the French defense expenditures in the early twentieth century, see Stevenson, 1996: 4; and Herrmann, 1996: 237.
42 On the reasons for the French technological inferiority, and the failure of the *Danton* class in particular, in the naval race of 1906, see Halpern, 2001: 45–6; and Walser, 1992: 141–8.
43 On the commitment for battleships in the French navy after Tsushima, see Halpern, 2001: 46–7.
44 On the British estimation of French naval power in 1909, see O'Brien, 1998: 31–2.
45 On the post-war state of the US Navy, see O'Brien, 1998: 62–7.
46 In 1900 the Japanese navy was in sixth place, and rose to fifth place for a few years before the war. It returned to sixth place during the war, and for the five years that followed it went up to fifth place. For the relative naval standing before, during, and after the war, see Evans and Peattie, 1997: 147.
47 On the growing role of the navy in Japanese politics after the war, see Masuda, 1982; Schencking, 2002, 2005.
48 During the war the Russian navy lost a total of 18 battleships (11 first-line and 7 second-line), 5 armored cruisers, 4 gunboats, and approximately 20 destroyers. See Mitchell, 1974: 269.
49 On the evolution of the Russian navy until World War I, see Mitchell, 1974: 267–82.
50 Evans, 2001: 28–33; Evans and Peattie, 1997: 129.
51 See, for example, Admiral Nagumo Chūichi's statement three weeks before the attack on Pearl Harbor. In Ike, 1967: 247.
52 For data on the accuracy rate, see Evans and Peattie, 1997: 125.
53 By 1904 the Royal Navy had developed the first targeting device. It also unified the fire from all the gun turrets by remote control using analogous computing machines to align the position of the ship with the target. On the improvement in gunnery systems, see Padfield, 1972: 183–5; Sumida, 1993: chs 3–5.
54 On the Japanese side, for example, about 370 torpedoes were fired, but only 17 hit the target (a success rate of about 4 percent). See Marder, 1961: 329. For reports on even lower success rates (about 2 percent), see Gray, 1975: 175; Lambert, 2001a: 74. Experts did not attach much value to the partial success of the Japanese torpedo attack in Port Arthur at the outbreak of the war since it was conducted at very close range and against stationary targets with no defense.
55 The speed of the torpedo increased from 35 kilometers per hour (19 knots) when launched at the maximum distance, to 83 kilometers per hour (45 knots) for almost double that distance.
56 For the evolution of torpedo range and speed, see Marder, 1961: 329.
57 For details of the losses both belligerents suffered, see Corbett, 1914, II: 446.
58 Liddell Hart, 1972: 145.
59 On the development of minesweepers before World War I (1914), see George, 1998: 230.

60 On the attitude of the Royal Navy to the mine before World War I, see Marder, 1961: 328–9.
61 During World War I both sides laid about 240,000 mines, resulting in the sinking of 216 warships and hundreds of merchant ships. See Hartmann and Truver, 1991: 15.
62 The need for new energy resources in the Royal Navy became evident in 1912 with the appointment of Fisher as chairman of a royal committee reviewing the possibility of supplying oil to the fleet. See Churchill, 1923: 137–8.
63 Toward World War I the German navy also began to use oil as a secondary fuel for its larger ships. It still relied on coal, however, for the fear of shortage of a stable supply of oil, as well as the assumption that the ship's coal storages served as additional shielding against torpedoes, particularly below the water level. See Epkenhans, 2001: 61–2.
64 On the development of supply ships in the twentieth century, see Wildenberg, 1996.
65 For the early history of submarines, see Compton-Hall, 1983; Middleton, 1976: ch. 1; Roland, 1978.
66 For the introduction of submarines into the Royal Navy, see Lambert, 1999: 38–72; Preston, 2001: 24–43.
67 On submarines in the Imperial Russian Navy, see Lambert, 1992: 148–9; Spassky, 1998.
68 On the Russian use of submarines during the Russo-Japanese War, see Mitchell, 1974: 233.
69 In a letter to Arnold While, March 12, 1904. In Marder, 1952: 305.
70 In a letter of April 20, 1904. In Marder, 1952: 308–9.
71 Add. Mss 49710, reprinted in Lambert, 2001b: 109–12.
72 On the impact of the war on the advocates of the submarine within the French navy, see Walser, 1992: 136.
73 Lambert, 1999: 234.
74 On September 22, 1914, the German submarine U-9 sank in less than an hour three British armored cruisers: HMS *Aboukir*, *Hogue*, and *Cressy*. During the entire war, Germany built 332 submarines. In George, 1998: 159.
75 The Wright brothers are usually credited with the first controllable, powered, heavier-than-air flight, which took place in Kitty Hawk, North Carolina, on December 17, 1903.
76 On the early development of ships as airplane carriers, see Humble, 1982: 6–11; Layman, 1989; Preston, 1979: 6–11; and Robbins, 2001: 11–67.
77 A year earlier it had again been the small Greek navy that had opened a stage in the new era when one of its airplanes dropped four bombs on a Turkish battleship during the Second Balkan War of 1913.
78 The last recorded incident of a battleship sinking another battleship took place on October 25, 1944 when the USN *Mississippi* hit the IJN *Yamashiro* with a salvo at 18,000 meters. Half a year later the world's largest battleship *Yamato* was also sunk by multiple hits of bombs and torpedoes dropped by about 380 airplanes.
79 Mahan, 1906: 142. See also Seager, 1977: 525–7.

18 The road to Jutland?

The war and the Imperial German Navy

Cord Eberspaecher

The centenary of the outbreak of the Russo-Japanese War has passed in Germany almost unnoticed. The war never entered German collective memory. This does not seem surprising at a first glance, considering today's impression that this war in northeast Asia rarely touched German interests, which were mainly focused on the European politics of the Great Powers. In 1904, the perception was different. The area known as the "Far East," and especially China, was of considerable interest to Germany. And the big and potentially dangerous neighbor in the European east was a major concern for the German Foreign Office, the army and the emperor. Bismarck had kept a loose alliance with the tsar's empire, but after the era of the "Iron Chancellor" the treaty with Russia expired. Although Germany was still interested in friendly relations and Wilhelm II trusted in the close family ties to the tsar, German diplomacy could not prevent Russia from seeking a new ally in Germany's arch-rival, France. Thus, the Russian engagement in northeast Asia seemed a distraction from European matters and was most welcome. When the emperor met Tsar Nicholas II in Reval in August 1902, his departure signal was: "The Admiral of the Atlantic greets the Admiral of the Pacific." This signal caused considerable irritation, mainly in Britain, which was the foremost seapower of the time.[1]

On the other hand, Germany's relations with Japan had cooled down after Germany had joined France and Russia in their initiative to prevent Japan from taking Port Arthur after victory over China in 1895. German diplomacy tried to restore the relationship with the new power in East Asia, but nonetheless many members of the German elite regarded Japan as a threat or still not to be taken seriously. Even during the Boxer Rebellion in China, German officers had talked about the "small yellow monkeys."[2] For the emperor, Japan became the personification of the "Yellow Peril." When he read about Japanese distrust toward Germany in a report by the German minister in Tokyo in August 1904, he even predicted that a Japanese victory over Russia would lead to the final battle between East and West. Led by the German emperor, Europe would have to fight Asia under Japan's leadership and the victorious side would dominate the globe.[3] Although officially neutral, German sympathies were with Russia; and, like the public opinion in most Western countries, even after the first setbacks Russia was expected to win in the long run. For example, German naval officer Oskar Kautter, stationed on the cruiser *Hansa* in 1904, hoped that Russia would finally keep the upper hand:

> because the Japanese would be carried away by their success in such a degree, that they would not be able to stop themselves. Japan is nice as a power of the second or third rank, but in the interest of every power involved in East Asia, it should not become a Great Power.[4]

Naval intelligence in the Russo-Japanese War

The Russo-Japanese War did not show a keen interest in the world's navies only because of political-diplomatic matters or questions about its cultural consequences. For the Imperial German Navy, as for every major Western navy, this was the most interesting incident since the Sino-Japanese War. Warships could only be sincerely tested under realistic circumstances. Maneuvers in peacetime could never bring the same results for future technical developments that actual battle could. Thus, it was customary to send military observers to every war where naval units were involved and collect as many reports as possible. What made the Russo-Japanese War even more attractive from this point of view was the fact that, in contrast to the conflicts between Chile and Peru in 1879–81 or between China and Japan in 1894–5, in 1904 two navies clashed that were to be considered first-rate in most aspects.

The role of the observer in East Asia and the Pacific would have naturally fallen to the German Cruiser Squadron, active in East Asia since 1894. But its value was limited as the German cruisers and gunboats were placed under orders to operate with utmost care in the northeast Asian waters and to keep away from possible places of action to avoid being involved.[5] For example, when the Baltic Fleet under the command of Vice Admiral Zinovii Rozhestvenskii approached Chinese waters in April 1905, the German cruiser squadron fell back on Tsingtao.[6] Another institutional and official channel for gathering information were the naval attachés. Military and naval observers were attached to many embassies and their duty was to report anything of interest in the field to their superiors. They were normally an accepted partner of the foreign state's army or navy and usually invited to parades, maneuvers, and other events. But from a naval attaché more was expected than reading the newspaper. Military observation has always been based somewhere in between diplomatic representation and espionage, even more so in an era when modern intelligence services had not yet emerged. Most naval or military attachés tried to enrich their reports beyond the level of official sources through informal or even illegal information and thus walked a thin line between the legal and illegal collection of information and espionage.[7]

Germany had installed a naval attaché in Japan in 1898. The initiative had come from the later head of the Imperial Naval Office, Admiral Alfred von Tirpitz. As commander of the cruiser division in East Asia he wrote in 1896, obviously because of impressions formed during the Sino-Japanese war, that it would be of greatest importance to gather more information about the Japanese fleet, as the main decision in future wars would take place between navies. And sufficient information about the navies in Japan or China could not be obtained from London, Paris, or St Petersburg.[8] In sharp contrast, however, to the mutual military representation in Europe and North America, military attachés in Japan were regarded as "legal spies." Every German naval attaché in Tokyo prior to World War I complained about Japanese secrecy and the cool restraint of their Japanese colleagues. Sometimes they were even observed by the police. Access to military property, participation in maneuvers, and the acquisition of naval intelligence being officially forbidden, the German side considered measures that ranged from inviting Japanese naval officers to German fleet maneuvers, in order to build up trust over the detachment of informal agents to collect information, to the systematic reduction of information given to the Japanese navy.[9]

These difficulties also faced lieutenant commander Konrad Trummler, who in 1904 had to face the difficult task of gathering information about Japanese plans and actions. Right after the Japanese attack on Port Arthur he asked for official material and about the possibility of witnessing the Japanese fleet during its operations. Trummler's request was not successful, and he was not even allowed to go near any of the Japanese men-of-war. The only result of his request to be present at the embarkation of troops sent to Korea was that his American colleague, who already had permission, was forced to leave Nagasaki only having seen some transports from a great distance. Although Japan installed a special liaison officer for the foreign naval attachés, Trummler kept complaining about Japanese secrecy; for example, he claimed that even official reports were only handed out to them after they had been released for the press.[10] In the end, Trummler never received information beyond official announcements and his reports contained little of interest about the war.[11]

Only the British attachés in Tokyo were an exception—as representatives of Japan's most important ally. Britain was eager to learn from the war in East Asia. Not only had the navy not been tested in major battle for about 100 years, since Trafalgar, but the Royal Navy faced increasing rivalry from the development of modern navies in Russia, France, Japan, the United States, Italy, and Germany. "Thus London had a very immediate need to know how the conflict was developing in Asia."[12] In February 1904, the Royal Navy had two attachés in Tokyo—Captain Ernest Troubridge and Captain Ricardo. Their presence, however, did not seem enough and Captain William Pakenham was sent as an additional observer. Troubridge felt that he was to be replaced by Pakenham and decided to leave accompanied by

Ricardo. This caused some fury in the Admiralty as they had never been ordered to leave their posts.

In the end, two additional officers, Captains Hutchinson and Jackson, were detached to assist Pakenham. Another attaché, Captain Eyres, was sent to work as an observer on the Russian side. He never reached Port Arthur and, when he eventually arrived in Vladivostok, was treated with grave suspicion and remained far from the main theater.[13] In comparison to Trummler, Pakenham enjoyed much greater freedom to visit naval facilities and ships and witness important operations, and notably he was on board Admiral Tōgō Heihachirō's battleship *Mikasa* during the battle of Tsushima.[14] On the other hand, the Japanese were careful not to let the gap between the English and other attachés become too wide: "While the British expected better treatment than the other Western countries who sent observers, the Japanese were worried about giving the impression that their war effort was being directed by the British."[15]

If Japan was an exception to the rule in one direction, Russia was an exception in the other. Not even in officially allied states did it seem as easy to get military intelligence as it did in the tsar's empire. Not only was the official exchange open to Western standards, but German agents obtained much more vital information by ways of friendship or bribery, for example paying Russian officers' debts. From the reports in the German archives it is very clear that, while the German navy was very much in the dark about the planning and operations of the Japanese, they knew almost everything about Russian decisions up to detailed accounts of the inner condition of the Russian fleet.

Circumstances were much easier for the German naval attaché in St Petersburg, Paul von Hintze, than for Trummler in Tokyo (Hürter, 1998). Not only was the atmosphere for naval attachés much more relaxed in the Russian capital, von Hintze also made good use of his friendship with several Russian officers. In June 1904, he could report to the head of the Imperial Naval Office, Alfred von Tirpitz, that several colleagues of the Russian navy had trusted him with Russian confidential information. He had been asked to keep this information absolutely secret—which meant for him that he would report his knowledge only to his direct superior and the emperor.[16] However, St Petersburg was too far from the main theater to attain information as precise as desired. Thus, shortly after the outbreak of hostilities, two naval officers, Albert Hopman and Hentschel von Gilbenheimb, were detached to Port Arthur directly.

The German naval attachés in Port Arthur

The most important step was to send additional naval observers and the reaction had to be quick, considering the time they would need to reach their posts. Wilhelm II had already signed an order for the designated naval attachés on February 13, 1904. In addition to quick and accurate reports, they were to collect any available news about modern weaponry, the use of tactics, or landing operations. To gather this information they were allowed to use every available means, "which do not collide with the principles of hospitality." In personal contact they were to exercise restraint, refrain from any comments about successes or failures, or give away information hinting at the state of the German navy.[17]

Hopman was at this time an officer in the admiral's staff in Berlin and started his journey in late February. Although he shared some of Wilhelm II's views about the struggle between the white and yellow races, Hopman regarded the war from a European point of view and saw Japan mostly as Britain's agent. His concern was that, in a future struggle between Russia on one side and Britain with the United States and Japan on the other, Germany's future would be doubtful.[18] In Colombo, he met the first Russian eyewitnesses—surviving members of the cruiser *Variag* traveling back to Europe. To Hopman it seemed almost unbelievable when he was told that nobody on the Russian side had really believed that the war would actually happen. The *Variag*'s captain had been under orders to avoid any hostile action until the arrival of a formal declaration of war, and to Hopman it needed "a considerable amount of Russian apathy to leave the commander of the *Variag* without any information in Chemulpo for almost two weeks."[19]

In Tsingtao Hopman met the Russian Major von Howen, who had been detached to the staff of Governor Alekseev. Howen claimed that the Russians had laid hands on Japanese operation plans even before the war. Although the Japanese army was quite capable and the navy was also respectable, there was no doubt that Russia would finally claim victory. Von Howen was of the opinion that Russia had not been prepared at the start of the war, but would gather its strength and succeed in the end.[20]

The opinion that apathy, indifference, and incompetence on the Russian side contributed decisively to Japanese victory is characteristic of Hopman's further reports. He arrived in China in April 1904, where he met von Gilgenheimb, who came from the staff of the cruiser squadron in East Asia. After Hopman and Gilgenheimb had received the necessary papers from the Russian legation in Beijing, they started their journey on April 13 via Tientsin and Shanhaikuan. Still under way, they learned about the loss of the *Petropavlovsk* and the death of Vice Admiral Stepan Makarov. Although no detailed information could be obtained, it became clear that this was a heavy blow for the defense of Port Arthur and that the hope for a decisive role for the navy had almost vanished.[21]

On their way they visited Russian troops in southern Manchuria. Both German officers were cordially invited and entertained with vodka. The Russians were quite confident about the final outcome of the war. In his memoirs, Hopman mentions a tall captain proudly displaying his huge scimitar, reminding the German of the fight between David and Goliath. After arrival in Port Arthur, the "Goliath" did not impress the German naval attachés. The Russians were still busy with unfinished fortifications, three battleships would not be ready for battle until June, and reinforcements were slow to arrive. Real or imagined Chinese spies were of great concern and Hopman reported that the plan to remove every Chinese from the city was only abandoned because the Russians lacked workers.[22]

Almost jokingly, Hopman portrayed the chaos that had occurred during torpedo boat operations during night-time. From the Russian side Hopman received information that they had been sent out repeatedly without cruisers and without clear orders. A central command had not existed, and after its installation, did not work as it lacked experience and was not familiar with the commanders of the boats. It seemed that, during operations, single boats or small groups went where they pleased. Signals did not work on either side and, in the dark, Russians and Japanese could not tell their own ships from the enemy's. One Russian captain told Hopman laughingly that once he sailed as "Admiral" in front of Japanese torpedo boats for about four hours. Because of these problems, the torpedo boats stopped attacks on other boats altogether and even the land batteries were forbidden to fire as they might hit their own ships. Hopman saw this as a harmless and unprofessional scrap that cost a few lives and did minor damage but without results worthy to speak of.[23]

The working conditions for the German attachés were good. Following some initial reluctance,[24] Alekseev allowed them to move freely around Port Arthur, to visit ships and wharves as they pleased, and to observe Japanese fleet movements from the eastern shore. Their reports were allowed to pass uncensored and unopened, Hopman's only concern being whether they actually arrived.[25] After Port Arthur had been cut off the reports had to be sent by Chinese junks to Chefoo, and from there sent to the German legation in Beijing. This connection was not very reliable and it seems that several messages were lost on the way.

The only other naval observer at the time of their arrival was the French naval attaché, Commander Comte de Cuverville. The relationship of the German attachés and their French comrade was cordial and they exchanged their experiences and opinions freely. Being French, he belonged to a nation allied with Russia and was treated even better by the Russian officials. Hopman, however, was satisfied that the Germans still had their advantage, because de Cuverville could not speak Russian, although he had been naval attaché in St Petersburg since 1901.[26] In early May another observer arrived —an American naval officer, Lieutenant Commander Newton McCully— whom Hopman characterized as kind, open-minded, but somewhat uncouth, but whose initiative seemed refreshing amidst the Russian apathy.[27] McCully had only reached Port Arthur after overcoming Russian reluctance by threatening official intervention by President Theodore Roosevelt. As he could speak neither Russian nor German, he was regarded with suspicion, many Russians believing he was English.[28]

The image of the Japanese changed considerably for the German observers. The "monkey" disappeared—even in the Russian view—and was replaced by a Japanese who had most of the virtues Germans claimed for themselves, such as punctuality, organization, and courage—in sharp contrast to the image of the Russians.[29] On April 24, Hopman reported the Japanese effort to block the entrance to Port Arthur's harbor. He admired the Japanese courage and was astounded that, on board the sunken ships, no Japanese sailors remained, either alive or dead. As Hopman guessed, the surviving crew had left the ship in time and escaped disguised in civilian clothes. He was particularly surprised about the results of the *Retvizan*'s artillery. Although the single shots had become a mighty roar, the Japanese steamers (blockships) had sunk comparatively late. Russian officers were of the opinion that grenades were less effective than normally considered and claimed that even torpedo boat attacks were by far not as dangerous as they looked.[30] On April 26, Gilgenheimb visited the damaged *Retvizan*. In his report he gave a short description of the attack and the damage done by the torpedoes. He noted that repairs were much more difficult than on the *Tsesarevich*, as the armor belt was affected and had to be taken partially off. His special interest was drawn by the ammunition that was still functioning after lying under water for about a month.[31]

On the same day, Hopman visited the armored cruiser *Bayan* and examined the damage. The Japanese grenades had exploded without much effort. The *Bayan*'s commander was of the opinion that even weak armor produced effective protection against these Japanese grenades, as they detonated on strike and splinters did not go through. Wood was easily damaged, but simple sacks filled with coal kept splinters off. Hopman concluded that explosive grenades without a delayed fuse were quite useless against armored ships and he assumed the Japanese ships were to be equipped with them. On the other hand, he was very critical of the Russian aiming procedures. After the battle started, the Russian ships had major problems in hitting their targets: "Whether they have the same procedure on every ship I cannot say. A unified and elaborated procedure is as likely missing as any education on the tactical level."[32]

The battle between the Russian squadron and the Japanese fleet on August 10 was the most interesting event for the German military observers in the war up to this date. Hopman noted that they did not notice the preparations and also had not been aware of the order for the squadron to leave Port Arthur. Hopman and Gilgenheimb were busy collecting every available piece of information and sending it to Berlin as quickly as possible. Shortly after the battle, Hopman reported the low spirits among the Russian officer corps: "Most of the admirals and commanders went out under the impression to be inferior not only in numbers, but also in leadership, in tactical, artillerist and technical training, and only to be able to make the breakthrough with extraordinary luck."[33]

Both attachés saw the reasons for the Russian defeat in bad preparation and lack of training. Hopman criticized the state of the Russian squadron as "materially and morally dissolute." He held Rear Admiral Vilgelm Vitgeft responsible for the disaster. Hopman blamed him for the "typical Russian conception" of "blind obedience to given orders as the highest military duty"—and the order for the squadron in Port Arthur to leave for Vladivostok as quickly as possible had been quite impossible to follow. He saw no basis on which to judge the Russian tactic during battle as the Russians had not fought according to tactical principles at all. Only Rear Admiral Pavel Ukhtomskii had acted correctly when he took the remaining ships back to Port Arthur, while the captains who sought neutral harbors made the mistake of taking their units out of the war. In quintessence, Hopman concluded: "The war lacked soul on the Russian side while in Japan nation, army and navy stood behind the war efforts with all their physical strength."[34]

In a more detailed account of the damage and the following conclusions, Hopman analyzed in his next report the state of the Russian ships after battle. Judging from the damage to the superstructure of the battleships, he remarked that ships of the line should not have any unarmored parts above water level at all. The deck of the *Peresviet* was a scene of devastation even after days of tidying up. This destruction had already begun in the first phase of battle at long distance and, although the main structure of the ship was not affected, it not only damaged morale, but caused fires, casualties, and poisoning by gas and reduced battle efficiency. In contrast, Russian officers pointed out the Japanese armored cruisers *Nisshin* and *Kasuga* as particularly difficult enemies because they had low superstructures and two-thirds of their sides were armored. Damage to the funnels reduced speed on most of the ships and raised the consumption of coal. Hopman especially stressed the effects of heavy artillery, while secondary artillery played only a minor role. He drew the following conclusions regarding the requirement of a modern battleship: it would require bigger displacement; better underwater protection; smaller superstructure; better protection of command towers without superstructure nearby; four guns of heavy caliber; the highest possible amount of secondary artillery of heavy caliber; some light artillery (as protection against torpedo boats, etc.); and nothing smaller.[35]

Hopman and Gilgenheimb had to leave their posts soon after August 10. Hopman was quite disappointed about the order of Wilhelm II, since he thought he could be more valuable if he stayed. He argued that the *New York Herald* would have paid 100,000 dollars for one man in Port Arthur, and complained that Germany had grown weak in the long period of peace: "I thought the Emperor would be tougher. *Ca ramollit* as Cuverville used to say when we talked about the Hurra-tone of the naval officers, of peace festivities etc."[36] They were required to leave Port Arthur together with the American and French representatives, as their security could no longer be guaranteed. De Cuverville intended to go to Vladivostok, as he thought he had seen enough and was not interested in being a witness "of a new Sevastopol."[37] Hopman left on a Chinese junk, which was soon stopped by the Japanese cruiser *Suma*. He was taken on board and thus attained the goal that the German naval attaché in Tokyo had tried to achieve in vain— to visit the Japanese fleet. After a warm welcome by the Japanese squadron, he was taken to Tsingtao. Gilgenheimb was less lucky. He too had left, together with the French attaché de Cuverville, on a Chinese junk, but neither ever reached their destination. About six months later, the Chinese police arrested the crew of a junk for the murder and robbery of the two Europeans.[38]

Hopman's expectations were surpassed in several respects. The proficiency and utmost politeness with which he was treated almost made him "forget that he was not amongst Europeans"—for him surely a high compliment! He was equally impressed with the passion and patriotism of the Japanese officers and pleased to hear that several had sympathies for Germany. The ships he visited were in good shape and their crews seemed to Hopman to be well trained.[39]

Lessons from the Russo-Japanese War

Early after the outbreak of the war, a growing number of articles on this topic were published in Germany. For German naval matters the *Marine Rundschau* (Navy Review) was definitely the most important. The first publication on the war provided an overview of the Russian and Japanese naval forces and soon after the question of the missing Japanese declaration of war was debated. The events were reported as soon as information was available and the German navy made good use of additional sources, for example by questioning the officers of the battleship *Tsesarevich* after their internment in Tsingtao about the battle of August 10. The second important naval magazine *Nauticus* also published a thorough analysis of the operations at sea in 1905. After the war was over, not only were several works about the Russo-Japanese War published by former military observers, journalists, and other writers,[40] but even more were translated as soon as they hit the bookshops.[41] The *Marine Rundschau* even announced a competition of articles comparing the naval battles of Trafalgar and Tsushima, two of which were published in 1907. The Imperial German Navy was also keen to get hold of unofficial or secret reports. In 1909, the Imperial Naval Office received a copy of the confidential report of a Russian ship's engineer and his experience in the war. Within days, several copies had been made and circulated.[42]

In late summer and autumn 1904, German naval authorities analyzed thoroughly the battle itself, and the tactics on either side, as well as the impact of heavy guns on armor. The first result was a "Short Summary of the Experiences Derived from the Russo-Japanese War," published as a confidential paper on November 14. It was mainly based on Hopman's reports from Port Arthur.[43] The report made a clear statement on the importance of the main artillery. Heavy guns had played the major role, secondary guns only a minor part. Equally important was to score as many hits as possible in short time. A higher frequency of fire was necessary, "because we see England pursuing the same goal with great energy."[44] The report also noted the absence of an organized system of communications. Not only had *Variag* been lost because the ship had been without any news about the political situation, but Governor Alekseev had also been completely unaware of public opinion in Japan. This lack of information was also seen as the reason why Russia had grossly underestimated the Japanese forces and entered the war almost unprepared. The logical conclusion was to organize a system of communications that would keep working after the official lines had been cut off—and these preparations had to be done in peacetime as it would not be possible to improvise after a war had started. These conclusions make clear that Germany was not much better prepared to gather sufficient information about a hostile country than the Russians were in 1904—and as World War I was to show, they could not make these deficiencies good until 1914.

In March 1905, the Naval Office finished a report on the results and conclusions of the war.[45] The information about the Russian side was based on the reports from the naval attachés in Port Arthur and the German government in Tsingtao, but was still considered far from complete. From the Japanese almost no news was available. Still, there had been reports about experiences of the war in several countries. More information was considered vital, as "it could be of decisive importance for the construction of our new built ships." It had been shown that light artillery had played a negligible role and even medium calibers had been hardly used. The sea battle of August 10 had been fought almost exclusively with heavy artillery. Hopman had stressed these points over and over again and the reports were in many aspects based on his opinion.[46] Yet the report recommended care in drawing conclusions and hinted at misinterpretations made after the battles at the Yalu river in 1894 in the Sino-Japanese War and near Santiago in 1898 during the Spanish-American War.

Naval mines played an important part in this war. Minefields had been used by both sides with success, but the Russians had been criticized for hampering their own actions and even endangering themselves by mistake. The main weakness was seen in the lack of organized minesweeping techniques and the conclusion was thus to install a functioning minesweeping division for the navy, which should be able to be deployed with the fleet. The effects of mines, torpedoes, and grenades on ship's armor were seen as especially important. A related problem was the proper storage of ammunition on board as the sinking of the *Petropavlovsk* and the *Hatsuse* was explained by detonations inside the ship after being struck from the outside. The most endangering types of ammunition were obviously loaded mines and torpedo heads, and the conclusion was mainly that mines should not be carried on board battleships at all. Every kind of grenade filled with explosive was to be stored as far away from the ship's side as possible and protected from all sides. Following the latest information, the navy's protection of the ship's bottom was not considered sufficient against mines and torpedoes. A stronger armor and additional bulkheads below the armored decks were suggested. Torpedo nets were considered of little use and it was decided not to reintroduce them.

The effects of grenades against unarmored parts of the ship were reported as devastating, but this was expected after earlier experiences. It was pointed out that although these effects did no vital damage the shocking impression of a deck full of debris was not to be underestimated. As this damage could not be completely avoided, the only lesson was to keep the superstructure as low as possible. Another problem was the severe damage to the funnels, which made it difficult to keep up enough steam or which let pieces fly into the engine rooms as had been the case on *Tsesarevich*, *Sevastopol*, *Peresviet*, *Bayan*, and *Askold*. As it was impossible to protect funnels with armor, the only conclusion was to keep them low as well.

The effects on armor were very much as expected. Of special concern were the armored command towers. In several cases shrapnel from explosions had entered the observation slits, causing heavy casualties among the ship's command. The countermeasure—to make the slits considerably smaller and to avoid any superstructure near the command towers—had been already taken effect in the German navy. So had the lesson from the Japanese cruiser *Iwate*, where the only direct hit on the command tower during the Russo-Japanese sea battles had not pierced the armor but broke almost every instrument loose, thereby killing or wounding almost every man inside. Instruments in German men-of-war had been installed away from the tower's armor for years, as the report contentedly noted. The deployment of the gun turrets on the Russian ships had proved satisfactory and the turret's armor had not been pierced. It was stressed that even turrets that had been directly hit stayed operable, splinters occasionally harming the crew but not the material.

In any case, according to the Naval Office report, the battleship remained the decisive unit: "It is indispensable to reach and keep naval supremacy. The strength of a fleet accordingly apart from the capacity of its personnel is measured in the number and strength of its battleships." The shipbuilding policy of every major navy proved this rule and, in contrast to several articles in the British press, displacement was also predicted to increase, as first news from the new British battleship *Dreadnought* proved. This last remark is quite interesting as it proves that the Imperial Naval Office was quite aware that a new type of battleship was being built in Britain. But it is equally interesting to see that the report neglected most of the conclusions from the Russo-Japanese War that had seemed obvious to the German observers in Port Arthur: the role of the medium calibers. Thus the German experts missed probably the most important element that made the HMS *Dreadnought* the prototype of a new era: the concept of the all-big-gun ship.

The report admitted that the role of the secondary battery had been judged as minor. This was explained by the great distance of the battles, but equally it was claimed that the consumption of ammunition had shown that later the secondary guns had been used as well. Equally, the damage on the Russian battleships had been attributed almost exclusively to heavy shells. The report stated that this could not be true, but the only reason for this point of view was that, in the damaged superstructure, it was difficult to judge how much damage had been done by grenades of which caliber. The report was firm in the belief that the destruction of the enemy could not be obtained by heavy artillery alone.

The report about the battle of Tsushima showed an even bigger reluctance to accept these new developments.[47] The voyage of the Russian squadron and the following battle were thoroughly analyzed on 83 pages, although it was admitted that the authors still lacked enough information— mostly from the Japanese side—to cover every detail. The reasons for the Russian defeat and the Japanese victory was the part the German navy was naturally most interested in: the lessons for future naval warfare and shipbuilding. It was already known that the experiences had consequences for the navies of Japan, Britain, and France. After the obvious effects of heavy artillery, the heavy guns were increased to 10–12 per battleship with a caliber of 305 millimeters (12 inches). Stronger armor was combined with a bigger displacement of 18,000–19,000 tons. The secondary artillery disappeared, but here the report already claimed that this came from a one-sided opinion about its uselessness. Additional changes were similar to the earlier German conclusions, for example a smaller superstructure and lower funnels. From the impressions about the lessons learnt by the British, German observers suspected a close exchange of opinions with the Japanese navy. The British principles also were a bigger displacement, more heavy guns of bigger caliber, and no secondary artillery. Increased secrecy in Britain was ascribed to the Japanese model. It seems clear that the German navy in principle knew about the building of the HMS *Dreadnought*, but was aware neither of its details nor that the concept was older than Tsushima and had only been confirmed by the lessons of the battles in East Asia during 1904–5. Nonetheless, France came to similar conclusions: the increased distances called for heavy guns of one caliber and accordingly the secondary artillery had to be abandoned.

When the report came to the lessons for the Imperial German Navy, the question of the right combination of guns was carefully avoided. It was stated that, although the battle of Tsushima had clearly been the first fully developed modern naval battle fought through to the end, consequences could only be drawn with great care. Similarly to the Sino-Japanese War and the Spanish-American War, it had been a fight between unequal adversaries. Japanese strategy and tactics were not tested in earnest. It was doubted that Tōgō would have had the same success against a more energetic opponent, as his tactics seemed to have been too static. Still, the

Japanese success was appreciated, but the authors of the report clearly looked down upon the young modern Japanese navy—which was somewhat ironic considering the short tradition of the Prusso-German navy when compared to old sea powers such as Britain and France.

The final conclusion of the report about Tsushima stated somewhat lamely that the most important lesson was that training in peacetime was the basis for the battle value of a fleet and a good weapon was only useful in the hands of capable leaders. The only other points mentioned were the education of officers and crews, continued training, and constant learning from experience—the question of shipbuilding and guns was completely avoided. How was this possible? The reports about the Russo-Japanese War were classified, so secrecy could not be the reason for avoiding a debate over such difficult questions. Other reasons have to be responsible for the reluctance to take up the consequences for the shipbuilding program that most of the other major navies were willing to accept, even more as the concept was far from odd or even completely new.

The most obvious result of the naval experiences of the war at sea in East Asia was the building of the British *Dreadnought*.[48] Every country with naval interests had watched the battles at sea closely and tried to learn from the available intelligence lessons for the men-of-war of the future. The most important lesson was the major role the heavy artillery had played in the encounters. The battle in August 1904 had been opened from hitherto unexpected distances of 8,000–9,000 meters. During the engagement the battle distance was reduced with grave consequences for both sides. The battle of Tsushima was started from 6,500 to 7,000 meters. These distances would have been judged impossible only ten years before. The effects of heavy shells were devastating, even against well-armored ships. In addition, the equipment of battleships with mixed calibers had proved difficult to operate during the engagements, as their difference could not be made out clearly and thus the aim proved hard to correct.[49]

The logical consequence was the all-big-gun ship. This idea had already occurred to the Italian engineer Cuniberti in 1903 and the Russo-Japanese War proved him right. After Tsushima, his plans drew considerable interest. The first results in shipbuilding were a last generation of Pre-Dreadnoughts, which still continued the old concept of mixed calibers, but upgraded the smaller guns almost to heavy artillery. Examples were the British battleships *Lord Nelson* and *Agamemnon*, the American *Connecticut* type, and the French *Danton*. Germany had followed a similar concept as far back as the 1890s with the *Brandenburg* class, but had refrained from full development of the concept due to the limits of the Kaiser-Wilhelm-Kanal, the main connection between the North and the Baltic Sea for the German fleet. Thus it fell to the Royal Navy to build the first fully developed ship of a new generation—HMS *Dreadnought*.[50] This revolution in the Royal Navy was already on its way when the Russo-Japanese War started. First Sea Lord Sir John Fisher believed that the Royal Navy could not rely only on superior numbers and thus initiated the concept of a new generation of fast capital ships. The naval operations of 1904–5 confirmed Fisher's plans. While he ignored contradicting reports from Pakenham, who "was not in favor of firing the guns in a broadside," Fisher was receptive to just the arguments needed for the main feature of the men-of-war he intended to build.[51]

While Admiral Fisher was shaping the British fleet of the future, his German colleague Admiral Tirpitz was more than reluctant to accept any changes to his naval concept. Of great interest concerning the German reaction to the news from the war at sea in East Asia was a discussion in the Imperial Naval Office on November 15, 1904, one day after the first report had been published. Admiral Tirpitz and the heads of every naval department were present. It was agreed that the material was satisfactory, but conclusions had to be drawn with care and also had to be made clear to the public. The foremost topic of discussion concerned the construction department. Most points were quickly agreed upon, for example the lower superstructure, better protection of command towers, lower funnels, and better underwater protection. Everyone agreed that the torpedo boat operations had not taught anything as both sides had lacked in tactics and organization. Most interesting was the question of future armament. In spite of the unmistakable statements in almost every report and Admiral von Eickstädt's opinion that even the large 210-millimeter (8.3-inch) secondary guns were not sufficient to pierce modern armor, Tirpitz was not willing to change his concept. He stressed the psychological effect of grenade explosions and the important role of the secondary guns when fighting at short distances—and Tirpitz made clear that, in his opinion, a naval battle would always be decided over short distances and the ships had to be designed accordingly.[52]

Tirpitz had reasons other than the lessons of the Russo-Japanese War on which he based his program to build a strong German battle fleet (Berghahn, 1971; Epkenhans, 1991; Hubatsch, 1955; Hobson, 2004). The biggest problem for Tirpitz was the *Reichstag*—the parliament—which had to approve the costs of the building program: "the very design of Tirpitz' navy law almost prohibited a move to an armament or speed that required greater displacement and cost, unless Great Britain forced Germany into it."[53] Thus Tirpitz was not interested in news that could be a potential threat to the budget of the navy. The protocol of the meeting in November 1904 shows not a celebrated genius building Germany's modern navy, but much more the administering bureaucrat. This meant that, although Germany had collected a vast amount of material to look for lessons from the Russo-Japanese War, and probably had the best information from the Russian side compared even to France, it structurally was not able to make adequate use of it. If Hopman's reports were the main basis for the later German *Dreadnought* conceptions,[54] as Epkenhans puts it, they did not cause the immediate reaction one would have expected from the highly qualified experts in the German naval staff.

However, the glorious role or the "spirit of the genius" often ascribed to Fisher had also dimmed. Fisher, as Jon T. Sumida has shown, was first appointed to save money and originally did not have the *Dreadnought*, but the *Invincible*, a new class of battlecruisers, in mind. While Germany aimed at better protection for ships, Fisher aimed at big guns and great speed. Although the new battle cruisers, similarly to the *Dreadnought* a few years earlier, made the existing heavy cruisers obsolete, as the battle of the Falklands showed in December 1914, the battle of Jutland revealed the vulnerability of the new type. Under conditions of World War I, Fisher's design seemed suddenly not so ingenious.[55]

The Russo-Japanese War was an important watershed in shipbuilding and observers saw the first large naval operations with modern battleships in history. But by only paying attention to the evolution of warfare it is easy to overlook that the war had strategic and political consequences as well. For Germany it meant that Britain and its ally held seapower in East Asia in their hands. The German Cruiser Squadron ceased to be an instrument of naval warfare. As World War I has shown, the German cruisers could only choose between war against trade shipping or return to Europe. Ironically, it was the new great power on the Asian stage that ended German rule in East Asia when Japan conquered German Tsingtao after the first months of the war. Hopman had already realized in 1905 that the consequences of Japan's victory went far beyond the conquest of Port Arthur: "The role of the white race as Lords in Asia has ended. This is the beginning of a new era in world history."[56]

Notes

1 See Hopman, 1924: 282. This chapter made use also of the following sources: Political Archive of the German Foreign Office, Berlin (PA-AA); Bundesarchiv-Militärarchiv, German Military Archive (BAMA); Nachlaß Albert Hopman, private family archive.
2 Stingl, 1978: 461.
3 Count Arco to Chancellor Bülow, August 11, 1904, with remarks, PA-AA, R 18816.
4 Kautter, 1910: 194.
5 Schlubach, 1958: 61.
6 *Ostasiatischer Lloyd*, 1905.
7 Meisner, 1957: 63–4.
8 Meisner, 1957: 23–4.
9 Giessler, 1976: 129.
10 Trummler to Tirpitz, 3 March 1904, BAMA, RM 3/2593.
11 Sander-Nagashima, 2005.
12 Towle, 1999: 158.
13 Towle, 1999: 158.
14 Widenmann, 1952: 203.
15 Towle, 1998: 24.
16 Hintze to Tirpitz, June 17, 1904, BAMA, RM 3/22.

17　Emperor Wilhelm II to Chancellor von Bülow, February 13, 1904, BAMA, RM 3/2593.
18　Hopman to his wife, February 4, 1904, Nachlaß Hopman.
19　Report Hopman, March 9, 1904, BAMA, RM 3/19.
20　Report Hopman, March 26, 1904, BAMA, RM 3/19.
21　Report Hopman, April 17, 1904, BAMA, RM 3/19.
22　Report Hopman, April 30, 1904, BAMA, RM 3/19.
23　Report Hopman, April 22, 1904, BAMA, RM 3/19.
24　Hopman, 1924: 290.
25　Report Hopman, April 22, 1904, BAMA, RM 3/19.
26　Hopman, 1924: 292.
27　Report Hopman, May 11, 1904, BAMA, RM 3/19.
28　Hopman, 1924: 297.
29　Stingl, 1978: 463.
30　Report Hopman, April 24, 1904, BAMA, RM 3/19.
31　Report Gilgenheimb, April 26, 1904, BAMA, RM 3/19.
32　Report Hopman, April 26, 1904, BAMA, RM 3/19.
33　Report Hopman, September 2, 1904, BAMA, RM 3/19.
34　Report Hopman, September 11, 1904, BAMA, RM 3/19.
35　Report Hopman, September 23, 1904, BAMA, RM 3/19.
36　Hopman, 2004: 115.
37　Hopman, 1924: 303.
38　Report of the German minister to China, Alfons Mumm von Schwarzenstein, July 7, 1905, BAMA, RM 4315.
39　Report Hopman, September 29, 1904, BAMA, RM 3/19.
40　For example, Janson, 1905; Lothes, 1910; Polmann, 1912; and Reventlow, 1906.
41　For example, Semenov, 1909.
42　Confidential note, undated, BAMA, RM 3/2596.
43　BAMA, RM 3/4313.
44　BAMA, RM 3/19.
45　BAMA, RM 4314.
46　Hopman, 2004: 113, 117–18.
47　Die Schlacht in der japanischen See, undated, BAMA, RM 3/5784.
48　Widenmann, 1952: 143.
49　Israel and Gebauer, 1991: 111.
50　Israel and Gebauer, 1991: 113.
51　Towle, 1999: 165–6.
52　Protocol, November 15, 1904, BAMA, 3/4314.
53　Fairbanks, 1991: 254.
54　Hopman, 2004: 40.
55　Fairbanks, 1991: 260.
56　Hopman, 2004: 126.

Bibliography

Adam, B.A. (1995) *The Vernacular Press and the Emergence of Modern Indonesian Consciousness (1855–1913)*, Ithaca, NY: SEAP.

Adams, C.C. (1968 [1933]) *Islam and Modernism in Egypt: A Study of the Modern Reform Movement Inaugurated by Muhammad 'Abduh*, New York: Russell and Russell.

Adhami, S. (1999) "The Conversion of the Japanese Emperor to Islam," *Central Asiatic Journal*, 43: 1–9.

Akashi, M. (1988) *Rakka ryusui: Colonel Akashi's Report on His Secret Cooperation with the Russian Revolutionary Parties during the Russo-Japanese War: Selected Chapters*, trans. C. Inaba, ed. O.K. Fält and A. Kujala, Helsinki: SHS.

Akmese, H.N. (2005) *The Birth of Modern Turkey: The Ottoman Military and the March to World War I*, London: I.B. Tauris.

Andaya, B.W. (1977) "From Rum to Tokyo: The Search for Anticolonial Allies by the Rulers of Riau, 1899–1914," *Indonesia*, 24: 123–56.

Anderson, B.R.O. (1966). "Japan, 'The Light of Asia'," in Josef Silverstein (ed.) *Southeast Asia in World War II: Four Essays*, New Haven, CT: Yale Southeast Asia Studies, pp. 13–50.

Anderson, B.R.O. (1991) *Imagined Communities: Reflections on the Origin and Spread of Nationalism*, revised edn, London: Verso.

Anderson, F.M. and A.S. Hershey (1918) *Handbook for the Diplomatic History of Europe, Asia, and Africa 1870–1914*, Washington, DC: GPO.

Andrew, C. (1968) *Théophile Delcassé and the Making of the Entente Cordiale*, London: Macmillan.

Andrews, C.F. (1912) *The Renaissance in India: Its Missionary Aspect*, London: Young People's Missionary Movement.

Arnold, G. (2002) *Historical Dictionary of the Crimean War*, Lanham, MD: Scarecrow Press.

Arthur, George (1920) *The Life of Lord Kitchener*, London: Macmillan.

Asada, A. (1961) "Japan's 'Special Interests' and the Washington Conference, 1921–1922," *American Historical Review*, 67: 62–70.

Asada, A. (1993) "From Washington to London: The Imperial Japanese Navy and the Politics of Naval limitation, 1921–1930," *Diplomacy and State Craft*, 4 (3): 147–91.

Ascher, A. (1988) *The Revolution of 1905*, vol. 1: *Russia in Disarray*, Stanford, CA: Stanford University Press.

Ascher, A. (2001) *P.A. Stolypin: The Search for Stability in Late Imperial Russia*, Stanford, CA: Stanford University Press.

Ashmead-Bartlett, E. (1906) *Port Arthur: The Siege and Capitulation*, Edinburgh: William Blackwood & Sons.

Aubert, L. (1906) *La Paix japonaise*, Paris: Armand Colin.

Austrian General Staff (1910–14) *Taktische Detaildarstellungen aus dem Russischjapanischen Kriege; im Auftrage des k.u.k. Chefs des Generalstabes*, 12 vols, ed. F. Beyer, Vienna: Verlag von Streffleurs Milit. Zeitschrift.

Baer, G.W. (1994) *One Hundred Years of Sea Power: The US Navy, 1890–1990*, Stanford, CA: Stanford University Press.

Bailey, T.A. (1934) *Theodore Roosevelt and the Japanese-American Crises*, Stanford, CA: Stanford University Press.

Bandō, H. (1995) *Porandojin to nichiro sensō*, Tokyo: Aoki Shoten.

Bank of Japan (Nihon Ginkō. Tōkeikyoku) (1966) *Meiji ikō hompō shuyō keizai tōkei* (Hundred-year Statistics of the Japanese Economy), Tokyo: Bank of Japan.

Banno, J. (1977) *Meiji: Shisō no jitsuzō*, Tokyo: Sōbunsha.

Banno, J. (1983) "External and Internal Problems After the War," in H. Wray and H. Conroy (eds) *Japan Examined: Perspectives on Modern Japanese History*, Honolulu, HI: University of Hawaii Press, pp. 163–9.

Barth, T. (1904) "Espérances de paix prématurées," *L'Européen*, 154 (November 12): 1–2.

Bartlett, C.J. (1994) *The Global Conflict: The International Rivalry of the Great Powers, 1890–1990*, London: Longman.

Batchelor, J. (1901) *The Ainu and Their Folk-Lore*, London: Religious Tract Society.

Bayly, C.A. (2004) *The Birth of the Modern World, 1780–1914: Global Connections and Comparisons*, Malden, MA: Blackwell.

Beale, H.K. (1956) *Theodore Roosevelt and the Rise of America to World Power*, New York: Collier Books.

Beasley, W.G. (1987) *Japanese Imperialism 1894–1945*, Oxford: Clarendon Press.

Beckett, I.F.W. (2001) *The Great War 1914–1918*, Harlow: Pearson Education.

Befu, H. (1995) "Swings of Japan's Identity," in S. Clausen, R. Starrs, and A. Wedell-Wedellsborg (eds) *Cultural Encounters: China, Japan, and the West*, Aarhus: Aarhus University Press, pp. 241–65.

Befu, H. (2001) *Hegemony of Homogeneity: An Anthropological Analysis of Nihonjinron*, Melbourne: Trans Pacific Press.

Behnen, M. (1985) *Rüstung, Bündnis, Sicherheit: Dreibund und informeller Imperialismus, 1900–1908*, Tübingen: Niemeyer.

Beillevaire, P. (2005) "Après *La Bataille*: L'égarement japonophile de Claude Farrère," *Les Carnets de l'exotisme*, 5 (Faits et imaginaires de la Guerre russo-japonaise): 223–46.

Benda, H.J. (1958) *The Crescent and the Rising Sun: Indonesian Islam under the Japanese Occupation 1942–1945*, The Hague: van Hoeve.

Bergere, M.-C. (1968) "The Role of the Bourgeoisie," in M.C. Wright, *China in Revolution: the First Phase 1900–1913*, New Haven, CT: Yale University Press.

Berghahn, V.R. (1971) *Der Tirpitz-Plan: Genesis und Fall einer innenpolitischen Krisenstrategie unter Wilhelm II*, Düsseldorf: Droste.

Bernard, W.S. (1998) "Immigration: History of US Policy," in D. Jacobson (ed.) *The Immigration Reader: America in Multidisciplinary Perspective*, Malden, MA: Blackwell Publishers, pp. 48–71.

Bernstein, H. (ed.) (1918) *The "Willy–Nicky" Correspondence: Being the Secret and Intimate Telegrams between the Kaiser and the Tsar*, New York: Alfred A. Knopf.

Berton, P. (1988) *Case Study in International Negotiations: The Russo-Japanese Alliance of 1916*, Pittsburgh, PA: Graduate School of Public and International Affairs, Pew Program in Case Teaching and Writing in International Affairs.

Berton, P. (1993) "A New Russo-Japanese Alliance? Diplomacy in the Far East during World War I," *Acta Slavica Iaponica*, 11: 57–78.

Best, A. (2002) *British Intelligence and the Japanese Challenge in Asia, 1914–1941*, Houndmills, Basingstoke: Palgrave.

Bickmore, A.S. (1868a) "The Ainos, or Hairy Men of Yesso," *American Journal of Science and Arts*, 45: 353–61.

Bickmore, A.S. (1868b) "The Ainos, or Hairy Men, of Saghalien and the Kurile Islands," *American Journal of Science and Arts*, 45: 361–77.

Bidwell, S. and D. Graham (1982) *Fire-power: British Army Weapons and Theories of War, 1904–1945*, London: Allen & Unwin.

Bieganiec, R. (2007) "Distant Echoes: The Reflection of the War in the Middle East," in R. Kowner (ed.) *Rethinking the Russo-Japanese War: Centennial Perspectives*, Folkestone: Global Oriental.

Bix, H. (2000) *Hirohito and the Making of Modern Japan*, New York: HarperCollins.

Black, J. (2002) Warfare in the Western World, 1882–1975, Chesham: Acumen.

Bond, B. (1965) "Doctrine and Training in the British Cavalry, 1870–1914," in M. Howard (ed.) *The Theory and Practice of War: Essays Presented to Captain B.H. Liddell Hart*, London: Cassell.

Boyce, D.G. (ed.) (1990) *The Crisis of British Power: The Imperial and Naval Papers of the Second Earl of Selborne, 1895–1910*, London: The Historian's Press.

Braginsky, V.I. and M.A. Boldyareva (1990) "Les manuscrits malais de Leningrad," *Archipel*, 40: 153–78.

Braisted, W.R. (1958) *The United States Navy in the Pacific, 1897–1909*, Austin, TX: University of Texas Press.

Braisted, W.R. (1977) "On the American Red and Red-Orange Plans, 1919–1939," in G. Jordan (ed.) *Naval Warfare in the Twentieth Century 1900–1945*, London: Croom Helm, pp. 167–85.

Brinton, C. (1938) *The Anatomy of Revolution*, New York: W.W. Norton.

Brockett, L.P. (1888) "Japan—I," *Baptist Missionary Magazine*, 68 (April): 96–9.

Brose, E.D. (2001) *The Kaiser's Army: The Politics of Military Technology in Germany during the Machine Age, 1870–1914*, Oxford: Oxford University Press.

Brunnert, H.S. and V.V. Hagelstrom (1912) *Present Day Political Organization of China*, Shanghai: Kelly and Walsh.

Bucholz, A. (1993) *Moltke, Schlieffen, and Prussian War Planning*, New York: Berg.

Bueb, V. (1971) *Die "Junge Schule" der französischen marine Strategie und Politik, 1875–1900*, Boppard am Rhein: Harald Boldt.

Bushnell, J.S. (1985) *Mutiny Amid Repression: Russian Soldiers in the Revolution of 1905–1906*, Bloomington, IN: Indiana University Press.

Bushnell, J.S. (2005) "The Specter of Mutinous Reserves: How the War Produced the October Manifesto," in J.W. Steinberg, B. Menning, D. Schimmelpenninck van der Oye, D. Wolff, and S. Yokote (eds) *The Russo-Japanese War in Global Perspective: World War Zero*, Leiden: Brill, pp. 333–48.

Butler, O. (2002) "Getting the Games: Japan, South Korea and the Co-hosted World Cup," in J. Horne and W. Manzenreiter (eds) *Japan, Korea and the 2002 World Cup*, London: Routledge, pp. 43–55.

Byram, L. (1908) Petit Jap deviendra grand! L'Expansion japonaise en Extrême-Orient, Paris: Berger-Levrault.

Cable, J. (1998) *The Political Influence of Naval Force in History*, London: Macmillan Press.

Cahiers de la guerre, Les (1916) "Verrons-nous les Japonais? Possibilités, conditions, conséquences d'une intervention japonaise en Europe," *Les Cahiers de la guerre*, 6.

Calman, D. (1992) *The Nature and Origins of Japanese Imperialism*, London: Routledge.

Cambon, H. (ed.) (1940–6) *Paul Cambon: Correspondance, 1870–1924*, 3 vols, Paris: Editons Bernard Grasset.

Cameron, M.E. (1931) *The Reform Movement in China, 1898–1912*, Stanford, CA: Stanford University Press.

Carr, E.H. (1961) *What is History?*, Harmondsworth: Penguin Books.

Carus, P. (1904) "The Yellow Peril," *Open Court*, 18 (July): 430–3.

Carus, P. (1905) "The Ainus," *Open Court*, 19 (March): 163–9.

Cary, O. (1976) *A History of Christianity in Japan: Roman Catholic, Greek Orthodox, and Protestant Missions*, vol. 2, Rutland, VT: Charles E. Tuttle.

Castex, R. (1904) *Le Péril jaune en Indo-Chine: Réflexions politiques et militaries*, Paris: H. Charles-Lavauzelle.

Cecil, L. (1996) *Wilhelm II: Emperor and Exile, 1900–1941*, Chapel Hill, NC: University of North Carolina Press.

Cecil, L.J.R. (1964) "Coal for the Fleet that Had to Die," *American Historical Review*, 69 (4): 990–1005.

Challener, R.D. (1973) *Admirals, Generals, and American Foreign Policy, 1898–1914*, Princeton, NJ: Princeton University Press.

Chamberlain, B.H. (1902) *Things Japanese*, London: John Murray.

Chapman, J. (2004) "Admiral Sir John Fisher and Japan, 1894–1904," in H. Cortazzi (ed.) *Britain & Japan, vol. V: Biographical Portraits*, Richmond, Surrey: Japan Library.

Charmley, J. (1999) *Splendid Isolation? Britain and the Balance of Power, 1874–1914*, London, Hodder & Stoughton.

Ch'en, J. (1961) *Yuan Shi-k'ai, 1859–1916: Brutus Assumes the Purple*, Stanford, CA: Stanford University Press.

Chirol, V. (1910) *Indian Unrest*, London: Macmillan.

Chirol, V. (1976) "Letter to G.E. Morrison, 7 July 1909," in Lo Hui-min (ed.) *The Correspondence of G.E. Morrison, I, 1895–1912*, Cambridge: Cambridge University Press, pp. 490–6.

Cho, T.-G. (1994) "Kŭndae ch'ogi ŭi yŏksa insi," in T.-G. Cho, Y.-U. Han, and C.-S. Pak (eds) *Han'guk ŭi yŏksaga wa yŏksahak*, Seoul: Ch'angjak kwa pip'yŏng, pp. 13–22.

Chow, T.S. (1960) *The May Fourth Movement: Intellectual Revolution in Modern China*, Cambridge, MA: Harvard University Press.

Chun C.W. (1970) "La France et la guerre russo-japonaise, 1895–1905," unpublished thesis, University of Paris.

Churchill, W.S. (1923) *The World Crisis*, London: Thornton-Butterworth.

Clark, C.A. (1904) "The Ainu of Japan," *Missionary Herald*, 100 (February): 63–6.

Clements, K.A. (1987) *Woodrow Wilson: World Statesmen*, Boston, MA: Twayne.

Combs, J.A. (1986) *The History of American Foreign Policy*, New York: Knopf.

Compton-Hall, R. (1983) *Submarine Boats: The Beginnings of Underwater Warfare*, London: Conway Maritime Press.

Connaughton, R.M. (1988) *The War of the Rising Sun and the Tumbling Bear: A Military History of the Russo-Japanese War 1904–5*, London: Routledge.

Conroy, H. (1960) *The Japanese Seizure of Korea: 1868–1910*, Philadelphia, PA: University of Pennsylvania Press.

Conroy, M.S. (1976) *Petr Arkadevich Stolypin: Practical Politics in Late Tsarist Russia*, Boulder, CO: Westview Press.

Coogan, J.W. (1994) "Wilsonian Diplomacy in War and Peace," in G. Martel (ed.) *American Foreign Relations Reconsidered, 1890—1993*, New York: Routledge, pp. 71–89.

Cook, T.F. (1993) "Heishi to kokka, heishi to shakai: Yōbei sekai e Nihon no Sannyū" ("Soldiers and the State, Soldiers and Society: Japan Joins the Western World"), in Junji Banno (ed.) *Nihon Kin-Gendaishi* (*A History of Modern and Contemporary Japan*), vol. 2: *Shihonshugi to "Jiyūshugi"* (*Capitalism and "Liberalism"*), Tokyo: Iwanami Shōten, pp. 257–98.

Copeland, W.R. (1973) *The Uneasy Alliance: Collaboration between the Finnish Opposition and the Russian Underground, 1899–1904*, Helsinki: Suomalainen tiedeakatemia.

Corbett, J. (1914) *Maritime Operations in the Russo-Japanese War 1904–5*, 2 vols, London: Admiralty War Staff.

Corbett, J.S. and E.J.W. Slade (1914) *Maritime Operations in the Russo-Japanese War, 1904–5*, 2 vols, London: Admiralty War Staff (reprinted, Annapolis, MD: Naval Institute Press, 1994).

Cortazzi, H. and G. Daniels (2002) *Britain and Japan*, London: RoutledgeCurzon.

Cosand, J. (1904) "A Pan-Religious Conference in Japan," *Missionary Review of the World*, 27 (August): 573–4.

Coté, J. (1996) "Communicating the Modern: Dutch and Vernacular Language Press and Indonesian Modernity Around 1900," paper presented at the 20th ASAA Conference, Monash University, Victoria, July 8–11.

Cox, G.P. (1992) "Of Aphorisms, Lessons and Paradigms: Comparing the British and German Official Histories of the Russo-Japanese War," *The Journal of Military History*, 56: 389–401.

Creese, H. (2004) "Three Transitional Texts: Turn of the Century Balinese Views of the World," in R. Cribb (ed.) *Asia Examined: Proceedings of the 15th Biennial Conference of the ASAA, 2004, Canberra, Australia*, Canberra: Asian Studies Association of Australia (ASAA) and Research School of Pacific and Asian Studies (RSPAS), The Australian National University.

Cronin J. (1996) *The World the Cold War Made: Order, Chaos, and the Return of History*, New York: Routledge.

Crowl, P.A. (1986) "Alfred Thayer Mahan: The Naval Historian," in P. Paret (ed.) *Makers of Modern Strategy: From Machiavelli to the Nuclear Age*, Princeton, NJ: Princeton University Press, pp. 444–77.

Crump, J. (1983) *The Origins of Socialist Thought in Japan*, London: Croom Helm.

Cumings, B. (1997) *Korea's Place in the Sun: A Modern History*, New York: W.W. Norton.

Current Opinion (1913) "Ethnological Basis of the Japanese Claim to be a White Race," *Current Opinion*, 55 (July): 38–9.

Dadabhai, N. (1917) *Speeches and Writings*, Madras: Nateson.

Dale, P. (1986) *The Myth of Japanese Uniqueness*, London: Croom Helm.

Daniels, R. (1977) *The Politics of Prejudice: The Anti-Japanese Movement in California and the Struggle for Japanese Exclusion*, 2nd edn, Berkeley, CA: University of California Press.

Danrit (pseudonym of E. Driant) (1909) *L'Invasion jaune*, 3 vols, Paris: Flammarion.

De Ceuster, K. (2002) "The Nation Exorcised: The Historiography of Collaboration in South Korea," *Korean Studies*, 25: 207–42.

DeForest, J.H. (1905) "The Japanese Environment and Christianity," *Missionary Herald*, 101 (April): 168–70.

Dennis, A.L.P. (1969) *Adventures in American Diplomacy, 1898–1906*, New York: Johnson Reprint Corporation.

Deringil, S. (2003) "Ottoman Japanese Relations in the Late Nineteenth Century," in S. Esenbel and C. Inaba (eds) *The Rising Sun and the Turkish Crescent: New Perspectives on the History of Japanese–Turkish Relations*, Istanbul: Bogazici University Press, pp. 42–8.

Dickinson, F.R. (2005) "Commemorating the War in Post-Versailles Japan," in J.W. Steinberg, B. Menning, D. Schimmelpenninck van der Oye, D. Wolff, and S. Yokote (eds) *The Russo-Japanese War in Global Perspective: World War Zero*, Leiden: Brill, pp. 523–43.

Dobson, S. (ed.) (2000) *The Russo-Japanese War: Reports from Officers Attached to the Japanese Forces in the Field (London 1905–6)*, Bristol: Ganesha Publications. "Introduction" available online at www.ganesha-publishing.com/russo_jap_into.htm (accessed January 2, 2006).

Dreifort, J.E. (1991) *Myopic Grandeur: The Ambivalence of French Foreign Policy Toward the Far East, 1919–1945*, Kent, OH: Kent State University Press.

Dua, R.P. (1966) *The Impact of the Russo-Japanese (1905) War on Indian Politics*, Delhi: S. Chand.

Dugdale, E.T.S. (1930) *German Diplomatic Documents, 1871–1914, vol. 3: The Growing Antagonism, 1898–1910*, London: Methuen.

Duiker, W.J. (1977) *Ts'ai Yuan-p'ei, Educator of Modern China*, University Park, PA: Pennsylvania State University Press.

Dunne, P.F. (1904) "Mr. Dooley on the War in the Far East," *St Louis Post-Dispatch*, August 28: 1B.

Duret, T. (1904) "La transformation européenne du Japon," *L'Européen*, 155 (November 19): 1–2.

Dutta, K.K. (1969) *The Year 1905: A Turning Point in Asian History: Proceedings of the Seminar on Studies in Asian History*, New Delhi: ICCR.

Duus, P. (1983) "The Takeoff Point in Japanese Imperialism," in H. Wray and H. Conroy (eds) *Japan Examined: Perspectives on Modern Japanese History*, Honolulu, HI: University of Hawaii Press, pp. 153–7.

Duus, P. (1995) *The Abacus and the Sword: The Japanese Penetration of Korea, 1895–1910*, Berkeley, CA: University of California Press.

Duus, P., R.H. Myers, and M.R. Peattie (eds) (1989) *The Japanese Informal Empire in China, 1895–1937*, Princeton, NJ: Princeton University Press.

Eckert, C.J., Lee, K.-B., Lew, Y.-I., Robinson, M., and Wagner, E.W. (1990) *Korea Old and New: A History*, Seoul: Ilchokak.

Edström, B. (1998) *Japan as a Model for Sweden*, Working Paper 47, Stockholm: Center for Pacific Asia Studies, Stockholm University.

Edström, B. (2002) "Introduction," in B. Edström (ed.) *Turning Points in Japanese History*, Richmond, Surrey: Japan Library, pp. 1–16.

Edwardes, M. (1967) *The West in Asia 1850–1914*, London: Batsford.

Edwards, E.W. (1954) "The Far Eastern Agreements of 1907," *Journal of Modern History*, 26: 340–55.

Ellis, J. (1975) *The Social History of the Machine Gun*, London: Croom Helm.

Elman, B.A. (2004) "Naval Warfare and the Refraction of China's Self-strengthening Reforms into Scientific and Technological Failure," *Modern Asian Studies*, 38: 283–326.

Epkenhans, M. (1991) *Die wilhelminische Flottenrüstung 1908–1914: Weltmachtstreben, industrieller Fortschritt, soziale Integration*, Munich: Oldenbourg.

Epkenhans, M. (2001) "Technology, Shipbuilding and Future Combat in Germany, 1880–1914," in P. O'Brien (ed.) *Technology and Naval Combat in the Twentieth Century and Beyond*, London: Frank Cass, pp. 53–68.

Erickson Healy, A. (1976) *The Russian Autocracy in Crisis*, Hamden, CT: Archon Books.

Esenbel, S. (2004) "Japan's Global Claim to Asia and the World of Islam: Transnational Nationalism and World Power, 1900–1945," *The American Historical Review*, 109: 1140–70.

Esthus, R.A. (1968) *Theodore Roosevelt and Japan*, Seattle, WA: University of Washington Press.

Esthus, R.A. (1986) *Double Eagle and Rising Sun: The Russians and Japanese at Portsmouth in 1905*, Durham, NC: Duke University Press.

Eto, S. (1986) "China's International Relations 1911–1931," in J.K. Fairbank and A. Feuerwerker (eds) *The Cambridge History of China, vol. 13: Republican China 1912–1949, Part 2*, Cambridge: Cambridge University Press, pp. 74–115.

Evans, D.C. (2001) "Japanese Naval Construction, 1878–1918," in P. O'Brien (ed.) *Technology and Naval Combat in the Twentieth Century and Beyond*, London: Frank Cass, pp. 22–35.

Evans, D.C. and M.R. Peattie (1997) *Kaigun: Strategy, Tactics, and Technology in the Imperial Japanese Navy, 1887–1941*, Annapolis, MD: Naval Institute Press.

Fairbanks, C.H. (1991) "The Origins of the Dreadnought Revolution: A Historiographical Essay," *International History Review*, 13: 246–72.

Fakhr al-Din, F.M. (1965) *Tarikh indunisia al-adabi wa-l-tahriri wa-l-islami*, Cairo: al-Dar al-qawmiyya li-l-thaqafa li-l-nashr.

Fält, O.K. (1976) "Collaboration between Japanese Intelligence and the Finnish Underground during the Russo-Japanese War," *Asian Profile* (Hong Kong), 4: 205–38.

Fält, O.K. (1979) "The Picture of Japan in Finnish Underground Newspapers during the Russo-Japanese War," in I. Nish and C. Dunn (eds) *European Studies on Japan*, Tenterden: Paul Norbury, pp. 130–3.

Fält, O.K. (1988) "The Influence of the Finnish-Japanese Cooperation during the Russo-Japanese War on Relations between Finland and Japan in 1917–1944," in

O.K. Fält and A. Kujala (eds) *Colonel Akashi's Report on His Secret Cooperation with the Russian Revolutionary Parties during the Russo-Japanese War: Selected Chapters*, Helsinki: SHS, pp. 177–95.

Fasseur, C. (1994) "Cornerstone and Stumbling Block: Racial Classification in the Late Colonial State in Indonesia," in R. Cribb (ed.) *The Late Colonial State in Indonesia: Political and Economic Foundations of the Netherlands Indies 1888–1942*, Leiden: KITLV, pp. 31–56.

Ferguson, N. (1999) *The Pity of War*, London: Penguin.

Ferguson, N. (ed.) (1995) *Virtual History: Alternatives and Counterfactuals*, London: Papermac.

Fischer, F. (1975) *War of Illusions: German Policies from 1911 to 1914*, London: Chatto & Windus.

Florinsky, M.T. (1947) *Russia: A History and Interpretation*, vol. 2, New York: Macmillan.

Foley, R.T. (2003) *Alfred von Schlieffen's Military Writings*, London: Frank Cass.

Foley, R.T. (2005) *German Strategy and the Path to Verdun: Erich von Falkenhayn and the Development of Attrition, 1870–1916*, Cambridge: Cambridge University Press.

Foreign Missionary (1877) "Aino Village in Japan," *Foreign Missionary*, 36 (December): 193–4.

Fountain, A.M. (1980) *Roman Dmowski: Party, Tactics, Ideology, 1898–1907*, New York: Columbia University Press.

France (1910–14) *La Guerre Russo-Japonaise de 1904–1905: Historique* (trans. of the Historical Account Published by the General Staff of the Russian Army), 14 vols, Paris: Chapelot.

France, A. (1991) *Sur la pierre blanche: Oeuvres III*, Paris: Gallimard, Pléiade (first edn: Calmann-Lévy, 1905).

French, D. (1987) "The Dardanelles, Mecca and Kut: Prestige as a Factor in British Eastern Strategy," *War & Society*, 5: 45–61.

Friedman, S.I. (1940) "Indian Nationalism and the Far East," *Pacific Affairs*, 13: 17–27.

Fujitani, T. (1996) *Splendid Monarchy: Power and Pageantry in Modern Japan*, Berkeley, CA: University of California Press.

Fuller, W.C. (1985) *Civil-Military Conflict in Imperial Russia 1881–1914*, Princeton, NJ: Princeton University Press.

Fuller, W.C. (1992) *Strategy and Power in Russia 1600–1914*, New York: Free Press.

Galai, S. (1973) *The Liberation Movement in Russia 1900–1905*, Cambridge: Cambridge University Press.

Gandhi, M. (1960) *Collected Works of Mahatma Gandhi*, vol. 4, Ahmedabad: Publications Division, Ministry of Information and Broadcasting, Government of India.

Gandhi, M. (1961) *Collected Works of Mahatma Gandhi, 1905–1906*, vol. 5, Ahmedabad: Publications Division, Ministry of Information and Broadcasting, Government of India.

Gandhi, M. (1967) *Collected Works of Mahatma Gandhi*, vol. 6, Ahmedabad: Publications Division, Ministry of Information and Broadcasting, Government of India.

Garner, J.W. (1904) "Records of Political Events," *Political Science Quarterly*, 19: 331–68.

Garraty, J.A. and P. Gay (eds) (1972) *The Columbia History of the World*, New York: Harper & Row.

Gasster, M. (1969) *Chinese Intellectuals and the Revolution of 1911: The Birth of Modern Chinese Radicalism*, Seattle, WA: University of Washington Press.

Gatrell, P. (1986) *The Tsarist Economy, 1850–1917*, New York: St Martin's Press.

Geifman, A. (2000) *Entangled in Terror: The Azef Affair and the Russian Revolution*, Wilmington, DE: Scholarly Resources.

Geiss, I. (1967) *July 1914: The Outbreak of the First World War—Selected Documents*, New York: Norton.

George, J.L. (1998) *History of Warships*, Annapolis, MD: Naval Institute Press.

German General Staff, Historical Section (1908–14) *The Russo-Japanese War*, 7 vols, London: Hugh Rees.

Germany (1910–11) *Der japanisch-russische Seekrieg 1904–1905: Amtliche Darstellung des Japanischen Admiralstabes* (The Official Report of the Japanese Admiralty), 3 vols, Berlin: E.S. Mittler & Son.

Germany (1911–12) *Der russisch-japanische Krieg: Amtliche Darstellung des Russischen Generalstabes*, 10 text vols., trans. Eberhard von Tettau, Berlin: E.S. Mittler & Son.

Gerschenkron, A. (1962) *Economic Backwardness in Historical Perspective: A Book of Essays*, Cambridge, MA: Belknap Press of Harvard University Press.

Giessler, K.-V. (1976) *Die Institution des Marineattachés im Kaiserreich*, Boppard am Rhein: Harald Boldt.

Gilbert, M. (1997) *A History of the Twentieth Century*, vol. 1, London: HarperCollins.

Gluck, C. (1985) *Japan's Modern Myths: Ideology in the Late Meiji Period*, Princeton, NJ: Princeton University Press.

Gokhale, G.K. (1918) *Speeches and Writings*, Madras: G.A. Natesan.

Goldrick, J. (1995) "The Battleship Fleet: The Test of War, 1895–1919," in J.R. Hill (ed.) *The Oxford Illustrated History of the Royal Navy*, Oxford: Oxford University Press, pp. 280–318.

Goldstein, E. (1994) "The Evolution of British Diplomatic Strategy for the Washington Conference," in E. Goldstein and J. Maurer (eds) *The Washington Conference, 1921–22: Naval Rivalry, East Asian Stability and the Road to Pearl Harbor*, London: Frank Cass, pp. 4–34.

Gooch, G.P. and H.W.V. Temperley (eds) (1926–38) *British Documents on the Origins of the War*, 11 vols, London: H.M. Stationery Office.

Gooch, J. (1974) *The Plans of War: The General Staff and British Military Strategy*, London: Routledge & Kegan Paul.

Gordon, M.L. (1899) "Japan's New Treaties and Their Effect on Mission Work," *Missionary Herald*, 95 (September): 363–5.

Gotō, K. (1997) *"Returning to Asia": Japan-Indonesia Relations 1930s–1942*, Tokyo: Ryukei Shosha.

Gotō, K. (2003) *Tensions of Empire: Japan and Southeast Asia in the Colonial and Postcolonial World*, Athens, OH: Ohio University Press.

Goudswaard, J.M. (1952) *Some Aspects of the End of Britain's "Splendid Isolation," 1898–1904*, Rotterdam: Brusse's Uitgeversmaatschappij.

Gough, B.M. (1988) "Maritime Strategy: The Legacies of Mahan and Corbett as Philosophers of Sea Power," *RUSI Journal*, 133 (4): 55–62.

Graham, D. (1982) "The British expeditionary Force of 1914 and the Machine Gun," *Military Affairs*, 46: 190–3.

Granville, J.A.S. (1985) "Diplomacy and War Plans in the United States, 1890–1914," in P.M. Kennedy (ed.) *The War Plans of the Great Powers 1880–1914*, Boston, MA: Allen & Unwin, pp. 23–38.

Gray, E. (1975) *The Devil's Device: The Story of Robert Whitehead, Inventor of the Torpedo*, London: Seeley, Service, & Co.

Great Britain, Committee of Imperial Defence (1906–10) *Official History of the Russo-Japanese War*, 5 vols, London: HMSO.

Great Britain, Committee of Imperial Defence (1910–20) *Official History (Naval and Military) of the Russo-Japanese War*, 3 text vols and 3 map vols, London: HMSO.

Great Britain, War Office, General Staff (1906–8) *Official History (Naval and Military) of the Russo-Japanese War*, 3 vols, London: HMSO.

Greenwood, J. (1971) "The American Military Observers of the Russo-Japanese War (1904–1905)," unpublished Ph.D. thesis, Kansas State University.

Griffis, W.E. (1904) *Dux Christus: An Outline Study of Japan*, New York: Macmillan.

Griffis, W.E. (1905) "Past and Present Christian Work for Japan," *Missionary Review of the World*, 28 (March): 183–4.

Griffis, W.E. (1906) *The Mikado's Empire*, 11th edn, New York: Harper & Brothers.

Griffis, W.E. (1907a) *The Japanese Nation in Evolution: Steps in the Progress of a Great People*, New York: Thomas Y. Crowell.

Griffis, W.E. (1907b) Promotional pamphlet, Folder 4, Box 1.2, Group 1, William Elliot Griffis Collection, Special Collections and University Archives, Rutgers University Libraries, New Brunswick, NJ.

Griffis, W.E. (1913) "Japan and the United States: Are the Japanese Mongolian?," *North American Review*, 197 (June): 721–33.

Griffith, P. (1994) *Battle Tactics of the Western Front: The British Army's Art of Attack 1916–1918*, New Haven, CT: Yale University Press.

Griswold, A.W. (1938) *The Far Eastern Policy of the United States*, New York: Harcourt, Brace.

Grove, E. (1995) *Big Fleet Actions: Tsushima, Jutland, Philippine Sea*, London: Arms and Armour.

Gulick, S.L. (1905) *The White Peril in the Far East*, New York: Fleming H. Revell.

Gulick, S.L. (1918) *American Democracy and Asiatic Citizenship*, New York: Charles Scribner's Sons.

Guo, T.Y. (ed.) (1963) *Jindai Zhongguo Shishi Rizhi* (Daily Record of Events in Modern Chinese History), *vol. 2: 1886–1911*, Taipei: Institute of Modern History, Academia Sinica.

Gwynn, S. (ed.) (1929) *The Letters and Friendships of Sir Cecil Spring-Rice*, 2 vols, London: Constable.

Hadler, Jeffrey (2005) "Immemorial Custom in the Balance: Haji Abdul Karim Amrullah, Datuk Sanggoeno Di Radjo, and 'Islam versus Adat' in 1919," unpublished manuscript.

Haimson, L. (1965) "The Problem of Social Stability in Urban Russia, 1905–1917," *Slavic Review*, 24: 1–22.

Hall, C. (1987) *Britain, America and Arms Control, 1921–1937*, London: Macmillan.

Hallock, H.G.C. (1905) "The Influence of Japan on China," *Missionary Review of the World*, 28 (October): 756–60.

Halpern, P. (2001) "The French Navy, 1880–1914," in P. O'Brien (ed.) *Technology and Naval Combat in the Twentieth Century and Beyond*, London: Frank Cass, pp. 36–52.

Hamilton, I. (1905) *A Staff Officer's Scrap Book during the Russo-Japanese War*, 2 vols, London: Edwin Arnold.

Hamka (Haji Abdul Malik Karim Amrullah) (1958) *Ajahku: Riwayat hidup Dr. H. Abd. Karim Amrullah dan perdjuangan kaum agama di Sumatera (Tjetakan kedua)*, Jakarta: Widjaja.

Harada, K. (1986) *Nichiro sensō no jiten*, Tokyo: Sanshodō.

Harcave, S. (1964) *First Blood: The Russian Revolution of 1905*, New York: Macmillan.

Harcave, S. (ed.) (1990) *The Memoirs of Count Witte*, Armonk, NY: M.E. Sharpe.

Harrell, P. (1992) *Sowing the Seeds of Change: Chinese Students, Japanese Teachers, 1895–1905*, Stanford, CA: Stanford University Press.

Harris, M.C. (1907) *Christianity in Japan*, Cincinnati, OH: Jennings & Graham.

Hartmann, G.K. and S.C. Truver (1991) *Weapons That Wait: Mine Warfare in the US Navy*, revised edn, Annapolis, MD: Naval Institute Press.

Hata, I. (1988) "Continental Expansion, 1905–1941," in P. Duus (ed.) *The Cambridge History of Japan: The Twentieth Century*, vol. 6, Cambridge: Cambridge University Press, pp. 271–314.

Hata, I. (1996) "From Consideration to Contempt: The Changing Nature of Japanese Military and Popular Perceptions of Prisoners of War through the Ages," in B. Moore and Kent Fedorowich (eds) *Prisoners of War and Their Captors in World War II*, Oxford: Berg, pp. 253–76.

Hatano, Y. (1968) "The New Armies: The First Phase," in M.C. Wright (ed.) *China in Revolution: The First Phase 1900–1913*, New Haven, CT: Yale University Press, pp. 365–82.

Hayne, M.B. (1993) *The French Foreign Office and the Origins of the First World War, 1898–1914*, Oxford: Clarendon.

Henning, J.M. (2000) *Outposts of Civilization: Race, Religion, and the Formative Years of American-Japanese Relations*, New York: New York University Press.

Herrmann, D.G. (1996) *The Arming of Europe and the Making of the First World War*, Princeton, NJ: Princeton University Press.

Hervé, G. (1904a) "Pour le Japon," *Revue de l'enseignement primaire et primaire supérieur (Revue sociale)*, 19 (February 7): 220–1.

Hervé, G. (1904b) "Contre l'alliance franco-russe," *Revue de l'enseignement primaire et primaire supérieur (Revue sociale)*, 25 (March 20): 292–3.

Hervé, G. (1904c) "L'opinion publique française et la guerre russo-japonaise," *Revue de l'enseignement primaire et primaire supérieur (Revue sociale)*, 1 (October 2): 5–6.

Hervé, G. (1904d) "Les défaites russes et les projets de mediation," *Revue de l'enseignement primaire et primaire supérieur (Revue sociale)*, 4 (October 23): 40–1.

Hervé, G. (1905) "La bataille de Moukden," *Revue de l'enseignement primaire et primaire supérieur (Revue sociale)*, 25 (March 19): 291–2.

Herwig, H.H. (1980) *"Luxury" Fleet: The Imperial German Navy, 1888–1918*, London: George Allen & Unwin.

Herwig, H.H. (1991) "The German Reaction to the *Dreadnought* Revolution," *International History Review*, 13: 273–83.

Herwig, H.H. (1997) *The First World War in Germany and Austro-Hungary*, London: Arnold.

Hirama, Y. (2004) *Nichiro sensō ga kaeta sekaishi*, Tokyo: Fuyō Shobō.

Hitchcock, R. (1891) "The Ainos of Yezo, Japan," in The United States National Museum (ed.) *Report of the United States National Museum*, Washington, DC: Government Printing Office, pp. 429–502.

Hitler, A. (1939) *Mein Kampf*, New York: Reynal & Hitchcock.

Hobson, R. (2002) *Imperialism at Sea: Naval Strategic Thought, the Ideology of Sea Power, and the Tirpitz Plan, 1875–1914*, Boston, MA: Brill Academic Publishers.

Hobson, R. (2004) *Maritimer Imperialismus. Seemachtideologie, seestrategisches Denken und der Tirpitzplan 1875 bis 1914*, München: Oldenbourg.

Hodgson, J.H. (1960) "Finland in the Russian Empire, 1904–1910," *Journal of Central European Affairs*, 20: 158–73.

Hong, S.-K. (2001) "Korean minjung's Resistance and the Growth of Modern Consciousness from 1876 to 1910 in Korea," *International Journal of Korean History*, 2: 137–56.

Hopman, A. (1924) *Das Logbuch eines deutschen Seeoffiziers*, Berlin: August Scherl.

Hopman, A. (2004) *Das ereignisreiche Leben eines "Wilhelminers": Tagebücher, Briefe, Aufzeichnungen*, ed. M. Epkenhans, Munich: Oldenbourg.

Horsman, R. (1981) *Race and Manifest Destiny: The Origins of American Racial Anglo-Saxonism*, Cambridge: Harvard University Press.

Hoston, G.A. (1986) *Marxism and the Crisis of Development in Prewar Japan*, Princeton, NJ: Princeton University Press.

Hoston, G.A. (1994) *The State, Identity, and the National Question in China and Japan*, Princeton, NJ: Princeton University Press.

Houge, R. (1964) *Dreadnought: A History of the Modern Battleship*, New York: Macmillan.

Hough, R.A. (1983) *The Great War at Sea, 1914–1918*, Oxford: Oxford University Press.

Howard, M. (1974) *The Continental Commitment: The Dilemma of British Defence Policy in the Era of the Two World Wars*, Harmondsworth: Penguin.

Howard, M. (1984) "Men Against Fire: Expectations of War in 1914," *International Security*, 9: 3–17.

Howard, M. (1986) "Men Against Fire: The Doctrine of the Offensive in 1914," in P. Paret (ed.) *Makers of Modern Strategy: From Machiavelli to the Nuclear Age*, Princeton, NJ: Princeton University Press, pp. 510–26.

Howard, M. (1997) "Europe on the Eve of the First World War," in H. Herwig (ed.) *The Outbreak Of World War I: Causes and Responsibilities*, Boston, MA: Houghton Mifflin, pp. 21–34.

Howarth, S. (1999) *To Shining Sea: A History of the United States Navy, 1775–1998*, Norman, OK: University of Oklahoma Press.

Hubatsch, Walther (1955) *Die Ära Tirpitz: Studien zur deutschen Marinepolitik 1890–1918*, Göttingen: Musterschmidt.

Hulbert, H.B. (1904) "The Russo-Japanese War and Christian Missions in the East," *Missionary Review of the World*, 27 (August): 570–2.

Humble, R. (1982) *Aircraft Carriers: The Illustrated History*, Secaucus, NJ: Chartwell Books.

Hume, D. (1777 [1975]) *Enquiries Concerning Human Understanding and Concerning the Principles of Morals*, ed. P.H. Nidditch, Oxford: Clarendon Press.

Hunt, M.H. (1987) *Ideology and US Foreign Policy*, New Haven, CT: Yale University Press.

Hürter, J. (1998) *Paul von Hintze: Marineoffizier, Diplomat, Staatssekretär. Dokumente einer Karriere zwischen Militär und Politik, 1903–1918*, Munich: Harald Boldt.

Hwang, M.-H. (1998) "Pukhan yŏksa hakkye ŭi minjok undongsa yŏn'gu tonghyang," in Han'guk minjok undongsa yŏn'gu hoe (eds) *Han'guk minjok undongsa ŭi saeroun panghyang*, Seoul: Kukhak charyo wŏn, pp. 33–57.

Iakovlev, N.N. (1957) *Vooruzhennye vosstaniia v dekabre 1905 goda*, Moscow: Gos. Izd-vo Politicheskoi Literatury.

Ienaga, T. (1904) "Japan's Claims against Russia," *Independent*, 56 (February 11): 303–4.

Ike, N. (ed.) (1967) *Japan's Decision for War: Records of the 1941 Policy Conference*, Stanford, CA: Stanford University Press.

Ikeda, K. (1982) "Japanese Strategy and the Pacific War, 1941–5," in I. Nish (ed.) *The Anglo-Japanese Alienation, 1919–1952*, Cambridge: Cambridge University Press, pp. 125–46.

Imbrie, W.M. (1906) *The Church of Christ in Japan: A Course of Lectures*, Philadelphia, PA: Westminster Press.

Inaba, C. (1992) "Polish-Japanese Military Collaboration during the Russo-Japanese War," *Japan Forum*, 4: 229–46.

Inoue, K. (1953) *Nihon gunkokushugi*, 2 vols, Tokyo: Tōkyō Daigaku Shuppankai.

Inoue, K. (1968) *Nihon teikokushugi no keisei*, Tokyo: Iwanami Shoten.

Iriye, A. (1966) *Nihon no gaikō: Meiji ishin kara gendai made*, Tokyo: Chūō Kōronsha.

Iriye, A. (1967) *Across the Pacific: An Inner History of American: East Asian Relations*, New York: Harcourt, Brace & World.

Iriye, A. (1972) *Pacific Estrangement: Japanese and American Expansion, 1897–1911*, Cambridge, MA: Harvard University Press.

Iriye, A. (1977) *From Nationalism to Internationalism: United States Foreign Policy to 1914*, London: Routledge & Kegan Paul.

Iriye, A. (1989) "Japan's Drive to Great-power Status," in M.B. Jansen (ed.) *The Cambridge History of Japan*, vol. 5, Cambridge: Cambridge University Press, pp. 721–82.

Israel, U. and J. Gebauer (1991) *Panzerschiffe um 1900*, Berlin: Brandenburgisches Verlagshaus.

Itō, I. (1929) *Katō Kōmei*, Tokyo: Kato Haku Denki Hensan Iinkai.

James, R.R. (ed.) (1974) *Winston S. Churchill: His Complete Speeches, 1897–1963*, London: Chelsea House.

Jansen, M.B. (1954) *The Japanese and Sun Yat-sen*, Cambridge, MA: Harvard University Press.

Jansen, M.B. (1965) "Changing Japanese Attitudes Toward Modernization," in M.B. Jansen (ed.) *Changing Japanese Attitudes Toward Modernization*, Princeton, NJ: Princeton University Press, pp. 49–83.

Jansen, M.B. (1975) *Japan and China: From War to Peace, 1894–1972*, Chicago, IL: Rand McNally.

Jansen, M.B. (1980) "Konoe Atsumaro," in A. Iriye (ed.) *The Chinese and the Japanese: Essays in Political and Cultural Interactions*, Princeton, NJ: Princeton University Press, pp. 107–23.

Jansen, M.B. (2000) *The Making of Modern Japan*, Cambridge, MA: Belknap Press of Harvard University Press.

Janson, A. von (1905) *Das Zusammenwirken von Heer und Flotte im russisch-japanischen Kriege 1904/5*, Berlin: R. Eisenschmidt.

Japan, General Staff (1906) *Meiji 37–8-nen sen'eki kanjō utushi*, 4 vols, Tokyo: Rikugunshō.

Japan, General Staff (1912) *Meiji 37–8-nen nichiro sensōshi*, 3 vols, Tokyo: Kaikōsha.

Japan, Ministry of Foreign Affairs (1944 [1971]) *Nichiro koshōshi*, Tokyo: Hara Shobō.

Japan, Ministry of Foreign Affairs Archives (1914) *Oshu Sensō kankei nichi-ei-ro-futsu shikoku no dōmei ni kansuru iken kōkan ikken*, Tokyo: Ministry of Foreign Affairs.

Japan, Ministry of Foreign Affairs Archives (1915–16) *Dayonkai nichiro kyōyaku teiketsu kankei ikken*, Tokyo: Ministry of Foreign Affairs.

Japan Weekly Mail (1904) "The Religious Bodies in Japan," *Japan Weekly Mail*, May 21: 580.

Al-Jarjawi (al-Girgawi), A.A. (1908) *Al-Rihla al-yabaniyya*, Cairo: al-Irshad.

Jessup, P.C. (1938) *Elihu Root*, 2 vols, New York: Dodd, Mead.

Johnson, H. (1994) *Breakthrough: Tactics, Technology and the Search for Victory on the Western Front in World War I*, Navato, CA: Presidio.

Jones, E.H. (1895) "Japan after the War," *Baptist Missionary Magazine*, 75 (December): 573–6.

Joseph, P. (1928) *Foreign Diplomacy in China, 1894–1900: A Study in Political and Economic Relations with China*, London: George Allen & Unwin.

Judge, E.H. (1992) *Easter in Kishinev: Anatomy of a Pogrom*, New York: New York University Press.

Jukes, G. (2003) *The Russo-Japanese War, 1904–1905*, Oxford: Osprey.

Jungar, S. (1969) *Ryssland och den Svensk-Norska Upplösning: Tsardiplomati och rysk-finländsk pressopinion kring Unionsopplösning från 1880 till 1905*, Åbo: Åbo Akademi.

Kahan, A. (1989) *Russian Economic History: The Nineteenth Century*, Chicago, IL: University of Chicago Press.

Kajima, M. (1976–80) *The Diplomacy of Japan, 1894–1922*, 3 vols, Tokyo: Kajima Institute of International Peace.

Kamil, M. (1904) *Al-Shams al-mushriqa*, Cairo: Al-Liwa'.

Kamil, M. (1906) *Matahari memancar*, trans. Abdullah bin Abdul Rahman, Singapore: Al-Imam.

Kaneko, K. (1904) "The Yellow Peril is the Golden Opportunity for Japan," *North American Review*, 179 (November): 641–8.

Kaneko, K. (1905) "The Far East after the War," *World's Work*, 9 (February): 5868–71.

Kaneko, K. (1929) *Nichiro sen'eki no hiroku*, Tokyo: Hakubunkan.

Kang, M.-G. (1990) "How History is Viewed in the North and in the South: Convergence and Divergence," *Korea Journal*, 30 (2): 4–19.

Kang, M.-G. (1999) *20 segi uri yŏksa*, Seoul: Ch'angjak kwa pip'yŏng.

Kang, M.-G., Kim, N.-S. and Kim, Y.-H. (eds) (1994) *Han'guksa*, vol. 12, Seoul: Han'gilsa.

Kang, S.-H. (1981) "Impact of the Russo-Japanese War on the Northeast Asian Regional Subsystem: The War's Causes, Outcome and Aftermath," Ph.D. dissertation, Northern Illinois University.

Kassim Ahmad (ed.) (1975) *Hikayat Hang Tuah*, Kuala Lumpur: Dewan Bahasa dan Pustaka.

Kautter, O. (1910) *Unter der Flagge Schwarz-Weiss-Rot vom Seekadetten bis zum Oberleutnant z. See*, Nürtingen: Self-published.

Kawakami, H. (1911 [1964]) "Nihon dokutoku no kokkashugi," in *Kawakami Hajime chosakushū*, Tokyo: Chikuba Shobō, pp. 185–210.

Kawamoto, K. (1984) "The Viet-Nam Quang Phuc Hoi and the 1911 Revolution," in S. Eto and H.Z. Schiffrin (eds) *The 1911 Revolution in China: Interpretive Essays*, Tokyo: University of Tokyo Press, pp. 115–27.

Kawamura, N. (2000) *Turbulence in the Pacific: Japanese-US Relations During World War I*, Westport, CT: Praeger.

Keene, D. (2002) *Emperor of Japan: Meiji and His World, 1852–1912*, New York: Columbia University Press.

Kennan, G. (1904) "Which Is the Civilized Power?," *Outlook*, 78 (October 9): 515–23.

Kennan, G. (1912) "Can We Understand the Japanese?," *Outlook*, 101 (August 10): 815–22.

Kennedy, P. (1980) *The Rise of the Anglo-German Antagonism, 1860–1914*, London: Allen & Unwin.

Kennedy, P. (1981) *The Realities Behind Diplomacy: Background Influence on British External Policies, 1865–1980*, London: Fontana Press.

Kennedy, P. (1983) *Strategy and Diplomacy, 1870–1945*, London: George Allen & Unwin.

Kennedy, P. (1988) *The Rise and Fall of the Great Powers*, New York: Random House.

Kennedy, P. (1989) *Strategy and Diplomacy, 1870–1945*, London: Fontana.

Kenny, L.M. (1976) "East versus West in *al-Muqtataf*, 1875–1900: Image and Self-image," in D. Little (ed.) *Essays on Islamic Civilization: Presented to Niyazi Berkes*, Leiden: Brill, pp. 140–54.

Ker, J.C. (1973) *Political Trouble in India, 1907–1917*, Calcutta: Editions India.

Kerr, G.H. (1945) "Kodama Report: Plan for Conquest," *Far Eastern Survey*, 14 (14): 185–90.

Kim, C.I.E. (1966) "Korea in the year of Ulsa," *Asian Survey*, 6 (1): 34–42.

Kim, C.I.E. and H.K. Kim (1967) *Korea and the Politics of Imperialism 1876–1910*, Berkeley, CA: University of California Press.

Kimitada, M. (1974) *Nichibei kankei no ishiki to kōzō*, Tokyo: Nansōsha.

Kita, I. (1906 [1959]) "Kokutairon oyobi junsei shakaishugi," reprinted in *Kita Ikki chōsakushū*, 2 vols, Tokyo: Misuzu shobō, vol. I, p. 213.

Kitaoka, S. (1978) *Nihon rikugun to tairiku seisaku*, Tokyo: Tōkyō Daigaku Shuppankai.

Knapp, A.M. (1897) *Feudal and Modern Japan*, vol. 1, Boston, MA: Joseph Knight.

Knapp, A.M. (1912) "Who Are the Japanese?," *Atlantic Monthly*, 110 (September): 333–40.

Knightly, P. (1975) *The First Casualty: The War Correspondent as Hero, Propagandist and Myth*, New York: Harcourt, Brace, Javanovich.

Kokovtsov, V.N. (1935) *Out of My Past: The Memoirs of Count Kokovtsov: Russian Minister of Finance 1900–1914, Chairman of the Council of Ministers 1911–1914*, Stanford, CA: Stanford University Press.

Kowner, R. (1998) "Nicholas II and the Japanese Body: Images and Decision Making on the Eve of the Russo-Japanese War," *The Psychohistory Review*, 26: 211–52.

Kowner, R. (2000a) "Japan's Enlightened War: Military Conduct and Attitudes to the Enemy During the Russo-Japanese War," in B. Edström (ed.) *The Japanese and Europe: Images and Perceptions*, Folkstone: Japan Library, pp. 134–51.

Kowner, R. (2000b) "'Lighter than Yellow, But Not Enough': Western Discourse on the Japanese 'Race,' 1854–1904," *Historical Journal*, 43: 103–31.

Kowner, R. (2001) "Becoming an Honorary Civilized Nation: Remaking Japan's Military Image during the Russo-Japanese War," *The Historian*, 64: 19–38.

Kowner, R. (2006) *Historical Dictionary of the Russo-Japanese War*, Lanham, MD: Scarecrow Press.

Kowner, R. (ed.) (2007) *Rethinking the Russo-Japanese War: Centennial Perspectives*, Folkstone: Global Oriental.

Krasnyi arkhiv (1924) "Russko-germanskii dogovor 1904 goda, zakliuchennyi v Berke," *Krasnyi arkhiv*, 5: 5–49.

Krasnyi arkhiv (1927) "Perepiska Nikolaia II i Mariia Federovny (1905–1906 gg.)," *Krasnyi arkhiv*, 22: 153–209.

Krasnyi arkhiv (1932) "Iz perepiski Nikolai i Mariia Romanovykh v 1907–1910 gg.," *Krasnyi arkhiv*, 50–1: 161–93.

Kublin, H. (1950) "The Japanese Socialists and the Russo-Japanese War," *Journal of Modern History*, 22: 322–40.

Kujala, A. (1980) "The Russian Revolutionary Movement and the Finnish Opposition, 1905: The John Grafton Affair and the Plans for an Uprising in St. Petersburg," *Scandinavian Journal of History*, 5: 257–75.

Kuropatkin, A.N. (1922) Dnevnik A.N. Kuropatkina, *Krasnyi arkhiv*, 2: 5–117.

Kusber, J. (1997) *Krieg und Revolution in Russland, 1904–1906: Das Militar im Verhaltnis zu Wirtschaft, Autokratie und Gesellschaft*, Stuttgart: Steiner.

Kusber, J. (2007) "Soldiers' Unrest in the Rear of the Front after the War," in R. Kowner (ed.) *Rethinking the Russo-Japanese War: Centennial Perspectives*, Folkstone: Global Oriental.

LaFeber, W. (1993) *The Cambridge History of American Foreign Policy*, vol. 2, Cambridge: Cambridge University Press.

Laffan, M.F. (1996) "Watan and Negeri: Mustafa Kamil's 'Rising Sun' in the Malay World," *Indonesia Circle* 69: 156–75.

Laffan, M.F. (2001) "Making Meiji Muslims: The Travelogue of 'Ali Ahmad al-Jarjawi," *East Asian History*, 22: 145–70.

Laffan, M.F. (2003) *Islamic Nationhood and Colonial Indonesia: The Umma below the Winds*, London: RoutledgeCurzon.

Laffey, J.F. (1989) "French Far Eastern Policy in the 1930s," *Modern Asian Studies*, 23: 119–49.

Lajpat, Rai, L. (1918) *Young India*, New York: B.W. Huebsch.

Lambert, A.D. (ed.) (1992) *Steam, Steel, and Shellfire: The Steam Warship, 1815–1905*, London: Conway Maritime Press.

Lambert, N.A. (1999) *Sir John Fisher's Naval Revolution*, Columbia, SC: University of South Carolina Press.

Lambert, N.A. (2001a) "Admiral Sir John Fisher and the Concept of Flotilla Defence, 1904–1909," in P. O'Brien (ed.) *Technology and Naval Combat in the Twentieth Century and Beyond*, London: Frank Cass, pp. 69–90.

Lambert, N.A. (ed.) (2001b) *The Submarine Service, 1900–1918*, Aldershot: Ashgate.

Lambi, I.N. (1984) *The Navy and German Power Politics, 1862–1914*, Boston, MA and London: Allen & Unwin.

Layman, R.D. (1989) *Before the Aircraft Carrier: The Development of Aviation Vessels, 1849–1922*, Annapolis, MD: Naval Institute Press.

Lea, H. (1909) *The Valor of Ignorance*, New York: Harper & Brothers.

Lee, C.-S. (1965) *The Politics of Korean Nationalism*, Berkeley, CA: University of California Press.

Lee, J. (2000) *A Soldier's Life: General Sir Ian Hamilton, 1853–1947*, London: Macmillan.

Lee, K.-B. (1984) *A New History of Korea*, Seoul: Ilchokak.

Lee, S. (1927) *King Edward VII: A Biography*, 2 vols, London: Macmillan.

Lehmann, J.-P. (1978) *The Image of Japan: From Feudal Isolation to World Power, 1850–1905*, London and Boston, MA: Allen & Unwin.

Lensen, G.A. (1959) *The Russian Push Toward Japan: Russo-Japanese Relations, 1697–1875*, Princeton, NJ: Princeton University Press.

Lensen, G.A. (1982) *Balance of Intrigue: International Rivalry in Korea and Manchuria, 1884–99*, 2 vols, Tallahassee, FL: The Diplomatic Press.

Lepsius, J., Mendelssohn-Bartholdy, A., and Thimme, F. (eds) (1922–7) *Die Grosse Politik der europäischen Kabinette, 1871–1914*, 40 vols, Berlin: Arbeitsausschuß Deutscher Verbände.

Leroy-Beaulieu, P. (1900) *La Rénovation de l'Asie*, Paris: A. Colin.

Lerski, J.J. (1959) "A Polish Chapter of the Russo-Japanese War," *The Transactions of Asiatic Society of Japan*, 3rd series, 7: 69–97.

Levine, I.D. (ed.) (1920) *The "Willy–Nicky" Letters: Letters from the Kaiser to the Czar*, New York: Frederick S. Stokes.

Levitsky, N.A. (2003) *Russko-iaponskaya voina* (reprint of the 1935 edn), St Petersburg: Terra Fantastica.

Lévy, C. (1995) "Les socialistes japonais et le péril jaune," *Les Carnets de l'exotisme*, 15–16: 129–43.

Lew, Y.-I. (1985) "Japanese Challenge and Korean response, 1870–1910: A Brief Historical Survey," *Korea Journal*, 25 (12): 36–51.

Li, K. (1994) "Zhao Erxun and the Political Situation in the Northeast during the Xinhai Revolution," in S. Eto and H.Z. Schiffrin (eds) *China's Republican Revolution*, Tokyo: Tokyo University Press, pp. 41–52.

Li, U.B. (1914) *Outlines of Chinese History*, Shanghai: Commercial Press.

Liddell Hart, B.H. (1930 [1972]) *History of the First World War* (originally: *The Real War, 1914–1918*), London: Pan Books.

Liddell Hart, B.H. (1944 [1972]) *Why Do We Not Learn from History?*, London: Allen & Unwin.

Lieven, D. (1980) "Pro-Germans and Russian Foreign Policy, 1890–1914," *International History Review*, 2: 24–54.

Lieven, D. (1983) *Russia and the Origins of the First World War*, New York: St Martin's Press.

Liew, K.S. (1971) *Struggle for Democracy: Sung Chiao-jen and the 1911 Chinese Revolution*, Berkeley and Los Angeles, CA: University of California Press.

Lin, Y.T. (1936) *A History of the Press and Public Opinion in China*, Chicago, IL: University of Chicago Press.

Literary Digest (1907) "What the Japanese War Rumors Mean," *Literary Digest*, 34 (June 22): 977–9.

Lone, S. (1988) "Of 'Collaboration' and Kings: The Ilchinhoe, Korean Court, and Japanese Agricultural-Political Demands during the Russo-Japanese War, 1902–1905," *Papers on Far Eastern History*, 38: 103–24.

Lone, S. (1994) *Japan's First Modern War: Army and Society in the Conflict with China, 1894–95*, New York: St Martin's Press.

Long, J. (1974) "Franco-Russian Relations during the Russo-Japanese War," *Slavonic and East European Review*, 32: 213–33.

Longuet, J. (1905) "Japon: les socialistes et le gouvernement japonais," *L'Européen*, 169 (February 25): 11.

Lothes, (Hauptmann) (1910) "Befestigte Flottenstützpunkte am Beispiel der Kwantung-Halbinsel (Port Arthur 1898 bis 1904)," *Vierteljahreshefte für Truppenführung und Heereskunde*, 7: 556–77.

Lowe, P. (1969) *Great Britain and Japan, 1911–1915: A Study of British Far Eastern Policy*, London: St Martin's Press.

Lu, H. (1956) *Selected Works of Lu Hsun*, vol. 1, Beijing: Foreign Language Press.

Luntinen, P. (1984) *French Information on the Russian War Plans, 1880–1914*, Helsinki: SHS.

McCormack, G. (1977) *Chang Tso-lin in Northeast China, 1911–1928*, Stanford, CA: Stanford University Press.

McDonald, D.M. (1992) *United Government and Foreign Policy in Russia, 1900–1914*, Cambridge, MA: Harvard University Press.

McDonald, D.M. (2005) "Tsushima's echoes: Asian Defeat and the Tsarist Foreign Policy," in J.W. Steinberg, B. Menning, D. Schimmelpenninck van der Oye, D. Wolff, and S. Yokote (eds) *The Russo-Japanese War in Global Perspective: World War Zero*, Leiden: Brill, pp. 545–63.

McGee, W.J. (1904) "Introduction," in J.W. Buel (ed.) *Louisiana and the Fair: An Exposition of the World, Its People, and Their Achievements*, vol. 5, St Louis: World's Progress Publishing, pp. i–xv.

Mackay, R.F. (1973) *Fisher of Kilverstone*, Oxford: Clarendon Press.

McKenzie, F.A. (1969 [1920]) *Korea's Fight for Freedom*, reprinted edn, Seoul: Yonsei University Press.

Mackenzie, S.P. (1999) "Willpower or Firepower? The Unlearned Military Lessons of the Russo-Japanese War," in D. Wells and S. Wilson (eds) *The Russo-Japanese War in Cultural Perspective, 1904–05*, Basingstoke: Macmillan, pp. 30–40.

McLean, R.R. (2003) "Dreams of a German Europe: Wilhelm II and the Treaty of Björkö of 1905," in A. Mombauer and W. Deist (eds) *The Kaiser: New Research on Wilhelm II's Role in Imperial Germany*, Cambridge: Cambridge University Press, pp. 119–42.

McLean, R.R. (2004) *Royalty and Diplomacy in Europe, 1890–1914*, Cambridge: Cambridge University Press.

MacMurray, J.V.A. (ed.) (1921) *Treaties and Agreements With and Concerning China, 1894–1919*, 2 vols, New York: Oxford University Press.

Mahan, A.T. (1890) *The Influence of Sea Power upon History, 1660–1783*, Boston, MA: Little, Brown, & Co.

Mahan, A.T. (1892) *The Influence of Sea Power upon the French Revolution and Empire, 1793–1812*, 2 vols, Boston, MA: Little, Brown, & Co.

Mahan, A.T. (1900) *The Problem of Asia and Its Effect upon International Policies*, Boston, MA: Little, Brown, & Co.

Mahan, A.T. (1906) "Retrospect upon the War between Japan and Russia," *National Review* (May): 142.

Major, J. (1978) "The Navy Plans for War, 1937–1941," in K.J. Hagan (ed.) *In Peace and War—Interpretations of American Naval History, 1775–1978*, Westport, CT: Greenwood Press, pp. 237–61.

Malozemoff, A. (1958) *Russian Far Eastern Policy 1881–1904: With Special Emphasis on the Causes of the Russo-Japanese War*, Berkeley, CA: University of California Press.

Mandal, S. (1997) "Natural Leaders of Native Muslims: Arab Ethnicity and Politics in Java under Dutch Rule," in U. Freitag and W.G. Clarence-Smith (eds) *Hadhrami Traders, Scholars and Statesmen in the Indian Ocean, 1750s-1960s*, Leiden: Brill, pp. 185–98.

Manning, R.T. (1982) *The Crisis of the Old Order in Russia: Gentry and Government*, Princeton, NJ: Princeton University Press.

Marder, A.J. (1940) *The Anatomy of British Sea Power: A History of British Naval Policy in the Pre-Dreadnought Era*, New York: Knopf.

Marder, A.J. (1952) *Fear God and Dread Nought: The Correspondence of Admiral of the Fleet Lord Fisher of Kilverstone: The Making of an Admiral, 1854–1904*, London: Jonathan Cape.

Marder, A.J. (1956) *Fear God and Dread Nought: The Correspondence of Admiral of the Fleet Lord Fisher of Kilverstone: Years of Power, 1904–1914*, London: Jonathan Cape.

Marder, A.J. (1961) *From Dreadnought to Scapa Flow: The Royal Navy in the Fisher Era, 1904–1919*, London: Oxford University Press.

Mark, E. (2003) "Appealing to Asia: Nation, Culture and the Problem of Imperial Modernity in Japanese-occupied Java, 1942–1945," Ph.D. dissertation, Columbia University.

Marks, F.W. (1981) *Velvet on Iron: The Diplomacy of Theodore Roosevelt*, Lincoln, NE: University of Nebraska Press.

Marks, S.G. (2005) "'Bravo, Brave Tiger of the East!': The Russo-Japanese War and the Rise of Nationalism in British Egypt and India," in J.W. Steinberg, B. Menning, D. Schimmelpenninck van der Oye, D. Wolff, and S. Yokote (eds) *The Russo-Japanese War in Global Perspective: World War Zero*, Leiden: Brill, pp. 609–27.

Marr, D.G. (1971) *Vietnamese Anticolonialism, 1885–1925*, Berkeley, CA: University of California Press.

Mason, J.W. (1997) *The Cold War, 1945–1991*, London: Routledge.

Masuda, T. (1982) "Kaigun gunbi kakuchō o meguru seiji katei, 1906–1914," in *Kindai nihon kenkyū, vol. 4: Taiehiyō sensō*, Tokyo: Yamakawa Shuppansha, pp. 411–33.

Mathews, J. (1957) *Reporting the Wars*, Minneapolis, MN: University of Minneapolis Press.

Matignon, J.J. (1907) *Enseignements médicaux de la Guerre Russo-Japonaise*, Paris: A. Maloine.

Matsumura, M. (1987) *Nichiro sensō to Kaneko Kentarō: Kōhō gaikō no kenkyū*, Tokyo: Shin'yūdo.

Matsuo, T. (1966) *Taishō demokurashi-no kenkyū*, Tokyo: Aoki Shoten.

Matsuo, T. (2001) *Taishō demokurashii*, revised edn, Tokyo: Iwanami Shoten.

Matsusaka, Y.T. (2001) *The Making of Japanese Manchuria, 1904–1932*, Cambridge, MA: Harvard University Press.

Matsusaka, Y.T. (2005) "Human Bullets, General Nogi, and the Myth of Port Arthur," in J.W. Steinberg, B. Menning, D. Schimmelpenninck van der Oye, D. Wolff, and S. Yokote (eds) *The Russo-Japanese War in Global Perspective: World War Zero*, Leiden: Brill, pp. 179–201.

May, E.R. (ed.) (1984) *Knowing One's Enemies: Intelligence Assessments Before the Two World Wars*, Princeton, NJ: Princeton University Press.

Meisner, H.O. (1957) *Militärattachés und Militärbevollmächtigte in Preußen und im Deutschen Reich*, Berlin: Rütten & Loening.

Mendel A.P. and T. von Laue (1965) "Comments to Leopold Haimson and Haimson's Reply," *Slavic Review*, 24: 23–56.

Menning, B. (1992) *Bayonets before Bullets: The Imperial Russian Army, 1861–1914*, Bloomington, IN: Indiana University Press.

Middleton, D. (1976) *Submarine, the Ultimate Naval Weapon: Its Past, Present and Future*, Chicago, IL: Playboy Press.

Miliukov, P.N. (1955) *Vospominanii*, 2 vols, New York: n.p.

Miller, E.S. (1991) *War Plan Orange: The US Strategy to Defeat Japan 1897–1945*, Annapolis, MD: Naval Institute Press.

Milner, A.C. (1995) *The Invention of Politics in Colonial Malaya: Contesting Nationalism and the Expansion of the Public Sphere*, Cambridge: Cambridge University Press.

Milton, G. (1999) *Nathaniel's Nutmeg: How One Man's Courage Changed the Course of History*, London: Hodder & Stoughton.

Minami, H. (1994) *Nihonjinron: Meiji kara konnichi made*, Tokyo: Iwanami Shoten.

Ministère des Affaires Étrangères (ed.) (1930–46) *Documents Diplomatiques Français*, 2nd series, 9 vols, Paris: Imprimerie Nationale.

Missionary Review of the World (1904) "Russia, Japan, and Korea," *Missionary Review of the World*, 27 (April): 300.

Mitchell, D.W. (1974) *A History of Russian and Soviet Sea Power*, New York: Macmillan.

Mitchell, R.H. (1983) *Censorship in Imperial Japan*, Princeton, NJ: Princeton University Press.

Miyaji, M. (1973) *Nichiro sensō seijishi no kenkyū*, Tokyo: Tōkyō Daigaku Shuppankai.

Mobini-Kesheh, N. (1999) *The Hadrami Awakening: Community and Identity in the Netherlands East Indies, 1900–1942*, Ithaca, NY: SEAP.

Mombauer, A. (2001) *Helmuth von Moltke and the Origins of the First World War*, Cambridge: Cambridge University Press.

Mombauer, A. (2002) *The Origins of the First World War: Controversies and Consensus*, London: Longman.

Monger, G.W. (1963) *The End of Isolation*, London: T. Nelson.

Morison, E.E. (1951–4) *The Letters of Theodore Roosevelt*, 6 vols, Cambridge, MA: Harvard University Press.

Morita, S. (1926) *Shinkei suijaku oyobi kyōhaku kan'nen no konchihō*, Tokyo: Jitsugyō no nihonsha.

Moritz, A. (1974) "Das Problem des Präventivkrieges in der deutschen Politik während der ersten Marokkokrise," Ph.D. dissertation, Berlin: Freie Universität.

Morrison, G.E. (1976) "Letter to V. Chirol," in Lo Hui-min (ed.) *The Correspondence of G.E. Morrison, vol. I: 1895–1912*, Cambridge: Cambridge University Press, pp. 369–71.

Morton, L. (1959) "War Plan Orange: Evolution of a Strategy," *World Politics*, 11: 221–50.

Mukōyama, H. (1974) "Amoi jiken to keishū jiken," *Kokugakuin Daigaku Kiyō*, 43: 35–54.

Murphey, W.R. (1970) *The Treaty Port and China's Modernization: What Went Wrong?*, Ann Arbor, MI: University of Michigan Press.

Myers, R.H. (1989) "Japanese Imperialism in Manchuria: The South Manchuria Railway Company, 1906–1933," in P. Duus, R.H. Myers, and M.R. Peattie (eds) *The Japanese Informal Empire in China, 1895–1937*, Princeton, NJ: Princeton University Press, pp. 101–32.

Nagazumi, A. (1969) "An Indonesian's View of Japan: Wahidin and the Russo-Japanese War," in F.H.H. King (ed.) *The Development of Japanese Studies in Southeast Asia: Proceedings of the Fourth Leverhulme Conference*, Hong Kong: Centre of Asian Studies, University of Hong Kong, pp. 72–84.

Nahm, A.C. (1988) *Korea: Tradition and Transformation*, Elizabeth, NJ: Hollym International Corp.

Najita, T. (1967) *Hara Kei in the Politics of Compromise, 1905–1915*, Cambridge, MA: Harvard University Press.

Nakamura, M. (1992) *Sengoshi to shōcho tennō*, Tokyo: Iwanami Shoten.

Naquet, A. (1904a) "L'alliance russe: La France est-elle engagée?," *L'Européen*, 119 (March 12): 1–3.

Naquet, A. (1904b) "Russie et Japon," *Annales de la jeunesse laïque*, 22 (March): 297–301.

Narasimha Murthy, P.A. (1977) *Lotus and the Chrysanthemum: India and Japan*, New Delhi: Japan Information Centre.

Narasimha Murthy, P.A. (1986) *India and Japan: Dimensions of their Relations*, New Delhi: ABC Publishing House.

Naster, W.R. (1996) *Power across the Pacific: A Diplomatic History of American Relations with Japan*, London: Macmillan.

Nation (1904) "Japan and the Jingoes," *Nation*, 79 (September 29): 254–5.

National Archive of India (1917) Home Department Proceedings, Political A, August, 1917, nos. 7–16.

Naudeau, L. (1909) *Le Japon moderne: Son evolution*, Paris: Flammarion.

Nehru, J. (1934–5) *Glimpses of World History, Being Further Letters to his Daughter, Written in Prison, and Containing a Rambling Account of History for Young People*, Allahabad: Kitabistan.

Nehru, J.L. (1949) *Glimpses of World History*, 4th edn, London: L. Drummond.

Neilson, K. (1989) "A Dangerous Game of American Poker: Britain and the Russo-Japanese War," *Journal of Strategic Studies*, 12: 63–87.

Neilson, K. (1991) "The Dangerous and Difficult Enterprise: British Military Thinking and the Russo-Japanese War," *War & Society*, 9: 17–38.

Neilson, K. (1995) *Britain and the Last Tsar: British Policy towards Russia, 1894–1917*, Oxford: Clarendon Press.

Neilson, K. (2002) "The Anglo-Japanese Alliance and British Strategic Foreign Policy, 1902–1914," paper presented at the STICERD conference, Glasgow.

Nesvoy (1904) "Lettre de Russie: le péril jaune," *L'Européen*, 132 (June 11): 9–10.

Neu, C.E. (1967) *An Uncertain Friendship: Theodore Roosevelt and Japan, 1906–1909*, Cambridge, MA: Harvard University Press.

Neu, C.E. (1987) *The Troubled Encounter: The United States and Japan*, Malabar: Wiley.

Neudeck, G. and H. Schröder (1904) *Das kleine Buch von der Marine*, Kiel and Leipzig: Lipsius & Tischer.

Nicholas II (1923) *Dnevnik imperatora Nikolaia II*, Berlin: Knigoizgatel'stvo "Slovo."

Nikolaevskii (Nicolaevsky), B. (1991) *Istoriia odnogo predatelia*, Moscow: Vysshaia shkola. [English version: *Aseff the Spy, Russian Terrorist and Police Stool*, Garden City, NY: Doubleday, Doran & Company, 1934.]

Nish, I.H. (1967) "Japan and the Ending of the Anglo-Japanese Alliance," in K. Bourne and D.C. Watt (eds) *Studies in International History: Essays Presented to W.N. Medlicott*, London: Longman, pp. 369–84.

Nish, I.H. (1976) *The Anglo-Japanese Alliance: The Diplomacy of Two Island Empires, 1894–1907*, reprinted edn, Westport, CT: Greenwood.

Nish, I.H. (1985) *The Origins of the Russo-Japanese War*, London: Longman.

Nishida, K. (1910 [1921]) *Zen no kenkyū*, Tokyo: Iwanami.

Notehelfer, F.G. (1971) *Kōtoku Shūsui: Portrait of a Japanese Radical*, Cambridge: Cambridge University Press.

O'Brien, P.P. (1998) *British and American Naval Power: Politics and Policy, 1900–1936*, Westport, CT: Praeger.

Ōe, S. (ed.) (1988) *Nichiro sensō no gunjishiteki kenkyū*, Tokyo: Chūō Kōronsha.

Oh, B.B. (1983) "Meiji Imperialism: Planned or Unplanned?," in H. Wray and H. Conroy (eds) *Japan Examined: Perspectives on Modern Japanese History*, Honolulu, HI: Hawaii University Press, pp. 125–30.

Oka, Y. (1982) "Generational Conflict after the Russo-Japanese War," in T. Najita and J.V. Koschmann (eds) *Conflict in Modern Japanese History: The Neglected Tradition*, Princeton, NJ: Princeton University Press, pp. 197–225.

Okamoto, S. (1970) *The Japanese Oligarchy and the Russo-Japanese War*, New York: Columbia University Press.

Okamoto, S. (1982) "The Emperor and the Crowd: The Historical Significance of the Hibiya Riots," in T. Najita and J.V. Koschmann (eds) *Conflict in Modern Japanese History: The Neglected Tradition*, Princeton, NJ: Princeton University Press, pp. 262–70.

Oleinikov, D. (2005) "The War in Russian Historical Memory," in J.W. Steinberg, B. Menning, D. Schimmelpenninck van der Oye, D. Wolff, and S. Yokote (eds) *The Russo-Japanese War in Global Perspective: World War Zero*, Leiden: Brill, pp. 509–22.

Ono, K. (2007) "Post Bellum Military Expenditures and Fiscal/Monetary Policy of Japan," in R. Kowner (ed.) *Rethinking the Russo-Japanese War: Centennial Perspectives*, Folkestone: Global Oriental.

Ono, S. (1935) *Gensui kōshaku Ōyama Iwao*, Tokyo: Ōyama Gensuiden Kankokai.

Ono, S. (1994) "A Deliberate Rumor: National Anxiety in China on the Eve of the Xinhai Revolution," in S. Eto and H.Z. Schiffrin (eds) *China's Republican Revolution*, Tokyo: Tokyo University Press, pp. 25–40.

Ostasiatischer Lloyd (1905) "Das deutsche Kreuzergeschwader in Ostasien," *Ostasiatischer Lloyd*, April 21.

Otte, T.G. (2000) "The Elusive Balance: British Foreign Policy and the French Entente before the First World War," in A. Sharp and G. Stone (eds) *Anglo-French Relations in the Twentieth Century: Rivalry and Cooperation*, London: Routledge, pp. 11–35.

Otte, T.G. (2003) "'Almost a Law of Nature'?: Sir Edward Grey, the Foreign Office, and the Balance of Power in Europe, 1905–1912," in E. Goldstein and B.J.C. McKercher (eds) *Power and Stability: British Foreign Policy, 1865–1965*, London: Frank Cass, pp. 77–118.

Otte, T.G. (2005) "'Wee-ah-wee'?: Britain at Weihaiwei, 1898–1930," in G. Kennedy (ed.) *British Naval Strategy East of Suez, 1900–2000*, London: Frank Cass, pp. 4–34.

Ovsyannikov, N. (2007) "The Impact of the War on the Constitutional Government in Japan," in R. Kowner (ed.) *Rethinking the Russo-Japanese War: Centennial Perspectives*, Folkestone: Global Oriental.

Padfield, P. (1972) *The Battleship Era*, London: Rupert Hart-Davis.

Painter, D.S. (1999) *The Cold War: An International History*, London: Routledge.

Paix-Séailles, C. (1904) "Contre la médiation," *L'Européen*, 150 (October 15): 1–3.

Pak, H. (1998) "Han'guk yŏksa hakkye ŭi minjok undongsa yŏn'gu tonghyang," in Han'guk minjok undongsa yŏn'gu hoe (eds) *Han'guk minjok undongsa ŭi saeroun panghyang*, Seoul: Kukhak charyo wŏn, pp. 3–32.

Pal, B.C. (1910) *The Spirit of Nationalism*, London: published privately.

Paléologue, M. (1934) *Un grand tournant de la politique mondiale, 1904–1906*, Paris: Plon.

Park, H.K. and Bae, J.-I. (1998) "Korea's territorial rights over Tokdo," *Korea Observer*, 29: 121–63.

Parkes, O. (1990) *British Battleships, "Warrior" 1860 to "Vanguard" 1950: A History of Design, Construction, and Armament*, new and revised edn, Annapolis, MD: Naval Institute Press.

Passin, H. (1982) *Encounter with Japan*, Tokyo: Kodansha International.

Philips, G. (2002) "The Obsolescence of the Arme Blanche and Technological Determinism in British Military History," *War in History*, 9: 39–59.

Pinon, R. (1906) *La Lutte pour le Pacifique: Origine et résultats de la guerre russo-japonaise*, Paris: Perrin.

Poeze, H.J. (1989) "Early Indonesian Emancipation: Abdul Rivai, van Heutsz and the Bintang Hindia," *Bijdragen tot de Taal-, Land- en Volkenkunde*, 145: 87–106.

Poeze, H.J. (1994) "Political Intelligence in the Netherlands Indies," in R. Cribb (ed.) *The Late Colonial State in Indonesia: Political and Economic Foundations of the Netherlands Indies 1888–1942*, Leiden: KITLV, pp. 229–45.

Poeze, H.J., C. van Dijk, and I. van der Meulen (1986) *In het land van de over-heerser: deel 1: Indonesiers in Nederland 1600–1950*, Dordrecht: Foris Publications.

Polivanov, A.A. (1924) *Iz dnevnikov i vospominanii*, Moscow: Vyshii voen Redaktsionny sovet.

Polmann, H. (1912) *Der Küstenkrieg und das strategische Zusammeenwirken von Heer und Flotte im russisch-japanischen Kriege 1904/05*, Berlin: Mittler und Sohn.

Porch, D. (1975) "The French Army and the Spirit of the Offensive, 1900–1914," in B. Bond and I. Roy (eds) *War and Society*, London: Croom Helm, pp. 117–43.

Porch, D. (1981) *The March to the Marne: The French Army 1871–1914*, Cambridge: Cambridge University Press.

Powell, E.P. (1904) "Some of the Reasons Why Americans Like the Japanese," *St Louis Daily Globe-Democrat Magazine*, 4 (April 17): 4.
Powles, C.H. (1961) "Abe Isoo and the Role of Christians in the Founding of the Japanese Socialist Movement: 1895–1905," *Papers on Japan*, 1: 89–129.
Pramoedya, A.T. (1982) *This Earth of Mankind*, trans. Max Lane, London: Penguin.
Prasad, B. (1979) *Indian Nationalism and Asia, 1900–1947*, Delhi: B.R. Publishing.
Pratt, J.W. (1965) *A History of United States Foreign Policy*, Englewood Cliffs, NJ: Prentice-Hall.
Preston, A. (1979) *Aircraft Carriers*, New York: Grosset & Dunlap.
Preston, A. (2001) *The Royal Navy Submarine Service: A Centennial History*, Annapolis, MD: Naval Institute Press.
Price, D.C. (1974) *Russia and the Roots of the Chinese Revolution, 1896–1911*, Cambridge, MA: Harvard University Press.
Price, D.C. (1984) "Anti-Imperialism and Popular Resistance in the Revolutionary Thought of Song Jiaoren," in S. Eto and H.Z. Schiffrin (eds) *The 1911 Revolution in China*, Tokyo: Tokyo University Press, pp. 61–80.
Price, E.B. (1933) *The Russo-Japanese Treaties of 1907–1916 Concerning Manchuria and Mongolia*, Baltimore, MD: Johns Hopkins University Press.
Pushkarev, S. (1985) *The Emergence of Modern Russia, 1801–1917*, Edmonton: Pica Pica Press.
Rankin, M.B. (1971) *Early Chinese Revolutionaries: Radical Intellectuals in Shanghai and Chekiang, 1902–1911*, Cambridge, MA: Harvard University Press.
Ras, J.J. (1968) *Hikajat Bandjar: A Study in Malay Historiography*, The Hague: Nijhoff.
Raulff, H. (1976) *Zwischen Machtpolitk und Imperialismus: Die deutsche Frank-reichpolitik, 1904–5*, Düsseldorf: Droste.
Rediger, A. (1999) *Istoriia moei zhizni: vospominaniia voennogo ministra*, Moscow: Kanon-Press.
Rediger, A.F. (1999) *Istoriia moei zhizni*, 2 vols, Moscow: Kanon-Press.
Régamey, F. (1904) *Le Japon en images*, Paris: P. Paclot.
Reid, A. (1969) *The Contest for North Sumatra: Aceh, the Netherlands and Britain 1858–1898*, Kuala Lumpur: Oxford University Press.
Reid, A. (1993) *Southeast Asia in the Age of Commerce 1450–1680*, New Haven, CT: Yale University Press/Silkworm Books.
Reinsch, P.S. (1905) "Japan and Asiatic Leadership," *North American Review*, 180 (January): 48–57.
Reventlow, E. (1906) *Der russisch-japanische Krieg: Armeeausgabe*, Berlin: C.A. Weller.
Reynolds, D.R. (1993) *China, 1898–1912: The Xinzheng Revolution and Japan*, Cambridge, MA: Harvard University Press.
Rhoads, E.J.M. (1975) *China's Republican Revolution: The Case of Kwangtung, 1895–1913*, Cambridge, MA: Harvard University Press.
Rich, N. (1965) *Friedrich von Holstein: Politics and Diplomacy in the Era of Bismarck and Wilhelm II*, 2 vols, Cambridge: Cambridge University Press.
Rich, N. and M.H. Fisher (eds) (1956) *The Holstein Papers*, 4 vols, Cambridge: Cambridge University Press.
Riha, T. (1969) *A Russian European: Paul Miliukov in Russian Politics*, Notre Dame, IN: University of Notre Dame.
Ritter, G. (1958) *The Schlieffen Plan: Critique of a Myth*, New York: Praeger.
Robbins, G. (2001) *The Aircraft Carrier Story, 1908–1941*, London: Cassell.

Rodell, P.A. (2005) "Inspiration for Nationalist Aspirations?: Southeast Asia and the 1905 Japanese Victory," in J.W. Steinberg, B. Menning, D. Schimmelpenninck van der Oye, D. Wolff, and S. Yokote (eds) *The Russo-Japanese War in Global Perspective: World War Zero*, Leiden: Brill, pp. 629–54.

Roff, W.R. (1967) *The Origins of Malay Nationalism*, New Haven, CT: Yale University Press.

Roff, W.R. (2002) "Murder as an Aid to Social History: The Arabs of Singapore in the Early Twentieth Century," in H. de Jonge and N. Kaptein (eds) *Transcending Borders: Arabs, Politics, Trade and Islam in Southeast Asia*, Leiden: KITLV Press, pp. 79–95.

Rogger, H. (1983) *Russia in the Age of Modernisation and Revolution 1881–1917*, London: Longman.

Röhl, J.C.G. (1994) *The Kaiser and His Court: Wilhelm II and the Government of Germany*, Cambridge: Cambridge University Press.

Röhl, J.C.G. (2004) *Wilhelm II: The Kaiser's Personal Monarchy, 1888–1900*, Cambridge: Cambridge University Press.

Roland, A. (1978) *Underwater Warfare in the Age of Sail*, Bloomington, IN: Indiana University Press.

Rolo, P.J.V. (1969) *Entente Cordiale: The Origins and Negotiations of the Anglo-French Agreement of 8 April 1904*, London: Macmillan.

Romanov, B.A. (1952) *Russia in Manchuria, 1892–1906*, Ann Arbor, MI: J.W. Edwards.

Roosevelt, T. (1906) "Sixth Annual Message," in *A Compilation of the Messages and Papers of the Presidents*, vol. 15, New York: Bureau of National Literature, pp. 7054–5.

Ropp, T. (1987) *The Development of the a Modern Navy: French Naval Policy, 1871–1914*, Annapolis, MD: Naval Institute Press.

Rosen, P.T. (1978) "The Treaty Navy, 1919–1937," in K.J. Hagan (ed.) *In Peace and War: Interpretations of American Naval History, 1775–1978*, Westport, CT: Greenwood Press, pp. 221–35.

Rosenberg, E.S. (1994) "Economic Interests and United States foreign policy," in G. Martel (ed.) *American Foreign Relations Reconsidered, 1890–1990*, London: Routledge, pp. 37–51.

Rosinski, H. (1977) *The Development of Naval Thought*, Newport, CT: Naval War College Press.

Rostunova, I.I. (ed.) (1977) *Istoriia russko-iaponskoi voiny 1904–1905 gg*, Moscow: Nauka.

Russia, Komissiia po opisaniiu Russko-iaponskoi voiny 1904 i 1905 godov (1910–13) *Russko-iaponskaia voina 1904–1905 gg.*, 9 vols (16 books), St Petersburg: A.S. Suvorina.

Russia, Morskoi Generalnyi Shtab (1912–18) *Voenno-Istoricheskaia kommissiia po opisaniiu deistvii flota v voinu 1904–05 gg., Russko-iaponskaia voina 1904–05 gg.*, 7 vols, St Petersburg: Russian General Staff.

Sablinsky, Walter (1976) *The Road to Bloody Sunday: Father Gapon and the St. Petersburg Massacre of 1905*, Princeton, NJ: Princeton University Press.

Sagan, S.D. (1988) "The Origins of the Pacific War," *Journal of Interdisciplinary History*, 18: 893–922.

St John, R.B. (1971) "European Naval Expansion and Mahan, 1889–1906," *Naval War College Review*, 23 (7): 74–83.

Sakurai T. (1907) *Human Bullets: A Soldier's Story of Port Arthur*, Tokyo: Teibi Publishing Co.

Sander-Nagashima, J.B. (2005) "Half a Century of Naval Relations: The German and the Imperial Japanese Navy from the End of the Nineteenth Century to the End of World War II," in C.W. Spang and R.H. Wippich (eds) *Japanese-German Relations, 1895–1945*, London: Routledge, pp. 40–57.

Sareen, T.R. (1979) *Indian Revolutionary Movement Abroad*, New Delhi: Sterling.

Sareen, T.R. (1986) *Japan and the Indian National Army*, New Delhi: Agam Prakashan.

Sareen, T.R. (1993) *Indian Revolutionaries, Japan and British Imperialism*, New Delhi: Anmol Publications.

Sato, S. (1998) "Japanese Expansionist Policy and the Question of Tokdo," *Korea Observer*, 29: 165–85.

Sazonov, S. (1928) *Fateful Years, 1909–1916*, London: Jonathan Cape.

Scalapino, R.A. and G.T. Yuand Yu (1985) *Modern China and Its Revolutionary Process: Recurrent Challenges to the Traditional order, 1850–1920*, Berkeley, CA: University of California Press.

Schencking, J.C. (2002) "The Politics of Pragmatism and Pageantry: Selling a National Navy at the Elite and Local Level in Japan, 1890–1913," in S. Wilson (ed.) *Nation and Nationalism in Japan*, London: RoutledgeCurzon, pp. 565–90.

Schencking, J.C. (2005) "Interservice Rivalry and Politics in Post-war Japan," in J.W. Steinberg, B. Menning, D. Schimmelpenninck van der Oye, D. Wolff, and S. Yokote (eds) *The Russo-Japanese War in Global Perspective: World War Zero*, Leiden: Brill, pp. 565–90.

Schiffrin, H.Z. (1970) *Sun Yat-sen and the Origins of the Chinese Revolution*, Berkeley, CA: University of California Press.

Schiffrin, H.Z. (1980) *Sun Yat-sen: Reluctant Revolutionary*, Boston, MA: Little, Brown.

Schimmelpenninck van der Oye, D. (2001) *Toward the Rising Sun: Russian Ideologies of Empire and the Path to War with Japan*, DeKalb, IL.: Northern Illinois University Press.

Schlubach, E.W. (1958) *Reisebriefe von 1903 bis 1905: Briefe eines jungen Seeoffiziers an seine Mutter während seiner Kommandierung im Kreuzergeschwader*, Hamburg: Hans Christians.

Schmid, A. (2002) *Korea between Empires, 1895–1919*, New York: Columbia University Press.

Seager, R. (1977) *Alfred Thayer Mahan: The Man and His Letters*, Annapolis, MD: Naval Institute Press.

Seager, R. and D.M. Maguire (1975) *Letters and Papers of Alfred Thayer Mahan*, 3 vols, Annapolis, MD: Naval Institute Press.

Semenov, V. (1909) *Rasplata* (The Reckoning), London: John Murray.

Serge'ev, A.A. (1932) "Vilgelma II o russko-iaponskaya voyna 1905 goda," *Krasnyi arkhiv*, IX.

Seton-Watson, H. (1967) *The Russian Empire, 1801–1917*, Oxford: Clarendon Press.

Seton-Watson, H. (1977) *Nations and States: An Enquiry into the Origins of Nations and the Politics of Nationalism*, Boulder, CO: Westview Press.

Sheffy, Y. (1998) *British Military Intelligence in the Palestine Campaign, 1914–1918*, London: Frank Cass.

Shillony, B.-A. (2005) *Enigma of the Emperors: Sacred Subservience in Japanese History*, Folkestone: Global Oriental.

Shillony, B.-A. and R. Kowner (2007) "The Russo-Japanese War: Its Significance and Memory from a Centennial Perspective," in R. Kowner (ed.) *Rethinking the Russo-Japanese War: Centennial Perspectives*, Folkestone: Global Oriental.

Shimana, M. (2001) *Nogi "shinwa" to nisshin, nichiro*, Tokyo: Ronsōsha.

Shimazu, N. (1998) *Japan, Race, and Equality*, London: Routledge.

Shin, D.-W. (2002) "Segyunseolgwa sikminji geundaeseong bipan (A Critique of the Germ Theory and Colonial Modernity)," *Yeoksa bipyeong*, 58 (spring): 341–63.

Shin, Y.-H. (1994) "The Sinminhoe's Independence Movement during the Last Years of the Chosŏn Dynasty," *Seoul Journal of Korean Studies*, 7: 13–44.

Shin, Y.-H. (ed.) (1995) *An Chung-gŭn yugojip*, Seoul: Yŏkminsa.

Shin, Y.-H. (2000) *Modern Korean History and Nationalism*, Seoul: Jimoondang.

Shin, Y.-H. (2001) *Ilche kangjŏmgi han'guk minjok sa*, vol. 1, Seoul: Sŏul Taehakkyo ch'ulp'anbu.

Shinobu, S. and J. Nakayama (eds) (1972) *Nichiro sensōshi no kenkyū*, revised edn, Tokyo: Kawade Shobō Shinsha.

Siebert, B. von (ed.) (1928) *Graf Benckendorffs Diplomatischer*, 2 vols, 2nd and augmented edn, Berlin: Walter de Gruyter.

Siegel, J. (2002) *Endgame: Britain, Russia and the Final Struggle for Central Asia, 1907–1914*, London: I.B. Tauris.

Sitaramayya, P. (1946) *The History of the Indian National Congress*, Bombay: Padma Publications.

Slattery, P. (2004) *Reporting the Russo-Japanese War, 1904–5: Lionel James' First Wireless Transmissions to the Times*, Folkestone: Global Oriental.

Smit, C. (ed.) (1957–62) *Bescheiden Betreffende de Buitenlandse Politiek van Nederland*, 5 vols, 3rd series, The Hague: Martinus Nijhoff.

Snyder, J. (1984a) *The Ideology of the Offensive: Military Decision Making and the Disasters of 1914*, Ithaca, NY: Cornell University Press.

Snyder, J. (1984b) "Civil–Military Relations and the Cult of Offensive, 1914 and 1984," *International Security*, 9: 108–46.

Sondhaus, L. (2001) *Naval Warfare, 1815–1914*, London: Routledge.

Song, C.-S. (1994) "Ilche ŭi sikminsahak," in T.-G. Cho, Y.-U. Han, and C.-S. Pak (eds) *Han'guk ŭi yŏksaga wa yŏksahak*, Seoul: Ch'angjak kwa pip'yŏng, pp. 304–24.

Spassky, I.D. (1998) *Submarines of the Tsarist Navy*, Annapolis, MD: Naval Institute Press.

Spiers, E. (1994) "The Late Victorian Army, 1868–1914," in D. Chandler (ed.) *The Oxford Illustrated History of the British Army*, Oxford: Oxford University Press, pp. 187–210.

Sprout, M.T. (1943) "Mahan: Evangelist of the Sea Power," in E.M. Earle (ed.) *Makers of Modern Strategy: From Machiavelli to Hitler*, Princeton, NJ: Princeton University Press, pp. 415–45.

Stanley, T.A. (1982) *Ōsugi Sakae: Anarchist in Taishō Japan, the Creativity of the Ego*, Cambridge, MA: Harvard East Asian Monograph.

Starr, F. (1904) *The Ainu Group at the Saint Louis Exposition*, Chicago, IL: Open Court Publishing.

Steinberg, J. (1970) "Germany and the Russo-Japanese War," *American Historical Review*, 75: 1965–86.

Steinberg, J.W., B. Menning, D. Schimmelpenninck van der Oye, D. Wolff, and S. Yokote (eds) (2005) *The Russo-Japanese War in Global Perspective: World War Zero*, Leiden: Brill.

Steiner, Z.S. (1959) "Great Britain and the Creation of the Anglo-Japanese Alliance," *Journal of Modern History*, 30: 27–35.

Steiner, Z.S. and K. Neilson (2003) *Britain and the Origins of the First World War*, 2nd edn, Basingstoke and New York: Palgrave.

Steltzer, H.G. (1989) *Die deutsche Flotte: Ein historischer Überglick von 1640 bis 1918*, Darmstadt: Societäts Verlag.

Stephan, J.T. (1994) *The Russian Far East: A History*, Stanford, CA: Stanford University Press.

Stevenson, D. (1996) *Armaments and the Coming of War: Europe, 1904–1914*, Oxford: Clarendon Press.

Stewart, A.H. (1904) "Baron Kaneko on the Yellow Peril," *New York Times*, February 21: 27.

Stewart, G.T. (2007) "The War and the British Invasion of Tibet, 1904," in R. Kowner (ed.) *Rethinking the Russo-Japanese War: Centennial Perspectives*, Folkestone: Global Oriental.

Stingl, W. (1978) *Der Ferne Osten in der deutschen Politik von dem Ersten Weltkrieg (1902–1914)*, Frankfurt am Main: Haag und Herchen.

Stockdale, M.K. (1996) *Paul Miliukov and the Quest for a Liberal Russia 1860–1918*, Ithaca, NY: Cornell University Press.

Stone, N. (1975) *The Eastern Front, 1914–1917*, London: Hodder & Stoughton.

Strachan, H. (2001) *The First World War: To Arms*, Oxford: Oxford University Press.

Straus, U. (2003) *The Anguish of Surrender: Japanese POWs of World War II*, Seattle, WA: University of Washington Press.

Straver, H., C.V. Fraassen, and J.V.D. Putten (eds) (2004) *Ridjali: Historie van Hitu. Een Ambonse geschiedenis uit de zeventiende eeuw*, Utrecht: LSEM (Landelijk Steunpunt Educatie Molukkers).

Subcommittee on Chinese-Exclusion Bill, House Committee on Foreign Affairs, United States Congress (1906) *Hearings on Chinese Exclusion*, Washington, DC: Government Printing Office.

Sukhomlinov, V.A. (1926) *Vospominaniia*, Moscow: Los. izd-vo.

Sumida, J.T. (1993) *In Defense of Naval Supremacy: Finance, Technology, and British Naval Policy, 1889–1914*, London: Routledge.

Sun, Y.S. (1913) "Zhong-ri qinshan gongxiang heping (Sino-Japanese Goodwill and Mutual Enjoyment of Peace)," in Guomindang (eds) *Guofu Quanji* (Collected Works of Sun Yat-sen), vol. II, 347, revised edn 1973, Taipei: Guomindang Party Commission.

Sun, Y.S. (1921) "Junren jingshen jiaoyu (The Spiritual Education of Soldiers)," in Guomindang (eds) *Guofu Quanji* (Collected Works of Sun Yat-sen), vol. 2, 481, revised edn 1973, Taipei: Guomindang Party Commission.

Sun, Y.S. (1924) "Pan-Asianism" (speech in Kobe, November 28, 1924), trans. and published in *The Vital Problem of China*, 1953, Taipei: China Cultural Service, p. 164.

Sundberg, J.R. (2004) "The Wilderness Monks of the Abhayagiravihāra and the Origins of Sino-Javanese Esoteric Buddhism," *Bijdragen tot de Taal-, Land- en Volkenkunde*, 160–1: 95–123.

Sweeney, A. (1980) *Reputations Live On: An Early Malay Autobiography*, Berkeley, CA: University of California Press.

Takahashi, K. (2005) "Japan-South Korea Ties on the Rocks," *Asia Times*, March 23. www.atimes.com/atimes/Japan/GC23Dh03.html/.

Takahashi, S. (1924) *Sanko iretsu*, Tokyo: Keibundo Shoten.

Takahira, K. (1904) "Why Japan Resists Russia," *North American Review*, 178 (March): 321–7.

Tani, T. (1966) *Kimitsu nichiro senshi*, ed. M. Inaba, Tokyo: Hara Shobō.

Tannenbaum, J.K. (1984) "French Estimates of Germany's Operational Plans," in E.R. May (ed.) *Knowing One's Enemies: Intelligence Assessment before the Two World Wars*, Princeton, NJ: Princeton University Press, pp. 150–71.

Tardieu, A. (1910) *La France et les alliances*, 3rd edn, Paris: F. Alcan.

Thomson, D. (1966) *Europe since Napoleon*, revised edn, Harmondsworth: Penguin Books.

Thongchai Winichakul (1994) *Siam Mapped: A History of the Geo-body of a Nation*, Honolulu, HI: University of Hawaii Press.

Tilak, B.G. (1920) *Speeches and Writings*, Madras: G.A. Natesan.

Till, G. (1995) "Retrenchment, Rethinking, Revival, 1919–1939," in J.R. Hill (ed.) *The Oxford Illustrated History of the Royal Navy*, Oxford: Oxford University Press, pp. 319–47.

Todd, M.L. (1898) "In Aino-Land," *Century*, 56 (July): 342–50.

Tokutomi, I. (1917) *Katsura Tarō den*, 2 vols, Tokyo: Katsura Kōshaku Kinen jigyōkai.

Tokutomi, I. (1933) *Kōshaku Yamagata Aritomo den*, Tokyo: Yamagata Aritomo-Ko Kinen Jigyōkai.

Towle, P. (1971) "The Russo-Japanese War and British Military Thought," *RUSI Journal*, 116: 64–8.

Towle, P. (1975) "Japanese Treatment of Prisoners in 1904–1905: Foreign Officers' Report," *Military Affairs*, 39: 115–17.

Towle, P. (1977) "The Evaluation of the Experience of the Russo-Japanese War," in Bryan Ranft (ed.) *Technical Change and the British Naval Policy, 1860–1939*, London: Hodder & Stoughton, pp. 65–79.

Towle, P. (1980) "The Russo-Japanese War and the Defence of India," *Military Affairs*, 44: 111–17.

Towle, P. (1998) "British Observers of the Russo-Japanese War," in S. Lone and P. Towle (eds) *Aspects of the Russo-Japanese War*, London: Suntory & Toyota International Centres for Economics and Related Disciplines, pp. 23–34.

Towle, P. (1999) "British Naval and Military Observers of the Russo-Japanese War," in J.E. Hoare (ed.) *Britain and Japan: Biographical Portraits*, vol. 3, Folkestone: Japan Library, pp. 158–68.

Trani, E.P. (1969) *The Treaty of Portsmouth: An Adventure in American Diplomacy*, Lexington, KY: University of Kentucky Press.

Travers, T.H.E. (1978) "The Offensive and the Problem of Innovation in British Military Thought, 1870–1915," *Journal of Contemporary History*, 13: 531–53.

Travers, T.H.E. (1979) "Technology, Tactics, and Morale: Jean de Bloch, the Boer War, and British Military History, 1900–1914," *Journal of Modern History*, 51: 264–86.

Travers, T.H.E. (1987) *The Killing Ground: The British Army, The Western Front and the Emergence of Modern Warfare, 1900–1918*, London: Allen & Unwin.

Travis, F. (1990) *George Kennan and the American–Russian Relationship, 1865–1924*, Athens, OH: Ohio University Press.

Trotsky, L. (1931) *Istoriia russkoi revoliutsii*, Berlin: Granit (English version: *The History of the Russian Revolution*, Ann Arbor, University of Michigan Press, 1957).

Tsuchida, M. (1998) "A History of Japanese Emigration from the 1860s to the 1990s," in M. Weiner and Tadashi H. (eds) *Temporary Workers or Future Citizens?: Japanese and US Migration Policies*, New York: New York University Press, pp. 77–119.

Tuchman, B.W. (1966) *The Proud Tower: A Portrait of the World before the War, 1890–1914*, New York: Macmillan.

Turk, R.W. (1978) "Defending the New Empire," in K.J. Hagan (ed) *In Peace and War: Interpretations of American Naval History, 1775–1978*, Westport, CT: Greenwood Press.

Turner, F.J. (1920) *The Frontier in American History*, New York: Henry Holt.

Ucar, A. (1995) "Japonlarin Islam Dunyasindaki yayilmaci siyaseti ve Abdurresid Ibrahim," *Toplumsal Tarih*, 4–20: 6–23.

Union of Soviet Socialist Republics (1931–9) *Mezhdunarodnye otnosheniia v epokhu imperializma: Dokumenty iz arkhivov tsarskogo i vremennogo pravitel'stv 1878–1917 gg*, Moscow: Central Executive Committee, Commission for the Publication of Documents of the Era of Imperialism.

United States Congress (1905–7) *Congressional Record*, Washington, DC: Government Printing Office.

United States Supreme Court (1922) *Takao Ozawa* v. *United States*, 260: 178–99.

United States War Department (1906–7) *Reports of Military Observers Attached to the Armies in Manchuria during the Russo-Japanese War*, 5 vols, Washington, DC: Government Printing Office.

Vagts, A. (1967) *The Military Attaché*, Princeton, NJ: Princeton University Press.

Valliant, R.B. (1974) "The Selling of Japan: Japanese Manipulation of Western Opinion, 1900–1905," *Monumenta Nipponica*, 29: 415–38.

van der Kraan, A. (2000) *The Dutch in Siam: Jeremias van Vliet and the 1636 Incident at Ayutthaya*, UNEAC Asia Papers no. 3, University of New England, Armidale, School of Economics.

van der Meulen, D. (1981) *Don't You Hear the Thunder? A Dutchman's Life Story*, Leiden: Brill.

van Evera, S. (1984) "The Cult of Offensive and The Origins of the First World War," *International Security*, 9: 58–107.

Vernadsky, G. (ed.) (1972) *A Source Book for Russian History from Early Times to 1917*, New Haven, CT: Yale University Press.

Verner, A.M. (1990) *The Crisis of Russian Autocracy: Nicholas II and the 1905 Revolution*, Princeton, NJ: Princeton University Press.

Vierhaus, R. (ed.) (1960) *Das Tagebuch der Baronin Spitzemberg: Aufzeichnungen aus der Hofgesellschaft des Hohenzollernreiches*, Göttingen: Vandenhoeck & Ruprecht.

Villiers, F. (1905) *Port Arthur: Three Months with the Besiegers*, London: Longmans Green.

Vogel, B. (1973) *Deutsche Russlandpolitik: Das Scheitern der deutschen Weltpolitik unter Bülow, 1900–1906*, Düsseldorf: Droste.

von Laue, T.H. (1963) *Sergei Witte and the Industrialization of Russia*, New York: Atheneum.

Walder, D. (1973) *The Short Victorious War The Russo-Japanese Conflict 1904–05*, New York: Harper & Row.

Waldron, P. (1998) *Between Two Revolutions: Stolypin and the Politics of Renewal in Russia*, Dekalb, IL: Northern Illinois University Press.

Walkin, J. (1962) *The Rise of Democracy in Pre-Revolutionary Russia*, New York: Frederick A. Praeger.

Walkin, J. (1963) *The Rise of Democracy in Pre-Revolutionary Russia: Political and Social Institutions Under the Last Three Czars*, New York: Praeger.

Walser, R. (1992) *France's Search for a Battle Fleet: Naval Policy and Naval Power, 1898–1914*, New York: Garland Press.

Warner, D. and P. Warner (1974) *The Tide and Sunrise: A History of the Russo-Japanese War 1904–05*, New York: Charterhouse.

Weinberg, R.E. (1993) *The Revolution of 1905 in Odessa: Blood on the Steps*, Bloomington, IN: Indiana University Press.

Weir, G.E. (1992) *Building the Kaiser's Navy: The Imperial Navy Office and German Industry in the von Tirpiz Era, 1890–1914*, Annapolis, MD: Naval Institute Press.

Wells, D. and S. Wilson (eds) (1999) *The Russo-Japanese War in Cultural Perspective, 1904–05*, New York: St Martin's Press.

Wesseling, H.L. (2000) *Soldier and Warrior: French Attitudes toward the Army and War on the Eve of the First World War*, Westport, CT: Greenwood.

Westwood, J.N. (1981) *Endurance and Endeavour: Russian History, 1812–1980*, Oxford: Oxford University Press.

Westwood, J.N. (1986) *Russia Against Japan 1904–05: A New Look at the Russo-Japanese War*, London: Macmillan.

Weulersse, G. (1903) *Le Japon d'aujourd'hui: Etudes socials*, Paris: A. Colin.

White, J.A. (1964) *The Diplomacy of the Russo-Japanese War*, Princeton, NJ: Princeton University Press.

Widenmann, W. (1952) *Marine-Attaché an der Kaiserlich Deutschen Botschaft in London 1907–1912*, Göttinger Beiträge für Gegenwartsfragen, Band 4, Göttingen: Harald Boldt.

Wildenberg, T. (1996) *Gray Steel and Black Oil: Fast Tankers and Replenishment at Sea in the US Navy, 1912–1992*, Annapolis, MD: Naval Institute Press.

Wildman, A. (1980) *The End of the Russian Imperial Army*, 2 vols, Princeton, NJ: Princeton University Press.

Williams, B.J. (1963) "The Strategic Background to the Anglo-Russian Convention of August 1907," *Historical Journal*, 9: 360–73.

Williams, B.J. (1974) "The Revolution of 1905 and Russian Foreign Policy," in C. Abramsky (ed.) *Essays in Honour of E.H. Carr*, London: Macmillan, pp. 101–25.

Willoughby, W.W. (1927) *Foreign Rights and Interests in China*, vol. 1, Baltimore, MD: Johns Hopkins University Press.

Wilson, G.M. (1969) *Radical Nationalist in Japan: Kita Ikki 1883–1937*, Cambridge, MA: Harvard University Press.

Wilson, K.M. (1985) *The Policy of the Entente: Essays on the Determinants of British Foreign Policy 1904–1914*, Cambridge: Cambridge University Press.

Wilson, K.M. (1993) "The Anglo-Japanese Alliance of August 1905 and the Defending of India: A Case of the Worst Case Scenario," *Journal of Imperial and Commonwealth History*, 21: 324–56.

Wilson, S. (1999) "The Russo-Japanese War and Japan: Politics, Nationalism, and Historical Memory," in D. Wells and S. Wilson (eds) *The Russo-Japanese War in Cultural Perspective, 1904–05*, Houndmills, Basingstoke: Palgrave, pp. 160–96.

Witte (Vitte), S.I. (1921) *The Memoirs of Count Witte*, 2 vols, ed. and trans. Abraham Yarmolinsky, Garden City, NY: Doubleday, Page.

Woodward, E.L. (1935) *Great Britain and the German Navy*, Oxford: Clarendon Press.

Worringer, R. (2006) *Islamic Middle East and Japan: Perceptions, Aspirations, and the Birth of Intra-Asian Modernity*, Princeton, NJ: Markus Wiener.

Wray, H. and H. Conroy (eds) (1983) *Japan Examined: Perspectives on Modern Japanese History*, Honolulu, HI: University of Hawaii Press.

Wright, M.C. (1968) *China in Revolution: The First Phase 1900–1913*, New Haven, CT: Yale University Press.

Yanagita, K. (1910 [1935]) *Tōno monogatari*, Tokyo: Kyōdo Kenkyūsha.

Yasuda, H. (1990) "The Modern Emperor System as It Took Shape Before and After the Sino-Japanese War," *Acta Asiatica*, 59: 38–58.

Yasukuni jinja (ed.) (1983) *Yasukuni jinja hyakunenshi, vol. 1: Shiryōhen*, Tokyo: Yasukuni jinja.

Yoshino, K. (1992) *Cultural Nationalism in Contemporary Japan*, London: Routledge.

Yu-Jose, L.N. (1992) *Japan Views of the Philippines: 1900–1944*, Manila: Ateneo de Manila University Press.

Za'ba (Zainal Abidin bin Ahmad) (1940) "Modern Developments [in Malay Literature]," *Journal of the Malayan Branch of the Royal Asiatic Society*, 18 (3): 142–62.

Zabecki, D. (1994) *Steel Wind: Colonel Georg Bruchmüler and the Birth of Modern Artillery*, Westport, CT: Praeger.

Zain, S.M. (1948) *Zaman baroe*, Batavia: J.B. Wolters.

Zilliacus, K. (1912) *Revolution und Gegenrevolution in Russland und Finnland*, Munich: Georg Müller.

Zolotarev, V.A. and I.A. Kozlov (1990) *Russko-iaponskaya voina, 1904–1905 gg. Borba na more*, Moscow: Nauka.

Zuber, T. (1999) "The Schlieffen Plan Reconsidered," *War in History*, 6: 262–305.

Zuber, T. (2002) *Inventing the Schlieffen Plan: German War Planning, 1871–1914*, Oxford: Oxford University Press.

Index

Breinigsville, PA USA
06 November 2009
227186BV00002B/3/P